FROM HERE TO THERE

A SELF-PACED PROGRAM FOR TRANSITION IN EMPLOYMENT

If everyone is thinking alike. . .
then somebody is not thinking.

- General George S. Patton

By:
LAWRENCE A. STUENKEL
Senior Partner and Founder
Lawrence & Allen, Inc.

The Most Complete
Job Hunting Guide Available

5th Edition

FACTS ON DEMAND PRESS

Fifth Edition
Published by Facts On Demand Press
www.fromheretothere.net

ISBN 1-889150-31-2
Printed in the United States of America

Publisher's Cataloging-in-Publication
(*Provided by Quality Books, Inc.*)

Stuenkel, Lawrence A.
    From here-- to there : a self-paced program for
transition in employment : the most complete job hunting
guide available / by Lawrence A. Stuenkel. -- 5th ed.
    p. cm.
    Includes index.
    ISBN: 1-889150-31-2

    1. Job hunting. 2. Career changes. I. Title.

HF5382.7.S78 2002   650.14
                           QBI02-200029

CONTENTS

THE AUTHOR SPEAKS

CHAPTER I
Planning the Trip and Getting Organized
If You Don't Know Where You Are Going, It's Hard to Get There.

CHAPTER II
The Road Map
Preparing An Action Oriented Resume. Where Have You Been & What Have You Done?

CHAPTER III
Guidelines for Writing Cover Letters
These Are Not Postcards.

CHAPTER IV
Developing Your Own Aggressive
Job Campaign by Telephone
Calling Collect Is Not an Option.

CHAPTER V
Developing Employment Opportunities Through
a Targeted Direct Mail Campaign
The Road Less Traveled.

CHAPTER VI
When Your Job Search Lacks Results,
Are You Pointing Yourself in the Right Direction?
Maybe It's Time to Check Your Bearing.

CHAPTER VII
Guidelines for Preparing for the Job Interview
It's Not the Final Destination, but You're Getting Close.

CHAPTER VIII
Evaluating and Handling the Offer of Employment
Checking Your Map and Compass One Last Time –
Are You There?

CHAPTER IX
Journey's End

This book is dedicated

to my good friend and a true partner,

Joy K. McLemore.

Thanks for going the extra mile!

INTRODUCTION

By Lawrence A. Stuenkel

In 1977, I was sitting very comfortably in a corporate position for a diversified manufacturing company headquartered outside of Chicago, Illinois. Through a series of sometimes strange, sometimes well-planned and executed events, I left corporate life to start the outplacement firm of Lawrence & Allen. The firm accepted its first client in 1978.

Since its inception, the charter of the firm has not varied. Our sole objective is to provide outplacement services to individuals as well as small and large groups of employees who have lost or will shortly lose their positions in corporate America and assist those people to transition into meaningful career continuing or alternative career positions.

This fifth edition of *From Here to There* represents my most complete and thorough analysis of the challenging task of finding new employment. The preceding sentence was actually used in the fourth edition. It was my desire to write the most complete job-hunting manual ever produced, and it was also my intent that the fourth edition would be so complete that a fifth edition would not be necessary for several years. Unfortunately, with the economy evolving as it has with mounting layoffs, plant closures, declining earnings, bankruptcies, restructuring and the sheer amount of people who are in the job market, I felt it was necessary to update this book with the fifth edition after one year. It reflects the latest information, technology, and my experience assisting people in the new millenium to change employers. It is designed for any individual with a salary between $35,000 and $350,000 per year. It is based on both my experiences and the experiences of others in our firm – having worked with all types of individuals that fall into the above-stated salary range.

To the best of my knowledge, no other author has attempted to write a "how to" book that has targeted as its readership individuals whose salary spread is over $300,000, i.e. from $35,000 to $350,000. Obviously job search and campaign tactics vary widely between the two salary points. Conventional wisdom might suggest that it would be better to write two different books with each targeted at a more focused salary range.

After careful study, I decided against it. Why? Because as I arranged my thoughts on various subjects, it became abundantly clear that some subjects (admittedly, not all) were equally applicable to whatever salary level an individual has achieved. My suggestion, therefore, is to read the entire guide, or, at least skim the sections you are absolutely, positively certain could never apply to you.

Securing employment is a constantly evolving process; the ideas and techniques we used to assist our clients twenty years ago are not the same methods or techniques we use today. In addition, the firm has conducted primary research on various aspects of job hunting. These research findings are shared with the reader under a heading called "Out-of-the-Box Thinking," which is recognized by the following "Out-of-the-Box" symbol:

"OUT-OF-THE-BOX THINKING"

There is one other symbol that we should describe and that is the symbol for "In-the-Box Thinking."

"IN-THE-BOX THINKING"

"In-the-Box Thinking" typifies thinking that is enclosed by either physical or artificial barriers to one's thought process. I will use this graphic to debase commonly held beliefs or old wives' tales that I feel might impede one's understanding of the employment process or techniques used to gain re-employment.

Initially, I would like to dispense with two "In-the-Box" thoughts that have persisted in the employment process longer than I have been in the Outplacement business.

First is the notion that a resume has to be limited to one page. This is nonsense! Expressed simply, a resume should get the story told and told succinctly. If it can be done in one page, fine. If it takes two pages, fine. If it takes some of a third page, fine. The sole objective should be getting the job done and **done right** – length be damned. The notion that employers today, in their search for qualified people, will not be interested in an individual with more than a one-page resume is not supported by our research into the screening process applicants are going through to gain employment.

Certainly, the number of telephone interviews and face-to-face interviews, as well as the increasing number of people involved in the consensus-interviewing process strongly suggests corporations have a heavy thirst to learn as much as they can about an applicant. Surely, this desire for more data and information does not support the theory, "companies only want one-page resumes," before an offer is extended.

The second is the notion that a job campaign will take one month of time for every ten thousand dollars of income the person had been previously enjoying. This, again, is utter nonsense. The length of time it takes a person to find suitable employment is conditioned upon the following factors.

FACTORS AFFECTING RE-EMPLOYMENT—
HOW LONG CAN I EXPECT MY JOURNEY TO TAKE?

Whether the search is commenced in the first, second, third, or fourth quarter of the year, employment rates vary by calendar quarter. Typically the employment market is the most aggressive with more people being hired during January, February, and March than any other quarter of the year. Most companies have their accounting or fiscal year coincide with the actual calendar year. Consequently, operating budgets including recruitment and hiring budgets are the fullest (fattest) during the first quarter of every new year. New programs as well as new products are introduced during this time. Bottom line, key additions to a company's staff are most likely to be added during the first quarter.

Conversely, fourth quarter, with the operating budget well spent, is the slowest quarter. This point is further driven by three major holiday periods during which key managers frequently choose to take their unused vacation time before it is lost. The end of the year makes for an especially slow period of recruitment.

- The skill status of the individual: Are the person's skills rusty, or even worse corroded, or does the person have current, state-of-the-art skills?
- Income level: If a person earns $250,000 per year, it is understandable that his or her type of search might take much longer than for a person who makes $35,000 per year.
- The professional background of the individual: The software-system designers are presently enjoying a very lucrative market. This may not be true for people in other professions. This country has always experienced one type of employee shortage or another. At one time, it was engineers, then teachers, then accountants – all have

seen the pendulum swing in their direction and then move away. The point, simply expressed, is **as business changes, demand for specific skills in professionals to lead those businesses also changes**.

In summary, believing that a person will be unemployed one month for every ten thousand dollars of income fails to incorporate the above factors. Equally important is the consistent observation that people who work hard on the job will also work hard trying to find new employment. I concur with this belief 100 percent. I have found that the average job hunter typically spends two hours a day or less working on his/her campaign. I initially felt that if a person were to spend eight hours a day working at his or her job, it should not be unusual to expect that he or she would spend eight hours a day looking for a new position. Realistically, this was too much to expect from almost everyone.

A more realistic expectation would be six hours per day. Eight hours is unrealistic because it does not take into account the frustrations that people have during a job search: the inability to get through to the right contact person, the delaying tactics of voice mail, the amount of rejection an individual can accept during a typical work day, and the sheer weight of some of the job-campaign tasks, which I fully admit are not always the most exciting or stimulating tasks to pursue, that can easily lead to boredom and frustration. Nevertheless, if a person will work hard six hours a day on a job campaign and pursue those tasks that are meaningful, as outlined in the following pages, it is my considered belief that the campaign will be both rapid and satisfying.

Obviously, all of the above items impact the time it takes to find and start a new employment relationship. Certainly, there are other not so "soft issues" – such as age, sex, minority status, whether the person "looks good," has a college degree, has a degree from the "right school," and has an advanced degree – that affect the employment process. Whether the individual has kept current in his or her craft or discipline and is knowledgeable about the frontier issues in his or her field that are emerging cannot be understated.

Finally, there is the factor of whether the person is employed or unemployed and how the hiring official views his/her employment status. Does being unemployed bring the connotation of "damaged goods"? Personally, I have felt that Lee Iacocca, former president of Chrysler Corporation, did more for lessening this stigma after his dismissal from Ford Motors by Henry Ford than any other individual.

Some people still believe and think along the following lines: *If you are good, you have a job! Oh! You don't have a job! (Pause.)* Such slanted thinking is terribly unfair, particularly as modern corporations adjust to offshore pressure, domestic competition, regulatory compliance, and new technologies producing downsizing, rightsizing, restructuring, re-engineering, realignments, layoffs, belt-tightening, lean organizations, hiring freezes, and my all-time favorite, hiring frosts.

What's the bottom line? We have all encountered one or more of these obstacles to gaining rapid employment. While unemployed individuals have more time to work on their campaign than employed individuals do, the process is never fast enough in regaining employment. The real answer, I believe, to the question, "How long will it take before I find my next position?" is fairly easy to explain. True, some individuals transition faster than others. Why? The answer lies within you. What makes a person run? Clients that I have worked with in Outplacement that transitioned the fastest were and are the ones that really wanted it to happen, and therefore worked hard at making it happen. People who work hard on the job, that give extra effort, are also the ones that work hard trying to find their next job.

Years ago, I was conducting a series of outplacement workshops for GTE, who was undergoing a reduction in staffing due to a shift in telephone technology. As a result of this shift, I met a pair of identical twin brothers who were losing their jobs. These gentlemen were long-time employees, had over twenty-five years of service, were overweight, non-degreed, and over fifty years of age. One brother constantly complained to anyone who would listen that it was wrong for the company to let him go and not recognize his twenty-five years of service. He knew no one would hire him since he was too old. This individual was a self-proclaimed prophecy. I don't think he ever found a job because he didn't put the effort into looking. His brother, on the other hand, applied himself to the task and was appropriately rewarded. Admittedly, he had to work very hard at his campaign, but he wasn't going to be denied. And he wasn't.

What my colleagues and I have learned is passed on in the following pages. This data has been compiled from a number of sources. Obviously, the experiences of our own clients, as they pursue their own job campaigns, have provided an abundance of resources. Not merely content with that, we have conducted our own research by interviewing human resource managers, employment managers, search consultants, and our own worthy competitors. With this understanding, I am pleased to share with you <u>From Here To There</u>.

Best wishes on your job campaign!

In the middle of difficulty lies opportunity.

- *Albert Einstein*

AS YOU START YOUR JOURNEY, MEET YOUR GUIDES

Robert T. Thomas	Manager of Manufacturing Operations, Monroe Manufacturing Corporation
Samuel A. Smith	National Account Executive, Nationwide Cards
Rosie M. Shannon	Senior Secretary, Quark Company
Harold J. Corona	Senior Vice President, UBR, Inc.
Norma M. Panetela	Vice President of Marketing, Millennium One
Jacob J. Robusto	Director of Technical Development, Better Products, Inc.

While all the names of the cast members are fictitious, their accomplishments and career paths are not. Each "guide" was selected to explain and amplify key points and different marketing strategies. In the forthcoming pages, you will find sample documents that illustrate the principles covered.

Each of these "guides" was selected because of his or her different background, career path, and salary level. However, all have one thing in common. They all used the principles explained in this guide and successfully completed their own job-hunting journeys – going *From Here to There*!

A brief note of explanation may be in order here. Lawrence & Allen, for whom I have been senior partner for twenty-five years, has had the opportunity to assist thousands of people to develop their marketing documents (i.e., resume, marketing letters, etc.). Consequently, the temptation to include "hundreds" of sample resumes might on first blush be appealing and add "bulk" to this guide. However, the appeal to emulate someone else's material all too often does not provide an original document or the strongest selling tool because it does not tell the individual's unique story.

My strategy, rather, is summed up in the following quote:

Give a starving man a fish
and he will eat today.
teach him to fish and he will
eat for life.

So, as you journey through this project, let Robert, Samuel, Rosie, Harold, Norma, and Jacob be your guides!

CHAPTER I.

PLANNING THE TRIP

AND

GETTING ORGANIZED

**If You Don't Know Where You're Going,
It's Hard To Get There.**

A WORD TO THOSE INDIVIDUALS
WHO MAY HAVE JUST RECENTLY BEEN SEPARATED
FROM THEIR EMPLOYERS

Just prior to the publication of this book, I was contacted by a syndicated columnist for an interview regarding advice to her readers as to what an individual should do upon separation. Specifically, she wanted to know when this type of information comes as a bolt out of the blue (i.e., being notified that your services are no longer required and you're being separated from the corporation), what should be the first step or steps the separated individual takes?

I told the reporter that this might be the shortest interview on record, as I would advise the person recently separated to do nothing. She pressed me and wanted to know why I would advise a person receiving this type of jolting information to do nothing. My answer to her was very simple. Individuals who receive this type of unexpected information are seldom in complete control of all their senses. Emotions start to run havoc; thinking is unclear or muddled at best. In short, the person is not in complete control of all the logic he or she needs to possess to go forward.

My best advice is to wait at least three or four days to allow the impact of the communication to register on the recipient and *then* request a meeting with the individual's human resource representative. At that meeting, a comprehensive and well-thought-out list of questions could be discussed in more detail. These subjects and other items usually are cov-ered in the separation agreement. These agreements attempt to clarify certain types of benefit questions and related issues. It is critical to understand three things: When do benefits start; how long do they run; and what are the costs or benefits to me? When reviewing the sample separation agreement at the employee and officer level, it is well to keep in mind that seldom is the individual able to converse authoritatively and knowledgeably on all these subjects upon notification of the separation. Therefore, following the proverb of "haste makes waste," take a few days to compose oneself and make a list of topics and subjects for further explanation.

SEVERANCE AGREEMENT

"A binding agreement between two or more persons or parties"

Simply stated, severance agreements are contracts and, as such, they can be entered into when an individual joins a company, leaves the company, or at any point in between. Typically, these agreements are designed by employers to protect employers' rights.

When an individual has involuntarily separated from an employer, he or she may receive a severance package that is contingent upon signing a separation agreement. These agreements are generally left to the individual to consider for a period of twenty-two days. The individual is encouraged during this "contemplated period" to seek the advice of outside counsel. Upon signing the separation agreement, the individual is entitled to receive separation pay, and by so doing, releases the company from any and all legal obligations. Typically after the agreement is "signed," there is a renege period, most frequently seven days, during which the individual has one more chance to change his or her mind and withdraw the signed separation agreement. After the renege period has passed, the agreement is considered signed and binding. Individuals who are separated and have signed these agreements generally are blocked from going to another company in the same industry or field. There is usually a non-solicitation period, most frequently for a specified period of time that an individual will not solicit or engage in any type of specific activities. These activities most frequently are spelled out as follows:

- "I will not, directly or indirectly, call on, solicit, perform services for, interfere with, or endeavor to entice away from the company any client or customer to whom the company has provided services at any time during the twelve months preceding the last day of the individual's employment with the company or any perspective client to whom the company has made a presentation at any time during the twelve months preceding the last day of the individual's employment with the company."

- "The individual will not directly or indirectly hire, attempt to hire, solicit for employment, or encourage the departure of any employee of the company for any individual who has been employed by the company at any time during the twelve months preceding the last day of the individual's employment with the company."

Additionally, these agreements can contain a promise not to say anything negative or disparaging about an employee's former company.

It is not unusual when an individual joins a company to have the new employee sign an intellectual property agreement. These agreements protect the employer's trade secrets, confidential marketing information, client or customer contact lists, or even pricing agreements.

During times of corporate downsizing, it is not unusual to find employees barred from either contacting their former coworkers or even discussing the details of their separation agreements. Non-disclosures are generally an accepted part of a separation agreement. Obviously, if an employee is bound by a non-compete clause, where the individual pledges not to go to work for a competitor, this agreement restricts individuals in their job searches.

More employers, as they are doing reference and background checks, are also asking potential employees if they have signed any non-compete agreements. The trend to restrict current or former employees' activities once they have left the business appears to be becoming more and more commonplace.

Keep in mind the following:

- Read all the print in all company application forms and employment agreements.
- Seek outside counsel regarding advice on whether such agreements are totally enforceable in your particular state.
- Keep copies of all agreements signed including any additional amendments or addenda to those agreements.

It is prudent to keep in mind that there is no mandatory federal or state law or regulation requiring any company to make severance payments or money payments to any employee absent a specific company policy or an individually contracted agreement. If severance is going to be paid, it is prudent to find out (1) if it's going to be paid in lump sum or paid on a weekly or every two-week, semi-weekly, semi-monthly basis; and (2) how long severance will continue and if there are other services that the company is going to afford to a separated individual. For example, outplacement services: what are the duration of the services and the type of services being provided?

If severance monies are being provided, does the company require a release to be signed by the separated individual? How long does the individual have to consider signing the release, and what are the alternatives if the release is not signed?

Medical Continuation

Is the company going to provide medical continuation under its group policy? If the company is going to provide medical coverage, for how long is this coverage, at what cost, and at the expiration of the coverage, is the individual able to assume the cost of the coverage? What are the conversion provisions for assuming individual medical coverage, etc.?

References

Verify what the company is going to say regarding past employment service to potential inquiring employers.

Benefits

In addition to medical benefits covered under COBRA, what is the effect of the separation on pension credits, 401K savings plan, unused but earned vacation and holiday pay?

Who is going to absorb the cost and for how long? What about such plans as eye care, dental, and prepaid legal programs? Does the prepaid legal program include seeking counsel for alleged wrongful discharge?

Purchase of Company Assets

Many times an employee will use company assets and at the point of separation may be granted the right to purchase those assets. For example, a car driven by a salesman or a laptop computer used in day-to-day activities would be helpful in the job campaign.

Other

In a separation, an employee should discuss how the company would like the other assets of the company returned. For example, credit cards, cell phones, telephone calling cards, keys to the building, file cabinets, desks, and preparation of final expense report or cash advances that are outstanding and left unclear.

Additional questions to consider might be: What is the effect of separation on any earned but unpaid bonus formulas? How are supplies to be returned? Are there any confidentiality agreements to be signed? How are patents that are pending to be handled? What about using a telephone calling card for a specific duration in the job-campaign process? How are proprietary documents to be returned, air travel cards? Does the employee get a receipt for all documents, materials, and assets returned to the company?

Separated individuals are well advised to discuss any prohibition against applying for employment with the company's competitor or remaining in the industry with another company. Were there any non-solicitation agreements or documents signed when the individual joined the company? Are there any conversion provisions available to assume premiums for life insurance, short-term disability, long-term disability, etc.? Are there any outstanding medical claims to be filed, or are there claims that have been filed but not paid? What are the employee's rights in the separation regarding the exercise of stock options? What is the time frame for exercising stock options? Certainly ask if severance payments are negotiable for extension if the employee is unable to locate suitable employment during the initial period of payments.

What is the effect of separation on tuition reimbursement? What about courses being taken or those already paid for but that not have been taken? For a recently terminated employee who might have relocated to a new city at the request of his new employer prior to separation, what obligation is the company going to assume to relieve an individual of new mortgage encumbrances? Would the company relocate the employee back to his old location? This is a scenario where no rule of thumb is available, but an in-depth discussion should be explored for potential options.

Certainly inquire whether the company is going to provide any assistance in the individual's job search. Are individual or group outplacement services going to be available? Where are these services located, and how long do they last?

Proprietary Documents/Materials to be Returned to the Company

Will the individual be given a receipt acknowledging return of same?

SEPARATION AGREEMENTS

The following are two sample separation agreements for your review. One is for the officer level, and one is for other employees leaving the organization. They are very similar in nature.

The key to separation agreements is to approach them in a very calm, non-emotional manner. Admittedly, it may be a difficult task when one is being separated to remain unemotional when discussing these various items. I am always reminded of the phrase, "Anger is only one letter away from danger." Successful negotiation of the elements included in the separation agreement is contingent upon complete professional demeanor, and as such, sound arguments must be put forward so that the employer will have ample opportunity to consider your request.

SAMPLE

OFFICER LEVEL SEPARATION AGREEMENT

Date:

To:

From:

The following sets forth our mutual agreement regarding your separation from _____ (the "Company").

1. **SALARY.**   Your last day of work shall be _____.   You will continue on the Company's payroll until

_____ or the date you commence new employment, whichever is earlier ("employment termination date"), at your current annual base-compensation rate of $_____. If you commence new employment prior to _____, you will be paid the equivalent of any remaining salary continuation through _____ in a lump-sum payment as additional separation pay and not as base compensation or salary.

2. **CASH PROFIT SHARING.** You will participate in Cash Profit Sharing at the Group 1 level for the current fiscal year (_____) with payments, if any, being paid in _____ and _____, 200_. For fiscal year _____, you will participate in Cash Profit Sharing at the Group IV level based on your current base compensation rate up to your employment termination date. Payments for fiscal year _____, if any, will be paid in ____ and _____, 200_. All separation pay or other lump-sum payments referred to in this letter shall not constitute earnings for purposes of calculating cash profit sharing pursuant to this paragraph.

3. **ANNUAL DISCRETIONARY BONUS.** You will be eligible to receive a payment from the Discretionary Bonus Plan for fiscal year _____ based upon an evaluation of your performance against your objectives. Any bonus amount that may be awarded will be calculated using actual base compensation paid during fiscal year _____. You will not be eligible to participate in the Discretionary Bonus Plan for fiscal year _____.

4. **SEPARATION PAY.** The Company will pay you separation pay in accordance with Company policy based upon your employment termination date. This amount will be paid to you in lump sum within thirty (30) days after your employment termination date, unless you decide to defer payment for up to two (2) years according to separation pay guidelines.

5. **RESTRICTED STOCK** Your interest in Restricted Common B Stock awarded you under the Company's Restricted Stock Plan will, in accordance with the provision of that Plan and as approved by the CEO, become vested as of your employment termination date. The Company has one hundred twenty (120) days after your employment termination date to exercise its option to repurchase your Restricted Stock. Since the Restricted Stock is not vested until your employment termination date, you may not offer to sell Restricted Stock back to the Company prior thereto. You will continue to receive dividends on your Restricted Stock so long as you are a stockholder on the appropriate record dates for payment of dividends. You shall be responsible for any tax or other payment necessitated by any payment to you pursuant to the Restricted Stock Plan.

6. **INCENTIVE CERTIFICATES.** Your Incentive Certificate units will mature on the earlier of their stated maturity date or your employment termination date in accordance with the Incentive Certificate Plan and as approved by the CEO. The payment to you for any appreciation of those Incentive Certificate units since their date of issuance will be handled by _____'s office. However, except for Incentive Certificate units maturing prior to your employment termination date, you cannot surrender your Incentive Certificate units prior to your employment termination date. Between now and your employment termination date, dividend equivalents (i.e., payments equivalent to common stock dividends) will be paid on the Incentive Certificate units you hold on the same date as common stock dividends if you are an employee of the Company on the record date.

7. **DEFERRED PROFIT SHARING.** You will continue to participate in the Deferred Profit Sharing and Savings Plan based on your base compensation rate up to your employment termination date. Your Deferred Profit Sharing and Savings Plan account will be determined as of the date of distribution of your account to you. You will receive further information regarding withdrawal of your account. All separation payments or other lump-sum payments referred to in this letter shall not constitute earnings for purposes of calculating Deferred Profit Sharing.

8. **HEALTH AND DISABILITY BENEFITS.** Benefits under the Company's Medical, Dental, Vision, and Prescription Drug Plans ("Health Care Plans") will continue in effect until the end of the month in which your employment termination date occurs if you pay the appropriate employee and/or dependent coverage premiums. At your option, you may extend either your Medical benefits exclusively or your Health Care Plans benefits for a period of up to eighteen months after termination of benefits by paying the full cost for your coverage and/or you and your covered dependents. Your Human Resources Benefit Specialist can provide you with more detailed information.

9. **LIFE INSURANCE.** Basic and Supplemental life-insurance coverage will continue in effect, subject to applicable plan provisions, until the end of the month in which your employment termination date occurs, provided you maintain membership and pay all appropriate premiums. There is an opportunity to convert any coverage that ceases upon termination at your expense.

10. **VACATION AND PERSONAL CHOICE HOLIDAYS.** Any remaining unused vacation and personal choice holidays, along with vacation and personal choice holidays you would accrue during the period prior to your employment termination date, are included in the salary continuation payments (paragraph 1).

11. **PENSION BENEFITS.** You are eligible to receive pension benefits under the Company's Retirement Plan at any time after you reach age fifty. Your pension benefit calculation will include service and earnings to your employment termination date. All separation or other lump-sum payments referred to in this letter shall not constitute earnings for purposes of calculating your pension pursuant to this paragraph. Please contact _____ with any questions.

12. _____ **MEMBERSHIP.** You will be able to continue membership and participation in _____ by payment of active employee dues through your employment termination date.

13. **FLEXIBLE SPENDING ACCOUNT FOR OFFICERS.** You will be eligible to use any unused balance of your 200_ allowance of $_____ anytime prior to your employment termination date. You will not receive a 200_ allowance.

14. **OUTPLACEMENT ASSISTANCE.** The Company will provide the services of the outplacement firm, Lawrence & Allen, Inc. to assist you in your efforts to secure other employment. Additionally, the Company will reimburse you for any reasonable job-search expenses, including preapproved significant travel expenses. Payment by the Company for reimbursable expenses pursuant to this paragraph shall be limited to a total aggregate reimbursement of $_____. Reimbursement will be based

upon receipt of the appropriate documentation. Either I or the Lawrence & Allen, Inc. outplacement executive can pre-approve significant travel expenses.

15. **DEATH STOCK PROVISIONS.** Your death prior to your employment termination date shall be deemed to be your employment termination date for the purpose of triggering the Company's repurchase options as provided in the agreement covering your Restricted Stock.

16. **RESTRICTIVE COVENANT.** You acknowledge and agree that you were a key executive directly responsible for both the business operations of the _____, as well as global business planning development for the _____. Accordingly, in consideration of the additional benefits and payments ("Payments") described above, which Payments you would not have been entitled under Company policy, you agree that, for a period of twenty-four (24) months after the execution of this letter (the "Period"), you will not engage, anywhere in the world, as either a principal, agent, consultant, employee, director, or otherwise for any of the following stated direct competitors (or any of their subsidiary or affiliate companies) of the Company's Division: _____, _____, _____, or _____. The phrase "Division" shall mean any portion of the business that manufactures, markets, sells, and/or distributes any product and/or service that is similar to, or competitive with, any of the Company's Division's products and/or services. Additionally, during the Period, you agree to not disclose to any person, firm, or corporation the name, position, or duties of any other person or persons employed by or associated with the Company, nor induce or attempt to induce any person or persons employed by or associated with the Company to leave the employment of or to discontinue his or her association with the Company. Finally, during the Period, you further agree to advise the Company in writing in advance and consult the Company when considering entering upon any activity that might violate the covenants of this paragraph. Any breach of this paragraph would not be readily or appropriately compensable in damages, and you expressly agree that each provision, restriction, and/or covenant shall be enforceable by injunctive relief.

17. **GOVERNING LAW AND VENUE.** The letter shall be construed under the laws of the State of _____, USA. You hereby irrevocably waive any objection that you may have now or thereafter to the laying of venue of any action or proceeding arising out of or relating to this letter being brought in the United States District Court for the _____ District of _____ or the Circuit Court of the State of _____ in _____, _____, and any objection on the ground that any such action or proceeding in either of such Courts has been brought in an inconvenient forum.

In consideration of the benefits and payments described above, you, on your own behalf and for your spouse, heirs, assigns, and representatives of any kind, hereby release and forever discharge the Company, its officers, directors, shareholders, employees, insurers, subsidiaries, and any affiliated companies from any and all claims, demands, rights, liabilities, and causes of action of any kind or nature, including claims under the Age Discrimination in Employment Act, known or unknown, arising or having arisen out of, in connection with, or during your employment with the Company. However, this release shall not apply to any of your rights under benefit plans that apply generally to former employees (subject to any benefit plan restrictions) of the Company, any claims based on facts arising after the date of execution of this Agreement, and your rights under this Agreement.

You agree to fully cooperate with the Company in any claim or matter, of or with third parties that may arise in the future to which you may have knowledge acquired during your employment with the Company.

In further consideration of the additional payments described above, you agree to keep strictly confidential, and will not disclose to any third part in any manner, directly or indirectly, the terms of this agreement and any confidential business or technical information of the Company, as well as any information regarding any business and/or personal affairs of any present or former directors, officers, stockholders, and/or employees of the Company or any affiliate or subsidiary companies of the Company to which you have been privy during the time that you were an employee of this Company in accordance with the requirements of this Agreement or as may be required by the Secrecy Agreement you signed.

You agree and understand that this Agreement sets forth and contains all of the Company's obligations to you and that you are not entitled to any other compensation of any kind or description.

We advise you to consult an attorney prior to signing this Agreement, especially in relation to the release stated above.

If you would like to discuss these terms further and include anyone else in the discussion, please contact me so that such a meeting may be arranged.

If you are in agreement with all of the terms stated in this letter, please sign both copies where provided below and return one (1) copy to me. We would appreciate receiving your response within twenty-two (22) days of receipt. You may revoke this Agreement within seven (7) days after you sign it, and if you do revoke this Agreement within the seven (7)-day period, this Agreement shall not become effective or enforceable.

_____

Accepted and agreed to this _____ day of _____, 200__

_____

NON- OFFICER SEPARATION AGREEMENT

Date:

To:

From:

The following sets forth our mutual agreement regarding your separation from the Company:

1. **SALARY.** Your last day of work will be _____ or the completion of your currently assigned project, whichever is earlier. You will continue on the Company payroll through _____ at your current base-salary level. If you secure new employment prior to that date, your employment with the company will be terminated and you will be removed from the Company's payroll as of the date you commence new employment. You will be paid the equivalent of any remaining salary continuation through _____, in a lump-sum payment as additional separation pay. You will not accrue additional vacation or personal choice days during any salary continuation period.

2. **SEPARATION PAY.** The company will also pay you separation pay equal to _____ weeks base salary. This amount will be paid to you in lump sum after your removal from the Company's payroll.

3. **HEALTH BENEFITS.** Benefits under the Company's Medical, Dental, Vision, and Prescription Drug Plans will continue in effect as provided in those plans. Your benefits specialist can provide you with more detailed information.

4. **LIFE INSURANCE.** Your life-insurance coverage under the basic life insurance plan will continue at a reduced level after your retirement. Your benefits specialist can provide you with more detailed information.

5. **UNUSED VACATION.** Any remaining vacation and personal choice holidays owed to you from _____ to _____ shall be paid in a lump sum by a separate check within fifteen (15) days of your removal from the Company's payroll. You are not eligible for additional vacation and personal choice holidays after _____.

6. **PENSION BENEFITS.** You are eligible to receive pension benefits under the Company's Retirement Plan at any time. Only base-salary earnings up to the date of your removal from the Company's payroll shall be utilized to calculate your pension benefits and shall not include any separation payments made pursuant to paragraphs 1 and 2 above. Your pension payments will commence in _____ if you choose your method of payment in a timely manner. However, you may defer the start of your pension. _____ of Human Resources can provide you with more detailed information.

7. **OUTPLACEMENT ASSISTANCE.** The Company will provide job-search assistance through Lawrence & Allen, Inc. to help in securing other employment. This service includes career counseling, resume development, networking techniques, interview training, and follow-up counseling. The Company will pay all fees and expenses of such services.

8. **FINANCIAL SERVICES.** The Company agrees to reimburse you up to Five Hundred Dollars ($500.00) for any financial consulting services, which you actually incur, from either a certified financial consultant or an attorney. Such reimbursement shall occur after the Company's receipt of validated statements relating to expenses incurred as a result of this Agreement or the transaction described herein. Said validated statements should be sent to _____ no later than _____.

In consideration of the benefits and payments described above to which you would not have been entitled under existing Company policy, you, on your own behalf and for your heirs, assigns, and representatives of any kind, hereby release and forever discharge the Company, its officers, directors, shareholders, employees, insurers, subsidiaries, and any affiliated companies from any and all claims, demands, rights, liabilities, and causes of action of any kind or nature, including, without limitation, rights and/or claims under the Age Discrimination in Employment Act, known or unknown, arising or having arisen out of, in connection with or during your employment with or separation from the Company. However, this release shall not apply to any of your rights under benefit plans that apply generally to former employees (subject to any benefit plan restrictions) of the Company, any claims based on facts arising after the date of execution of this Agreement, and your rights under this Agreement.

In further consideration of the additional payments described above, you agree to keep strictly confidential, and will not disclose to any third party in any manner, directly or indirectly, the terms of this agreement and any confidential business or technical information of the company, as well as any information regarding any business and/or personal affairs of any present or former directors, officers, stockholders, and/or employees of the Company or any affiliate or subsidiary companies of the Company to which you have been privy during the time that you were an employee of this Company in accordance with the requirements of this Agreement or as may be required by the Secrecy Agreement you signed.

You agree to cooperate with the Company in any claim or matter, which may arise in the future, to which you may have knowledge acquired during your period of employment.

You agree and understand that this Agreement sets forth and contains all of the Company's obligations to you and that you are not entitled to any other compensation of any kind or description.

We advise you to consult an attorney prior to signing this Agreement, especially in relation to the release stated above.

If you would like to discuss these terms further and include anyone else in the discussions, please contact me so that such a meeting may be arranged.

If you are in agreement with all of the terms stated in this letter, please sign both copies where provided below and return one (1) copy to me. We would appreciate receiving your response within twenty-two (22) days after your receipt. You may revoke this Agreement within seven (7) days after you sign it, and if you do revoke this Agreement within the seven (7)-day period, this Agreement shall not become effective or enforceable.

_____

Accepted and agreed to this
_____ day of _____, 200_

_____

GUIDELINES FOR SEPARATION

If you are still employed but know you will be separated in the near future, please keep the following guidelines in mind when you leave your current employer:

☑ Leave graciously. Your behavior and attitude can "make" your reputation. Even if you feel angry, try not to show it, and do **not** show dissension.

☑ Do not make the individual who separates you feel guilty. Do you really know that he or she was part of the decision or just the messenger? Additionally, he or she may be a future source for a reference or recommendation.

☑ Get specific information on severance (amount, duration, conditions), benefit continuation, bonuses, profit sharing, etc. Find out whom to call in the future should you have additional questions. Where are your employment records to be kept in the event your plant is closing or there is a change in ownership of your company?

☑ Try to assure an orderly transition. Leaving your work in good order attests to your sense of responsibility. Leave priority or "to-do" lists.

☑ If possible, take along the business cards of your colleagues outside the company that you have collected over the years and your telephone-address book. These may be utilized to network in your job campaign.

☑ Leave the impression with your former colleagues that you are confident about the future. Do not feel sorry for yourself or ask coworkers to feel that way. They are more likely to retain positive memories of you. **Final words, actions, and attitudes are usually what are remembered and what you want passed on.**

☑ Do not take a vacation to "think things over." You probably cannot afford it, and the sooner you start looking for another job, the sooner you will find one.

**Remember, how you leave your job today . . .
is how I will remember you tomorrow.**

DEALING WITH THE FAMILY

When discussing your recent separation with the family, keep in mind the following guidelines:

☑ Be honest. Showing and sharing your concern about your search for a new position is not a sign of weakness. Rather, it indicates you recognize that your family can pull together as a team during a difficult time. Your confidence in your family will help reinforce their confidence in you.

☑ Your spouse can help reduce pressures on you if you communicate with each other.

☑ Your spouse or children can cover your telephone at home if you are unable to take calls at the office or if you are out. Impress upon them the importance of taking accurate messages. This topic is covered in detail in Chapter IV.

☑ Your spouse is probably a valuable source of advice for reducing expenses during your search period. Discuss controlling household-operating expenses during your job search period.

☑ Discuss the progress of your search with your family.

☑ Explore the implications of possible relocation. If the children are old enough, include them. A job search can be a positive instructive experience for children if their security is not threatened. If moving from the community and school are likely, let the children in on these matters. Do not drop a bombshell on them. If you anticipate moving to take advantage of an opportunity, your children are more likely to reflect your attitude if you share your excitement with them. They can sense your feelings anyhow, so talk about these feelings. Remind the children that they can visit old friends during vacations and holidays. Carry through on your intentions.

☑ Spending a great deal of time on your job search may not leave you time for such things as lawn mowing, major repairs, or projects around the house. Ignore these tasks until the weekend or assign them to another member of the family.

☑ Your spouse and older children can help you do research on prospective employers, etc., at the local library. Or they can be messengers, bringing books from the library, for example.

☑ If someone in your family can type, they can help send letters to prospective employers.

☑ Members of the family can look up out-of-town names and addresses (of employment agencies, recruiters, companies, etc.) in directories at the main office of your local telephone company or search the Internet for them.

☑ Tell your family whom you have contacted, and still plan to contact, so that they can act intelligently if they receive a telephone call from one of your prospects.

ENROLLING A SPOUSE IN THE JOB CAMPAIGN PROCESS

As an integral part of our outplacement-consulting practice, my firm has always encouraged the outplaced individual to invite his or her spouse to visit our offices. I find this extremely important, especially if the spouse does not work outside of the home.

Since many spouses derive self-esteem, ego, and security from the position of the co-captain on the marriage team, when that individual loses his or her position, the support base is shaken significantly. To reassure a spouse about what activities take place at an outplacement consultant's office, we invite him or her in to take a look firsthand. If necessary, we offer counseling from our psychologist, as well as to chat about campaign strategy and what the market is for the person who's just starting his or her job campaign. Invariably we come to a question that is raised, "What can I do to help my wife's or my husband's campaign?" Therefore, I have organized the following list of activities, which will accelerate re-employment plus make the spouse feel an integral part in helping his or her husband or wife secure gainful re-employment.

The objectives of the following activities are twofold. First, to assist in the job campaign activities and to alleviate the job hunter of those activities that can best be handled by someone else, i.e., the spouse. Remember the old economics principle of "The Law of Comparative Advantage." If I am the best attorney in town, and I am also the fastest and best typist in town, the law of comparative advantage says that I should do what I do best to leverage my income. While I can be the best lawyer and best typist, obviously I can make more money trying cases than I can typing briefs. Second, the job hunter is now free to work on those job campaign activities that only he or she can perform himself or herself. These type of activities would take the form of personal follow-up calls, specific decisions on the job campaign that only the job hunter can make, and to explore various alternatives with networking contacts, as well as to request informational interviews about future growth opportunities within various industries and, of course, to target specific companies.

Several of the items listed have to do with perusing the Internet, preparing E-mail responses, downloading information on identified companies, etc. Under a separate section in this book, I discuss the hard facts about using the Internet in your job campaign. The bottom line is too many people waste too much time on the Internet because less than probably 5 to 7 percent of the jobs currently being filled are filled through the Internet. This is an activity that draws many job hunters only to be disappointed when they realize that the amount of effort going into using the Net is highly disproportionate to the results that the Net produces. Therefore, many of these activities can be delegated to the spouse to cruise the Net and even prepare responses back to positions that are posted on the Net.

- Check career Web site listings for appropriate ads. (See Chapter II for complete listing of Web sites).

- Prepare E-mail responses to posted positions on the Web.

- Research information on companies: verifying addresses, current names, titles, and phone numbers.

- Input information to a database for subsequent list-merging programs.

- Identify key contact individuals within organizations; verify titles, current addresses, and phone numbers.

- Keep track of job-hunting expenses.

- Review all proposed purchases for absolute need.

- Become proficient in word-processing programs including list processing.

- Read newspapers, particularly the business section, to identify potential companies or individuals for contact, economic trends, and companies moving into the area.

- Prepare letters for mailing.

- Reserve the "honey-do" assignments for the weekend.

- Encourage and participate in an exercise program to be done with the job hunter.

- Seek out or start a spouse support group.

- Keep your ears open for comments that may be dropped during a social conversation that could be important to the job search.

- Purchase and install an envelope feeder if your computer does not have one.

- Tap in to your spouse's network. Send these individuals a couple of resumes.

- Have your spouse update last year's Christmas-card list that now becomes your personal networking database.

MAINTAINING A POSITIVE ATTITUDE

The biggest disease today is
not leprosy or tuberculosis,
but rather the feeling of
being unwanted.

-   Mother Teresa

All of us have patterns in our lives. We follow routines during most days and have a certain satisfaction in the regularity of these patterns. When something happens to disrupt one of these major patterns, such as our work activities, it can be a challenging time for us. Any serious loss or unwelcome change in life patterns can trigger unhappiness and sad feelings. Change, however, can be challenging and can provide the opportunity to expand our horizons.

It is not uncommon for persons who face the challenge of a search for a new position to experience strong emotions. For many, coping with job loss is much like coping with the loss of a loved one. One may have to go through a similar process of grieving. The severity of the loss experienced will depend on the degree to which the person's identity has been tied to his or her job. People with other outlets that give them a strong sense of persona will weather the loss somewhat better. Finding healthy ways to deal with the pain of the loss can be immensely helpful.

Many research studies have documented the seriousness of job loss and the aftermath of this experience. It is important that you be alert to these possible negative aftereffects and work to turn this normally traumatic experience into a more meaningful one.

When the news of separation is first received, emotional denial may occur. Anger and frustration can follow this initial denial. You may feel tense, anxious, nervous and upset. Internal bargaining with oneself sometimes is experienced. The optimal outcome of these transitional stages is acceptance and commitment to the future.

By understanding how these disruptions in the patterns of our lives affect us and by following some simple tips, we can lessen the physical and emotional impact of these stressful experiences. The impact will vary from individual to individual in terms of tolerance to disruptive events. However, there are some methods that have proven helpful in recovering and continuing to maintain mental and emotional equilibrium in the face of pattern disruption. These include honest inventory taking, planning, consistency, exercise, and patience.

A daily personal inventory can be useful to take stock of one's emotional temperature, so to speak. This inventory can provide an opportunity to identify needs to ventilate anxiety, frustration, and general issues that occur on a daily basis. Sharing these perceptions with a trusted confidant who is supportive can be of great benefit. Discuss problems and be positive.

It will be important to use your time wisely. Do not overload yourself; do not procrastinate. Make lists of tasks to be completed and pace yourself appropriately. This will lessen the chance that you will feel overwhelmed by the task at hand.

Maintaining good health habits will never be more important than when you are in an anxiety-generating and stressful situation. Exercise regularly, eat right, get enough sleep, and do not abuse alcohol or other drugs. Regular physical exercise can be of great benefit.

If you have not been exercising regularly, you may need to gradually work up to an adequate exercise program. Changes in your level of physical exercise should not be attempted without the recommendation and supervision of your personal physician. Finding an exercise schedule and program that is enjoyable is also critical to maintaining it over time.

A time of transition and change in patterns can be an excellent time to change your personal habits. Be kind to yourself and acknowledge your successes. Reflect on your abilities and accomplishments. Share your thoughts and feelings with someone you trust. Do things you enjoy. Quit smoking and reduce caffeine intake if possible. Schedule leisure time. Seek out new interests and, by all means, seek professional help if you experience sustained feelings of depression or anxiety.

Finally, be patient. Be persistent and consistent. Do not entertain feelings of "giving up" when things do not seem to go smoothly. Once you have successfully maneuvered through the turbulent waters of the initial separation experience, do not let yourself get bogged down by feelings of rejection, frustration, and disillusionment that may come as your campaign progresses. Rome was not built in a day. You may not find a new, satisfying position in a short period of time. Every interview will not turn into an offer of employment. Be on your guard. Continue to practice positive behaviors previously suggested.

When setbacks and disappointments occur during your campaign, it will be important for you to sometimes engage in self-talk. Continue to reinforce your own knowledge of your achievements and strengths. Change views and ideas that lead to discouragement and self-defeating behaviors. Work to eliminate unwanted, negative thoughts through substitution of positive thoughts.

Utilize your support network. It will be important to maintain a positive attitude as you progress through the campaign to locate a new position. It is often helpful to have the family or other loved ones actively involved. Those closest to us can offer emotional support that involves understanding, patience, affection, and encouragement. Suggestions are made on page 20 of this guide as to how your family and loved ones can play an active, practical role in your campaign.

Publications that may be helpful as you face the emotional challenge of the rigors of a search for a new position are *Feeling Good* by David Burns, M.D., and *Pathfinders* by Gail Sheehy. Each of these publications is available in paperback at many bookstores. In addition, you will likely find copies at your local public library.

SIGNIFICANT LIFE-EVENTS SURVEY

The following instrument is designed to measure stress in terms of life changes. Studies have revealed a consistent relationship between the number of stressful events in a person's life and that person's emotional and physical health.

Research has shown that more than 50 percent of the people whose life-change units summed up to between 200 and 300 in a single year exhibited health problems the following year; 79 percent of the people whose scores summed to over 300 became ill the following year. These are probabilities, however, and not certainties. Awareness can be the first line of defense so that preventive measures can be taken.

For people whose life-change unit values were high, interesting research has shown that persons whose attitudes toward life could be rated high on involvement, feelings of control, and positive responses to change remained much healthier than the persons who scored low on these dimensions. The most important factor appeared to be attitude toward change. People who view change as a challenge are apt to experience less stress and to turn situations to their advantage. The personality characteristics of stress-resistant or **hardy** individuals have been summarized in capsule form by the terms **commitment**, **control**, and **challenge**.

Stress can increase the probability of illness, but it does not have to. People who view the world as an interesting place, who seek to learn from their experiences, and who believe they have some control over the events in their lives seem to cope more adequately in their life situations. These **attitudes** coupled with the following behaviors seem to be most effective in nurturing good health: no smoking, good nutrition habits, moderate weight, moderate or no alcohol, regular exercise, and regular sleep habits.

SIGNIFICANT LIFE-EVENTS SURVEY

(Adapted from the Holmes and Rahe Social Readjustment Rating Scale, after Holmes and Rahe, 1967.)

Please circle the number before any event that you have experienced within the past year.

Name: _____

1.   Death of Spouse
2.   Divorce
3.   Marital Separation
4.   Jail Term
5.   Death of a Close Family Member
6.   Personal Injury or Illness
7.   Marriage
8.   Loss of Job
9.   Marital Reconciliation
10. Retirement
11. Change in Health of Family Member
12. Pregnancy
13. Sex Difficulties
14. Gain of New Family Member
15. Business Readjustment
16. Change in Financial State
17. Death of a Close Friend
18. Change to a Different Line of Work
19. Foreclosure of Mortgage
20. Change in Responsibilities at Work
21. Son or Daughter Leaving Home
22. Trouble with In-Laws
23. Outstanding Personal Achievement
24. Spouse Begins or Stops Work
25. Begin or End School
26. Change in Living Conditions
27. Change in Personal Habits
28. Trouble with Boss
29. Change in Work Hours or Conditions
30. Change in Residence
31. Change in School
32. Change in Recreation
33. Change in Church Activities
34. Change in Social Activities
35. Change in Sleeping Habits
36. Change in Eating Habits
37. Vacation
38. Major Religious Holiday
39. Minor Violations of the Law

SIGNIFICANT LIFE-EVENTS SURVEY

(Adapted from the Holmes and Rahe Social Readjustment Rating Scale, after Holmes and Rahe, 1967.)

ANALYSIS
( ) = Point Value

1. Death of a Spouse (100)
2. Divorce (73)
3. Marital Separation (65)
4. Jail Term (64)
5. Death of a Close Family Member (63)
6. Personal Injury or Illness (53)
7. Marriage (50)
8. Loss of Job (47)
9. Marital Reconciliation (45)
10. Retirement (45)
11. Change in Health of Family Member (44)
12. Pregnancy (40)
13. Sex Difficulties (39)
14. Gain of New Family Member (39)
15. Business Readjustment (38)
16. Change in Financial State (38)
17. Death of a Close Friend (37)
18. Change to a Different Line of Work (36)
19. Foreclosure of Mortgage (34)
20. Change in Responsibilities at Work (29)
21. Son or Daughter Leaving Home (29)
22. Trouble with In-Laws (29)
23. Outstanding Personal Achievement (28)
24. Spouse Begins or Stops Work (26)
25. Begin or End School (26)
26. Change in Living Conditions (25)
27. Change In Personal Habits (24)
28. Trouble with Boss (23)
29. Change in Work Hours Or Conditions (20)
30. Change in Residence (20)
31. Change in School (20)
32. Change in Recreation (20)
33. Change in Church Activities (19)
34. Change in Social Activities (18)
35. Change in Sleeping Habits (15)
36. Change in Eating Habits (15)
37. Vacation (13)
39. Major Religious Holiday (12)
40. Minor Violations of the Law (11)

0 – 150 pts   No significant problems predicted.
150 – 199 pts   Mild life crisis (33 percent chance of physical or emotional problems).
200 – 300 pts   Moderate life crisis (50 percent chance of physical or emotional problems).
Over 300 pts   Major life crisis (80 percent chance of physical or emotional problems).

COPING FINANCIALLY

Beware of little expenses.
A small leak will sink a great ship.

-   Benjamin Franklin

Make cutting expenses a family project.   Do not try to carry the dual burdens of finding a job and holding the line on cash outflow. With your spouse or family members, draw up an honest financial income and outflow chart. Try to keep all family members aware of your situation. Be sure there is agreement on all expenditures. In other words, ask this question: **"Do we *have* to buy it?"**

Draw up a family operating budget or trim the current one. Now is a good time. The better you organize your finances, the longer you can look for the right position. Establish a budget that is tight and stick to it without exception. You will be amazed at all the items you can cut out or, at least, reduce.

If possible, plan a budget with your family that will carry you for a six-month period. **This means reducing your living expenses by one-third.**   If you observe the recommended job search regimen, the odds are that you will find another position before your severance runs out, but be on the safe side.

Stop using credit cards. Pay cash, especially if credit costs money.

Make a list of all creditors and advise them of your financial situation. **DO NOT STOP PAYING BILLS.** As long as you make a token payment to your creditors, you will generally find them to be understanding and accommodating. If you will be unable to meet finance payments on a regular basis, write or telephone your creditors and offer to stay current with interest payments. Most creditors will cooperate with such reasonable requests, especially if your payments are current and you have had a good record of being prompt. Even if denied, your request will *not* endanger your status if your payments are up to date. Keep copies of all payments made to creditors or letters written to explain your temporary predicament. Do not be intimidated by computer printouts that warn that your credit status is in jeopardy. You are paying something on your bills, and this will be important in the unlikely event that the situation should go to Small Claims Court or a collection agency.

Reassess your assets. You may have little cash available, but what about stocks, bonds, a second mortgage or a home equity loan, disposing of your second car, a loan on life-insurance policies, dropping club memberships, or even selling art treasures and other valuables?

Do not hire outside experts to help you plan for this period.   Between this professional Outplacement program and your own contacts, you will be amazed how much assistance you can get without tapping into your financial resources.

Many banks offer family budgeting forms free of charge. Ask your bank if they have such forms available.

Do not use your money to start your own business. You may not be in the most objective state of mind at this time, **do not deplete your cash reserves when you have little incoming cash flow.** Beginning your own business may seem like a viable alternative to corporate employment but is risky under the best of circumstances. If you are determined to embark upon business for yourself, plan to do so, but do it on your own terms – not as a result of your ex-employer's terms.

Apply for every kind of benefit for which you are eligible. Do not forget unemployment insurance! It may not be much, but it will help with the management of your funds during this transition period.

Do not apply for unnecessary loans to cover this period. Loans are extremely expensive and should only be used as a last resort. Also, remember that lending institutions could be hesitant to loan money, even if you have collateral, because you are seeking employment. What you do not need at this time is disappointment and frustration.

For those of you who want a detailed assessment of your financial status and a planning guide for the period of unemployment, **please see the following Financial Planning Guide.** This section also includes a guide to tax-deductible expenses incurred during your job campaign.

LIST THREE (3) EXPENSE ITEMS TO CUT BACK OR ELIMINATE

My Choice   My Spouse's Choice

1. _____   _____

2. _____   _____

3. _____   _____

If you and your spouse agree – great! If you don't – negotiate and be flexible.

FINANCIAL PLANNING GUIDE

The starting point for any financial plan involves a close, hard look at anticipated expenses. If you are married, it would be wise to sit down with your spouse and approach financial planning with the assumption that you will be out of work for three to six months. Any unfounded optimism at this stage would only leave you in a more difficult position at a later date.

On the next few pages is a general financial planning guide for anyone who finds him or herself suddenly unemployed. The original source for this guide came to us through the courtesy of the Dow Chemical Corporation and the TRW Corporation.

I have divided this guide into three basic sections:

1. **Anticipated Cash Flow** – Your projection of expenses during the period of unemployment.
2. **Present Cash Position and Anticipated Cash Flow** – Your present cash position and your estimates of possible cash inflows.
3. **Supplemental Income from Sales of Assets, etc.** – Your potential need to identify sources of additional cash through the sale of assets.

1.   **ANTICIPATED CASH FLOW**

The following is a list of the types of expenses that are routinely incurred by most individuals. They are only intended as a general guide. However, we have found that the people who work through this budgeting exercise are likely to bring areas for potential savings into focus.

One extra expense that we have listed will involve the cost of your job campaign. You will have to make an allowance for expenses related to such items as computer lease, typing fees, stationery, stamps, extra weekly periodicals, phone charges, added transportation, dry cleaning, etc. There can be little doubt that it will cost money for you to find a good job. We advise that you do your best to provide the funds that will enable you to proceed with maximum speed.

FINANCIAL PLANNING

EXPENSES	MONTHS					
	1	2	3	4	5	6
Bills and Other Debts Presently Outstanding						
Interest on Debts						
Mortgage (and/or rent)						
Life-Insurance Premium(s)						
Medical-Insurance Premium(s)						
Automotive-Insurance premium(s)						
Other Installment Payment Obligations						
Property Taxes						
Tuition Payments						
Club Dues						
Contributions						
Gifts						
Lessons: Music, Tennis, etc.						
Food						
Clothing						
Housewares						
Personal Items (Cosmetics, toiletries, etc.)						
Drugs and Medical Supplies						

EXPENSES	MONTHS					
	1	2	3	4	5	6
Household Operations:						
Heating						
Electricity						
Water						
Other						
Subscriptions/Newspapers, Magazines, etc.						
Automotive Expenses:						
Gas						
Maintenance						
Local Transportation (taxi, bus, etc.)						
Other Travel						
Laundry and Dry Cleaning						
Entertainment						
Barber/Beauty Shop Expenses						
Other:						
TOTAL – ALL OF THE ABOVE						
Estimated Job Campaign Costs:						
GRAND TOTAL (Anticipated Expenses)						

2. PRESENT CASH POSITION AND ANTICIPATED CASH FLOW

Listed below are general categories that should be sufficient for you to identify your present cash-flow position and anticipated cash inflow. Those items that exist as totals, rather than monthly income, should be evenly divided among six months. Once you complete these estimates, compare your cash availability with forecasted expenses from Section 1.

PRESENT CASH POSITION

(including assets, which can be readily converted to cash as required)

ASSETS	MONTHS					
	1	2	3	4	5	6
Cash:						
Checking Account						
Savings Account						
Credit Union, etc.						
Stocks/Bonds						
Cash Value Life-Insurance Policy						
Leases/Land Contracts						
Other						
TOTAL:						

ANTICIPATED CASH FLOW

CASH FLOW	MONTHS					
	1	2	3	4	5	6
Severance Pay						
Unused Vacation Pay						
Retirement Funds						
Pay in Lieu of Pension/Stock Savings Plan						

CASH INFLOW	MONTHS					
	1	2	3	4	5	6
Unemployment Compensation						
Interest from Savings Account						
Interest from Bonds						
Dividends from Stocks						
Tax Refund						
Collectable Debts Owed to You						
Income Generated by Part-Time Job						
Other						
TOTAL (Anticipated Cash Position)						

3.   SUPPLEMENTAL INCOME FROM THE SALE OF ASSETS, ETC.

As I mentioned before, you should approach financial planning with the point of view that you may be unemployed for some time. In completing Sections 1 and 2, you may very well find that you are not going to have the cash required for surviving this difficult period. If your situation is very tight, you should obviously attempt to hold down many expenses that would otherwise be normal. Here we refer to things such as entertainment expenses, gifts, contributions, lessons for the children, extra telephones, etc. You should also consider a garage or rummage sale of assets that otherwise might be unused.

If the situation looks very negative, you will have to face up to the possibility of selling certain assets. This is a step that should only be taken after you have exhausted all other avenues for cash generation or expense reduction.

The following is a listing of some of the categories you might examine as sources of extra cash.

SUPPLEMENTAL INCOME	MONTHS					
	1	2	3	4	5	6
Automobiles (Second Car)						
Automobiles (First Car)						
Sporting Equipment (boats, planes, motorcycles, snowmobiles, campers, etc.)						
Expensive Cameras (or other hobby equipment)						

Jewelry						
Musical Equipment						
Stamp/Coin Collection						
Works of Art						
Unused Furniture						
Old Clothing						
Other Equipment (unused lawn and farm)						
Secondary Properties						
Your Home						
Other						
TOTAL (Supplemental Income)						

SUMMARY COMMENTS ON FINANCIAL PLANNING

This very short guide can help you identify those potential expenses that might be reduced or eliminated. When you are unemployed, it is sometimes difficult to channel funds to the places where they are most needed without actually going through a budgeting exercise. If you are unemployed for some time, it would be wise for you to consider early communication with any creditors you may have. If you speak to them before you get behind in any payments, you will probably receive better consideration from them as you go along.

Some other things you may wish to consider would include:

1. Borrowing against your life-insurance policy rather than cashing it in. Most policies offer a lower interest rate than is currently available and, in the future, a varying payment schedule.
2. A single-source loan to consolidate smaller debts. It will be difficult to get a loan from a financial institution while you are unemployed. However, if you have collateral, it is possible. You may be able to secure a loan at a lower interest rate than the interest you will be charged by retail stores and credit card firms.
3. If you are really feeling pressed, sooner or later you may have to consider selling your home. A respected realtor with whom you can frankly review your problem will prove invaluable.

At the time you find yourself unemployed, you should also check into the prevailing government programs. For example, the Federal Food Stamp Program, government programs for paying the travel and interviewing expenses of technical personnel, state funding programs, and others.

GUIDE TO TAX- DEDUCTIBLE JOB-SEEKING EXPENSES

The following guide can help you to determine which expenses incurred during your job campaign are tax deductible. The original source for this guide came to us through the courtesy of David P. Lauzen, David P. Lauzen and Company, and selected IRS publications.

In general, any expenses incurred while looking for a new job in your present occupation are deductible. This is true whether you actually obtain a new job. If you are unemployed, you may deduct the expenses of looking for a job in your most recent occupation. Expenses incurred while looking for a job in a different occupation are not deductible, even if you obtain a new job. (For further definition of "different occupation," please refer to the Research Institute of America's Tax Guide, Volume 2, paragraph 16501 or IRC Section 62 (a)(1).

We have divided this guide into four (4) basic sections:

1. **Basic Expenses** – incurred during your job campaign.
2. **Travel Expenses** – incurred during your campaign.
3. **Moving Expenses** – incurred when you accept a position in a different location.
4. **Miscellaneous Expenses** – incurred as you conduct your job campaign.

1. BASIC EXPENSES

All of the items that follow may be tax deductible if you are seeking employment in the same business or trade:

- Resumes (i.e., cost of printing, professional help in writing, etc.)
- Postage
- Telephone bills
- Typing fees
- Stationery and all other types of consumable office supplies.

Remember that, as a taxpayer, you may be engaged in more than one trade or business and that the job campaign costs with respect to *any* of your trades or businesses may be tax deductible. Thus, a full-time attorney and a part-time lecturer was allowed to deduct job campaign costs of seeking a full-time teaching position (Rev Rule 78-93, 1978-1 CB 38). Please seek the advice of an accountant or tax expert to determine the suitability of deductions.

2. TRAVEL EXPENSES

Travel expenses when looking for a new job while still in your present occupation are deductible. The trips must be made primarily to look for a new job. Deductible travel expenses include transportation expenses to and from the area, food, lodging, and transportation while there.

Local transportation to look for a new job in your present occupation may be deductible. Transportation from home to an interview is **nondeductible commuting**. The cost of transportation from your present job to a job interview or outplacement firm, from an outplacement firm to a job interview, from one job interview to another, and from a job interview to the present job location is deductible. That way you will most likely generate the largest possible deductible mileage amount and smallest commuting amount.

When calculating automobile expenses, the standard mileage rate for year 2002 is 36.5 cents per mile.

3.   MOVING EXPENSES

If you elect to move in order to work for a new employer, you may be able to deduct the cost of moving your household to your new business location. The following paragraphs describe the parameters that must be met in order to deduct moving expenses:

Distance: The new principal place of work must be at least fifty miles farther from your old residence than your old residence was from your former place of work. For example, if your old job was three miles from your former home, you new job must be at least fifty-three miles from that former home.

Full-Time: You must be a full-time employee for at least thirty-nine weeks during the 12-month period immediately following the move to your new job location. You may have already obtained work in the new place at the time of your move, or you may secure employment after your move. Your family does not have to arrive with you, and your new household need not be established at that time.

Closely Related: Moving expenses must be closely related to the date that you begin work. In general, you may deduct expenses incurred more than one year after you begin work at the new location only if you can show that circumstances prevented you from completing your move earlier.

Travel expenses, including lodging but not meals, for yourself and your family while en route to your new residence are deductible. You may also deduct the cost of gas and oil for your car if you keep an accurate record of each expense or deduct 36.5 cents a mile. Parking fees and tolls are also deductible. General car repairs, maintenance, insurance, and depreciation are not deductible. The actual costs of moving your household, including the cost of transportation from your old residence to your new one and the cost of packing, storing, and insuring household goods for thirty consecutive days, are deductible. You may deduct the cost of shipping your car and any household pets.

Nondeductible moving expenses include:

- Pre-move house-hunting expenses
- Temporary living expenses

- Meal expenses
- Expenses of getting or breaking a lease
- Expenses of buying or selling a home

4. MISCELLANEOUS EXPENSES

Professional or trade association dues are deductible only if the membership benefits you in your field of desired employment. Subscriptions to professional publications or journals in your field are also deductible.

Please note that the information included in this workbook is of broad general usefulness to job seekers. Lawrence & Allen, Inc. advises that all individuals seek the advice of appropriate tax counsel to be apprised of any recent additions or changes in the tax law.

IRS publications you may want to refer to include:

- 463 (Travel, Entertainment, and Car)
- 508 (Educational Expenses)
- 521 (Moving Expenses)
- 529 (Miscellaneous)
- 535 (Business Expenses)

5. If you purchased this guide – Yes! The cost is deductible!

ADDITIONAL JOB-HUNTING EXPENSES

These expenses when looking for a new job in a taxpayer's present line of work are tax deductible, even if a new job is not found. However, expenses of looking for a new job in a new trade or business, even if a job is found, are not deductible.

Deductible job-hunting expenses include:

- Fees paid to employment agencies and executive recruiters
- Cost of assembling portfolios of work
- Career counseling to improve position in trade
- Fees for legal and accounting services or tax advice relating to employment contracts
- Advertising for a new job in present field
- Transportation costs to job interviews
- Long-distance telephone calls to prospective employers
- Newspapers and business publications bought for employment ads
- 50 percent of meals and entertainment expenses directly related to job search
- Out-of-town travel expenses include meals, lodging, and local transportation if the trip is primarily to look for a new job. If the main purpose of the trip is personal, travel costs are not deductible. However, out-of pocket job-hunting expenses at the destination are still deductible.
  Tax Court: A nurse practitioner made a trip from her home in New York to her son's home in Los Angeles. During the three-week stay, she conducted a job search, making telephone calls and sending resumes to several prospective employers. The Tax Court denied her deduction for travel expenses, stating that the reason for the trip was primarily personal. However, the Court allowed travel expenses from a similar trip made approximately one year later. For the second trip, which lasted two weeks, the taxpayer produced a daily log showing attendance at job interviews and follow-up phone calls to companies to which she had previously given her resume. The Court decided the second trip was primarily for job-seeking purposes (Murata, TCM 1996-321). Thus, the key to her success on the second trip was simply *DOCUMENTATION – PROVE IT OR LOSE IT!!!*

Deductible Home Phone Calls:

- Long distance business calls
- Extra cost of a second phone installed in home for business use.
- Extra features such as call waiting or call forwarding

REMEMBER

1. Keep track of everything!
2. The first and last stop every day should be the Outplacement office – thus making all mileage in between deductible. Example: Mileage from your home to an interview is considered a commute and is not deductible.

THE 2-PERCENT RULE

While certain job-hunting expenses are tax deductible, these expenses are considered miscellaneous deductions and are therefore subject to the 2 percent rule or floor. Expressed succinctly, allowable job campaign expenses are deductible, but only insofar as they exceed, along with all other miscellaneous deductions, 2 percent of an individual's adjusted gross income (IRS Publication 529 – Miscellaneous Deductions). A spouse's miscellaneous deductions may also be included if a joint return is filed. Thus, "bunching" deductions into a year, which includes a job campaign, may be very worthwhile.

For example, if:

Adjusted **G**ross **I**ncome equals	$100,000
Total job hunting expenses equal	$ 3,000
Less 2 percent of AGI	$ -2,000
Amount of deductible expenses	$ 1,000

UNEMPLOYMENT INSURANCE BENEFITS
AND JOB SERVICE

WHAT ARE UNEMPLOYMENT INSURANCE BENEFITS?

Unemployment Insurance Benefits, under a state-operated insurance program, are designed to partially compensate you for loss of wages when you are out of work. If you meet the requirements of the law, the benefits enable you to have an income until you can return to full-time employment. Unlike Social Security, which you pay through payroll deductions so that you can have a benefit when you retire, you do not pay any part of your wages toward unemployment insurance benefits. This plan is funded by taxes paid by your company and other companies.

ELIGIBILITY REQUIREMENTS

To qualify for unemployment insurance benefits, you must meet eligibility requirements that may differ in each state. If you do qualify, benefits will be paid to you as a matter of right. Benefits are not based on need and are not charity or welfare.

This program is administered by your State Department of Workforce Development – Unemployment Insurance Division and is operated through local offices in cities throughout the state. Specific names vary by state.

You should file a claim with your local unemployment Insurance Office during the first week after you have been separated or as soon as possible after that date. Many claim applications are now filed by using an automated telephone system, which will walk you through each step of the process.

Usually, there is a waiting period (example: one week) during which benefits are not paid. In many states, this waiting period may not start until you apply. Therefore, to be on the safe side, do not delay. The longer you delay filing, the more you may be delaying receipt of your first unemployment insurance check.

Since many separations take place on a Friday, the telephone lines and office will be busy on Monday morning. If you are separated on Friday before the end of the normal business day, you should call your nearest unemployment insurance office on the same day. Most individuals who are separated on Friday will wait until Monday morning to file a claim. You can imagine how crowded it would be on Monday. You may want to beat the crowd.

Although the eligibility requirements for your state may be different, examples of some (but not all) requirements may include the following:

1. You are unemployed during each week in which you claim benefits.
2. During each week in which you claim benefits, you were able to work, available for work, and actively looking for work.
3. You were registered for work with the Job Service (a component of the Department of Workforce Development).
4. You have served the appropriate waiting period (example: one week).

REASONS FOR DISQUALIFICATION

Although each state differs as to the reasons for rejecting your claim or stopping payment of your benefits, examples of some of the reasons may include the following:

1. Voluntarily quit your job (unless you quit because of health or other acceptable reasons).
2. You were discharged for misconduct connected with your work (which generally does not include poor job performance).
2. You failed, without good cause, to apply for or accept a suitable job offered to you.
3. For the same week for which you claim benefits, you will be paid, or will have already received, vacation pay, separation pay, wages in lieu of notice, workers' compensation pay, or pension/retirement plan benefits.

HOW MUCH WILL I RECEIVE?

The weekly amount of unemployment benefit varies by state. As an example, the state of Wisconsin unemployment benefit is computed based on 4 percent of the total high quarter wages from all covered employment. State law determines the minimum and maximum rates. For the year 2001, the Wisconsin maximum weekly rate was $313 while South Carolina had a weekly maximum of $268. These rates will change on a yearly basis.

A typical time period that you may be eligible to receive benefits is thirteen weeks with a possible extension to twenty-six weeks. This again varies by state. Be sure to inquire about length of benefit availability with your local unemployment insurance office.

Remember that your unemployment benefit is considered taxable income and is a limited resource. Do not rely on it as a sole means of support.

WHAT INFORMATION SHOULD I HAVE READY WHEN I FILE A CLAIM?

1. Social Security Number.
2. Employer names, addresses, telephone numbers, and dates of employment for the past eighteen months.
3. Evidence of earnings, such as check stubs and withholding statements.
4. Driver's License number.

WHAT INFORMATION SHOULD I BE PREPARED TO PROVIDE WHEN I FILE A CLAIM?

1. Why you are unemployed.
2. Wages received, including separation pay, vacation pay, pension/retirement plan pay, or any other earnings.
3. Names and birth dates of children under age eighteen, supported by you or names of older children supported by you who cannot work because of illness or disability.
4. Social Security number, if any, of spouse (if supported by you) and information about his/her employment during the past two (2) years.
5. Information documenting all efforts to find another job.

WHAT IS THE CLAIMS PROCEDURE?

Although the procedure varies with every state, it usually starts when you file a claim with your local unemployment insurance office. A notice will be sent to your last employer (and, in some cases, to your previous employer). If the company protests your claim, there will be a series of steps in which an administrator or deputy from the Department of Workforce Development will act as a "judge" in objectively determining the facts and will reach a conclusion as to whether you are eligible for benefits.

In most cases, when your separation is due to downsizing, plant closing, restructuring, reengineering, performance related reasons, etc., the company may not protest this claim but, instead, may encourage you to file for unemployment insurance benefits.

WHAT IS THE STATE JOB SERVICE?

The purpose of the State Job Service (or Job Center as they may be called in different states) is to help you find a job. To qualify for unemployment insurance benefits, you must register for work with the Department of Workforce Development, and you must report to the office whenever you are asked to do so. If you do not meet these requirements, your benefits may be affected.

The Job Service, depending upon the state, may also counsel workers with special problems, provide special assistance for veterans, provide selective placement of workers who are handicapped, and administer vocational/aptitude tests to help determine how successful applicants will be in particular jobs.

Applicants may be entered in a computerized system that can be accessed to fill job orders. When an employer is seeking candidates for employment openings, the system may identify the applicant's most important former position. This may increase the potential of being referred for job openings and also help claimants meet job search requirements to preserve eligibility for unemployment insurance benefits.

Your state may have a computerized system or Job Net to link employers and job seekers. This system would be available at your local Job Service office and may also be accessed via a Web address on the Internet.

Job listings typically range from service to manufacturing including management, professional, clerical, and technical opportunities.

Job Service and computerized job posting are a free service provided by your state. This is an excellent resource for learning about employment opportunities in an efficient manner and should be used as one part of your job campaign.

QUESTIONS TO ASK YOUR JOB-SERVICE REPRESENTATIVE

1. Will part-time employment bar me from collecting unemployment compensation?
2. What does "actively looking for employment" mean?
3. Do I have to actually visit an employer's place of business to be considered actively looking for employment?
4. Does rejecting an offer of employment bar me from collecting unemployment compensation?
5. Is unemployment compensation taxable?

6. Does your Job Service recognize E-mail, telephone calls, and/or letter campaigns to potential employers as "actively" looking for employment?
7. What records must I keep to maintain my eligibility for unemployment compensation?

TO TEMP OR NOT TO TEMP?
That Is the Question

One of the options you may want to consider during your job search is that of temporary employment. Not only does working temporary job assignments provide cash flow, but more and more employers are utilizing temporary services to provide a pool of potential full-time workers from which to draw. These workers are most often production and clerical, but temporary personnel are filling technical, legal, medical, professional, and management positions.

One of the most important aspects of working as a temporary is understanding your relationship with the temporary service. The service is your employer while you are on a temporary assignment. It is not an agency representing you. The service provides client companies temporary personnel to perform various work assignments and bills the company for the work done. In turn, the service pays the temporary employee an hourly rate for the number of hours worked. The difference between the pay rate and the bill rate is where the temporary service makes its profit. That difference must be large enough to cover the applicable payroll taxes, benefits cost, recruiting costs, etc., and allow for a reasonable profit. Most services pay weekly, although some that employ manual laborers pay on a daily basis.

Working as a temporary employee has become a career choice for some. The flexibility of work schedules and variety of assignments provides a lifestyle that appeals to many. However, the nature of temporary jobs is that assignments may be sporadic, with no guarantees of working forty hours per week. If this is the case, you will be working temporary part-time. If you are offered a long-term assignment (four or more weeks) working forty hours per week, you will be considered as employed temporary full-time. The amount of work you will be offered is directly related to your skills and performance, the local job market for temporary personnel, your pay requirements, and your flexibility to accept a variety of assignments.

Choosing a temporary personnel service can require a bit of research. Talk with friends and acquaintances that have worked as temporary employees. Ask which service(s) they recommend. If you don't know anyone to ask, look in the Yellow Pages of the telephone book under "Employment Contractors – Temporary Help" or read the want ads in the newspaper. Usually, temporary services advertise available positions. Some of the leading national temporary services are Norrell, Olsten, Kelly, Adia, Talent Tree, Uniforce, Interim Personnel, Manpower, Remedy, and Today's Temporary. Most national services offer benefits such as the availability of medical and dental insurance, vacation and holiday pay, free training, and bonuses. Some even offer profit sharing, 401K plans, child-care allowances, and lunch pay. In addition to national services, there are many regional and local services. However, these smaller services seldom offer benefits to their employees. Remember, when you are on assignment, you are an employee of the temporary service.

It is acceptable to work with more than one temporary service. As you accept work assignments from various services, you will discover that some jobs offered will fit your needs better than others. A word of caution: **Do not back out after having accepted a job assignment without providing sufficient time for the service to find a replacement.** You do not want to develop the reputation of being untrustworthy. Working as a temporary employee will be part of your job history and could be subject to reference checking by a potential employer.

After selecting a service, call to schedule an appointment to talk with a representative about working as a temporary employee. This meeting will be an interview – dress accordingly. Take with you a resume or information detailing previous work history and a list of references. Be prepared to complete an application and undergo a skill evaluation. If the interview goes well and you meet the service requirements to work for the company, you will probably be offered an assignment.

Flexibility is the key to becoming a successful temporary employee. Many factors associated with the assignment are subject to change. Frequently, the length of the assignment changes. Should this happen, advise your service representative that you will be available for another assignment sooner than expected. Should the assignment be extended and you are unable to work beyond your original commitment, notify your temporary service so that a replacement worker can be assigned.

In today's labor market, with the shortage of available, qualified workers in many areas of the country and the cost of recruiting these workers, the temp-to-perm hiring method is becoming more prevalent within the business community. This method allows the client company to fill a position with a temporary employee and evaluate his or her performance. If the performance is satisfactory, the company may make an offer of employment, and, upon acceptance, may add the worker to the organization's payroll after paying a temp-to-perm or cost recovery fee to the service. Often the temporary service will require the individual to remain on the service's payroll for a specified number of weeks before converting to the client company's payroll. Whatever the method chosen to compensate the service, the temporary employee is not responsible for paying the fees. That issue is between the service and the client company. However, the temporary employee is obligated to honor the service's temp-to-perm policy. The temporary service's application and subsequent time sheets are contracts and by signing these documents, the temporary agrees to abide by the service's policies.

The downside to working as a temporary employee is that it limits the time you have available to work on your job search campaign. However, depending on your circumstances, being a temporary employee certainly can offer assistance in the form of income, contacts, information on available full-time positions, and visibility to potential employers who have the opportunity to see the quality of your work.

Take a close look at temporary employment and consider the pros and cons to see if it fits into your job search strategy.

QUESTIONS TO ASK WHEN INTERVIEWING WITH A TEMPORARY SERVICE

1. How often do you get requests for my skills?
2. Who are some of your client companies?
3. When is my time sheet due?
4. With which banks have arrangements been made for check cashing?
5. Do I pick up my check here or is it mailed?
6. When is payday?
7. Who will probably be calling on me for an assignment?
8. What should I do if I don't like the job?
9. Do you often have temp-to-perm assignments?
10. What should I do if I am offered a position with the client company?
11. Will my performance be evaluated?
12. Will you share with me any feedback from the client on my work performance?
13. What happens if I feel the feedback is incorrect?
14. What happens if I decline an assignment?
15. Will I be penalized if I can't complete an assignment?

QUESTIONS TO ASK WHEN OFFERED AN ASSIGNMENT

1. Where is the assignment?
2. What is the work schedule and start date?
3. What is the pay rate?
4. What is the length of the assignment?
5. Could the assignment develop into a temp-to-perm opportunity?
6. What are the responsibilities of the assignment?
7. To whom do I report?
8. What is the dress code?
9. Is parking provided?
10. How long is the lunch break? Are eating establishments nearby?
11. Have you worked with this client before?

MARKETING YOURSELF IN THE NEW MILLENNIUM

Choose a job you love,
and you will never have to work
a day in your life.

- Confucius

The job market has changed significantly in the last five to ten years. To navigate effectively through these waters, it is extremely important that you understand some of these changes. First and foremost, the number of qualified job applicants in the market has increased due to ongoing corporate restructuring. Additionally, you will be competing with other individuals who are employed but looking to make either a job or career change. Therefore, the importance of learning how to successfully sell yourself in your job market is quite significant.

Conducting a successful job campaign is, in simple terms, learning how to market yourself. **In fact, a successful job campaign depends on a combination of 20 percent skills and 80 percent marketing**. Once you are employed, these ratios will change their respective positions.

Ten years ago it was more common for individuals to locate suitable positions through advertisement or by simply walking into a company and filling out an application. In today's job market, only about 10 percent to 15 percent of jobs are found through advertisements.

The two most effective ways to find jobs today are networking (which is the process of contacting individuals that you know, seeking their advice and assistance, and asking if they can refer you to other individuals), and marketing yourself directly to companies.

Additional processes that have changed include interviewing, resume construction, using E-mail for responding to electronic ads, follow-up, interview follow-up, and salary negotiations. All of these topics and many more are covered in the following pages. Even if you have searched for a job once or twice within the last ten years, I strongly encourage you to make use of this guide. We, at Lawrence & Allen, make it our priority to keep up with the latest trends in job seeking. It is our desire to share with you what we have learned and a little bit more about the process of successfully locating a new position.

Within GE, we've got to upgrade workers' skills through intense and continuous training. Companies can't promise lifetime employment, but by constant training and education, we may be able to guarantee lifetime employability.

- Jack Welch
Chief Executive Officer
General Electric, 1993

EMPLOYMENT VS. JOB SECURITY

Expressed simply, there is no such thing as job security – only employment security.

No job ever remains the same. It is in a constant state of evolution – and if the position or job ceases to evolve, it ceases to exist altogether.

The best and simplest example is the village blacksmith. Even the simple task of placing shoes on horses to protect the bottoms of their feet has undergone a significant evolution. In the early days, the famous picture of the village blacksmith working at his forge and anvil "under the spreading chestnut tree" was a common sight on Saturdays when the farmers would bring their horses and mules into town for shoeing. The blacksmith would also forge iron into plow blades and perform minor farm-equipment repair.

Contrast this somewhat romantic picture of the sweating blacksmith with the modern-day blacksmith.

First, the blacksmith is no longer called a blacksmith. He is called a farrier. The nature of the craft of protecting horses' feet has changed radically. No longer do owners of livestock bring their animals to the blacksmith shop. Rather, the farrier travels to his customers in a custom pick-up truck or van (an example of commitment to the customer.) Second, he no longer repairs farm plows or farm equipment. The local John Deere dealer now handles this.

In his van, the farrier has battery-charged bellows to heat the horseshoes. Even the fire has changed. No longer are coal and embers used to heat iron, but rather portable furnaces are used, fueled by propane gas. The nature of the horseshoe has changed from pure iron to the addition of boron and/or aluminum. To protect the inner hoof, polyurethane-filled pads with silicone jell have been introduced. No longer is the farrier charged with only protecting horses' hooves. Now he must protect the feet as well as make corrections on the angle of the foot for proper movement. How well the horse moves is now the key to its care. As the farrier's role has changed, so too the horse's role.

Even the modern-day farrier is subject to the process of subcontracting or outsourcing. Previously, the blacksmith would take an iron bar, heat it, bend it, and fit it to the horse's hoof. Now, the modern-day farrier buys the "shoe" as a preformed blank, requiring less time to fit the shoe to the horse.

Changes in climate also affect the farrier's position. With winter frost and snow, boron is applied to iron shoes to sharpen the edges. "Snowpads" are placed on the inside of horses' hooves to protect from snow accumulation, which would throw off the horse's movement and possibly cause a fall.

Even the peak hours have changed. The old blacksmith would have his biggest day on Saturday when people would come into town. Today the farrier's task is done on a Monday through Friday schedule. Saturday is a light day because farriers charge time and one-half, and they require animal delivery during off-hours.

In summary, even some of society's oldest jobs constantly change and evolve. Without this change, the farrier's job—and others, as we used to know them—would not exist in their present form. All jobs change. The benchmark for true job security is whether a person will continue to learn and change while performing the duties and executing the responsibilities of his or her position. If the individual ceases to learn from the position, then the position, and hence the individual, becomes a high target or probability for elimination. It is this one simple question that you can ask yourself, "Do I continue to learn from this position?" If the answer is no, you might be reading this Outplacement guide a second time.

I do not want you to make this mistake! I want you to focus on the important elements of your career. To do this, please begin by answering the following questions:

1. **What do you want to do?** What tasks and functions do you enjoy performing and do well (i.e., planning, managing, designing, implementing, analyzing, administering, investigating, etc.)? What job objectives will challenge you to use your best skills?

2. **Where do you want to do it?** Do you have any geographic restrictions? What industries interest you?

3. **What working conditions do you want** (i.e., a variety of responsibilities, the chance to be creative, chance of promotion, etc.)?

4. **What is your definition of success?** (Consider your immediate personal and professional priorities; how do these relate to your long-range goals in terms of career and family?)

5. **Does your spouse work outside of the home?** At the present time, slightly over 60 percent of married couples have dual careers. If your co-captain has a career outside the home, how does that impact your decision on furthering your career? Are you willing to relocate in your next position? What amount of overnight travel would be acceptable?

    Significantly, perhaps, many good companies recognize when they recruit good talent that either the husband or wife on the marriage team is also actively pursuing his or her own career. These companies many times will offer, if requested, partner relocation assistance. Similar to Outplacement, this service is given to the trailing spouse to facilitate his or her continued career for the benefit of the hiring company. This option should not be treated lightly as it does assist both partners in the marriage to continue their respective careers.

6. **Which of the above answers are fully fixed in your mind and are not negotiable?** To help you focus even further, I have provided two exercises to aid you in identifying what is most important to you in a position and what skills you have and will enjoy using. Please complete the following exercise.

WORK, WHAT'S IN IT FOR ME?

People have many different ideas about what is most important in a job. First, look over the list below and check the column that best describes your opinion about each item.

Then look over your list. In the last column, rank the items from 1 (most important) to 16 (least important).

Aspect of a Job	Very Important	Somewhat Important	Not Important at All	I Don't Know	Rank
A high salary					
Enjoy kind of work					
Plenty of vacation					
A chance to help others					
Regular working hours					
A chance for promotion					
Job security					
Duties spelled out clearly					
Friendly coworkers					
Pleasant surroundings					
A good boss					
A chance to supervise others					
Good health insurance/benefits					
A chance to continue education					
A variety of responsibilities					
A chance to be creative					

Would you say you have a clear idea of what's important to you? Why/why not?

WHAT SKILLS DO YOU HAVE AND MOST ENJOY USING?

Generally speaking, all skills divide into six clusters or families. To see which ones you are attracted to, try these exercises.

Below is an aerial view of a room where a party is taking place. At this party, people with the same or similar interests have all gathered in the same area of the room – as described below:

People who have athletic or mechanical ability; who prefer to work with objects, machines, tools, plants, or animals or to be outdoors.

GROUP A

People who like to work with data; who have clerical or numeric ability; who carry things out in detail or follow through on other's instructions.

GROUP B

People who like to work with people – influencing, persuading; who like to perform, lead, or manage for organizational goals or economic gain.

GROUP C

The Party

People who like to observe, learn, investigate, analyze, evaluate, or solve problems.

GROUP D

People who have artistic, innovative, or intuitional abilities, and who like to work in unstructured situations, using their imagination or creativity.

GROUP E

People who like to work with people – to inform, enlighten, help, train, develop, or cure them or are skilled with words.

GROUP F

1. Which area of the room would you instinctively be drawn to – the group of people you would most enjoy being with for the longest time? (Put aside any question of shyness or whether you would have to talk with them.) Write the letter for that group here: ____

2. After fifteen minutes, everyone in the area you have chosen leaves for another party across town, except you. Of the groups that still remain, which would you be drawn to the most – the people you would most enjoy being with for the longest time? Write the letter for that group here: ____

3. After fifteen minutes, this group, too, leaves for another party, except you. Of the groups that remain now, which would you be drawn to the most – the people you would most enjoy being with for the longest time? Write the letter for that group here: ____

4. Now underline the skills in each area that you like best. The underlined skills in the group(s) you have selected will indicate both the key skill sets you have, enjoy using, and will probably want to "sell" to prospective employers.

CHAPTER II.

THE
ROAD MAP

**Preparing An Action Oriented Resume.
Where Have You Been & What Have You Done?**

HOW ARE YOU GOING TO SELL YOURSELF?
PREPARING YOUR RESUME

"The world cares very little about what a man or woman knows;
it is what the man or woman is able to do that counts."

- Booker T. Washington

You may ask yourself, "What is a resume, and what purpose does it serve?" Many people have differing opinions about what constitutes an effective resume. You have your own ideas about this subject. Let me suggest that you immediately set aside all of the advice you have been given about resumes in the past and open yourself up to some reliable, effective, and proven methods of constructing a resume. But first, let me define the resume, what it is, and what it does.

Your resume is an extremely important tool – a personal advertising brochure – that allows you to communicate with a number of audiences. **Your resume cannot say everything you want to say or need to say about yourself and your accomplishments, but it can provide the reader with a significant "taste" of your skills and accomplishments.** In a sense, your resume can be likened to a meal carefully prepared by a superb chef. It may not inform the reader of all the dishes you are capable of preparing, but if it is done well, the reader will say, "Wow, what a fantastic cook! I want to see what this person can do for me!"

The purpose of your resume is to entice the reader and create enough interest to secure an interview. If you feel that the resume is the **most** important ingredient in your job search, you are wrong. **YOU** are the most important ingredient and the most effective marketing tool, but your resume can get a "foot in the door."

Not only is a resume a tool in securing an interview, it is also an effective means by which you can organize your career history. A resume allows you to present the important events in your career clearly and concisely. It also lets you highlight the things you believe are most important about you.

Your resume is the personal advertising document you create. It will support your job marketing strategy in the following areas:

1. All hiring officials will request a resume.
2. Newspaper and trade journal advertisements will normally ask for a resume.
3. Search firms and employment agencies will want to see your resume – it will become part of their files.
4. Your personal contacts may distribute your resume to certain key people with a cover letter from them.
5. Your resume will become a script to refer to when you interview.
6. Your resume can go where you can't go – through the office mail slot!

Therefore, your resume should be a part of you – it should **sound** like you. I want your resume to help you secure an interview and the interviewer to know enough about you so that he or she can interview you properly. I want the interviewer to interview you effectively and attentively by using the "script" that you have prepared and with which you are familiar.

In a resume, you give facts about your background in an easy-to-read manner. You should avoid self-praise and self-evaluative comments about yourself, such as "hard working, dedicated, innovative, team player, focused," etc. Evaluative comments by others, including comments by consultants, psychologists, and references are in poor taste. Most top executives in major companies who will be reading your resume regard overselling unfavorably. However, state factually and quantitatively (using numbers) your specific achievements such as sales increases, cost reductions, products developed, and awards won.

RESUME CHECK LIST

Be sure your resume includes or does the following:

☑ Contains full name, address and telephone number, including area code. An E-mail address should be placed below your telephone number (if you have one).

☑ Does not use personal pronouns – i.e., "I", "we" or "they."

☑ Summarizes your experience in a few opening statements – not an objective. An objective is too limiting. A Summary of Experience will give a broad overview of the breadth and depth of your experience and background. The Summary of Experience section clarifies for you and your reader what you are "selling," what you are going to bring to the party. It does not indicate what you want from the company or life in general. (Examples of Summary of Experience paragraphs are provided later in this section.)

☑ Accounts for all time from college, or the first full time job, to the present. Gaps in employment history dates are interpreted negatively. It appears that the writer is trying to avoid or hide something.

☑ Lists the names and dates by year, not by month, of all employers, including your present employer.

☑ Describes, in brief, each company or division where you worked, particularly the product line and number of employees at this location. If appropriate, also include sales volume, standing within industry, key markets served, and areas of technical excellence.

☑ Defines the different positions you held with each employer, with dates – year, not by month – for each position. Lists all functions and positions held. Indicates the title of your supervisor, plus numbers and types of people you supervised, including total personnel for whom you were responsible. Describes both your own job function and how your job fits into the organizational structure.

☑☑☑ **MOST IMPORTANT!** Describes quantitatively your actual accomplishments in each function, (i.e., increased sales from $1,000,000 to $2,000,000 in two years, negotiated three new union contracts without wage increases, etc.) Do not dilute your resume with excessive descriptions of early jobs or experience irrelevant to your objectives. Remember, your most recent track record of accomplishments (defined as your last two to five years) is your best predictor of future success! See Resume Samples 1-6 for good examples of quantifying accomplishments with numbers.

Expressed simply, business is not, has not, and will not be a spectator sport. Business and the men and women who work in businesses are measured by their contributions. The contributions that are the most eye catching are those that fall into three simple categories: those that generate revenue, those that reduce cost(s), and those that do some of both. The further an individual is removed from making contributions in one of these three areas, the closer he/she becomes to being labeled as "overhead" or is assigned to "special projects."

What, in my mind, separates a hard hitting resume from the majority of the "job descriptions," that are passed out as resumes is simply this – does it tell what you did, your accomplishments, or does it detail the responsibilities of your job? Being responsible for a function or several functions does not tell the reader of your resume how, if ever, these responsibilities were discharged, nor if they were discharged successfully. And how did you measure success? Fortunately, in business success is measured by using numbers and more numbers.

If more people would spend more time measuring their contributions rather than articulating their hobbies and other interests, their resumes would be vastly improved. For example, including that one coaches little league baseball, while admirable from the civic-minded perspective, also suggests that you would be leaving sharply at 4:00 or 4:30 p.m. every Tuesday or Thursday. Hobbies clutter up a resume!

When quantifying your accomplishments, the "Net Results:" should be expressed in their full numeric form. If the sales went to $2,000,000, use the dollar sign followed by the seven digits. Why? Because numeric symbols in a field of alpha characters have greater visibility and recognition. They jump off of the paper better than if they were expressed as "two million dollars."

For even greater recognition, have your numbers fall at the end of the sentence. For Example:

> "Increased sales from $1,000,000 to $2,000,000 in two years."

Better yet would be:

> "Increased sales in two years from $1,000,000 to $2,000,000."

☑ Lists all degrees, including the word "Degree." For example, don't say "B.S., Business," but rather "B.S. Degree, Business Administration." Include the date the degree was obtained, names of colleges, and locations. Major extracurricular activities and positions of leadership should be mentioned. If no college degree, list highest academic level achieved. Professional engineers and CPAs should include date and state of examination.

☑ If appropriate, after the Education section, include a Technical Summary of computer hardware (i.e., IBM 360, AS 400, etc.), software programs (i.e., Lotus 1-2-3, PowerPoint, etc.), programming languages (i.e., C, C++, Cobal, etc.), and operating systems (i.e., SAP, MRPII, etc.).

☑ Includes U. S. citizenship, if appropriate.

☑ Indicates the number and field of patents granted, pending, or "applied for" and published articles.

KEEP IT BRIEF: But remember the objective is not brevity – but to get the job done – and done right in a focused manner!! To keep your resume brief and to the point, check these items:

☑ Do not start writing with the objective that your resume will not exceed a certain number of pages. Instead, tell your story.

☑ Do not list references or state that they will be furnished upon request. Prepare a list of three references on a separate sheet of paper so that if you are requested to provide references, you have them available.

☑ Avoid irrelevancies such as name of spouse or children and excessive listing of short educational courses or hobbies.

☑ Keep military experience brief. Give dates, branch of service, highest rank attained, and short description of responsibilities.

☑ Do not include salary history, and do not date the resume. Salary information always goes in the accompanying cover letter. This subject will be discussed later.

☑ Do not include reason for leaving previous positions/companies or most recent employer. This topic can best be handled verbally.

☑ Avoid all references to health (i.e. Health: Excellent).

☑ Finally, your resume should tell a story. What is the story you want the reader to read?

HELPFUL TIPS

In your final editing, remember:

1. Rewrite your text as many times as necessary to have a fluid style. It is helpful to have a personal friend edit your resume to be sure your meaning is clear. However, the final draft should be your own.

2. Proofread for typing and spelling errors. Most resumes have several. Errors are most likely to occur in your name, address, telephone number, dates, numbers, and technical terms. Two typewritten pages is the customary length – but, if need be, feel free to go onto a third page.

3. I recommend a good quality 8 1/2 x11” white bond paper and suggest you avoid unusual colors, special or fancy bindings, etc.

4. Staple the two or three sheets together before you send them out. Use No. 10 business envelopes, and do not include a return address on the envelope.

5. Never forward an out-of-date or “patched up” resume.

6. Proof your name, telephone number, and zip code once again!

7. Resumes that use bullet points facilitate skimming and draw attention to your accomplishments. Additionally, write in the past tense with action verbs to demonstrate successful execution of your responsibilities.

8. If you fax or E-mail your resume, always follow up with a hard copy.

QUANTIFYING YOUR ACCOMPLISHMENTS

Every individual should have a results-oriented resume that informs the reader of specific accomplishments and the results of these accomplishments. Corporations want to hire individuals who can identify problems, design solutions, and implement these solutions. Corporations also want to hire individuals who can either make money or save money! When you write your accomplishments, keep this in mind and always ask yourself, **"How did the results of my actions make or save the company money?"**

When composing these results, you must do the following:

1. Quantify your accomplishments!

2. **Quantify your accomplishments!!**

3. **QUANTIFY YOUR ACCOMPLISHMENTS!!!**

And to quantify your accomplishments, you must use:

1. Numbers!

2. **Numbers!!**

3. **NUMBERS!!!**

Numbers have an extremely positive effect on a resume because they stand out and grab the reader's attention. In addition, society places value on things with numbers. **NUMBERS TALK!** Compare the following statements:

"He resides in a nice house in the country."

OR

"He resides in a nice $950,000 house in the country."

Which statement has more impact on you? What images arise in your mind when thinking of a nice house or a nice $950,000 house? Do you see iron gates, a circle drive, a swimming pool, gardens, a tennis court, trees, etc.?

The same is true with your resume. Another example is this:

- Designed and implemented a program that reduced production time, saved the company money, and increased product sales.

- Designed and implemented a program that reduced production time by 26 percent in a six-month period. **Net Result:** Reduced labor costs by 13 percent, which contributed to an increase in profits of $150,000.

Get the point? Remember, it will take more effort in the initial writing stages to quantify your accomplishments, but the results of these efforts will reward you with more interviews and more opportunities for job offers. A resume with specific, quantified accomplishments is far superior to a resume that simply lists duties and responsibilities.

To create a superior resume takes time and effort. If you compose and write your resume in two hours, the final document will look like it took you two hours to write – UGH!!

A logical point to consider is where are these numbers that represent your quantified accomplishments found? It is obvious that these numbers should not be figments of one's imagination but carefully documented and researched quantifiable results of your activities and achievements. The most obvious source for numbers to include in your resume comes from your own memory. Unfortunately, this source is rather ephemeral in the sense that our memory begins to fade, and you will probably be unable to recall all of the numbers that you need to complete your resume. A second viable source for the numbers would be your own performance evaluation. If you have not been given a copy of past performance evaluations, perhaps requesting a copy from Human Resources would revive information to jog your memory or even document appropriate quantifiable achievements. Third, many companies have performance based on MBOs (Management by Objectives). Look at the results of these reviews. Solid MBOs are always accompanied by quantification.

Should the above three sources not provide you with sufficient detail, consider asking your former boss or, in the case of a downsizing or impending office or plant closure, your current boss the following, "I am constructing my resume, and do you remember when we worked on _____? What was the result of those activities?" Nothing adds more credibility than being able to supply quantified accomplishments as reported by your boss. Possibly these same numbers were used in his or her own resume. If your immediate supervisor throws up his or her arms and says, "Regretfully I can't remember what those results were," ask him/her to provide an estimate. Be sure to make this estimate conservative. If you are asked in the future where these numbers come from, you can indicate a truthful response, "They came from my boss." If all other sources fail – documentation is lost, your boss can't remember, no accurate record remains, or there was never a recorded documentation in the first place – then it is considered ethical to provide your own estimate of what the results were. Remember, this estimate should always be expressed in a conservative mode. If verified, you want the person commenting on the quantification of results to say, "Yes, that seems about right; if anything it is low." Nothing destroys the credibility or viability of a resume quicker than to have exaggerations that can't be substantiated.

TRAIL MIX

> **Definition:** *A snack to tide hikers on their journey, usually composed of dried nuts, cereal mix, and/or dried fruit, including raisins. It can be consumed while an individual is hiking or at his or her trail camp for extra strength.*

In this edition of *From Here To There,* I have provided a CD-Rom. This CD-Rom contains a number of topics that are designed to assist in the organization of your campaign. The PC compatibility needs for the *From Here To There* CD-Rom are as follows:

Windows 95 or higher
Internet connection with a browser
Adobe Reader (this program is provided on the CD-Rom).

The following is the table of contents:

I. Job Search Plan Worksheet
   a. Job Search Plan Review
   b. Network Datasheet
   c. Financial Planning for the Journey from Here . . .to There

II. The Perfect Resume Builder

   a. Organizing Your Facts: Position Specific Tips
      This section of the Trail Mix was developed for various professions. These materials present you with a particular set of questions designed to prompt you to recall important information that should be included in your resume. Use these tools and these questions to jog your memory regarding your career accomplishments. The following fact sheets are included:

Accounting	Manufacturing Personnel
Auditor	Marketing & Sales
Clerical/Secretarial	Materials Management
Contract Management	Purchasing
Controller	Quality Assurance Control
COO-Lending & Leasing	Retail
Engineer	Senior Credit Officer
Finance	MIS/IS Technical
Human Resources	Technician
Logistics/Physical Distribution	Treasurer

   b. Resume Builder
   c. Resume Editor

III.   Ad Response Worksheet

IV.   Error Free Phone Message

V.   Interview Replay Worksheet

VI.   Check List for Evaluating Job Offers

It would be appropriate at this time to insert the CD-Rom and review the section on Organizing Your Facts. The CD-Rom is located in the pouch attached to the back inside cover of this book and is designed to assist you in constructing your resume. Layout, margins, spacing, and prompts have been provided for you to construct your own "perfect" resume.

Focus Time – Cutting To The Quick

Can you complete any of these statements?

When constructing your resume, think about ways in which you:

- Increased R.O.I.

- Improved gross profits

- Augmented sales

- Increased market share

- Improved market penetration

- Improved productivity

- Lowered costs

- Reduced employee turnover

- Cut new product launch time

- Recruited, hired and trained how many people

- Improved cash availability

- Developed budgets

- Affected re-capitalization

- Reduced operating expenses

- Arranged moratorium with creditors

- Negotiated settlements

- Planned and executed moves

- Negotiated leases

- Collaborated with architects, contractors, builders, and zoning authorities

- Reduced inventory

- Reduced customer complaints

- Enhanced community relations

- Improved product quality

- Instituted cost controls

- Set new goals and objectives

- Devised new strategies

- Reversed negative cash flow

- Reduced new contract cancellations

- Discouraged union organization

- Recovered __percent of uncollectable receivables

- Designed and implemented new products, systems, forms, etc.

- Eliminated obsolete ____

- Set all-time record for ____

- Discovered ____

- Invented ____

- Earned____

- Extended payable cycle from ___days to ___ days

- Increased inventory turns ____

- Revitalized

- Planned and developed new product line(s), which added sales of $_____.

- Developed, proposed and implemented ____

- Compromised lease (or other liabilities) of $____ for $____ -payable over ___ years

- Reduced:
  overhead
  ROCE
  employee head-count
  flow time
  cycle time
  inventories
  interest expenses
  bank debt
  financing
  audit fees
  losses
  product development time

- Decreased day's outstanding receivables from __ to __ day's.

- Key team player, which ____

- Increased:
  sales
  ROCE
  margins
  profits
  productivity
  quality acceptance rate
  cash flow
  operating efficiency
  key accounts
  PBT
  market share

- Improved EBITDA

- Increased sales per employee by____

- Reduced rejected units from ____PPM to ____PPM

Remember: The above are all key indices by which business performance is measured. Without measurement there is no movement or progress.

RESUME SENTENCE OPENERS

Bullet points make it easy to skim and draw attention to your accomplishments. Resumes are written using past-tense action verbs to show how well you executed your responsibilities.

All bullet points must use the past tense to be consistent throughout the resume, whether you are presently employed or unemployed. Weak words to avoid using are "coordinated," "assisted," "administered," and "involved," as these are vague and non-descriptive. The following are sentence openers to be used with accomplishments.

Accelerated	Implemented	Scheduled	Traded
Accomplished	Improved	Serviced	Trained
Achieved	Increased	Set up	Transferred
Approved	Introduced	Simplified	Translated
Completed	Invented	Sold	Trimmed
Conceived	Launched	Solved	Tripled
Conducted	Maintained	Spearheaded	Turned
Consolidated	Negotiated	Started	Uncovered
Created	Organized	Streamlined	Unified
Delivered	Performed	Strengthened	Unraveled
Demonstrated	Processed	Stressed	Utilized
Designed	Programmed	Stretched	Vacated
Developed	Promoted	Structured	Waged
Directed	Proposed	Succeeded	Widened
Doubled	Purchased	Summarized	Withdrew
Eliminated	Recommended	Superseded	Won
Established	Redesigned	Supervised	Worked
Expanded	Reduced	Terminated	Wrapped
Generated	Reorganized	Traced	Wrote
Identified	Revised	Tracked	

 Remember – Good resumes use good, strong past-tense action verbs!

It is strongly suggested that you avoid **weak** words such as:

Coordinated   Involved   Participated   Administered

UGH! Absolutely the worst word to have on a resume!

SAMPLE RESUMES

SAMPLE 1

Great looking resume! Excellent job!

ROBERT T. THOMAS
1234 Main Street
Anywhere, State 99999
(765) 555-1212
E-Mail: (Optional)

Details what Mr. Thomas is selling.

Summary of Experience

Twenty (20) years of diversified manufacturing experience in both heavy equipment and light appliance operations. Extensive background in materials management, production planning, production management, and inventory control. Work environments have included both union and non-union manufacturing operations.

Describes last employer.

1980 to Present

Monroe Manufacturing Corporation, Plantville, U.S.A.
A publicly held $140,000,000 corporation producing a diversified line of kitchen

"Present" indicates current or last job.

Indicates reporting relationship.

1983 to Present

Manager of Manufacturing Operations: Responsible to the General Manager For all manufacturing operations including metal fabrication, machine shop, plastic fabrication, assembly, painting and finishing, packing, warehousing, and receiving and shipping departments.

Concise description of major responsibilities.

- Directly supervised a management staff of 1 general foremen, 9 department foremen, plus 145 hourly, union, and clerical employees.

Good quantification of accomplishments

- Redesigned and modernized the layout of 3 departments in a 150,000 square-foot plant increasing the flow of raw materials, subassemblies, and finished goods. **Net Result:** Increased production in the first year without additional equipment or manpower by 9.9% or $3,600,000.

Have numbers fall at sentence end to increase visibility.

Bullet points indicate major accomplishments!

- Proposed, developed, and implemented the introduction of numeric control (NC and CNC) machining equipment. **Net Result:** Achieved first year labor savings of $250,000.

- Reduced material scrap and defective workmanship by developing a new Quality Assurance Program. **Net Result:** Generated $138,000 savings first year.

Good use of numbers.

- Established first Company and Union Safety Committee. **Net Result:** Reduced accidents by 55% and saved $54,600 in workmen's compensation claims.

Use of percentages and actual dollar amounts doubles effectiveness.

1982 to 1983

Production Control Supervisor: Responsible to the Manager of Manufacturing Operations for scheduling of production for all product lines.

- Introduced an "ABC" Inventory Control System. **Net Result:** Reduced purchasing requirements the first year by $68,000.

- Established first Materials Management Committee that integrated the functions of production, sales, purchasing, and inventory control. **Net Result:** Eliminated all parts and subassembly shortages while more closely tying production requirements to anticipated customer demands.

- Promoted to Manager of Manufacturing Operations.

1980
to
1982

General Foreman: Responsible for the supervision, selection, and training of 9 department foremen.

- Installed new plating process for finished goods. **Net Result:** Trimmed processing time by 50%.

- Developed new packing process. **Net Result:** Eliminated all returned or damaged goods and generated a first year savings of $31,000.

- Promoted to Production Control Supervisor.

1970 to
1980

Burro Crane, Incorporated, Hometown, U.S.A.
A privately held $20,000,000 company producing 15-ton industrial railroad cranes.

1974
to
1980

General Foreman: Responsible for 4 departments, including Structural Shop, Machine Shop, Subassembly Department, and Final Assembly Department, supervising 110 people with a budget of $4,000,000.

- Increased production rate by 50% from 2 cranes per month to 3 cranes per month by improved production management techniques.

No need for more details on earlier employment.

- Combined limited second shift operation with first shift. **Net Result:** Reduced shift premiums by $125,000.

1971
to
1974

Foreman, Machine Shop

- Promoted to General Foreman.

1970
to
1971

Lead Machinist: Responsible for operating a variety of machines, setting up equipment and instructing other operators.

- Promoted to Foreman.

Education:

B.S. Degree – Industrial Management, U.S.A. University, 1975 (Evening Program)

IMPORTANT: Without the word "Degree," graduation may not be understood.

Another great job!

SAMUEL A. SMITH
536 Longmeadow Circle
Anywhere, State 60174
(312) 552-1732

Double-check the accuracy of your telephone number.

Summary Statement.

Summary of Experience

More than nineteen (19) years of extensive and diversified experience in sales, sales training, and market development. Specific assignments include creation, development and implementation of market plans, sales and merchandising programs, training and evaluating sales personnel, and establishment of Master Distributor Plans.

1970 to
Present

Nationwide Cards, Incorporated, Kansas City, Missouri
A $2,000,000,000 producer and distributor of greeting cards, gifts and decorative accessories, along with Crayola brand products and real estate development holdings.

1985
to
Present

National Account Executive: Responsible to the Sales Director of Specialty Store Development for successful accomplishment of both corporate and retail sales goals. Developed sales and merchandising programs, planned inventory levels, and maintained liaison between Nationwide and the accounts management. Responsible for 2 national accounts with sales in excess of $12,000,000.

Excellent use of strong action verbs.

- Managed the national account activities of 95 nationwide sales representatives in 30 states. Achieved a 75% increase in sales in 4 years. Sales 1992-to-date were 16% ahead of 1991, or $7,980,000.

Note use of numbers to quantify accomplishments.

- Directed the merchandising and installation of 38 new accounts within a 3-month period in 1988. **Net Result:** $1,100,000 in additional sales.

- Developed and implemented new merchandising concepts to increase sales in high-density displays. This system replaced product with a history of lower sales and profits, increasing overall department sales by 8%.

- Achieved membership 7 consecutive years in Nationwide Crown Club for sales excellence.

- Created and implemented year-round sales and merchandising plans which were used by accounts in updating and changing product mix to reflect key seasonal changes that maximize sales at peak selling periods. **Net Result:** An additional 5% increase in total department sales.

1981
to
1985

Senior District Training Manager: Reported directly to the Senior District Sales Manager with responsibility for the development, planning, organization, and implementation of an effective sales and retail training program. This district included 600 accounts and $65,000,000 in sales.

- Supervised, trained, motivated and scheduled 3 Retail Installation Coordinators who were responsible for the installation of all new and remodeled accounts. 2 of these 3 were promoted and are progressing in their careers.

- Supervised the activities of designated trainers who were responsible for the initial sales training of 10 new account representatives.

- Developed and launched a retail training program which was utilized by Nationwide with a national drug store chain.

- Conducted key presentations at all sales meetings. These sessions were informational and motivational in matter.

- Promoted to National Account Executive.

1979
to
1981

Market Development Manager: Reported to the District Sales Manager with responsibility for establishing and executing master distribution plans, developing contact with shopping center developers, and creating pro forma operating and cash flow statements.

- Increased market penetration significantly by generating $900,000 in new business through directing target programs for 10 sales territories including the identifying of new account opportunities and new locations.

- Promoted to Senior District Training Manager.

1975
to
1979

Multiple Account Coordinator: Responsible for development and implementation of sales programs for multiple management, which included creative merchandising plans and training of in-store personnel.

- Expanded multiple sales in excess of 80% through an aggressive plan of remodeling and new store openings.

- Promoted to Market Development Manager.

1970
to
1975

Account Manager-Senior Account Manager: Responsible for meeting sales quotas, maximizing retail sales and acquiring new accounts.

- Consistently exceeded objectives by selling in excess of $800,000 annually.

- Promoted to Multiple Account Coordinator.

Education: Master of Business Administration Program, Lewis University, Romeoville, Illinois, 1970.

Graduate work: University of Iowa.

BA Degree, Business Administration, St. Ambrose University, Davenport, Iowa, 1982.

Military Service: Army National Guard (Sergeant E-5), obligation completed.

ROSIE M. SHANNON
1424 Washington Avenue
Anywhere, State 99999
(765) 555-5429

Summary of Experience

Over nine (9) years of diversified secretarial experience in the marketing and service departments of a major manufacturing corporation. Utilized all secretarial skills including typing at 90 wpm and shorthand at 120 wpm. Skilled in WordPerfect 5.1, DBASE III, and Lotus 1-2-3. Proficient on dictating equipment, fax machines, and Merlin telephone systems.

1981 to
Present
Quark Company, Hometown, USA
A division of Electronic Corporation of America, a $20,000,000,000 manufacturer and wholesaler of consumer and industrial electrical products.

1983
to
Present
Senior Secretary: Responsible to the Product Service Manager and staff for administrative functions in the Service Department.

- Revised and maintained division-wide cross-reference publication master index. **Net Result:** Reduced time previously required to research and resource information by 40%.

- Participated in selection of word processing system for Service Department.

- Distributed new machine modification notices and operating instructions to Service Managers throughout the United States.

- Entered and maintained machine field modification file on computer, compiling and distributing quarterly status reports to field personnel throughout the United States.

- Received and directed telephone inquiries throughout the division utilizing a Merlin 30-line Queued Call Console.

- Prepared travel arrangements for 10 employees in the service department.

- Maintained a list of 850 products built in the Franklin plant.

- Assisted Manager in organization and preparation of the monthly departmental report.

Note use of numbers to quantify accomplishments.

1981 to 1983	**Secretary/Clerk**: Responsible to Product Manager and staff for secretarial and clerical functions in the Marketing Department.

- Maintained inbound sales order log and sales order file; processed incoming sales orders and distributed throughout the plant.

- Typed letters, made reservations and all other arrangements in the plant visitor program.

- Maintained inbound, build, shipment, finished goods, and backlog report on computer utilizing Basic language.

Education:

Kirk Community College; Commenced work on Associate of Applied Arts Degree in Business Administration, Plantville, USA, 1988.

Institute of Business, Secretarial Science Degree, Anytown, USA, 1978.

Professional Affiliations:

Secretaries Network Club of the United States.

Very strong resume!

HAROLD J. CORONA
120 South Carol Street
Milwaukee, Wisconsin   53706
(414) 333-1111
HJCorona@execpc.com

Summary Statement.

Summary of Experience

Senior level executive with twenty (20) years of diversified experience in a worldwide consumer products industry. Background portfolio of international and domestic acquisitions and divestitures, strategic planning, finance, corporate audit, controllership, SEC filings, turnarounds, streamlining costs, operations analysis, IS, banking relations, tax planning, building management teams and worldwide market penetration.

1980 to
Present

UBR, Inc., New York, New York
A publicly held $80 billion worldwide consumer products manufacturer and marketer.

1997
to
Present

Senior Vice President - Finance, Strategy and IS, Ubermacher, Milwaukee, Wisconsin (A $5 billion wholly owned operating company of UBR, Inc.): Responsible to the Chairman and CEO for all domestic/international financial functions, tax, banking, strategic planning and financial forecasting, and IS. Acted as liaison to parent organization for all financial performance reports, forecasting, and strategy..

- Designed and directed the implementation of a major company restructuring including corporate, sales, marketing, and production functions. **Net Result:** Streamlined the decision-making processes and administrative layers, saving over $30,000,000 annually.

- Negotiated with international partner to reduce import product prices and led the consolidation of administrative offices for importer. **Net Result:** Saved over $3,000,000 annually in import pricing and over $5,000,000 in costs.

Focus on results.

Quantify!!!
Gets
reader's
attention.

- Directed 2 major transforming initiatives that examined, with investment bankers and 2 separate international alliances each totaling over $1,000.000,000. **Net Result:** Produced total analysis of each alliance and elected not to proceed.

- Directed the strategic analysis of projects including international distributorships, internal initiatives and acquisitions. **Net Result:** Created proposals with projected savings of over $9,000,000 and revised or established 4 international alliances/distribution agreements. Analysis resulted in the rejection of purchase of 2 brands and a brewery.

- Directed purchase negotiations of the 2 organizations. **Net Result:** Acquired companies for under $19,000,000, and increased market position over 10%.

1996
to
1997

Vice President - IS & Financial Analysis, UBR, Inc., New York, New York: Responsible for planning, directing all financial forecasting and budgeting, and IS worldwide. Appointed to Board of Directors.

- Directed preparation of financial status reports to advise Board of Directors, CFO, and CEO of debt position and maturities, stock buyback, cash flow, income. Consolidated all 6 operating companies' budgets into 1 corporate budget.

Use
action
verbs.

- Created a team oriented financial forecasting, budgeting and IS cost savings process with each operating company and maximized purchasing synergies of over $800,000,000 of worldwide

IS investments annually. **Net Result:** Generated accurate forecasts & budgets, and established a 5-year telecommunications agreement with savings of over $200,000,000.

- Promoted to Senior Vice President - Finance, Strategy and IS, Ubermacher.

1994
to
1996

Vice President - Corporate Audit, UBR, Inc., Rye Brook, New York: Responsible for all audit and business control advisory functions worldwide. Total staff included 158 with 4 offices in Europe, 4 in the United States, and 2 offices in Asia/Pacific.

- Directed the development and mentoring of high-performance employees. **Net Result:** Promoted and transferred over 20 key employees each year into general business assignments.

- Partnered with Treasurer and established a commercial paper (short-term debt) monitoring and tracking system. **Net Result:** Controlled over $3,000,000,000 of annual short-term debt.

- Led the development of a European business unit treasury cash netting system. **Net Result:** Reduced annual short-term debt by $20,000,000.

- Directed and participated in over 10 major due diligence reviews on acquisition and divestiture of businesses.

- Partnered with General Counsel and Controller on preparation of 10Q and 10K SEC filings.

- Promoted to Vice President - IS & Financial Analysis, UBR, Inc.

1988
to
1994

Director of Corporate Audit, UBR, Inc., Rye Brook, New York: Responsible for all corporate audit activity for the corporation.

- Performed due diligence reviews in over 12 acquisitions. **Net Result:** Identified key cost savings and problem areas.

- Promoted to Vice President - Corporate Audit.

1982
to
1988

Corporate Audit Manager, Richmond, Virginia; Milwaukee, Wisconsin; and New York, New York: Responsible for all audit activity in operating companies.

- Promoted to Director of Corporate Audit.

1980
to
1982

General Accountant, MVC Company, Mission Viejo, California.
A wholly owned operating company of UBR, Inc., specializing in land planning and development.

- Promoted to Corporate Audit Manager, UBR, Inc.

1975 to
1980

Circle K Corporation, Phoenix, Arizona

Investor Relations/General Accounting

Education: B.A. Degree - Accounting, University of Wisconsin, Madison, Wisconsin, 1975.

**Professional
Certifications:**   Wisconsin State Certified Public Accountant (CPA).
Certificate in Management Accounting (CMA).
Certified Internal Auditor (CIA).

Excellent quantification of accomplishments. It tells a great story!

NORMA M. PANETELA
777 Career Drive
Hightown, State 99999
(555) 555-1234
Npanetela@dot.net

"Sound Byte" of career experience.

Summary of Experience

Senior level professional with over eighteen (18) years of diversified experience in worldwide consumer products industries. Extensive background in domestic and international business management, P&L, strategic planning, marketing, sales management, turnaround and new product development.

1993 to Present   **MLM, Inc.**, New York, New York
A publicly held $80 billion worldwide consumer products manufacturer and marketer.

1994 to Present   **Vice President Marketing, Millennium One**, New York, New York
Responsible to the CEO of this $5,000,000,000 division for new product development and all domestic marketing, direct management of 171 employees, and up to $900,000,000 marketing investment annually. Member of the Chairman's Executive Committee.

Action verbs

- Maintained growth of $1,500,000,000 Millennium Melt brand in declining industry. **Net Result:** Produced revenues $22,000,000 over budgeted plan.

Highlight results.

- Directed the overall marketing strategy for trademark brands. **Net Results:** Exceeded financial goals by $80,000,000 in sales and $27,000,000 profit.

- Directed the marketing strategy for an independent subsidiary. **Net Result:** Exceeded profit goals by over 80%.

Use percentages to quantify.

- Developed a geographically based portfolio strategy. **Net Result:** Increased focus and efficiency of $900,000,000 marketing investment and directed sales force priorities.

- Developed new concepts for in-market testing for multiple brands. **Net Result:** Tested in-market 4 new brands and launched industry-first packaging innovation.

1993 to 1994   **Vice President, Brand Management, Millennium One**, New York, New York
Responsible to Senior Vice President Marketing and International for full P&L and strategic planning for 16 established domestic brands.

- Developed and implemented a turnaround strategy to reverse a 5-year decline. **Net Result:** Restored volume growth and exceeded plan by $65,000,000 in revenue and $23,000,000 profit.

- Directed the successful launch of 5 new products and line extensions. **Net Result:** Increased premium brand volume by 6% and 1.7pp category share.

- Initiated the consolidation of media planning and buying at 1 agency. **Net Result:** Reduced system costs by 15%, or $6,000,000.

- Promoted to Vice President Marketing.

1988 to 1993	**PepsiCo, Inc**, Purchase, New York A $28,000,000,000 publicly held worldwide consumer products company specializing in the beverage, salty snacks, and restaurant industries.

1992 to 1993	**Vice President, International Marketing, Pizza Hut International**, Wichita, Kansas. Responsible to the President for providing marketing leadership for operating companies and franchisees of this $1,400,000,000 division in 72 countries.

- Developed and redefined the corporate marketing function's role and strategic framework. **Net Result:** Increased globally the consistent development and application of brand equities and identity.

- Spearheaded a multi-national initiative to contemporize marketing strategy. **Net Result:** Tested new concepts in Australia and Canada.

1991 to 1992	**Smiths Crisps, Ltd.**, Theale, United Kingdom A $650 million subsidiary of PepsiCo Inc., producing and marketing salty snacks.

Marketing & Sales Director: Responsible to Managing Director for all marketing functions and the direct management of a 245-member sales force.

- Designed and implemented a DSD sales strategy. **Net Result:** Exceeded volume plan by 4% in a declining market, and generated margin growth of over 1.4pp.

- Directed the restructuring of the sales organization. **Net Result:** Saved $400,000 annually in operational costs and improved sales focus and control.

- Promoted to Vice President, International Marketing, Pizza Hut International.

1989 to 1991	**Marketing Director**, United Kingdom Responsible to Managing Director for full P&L and strategic planning for a diverse portfolio of 18 snack brands with $65,000,000 turnover.

- Designed and directed a turnaround strategy for a loss-making potato chip business.
- **Net Result:** Generated a $6,000,000 profit in 12 months.

- Promoted to Marketing & Sales Director.

1988 to 1989	**Director, International Marketing, PepsiCo Foods International,** Dallas, Texas Responsible for marketing leadership, and counsel to 11 operating companies throughout Europe, Australia and Far East, including equity, joint venture, and start-up.

- Promoted to Marketing Director of Smiths Crisps, Ltd. in United Kingdom.

1981 to 1988	**General Foods Corporation, Maxwell House Division**, White Plains, New York A division of General Foods Corporation producing and marketing coffee brands.

Product Group Manager: Responsible for full P&L of $800,000,000 Maxwell House ground coffee brands, with a marketing budget of over $130,000,000.

- Promoted 4 times during period.

Education:	Harvard Graduate School of Business Administration, Cambridge, Massachusetts, MBA Degree, Marketing, 1981. University of Reading, Reading, United Kingdom, BA Degree, Economics, 1976.

JACOB J. ROBUSTO
3361 Innovation Lane
Tampa, Florida   33761

(813) 555-1212
JJrobusto@aol.com

Summary of Experience

Over fourteen (14) years of diversified experience within the commercial, consumer and service products industries. Extensive background in recognition, analysis, development, and commercialization of new products and services for emerging markets involving complex integration of technical/business issues. A seasoned visionary for ideation sessions, strategic planning, marketing, team building, business, and technology assessment.

1986 to Present	**Better Products, Inc.**, Tampa, Florida
	A privately held $5,000,000,000 global marketer of consumer products.

1990 to Present — **Director of Technical Development**: Responsible for creating and managing new product and service opportunities for North American Professional Business Group.

- Succeeded in presenting and closing the sale of Electronic Fly Trap to the McDonald's Corporation. **Net Result:** Generated $1,000,000 in sales the first year of launch. Projected sales of $10,000,000 within 3 years globally.

- Launched new Protector Consumer Electronic Fly Trap in 5 months to test specialty markets using catalog distribution systems. **Net Result:** Positioned product to be mainstreamed into the ZAP product line.

- Succeeded in presenting and closing the sale of Electronic Fly Traps to K-Mart and Wal-Mart Corporations. **Net Result:** Generated $3,000,000 in sales.

- Directed the design and development of a new patented non-pesticidal flea trap for ZAP consumer markets. **Net Result:** Positioned product for national launch in 1995.

- Designed customized sanitation programs for top 30% of the retail food industry. **Net Result:** Retained the $12,000,000 annual Wal-Mart account, and secured national accounts including K-Mart Super Centers and Target.

- Commercialized new fire protection coating for hood and duct systems. **Net Result:** Reduced labor costs by 50% and chemical costs by 40%.

1986 to 1990 — **New Business Development Manager**: Responsible for creating new products, services, and business opportunities for the Worldwide Service Business Group.

- Developed and commercialized an innovative and patented non-contaminating, non-pesticidal flying insect control trap creating a new market worldwide. **Net Result:** Generated $50,000,000 in incremental sales since its launch in 1988.

- Created revolutionary patented pesticide application equipment using electrostatics, "cryogenics" and pulsation. New design used less pesticide and reduced chemical costs. **Net Result:** Generated new incremental sales of $2,000,000.

- Served as founding member of the Corporate Entrepreneurial Seed Fund that guides and champions new product ideas. **Net Result:** Provided an environment to promote innovation and creativity that launched products including fly and flea traps, and fly line cleaner.

- Promoted to Director of Technical Development. ◄——— *Indicate promotions.*

1983 to
1986

American Sanitation Institute, St. Louis, Missouri
Consultants to the food processing, storage and distribution industry.

Vice President and Executive Director: Responsible for the development of service programs for clients. Created strategies and tactics to negotiate with Federal and State Regulatory Agencies. Directly responsible for 30 field specialists, 17 corporate, and 12 manufacturing and regulatory personnel.

- Provided expert defense for a client involved in the largest business seizure in history of FDA. **Net Result:** Succeeded in defense of the $350,000,000 privately held company.

- Developed incentive programs and training sessions for 30 field specialists. **Net Result:** Increased sales of field specialists by 9% in a saturated market.

1980 to
1983

United States Air Force, Washington, D.C.

Captain - Defense Pest Management Information Analysis Center: Responsible for consultations to Army, Navy, and Air Force personnel on a global basis.

- Developed an early warning medical system for the D.O.D. that assessed the risk for combat troops to diseases around the world. **Net Result:** Experienced no0 loss of military personnel from arthropod borne diseases, including poisonous snakes and plants in Iran.

- Awarded the Tri-Service Commendation Medal for developing the Disease Vector Ecology Profile Program.

1971 to
1980

University of California, Davis, California

Responsibilities included positions as Research Associate and Teaching Assistant for the Departments of Entomology, Veterinary Microbiology, Nematology, and the School of Medicine.

- Designed and developed the Aquatic Insect Monitoring System (AIMS) chambers and JCL Insect Traps. **Net Result:** Established JCL Traps as the standard in monitoring procedures for Lake County Mosquito Abatement District.

- Derived a formula that made possible the large scale application of a fungus to control vectors of Malaria, Encephalitis, Yellow Fever, Dengue, and Elephantiasis. **Net Result:** Reduced labor to rear/colonize fungal spores by 53% and materials by 60%.

Education:

M.B.A. Degree - Management/Administration, Central Michigan University, Mount Pleasant, Michigan, 1982.
Ph.D. Degree - Entomology University of California, Davis, California, 1979.
B.S. Degree - Zoology, University of California, Davis, California, 1973.

THE BEFORE AND AFTER OF GOOD RESUMES

What follows are the resumes of three individuals that we had the opportunity to work with in our outplacement business. I selected these resumes because they demonstrate a number of points. Each individual came into our office ready to start his or her marketing campaign with the following resumes. Each one thought the resume he or she had completed was strong and ready to be sent to various search firms, networking contacts, and corporations or to respond to various Internet ads or print media.

With some diplomacy, we indicated to each person that while we did not think his or her respective resume was wrong, we felt that it might be prudent if we spent a little more time on each document. We tried to include the accompanying points on resume construction that precede this section and basically ratchet the resumes up a full notch or two. All three individuals agreed that since the additional time was actually an investment in themselves and their careers, it was a prudent thing to hold off sending their existing resumes until they could compare their "before edition," with the "after edition." All three people elected to use the revised "after" edition in their job campaigns.

What follows is each individual's original resume unedited or corrected. Following each resume is a critique and analysis of the original document. Following the critique and analysis is the revised or "after" edition of the document. In each of the "makeovers," we tried to encompass the following points:

1. A cleaner layout – for easy reading or skimming.
2. More quantification of accomplishments – for greater impact.
3. Double-spacing of key data to allow greater visual skimming and impact.
4. Elimination of lines and boxes to present a resume with as much white space so that the readers eye would not be distracted and could skim the document easily.
5. In addition, certain information was deleted with emphasis strictly on major accomplishments. Hobbies and activities that were not related to one's career were deleted.

After you review each resume in its original form, you can then read the comments and analyses that were incorporated to redo the resume, thus producing a stronger document. After the comment section, the revised resume has been reproduced for your review.

J. DONALD FINDERS
104 Lake View Drive
Brookfield, Wisconsin 53005
Office Phone: (555) 111-2222   Home Phone: (555) 111-2000

MARITAL STATUS	Married
BIRTH DATE	April 8, 1947
PERSONAL OBJECTIVE	Research Engineer, specializing in the design and development of internal combustion engines.
EDUCATION	City Colleges of Chicago, Diploma in Arts in Engineering, 1973.
	Vanderbilt University, Nashville, Tennessee, Bachelors Degree in Mechanical Engineering, June, 1976.
MILITARY SERVICE	U.S. Air Force, serving from May, 1967, to February, 1971. Honorable discharge.
EXPERIENCE 1976-1987	Employed by Lakeland Marine Corporation, Outboard Section, North Shores, Illinois, after graduation. Last position held was Project Engineer, concerned with advanced concept engine design.
1987-1990	Employed by NC Engineering, Gastonia, North Carolina as Senior Staff Engineer, concerned with two-stroke engine design and development.
1990 to present	Employed by Wisconsin Marine, Brookfield, Wisconsin as Lead Project Engineer, concerned with low emission, two-stroke engine concepts.
ABILITIES	Have specialized in two-stroke cycle, spark ignition engines. Have experience with computer modeling of both two and four-stroke engine gas dynamics and mechanical kinematics. Experienced with carburetion and fuel injection systems, pressure-charging systems, inlet exhaust system dynamics and tuning, bearing load analysis, and engine balancing. Have the ability to write clear and concise engineering reports.
ACCOMPLISHMENTS	Patents: U.S. Patent 4,373,475; Internal Combustion Engine. U.S. Patent 4,340,018; Internal Combustion

Engine Having a Wet-Type Cylinder Liner and Process for Manufacturing Same. U.S. Patent 4,512,291; Internal Combustion Engine. U.S. Patent 6,055,962; Fuel System for an Internal Combustion Engine.

Publications Authored: "Performance Testing a 30 Cubic Inch Bourke Engine," Sport Aviation Magazine, March, 1980. "Design of a Two-Stroke Cycle Spark Ignition Engine Employing a Scotch-Yoke Crankshaft Mechanism", SAE Paper 851518, September, 1985.

Designed, engineered, and constructed successful running prototypes of a light aircraft engine employing a novel mechanical arrangement.

Designed and engineered a high performance, 3-cylinder, outboard boat racing engine for Mod-50 class. This was a highly successful engine that was in limited production and held several class records.

Engineered and successfully tested hydraulically boosted, power steering system for large displacement, racing outboard engine application.

Designed and engineered three small displacement, single cylinder, air-cooled chain saw engines, two of which are currently in production.

Designed and engineered 116cc and 60cc displacement air compressors for two-stroke DFI engine applications. The 116cc unit is in current production.

Designed, engineered, and constructed prototype Stirling engine powered generator set that has met initial design targets.

PROFESSIONAL SOCIETIES

Member of the Society of Automotive Engineers and the American Society of Mechanical Engineers.

LEISURE

Interested in engines of all types. Interested in aircraft and aviation. Enjoy music, playing jazz guitar, and performing on a regular basis.

REFERENCES

Will be furnished upon request.

Comments on the Resume of Donald Finders

Mr. Finders, under his personal information of address and phone number, has chosen to list his office phone number. Certainly sending out a resume with your office/work telephone number is a signal of company disloyalty. The inclusion of the office or work telephone number clearly suggests that Mr. Finders was indeed conducting his job campaign on his employer's time and that potential employers should feel free to contact him at his office. This is negative as it communicates disloyalty and using company resources for personal gain. Company resources, of course, should only be used for fulfilling company objectives.

Marital Status: This section is not needed, and it was deleted in the revised copy. Certainly, being married does not suggest that the individual is a harder worker than a single person.

Birth Date: It is not necessary to indicate your date of birth. In an interview, this would be considered an illegal and discriminatory question.

Personal Objective: Again, this is not necessary: therefore, it was deleted. What your objective is has no relationship to what the company may or may not be looking for in the successful candidate. A stronger approach is to replace a Personal Objective with a Summary of Experience. This four- or five-line paragraph simply indicates in a very concise, succinct manner those skills that you have and are interested in bringing to a potential employer. Titles, which most Personal Objectives use, are misleading and are seldom accurate and do not translate clearly to all organizations.

Education: While this is indeed an important section, I have always felt it is not the fact that you concluded your degree and made it to the auditorium for graduation ceremonies, but what you did with the educational opportunities that you had acquired. How has your education facilitated an employer's business? Therefore, the educational section was repositioned at the end of the resume.

Military Service: Although important, it occurred more than thirty years ago, and therefore, was also repositioned at the end of the resume.

Experience Section 1976 - 1987: This was a little vague, and although it indicated eleven years of experience, many people are not aware of what this particular company did so we defined the size of the organization ($1.4 billion), where it was located, what city, what state and what the company does at that location – just a little bit more information.

1987 - 1990: With the next position, we again have provided the reader with a little more definition of what Mr. Finders' company during this time period actually produced and where it produced it – city and state.

Mr. Finders, in these two positions, has indicated what his last position was, but there are no accomplishments. He does not indicate any achievements, quantitatively and whether there were additional positions prior to the one listed as the last position.

This type of resume is called the "flipper." It is called the flipper because you must flip back and forth between page one and page two and try to determine what accomplishments were achieved during what period of time. It is confusing at best and in the revised copy everything was organized by sequence.

It is interesting that Mr. Finders listed his most recent job last and listed his very first job at the top of the employment section. Just the opposite of how it should be listed. You always want to show your most recent job first and then go back in time.

Abilities and **Accomplishments**: These sections, in my opinion, are absolute unqualified disasters. We have no idea how Mr. Finders' engineering talents made the product more reliable, increased the quality, increased the ease of manufacturing, or what he actually did. Basically, he states no accomplishments or results of what he accomplished. We have a very extensive list of publications, which again do not state specifically how they benefited the company or the product line for which he was assigned.

Patents are impressive, but again, without further elaboration of how they impacted the company's product line, they are passive at best. There must be some relationship between the patents granted and how the company benefited from these innovations.

Finally, I thought listing his **Professional Societies** was a good idea, but was at a loss to explain how citing his **Leisure** activities and the phrase "**References** will be furnished upon request" enhances his document; consequently, on the revised resume these items were eliminated.

In the revised document the layout was much improved. We know where he worked, for whom and what the companies do, etc., and, most important, what Mr. Finders' specific accomplishments were. These accomplishments incorporated excellent use of numbers, and the indications of his patents, inventions and publications were formatted in a much more concise manner.

Note how the accomplishments cited on page one of his resume end with the Net Result, i.e., how the company benefited from his accomplishment. Quantification or numbers that could be obtained were inserted to add extra impact. The layout is clean without excessive and distracting lines or boxes.

J. DONALD FINDERS
104 Lake View Drive
Brookfield, Wisconsin
(555) 111-2000
<u>dfinders@milwpc.com</u>

<u>**Summary of Experience**</u>

More than twenty (20) years in engineering and design of internal combustion engines. Extensive background in computer modeling of engine gas dynamics for both two-stroke and four-stroke cycles, carburation, fuel injection systems, pressure-charging systems, inlet and exhaust system dynamics and tuning, kinematic analysis bearing load analysis and engine balancing.

1990 to **Wisconsin Marine**, Brookfield, Wisconsin
Present A $1.4 billion division of Brunswick Corporation, specializing in the design, production and marketing of marine engines, propulsion drives and accessories worldwide.

<u>**Senior Project Engineer IV, Applied Technology**</u>: Responsible for development of low emission engines and related systems involving design, testing, and product transition into production status.

- Created and engineered high-speed, compact air compressor for implementing direct-cylinder, air assisted fuel injection systems to two-stroke outboard engines. **Net Results**: Developed new technology not yet commercially available.

- Supervised design of air compressor for Optimax fuel system, the world's first production, direct cylinder injected, low emissions, V-6 outboard engine. **Net Results**: Provided key component in project and sold 70,000 units in four (4) years.

- Designed induction and exhaust systems for a two-cylinder, four-stroke, 25 horsepower outboard using computer modeling. **Net Results**: Reduced developmental time by 75% over traditional methods.

- Designed induction and exhaust systems for a two-cylinder, four-stroke, 25 horsepower outboard using computer modeling. **Net Results**: Reduced development time and met all performance criteria.

- Engineered and supervised design of air compressor for fuel system for 3-cylinder Optimax engine. **Net Results**: Provided key component to engine fuel system.

- Supervised design of motoring text stands and test procedures for all compressor performance and endurance testing. **Net Results**: Performed internal tests under budget and established durability and performance quidelines.

- Performed thermodynamic analysis and conducted complete dynamometer performance tests on high-speed, compression-ignition engine concept. **Net Results**: Proved concept validity and wrote a technical report for use in determining future strategy.

- Invented several novel concepts concerning fuel systems, two of which are patented. **Net Results**: Added additional patent coverage to Optimax technology.

- Performed advanced technical support assisting project engineers to optimize engine balance and analyze bearing loads. **Net Results**: Increased product durability, reliability, and functionality.

1987 to	**NC Engineering**, Gastonia, North Carolina
1990	A manufacturer of chain saws and hand-held lawn and garden products.

Senior Staff Engineer: Responsible for two-stoke engine design and development.

- Engineered and supervised design and development of three (3) single cylinder, air-cooled chain saw engines through product launch. **Net Results**: Established improved standard of performance for power output, low vibration, and durability.

- Simplified manufacturing by utilizing numerical machining equipment. **Net Results**: Reduced warranty claims, and incurred greater accuracy and repeatability in components allowing consistent performance.

1976 to	**Lakeland Marine Corporation**, North Shores Illinois
1987	A manufacturer of boat propulsion systems.

Project Engineer, High Performance Group: Reponsible for the development of advanced concept engines and systems.

- Designed and engineered a high performance, 3-cylinder, outboard racing engine. **Net Results**: Exceeded performance specifications, increased durability by 300%, and held several class records.

- Engineered and implemented hydraulically assisted power steering system for large displacement, racing outboard application. **Net Results**: Reduced driver fatigue, offered more precise steering, and improved safety.

- Engineered and designed a turbo-charged and fuel injected induction system for production V-6, two stroke outboard as a proof-of-concept demonstrator. **Net Results**: Set new standards for highest power and performance achieved.

Education: Bachelor's Degree in Mechanical Engineering, Vanderbilt University, Nashville, Tennessee, 1976

Inventions: Patents: U.S. Patent 4,373,475; Internal Combustion Engine
U.S. Patent 4,340,081; Internal Combustion Engine Having a Wet Type Cylinder Liner and
    Process for Manufacturing Same
U.S. Patent 4,515,291; Internal Combustion Engine
U.S. Patent 6,055,962; Fuel System for an Internal Combustion Engine
U.S. Patent 6,112,707: Engine Fuel System with a Supercharged Air Compressor

Professional Societies: Member of Society of Automotive Engineers (SAE) and American Society of Mechanical Engineers (ASME)
Active participant in the Wisconsin Small Engine Consortium (WSEC).

Military Service: U.S. Air Force, Honorable discharge, 1971

Dianne M. Keepers
1000 Pleasant View Avenue
Brookfield, Wisconsin 53005
414-555-1010

Professional Experience

ANC Capital Corporation (*Lake Shores, IL*)	Vice President and Finance Counsel	1999 to Present
ANC Global, N.V. (*Brookfield, WI*)	Senior Counsel	

- Responsible for and manage combined global financial services for an $11 billion equipment finance company

  - Provide advice relating to exit agreements on two financial services joint ventures in Europe

  - Assist in the creation and establishment of an Irish bank (Summer, 2000) and branches in various European countries.

  - Lead the New Central Credit and Arca Credit teams (U.S. and Canadian) in merging retail contracts, security agreements, guarantees and loan agreements into one set of forms

  - Integrating each company's open account credit card program under which credit is extended to retail customers for direct purchases of parts and labor from Arca and New Central dealers

  - Manage financial legal services for business units in Canada, Australia, Latin America (including Brazilian Bank) and Europe.

- Manage continuous funding of the combined companies, including asset-backed securitizations, bank agreements, commercial paper programs, medium term note programs and other funding alternatives.

  - First combined asset-backed securitization of over U.S. $1 billion was closed in March, 200q

- Manage the collection activity of ANC Capital

- Manage outside counsel and negotiate fee structures

- Manage and lead a staff of professionals and administrative personnel

Arca Capital Corporation	Vice President and Senior Counsel	1987-1999
Arca Corporation (*Brookfield, WI*)	Senior Counsel	

- Responsible for the global financial service business of Case Capital Corporation ($8 billion equipment finance company

  - Launched open account credit card in the U.S. and Canada where customers have a line of credit to purchase parts and labor from Arca dealers

  - Established an insurance brokerage program under which our insurance agency offers various insurance products (underwritten by insurance companies) that may be financed by Arca Credit along with the purchase of Arca equipment.

  - Established "Soris Financial" brand name and program under which non-Arca equipment is financed

  - Created all U.S. and Canadian retail contracts, guarantees, security agreements, promissory notes and other forms used to finance the sale of equipment and lien perfection procedures

  - Drafted and managed wholesale security agreements and other forms utilized when Arca/Arca Credit finances the sale of equipment to Arca dealer.

- Maintained all state licenses required for the financing provided by Arca Credit

- Managed compliance with all state laws relating to financing (disclosure requirements, maximum interest rates/time price differential, late charges, processing fees, etc.)

- Launched Arca Credit's commercial marine financing program

- Launched Arca Credit's commercial lending finance program (acquisition loans, real estate loans, working capital loans and borrowing base loans)

- Managed funding of Arca and Arca Capital, including asset-backed securitizations, bank agreements, commercial paper programs, medium term note programs and other funding alternatives. On the average, Arca Credit closed two U.S. and two Canadian asset-backed securitizations each year. Closed one wholesale warehousing facility (revolving) and one retail (revolving) warehousing facility. Closed various bond and medium term note programs in the U.S., Canada and Australia.

- Managed, drafted, reviewed various types of supply contracts, software license agreements, consulting and other types of agreements

- Managed the collection activity of Arca Capital

  - Centralized replevin/bankruptcy activity from multiple state firms to two national firms

- Managed and lead professional and administrative staff

White & Herschel *(Milwaukee, WI)*	Associate	1986-1987

- Represented various parties in bankruptcy cases and in real estate matters.

- Prepared loan documents.

Harter & Black *(Dallas, TX)*	Associate	1985-1986

- Represented debtors, secured creditor and unsecured creditors in bankruptcy cases under Chapters 7 and 11 of the Bankruptcy Code

Goodman, Udale, Varner, Melton & Anderson *(Dallas, TX)* (now defunct)	Associate	1982-1985

- Represented various parties in bankruptcy cases. From January 1983 to April 1985 a substantial amount of my time was devoted to the Braniff Airways, Inc. Chapter 11 bankruptcy case as the firm was co-counsel to the Unsecured Creditors' Committee

- Prepared loan documents

Education

Hamline University School of Law	Juris Doctor	1982

Rank 3 of 141, Silver Gavel Honor Society, American Jurisprudence Awards, Torts, Corporations, Family Law and Creditor-Debtor Rights, Moot Court, Primary Editor of Law Review

University of Wisconsin, Milwaukee	B.A., International Relations	1977

Admissions

State Bar or Wisconsin
State Bar of Texas (Inactive)

Analysis of the Resume of Ms. Dianne M. Keepers

Ms. Keepers' resume as originally presented is fairly simplistic. First, Ms. Keepers failed to put down her home E-mail address, which we find fairly typical. We deleted the phrase **Professional Experience** from her resume, as that was obvious. We also inserted a **Summary of Experience** to frame in the reader's mind what this person has to offer or could bring to their organization. Throughout the two page resume we have numerous lines or bars going across the resume. It is also well to keep in mind that it is always better to have a clean resume that will facilitate easy reading or skimming. New software programs seem to invite lots of graphics, lines, boxes, etc., and they distract from the presentation. So, we took those out as well.

The other major deficiency in the first draft was that Ms. Keepers absolutely failed to quantify any of her accomplishments. She gave us a litany of what she did but not the results, achievements, or accomplishments of her activities. When we "bulletized" the accomplishments with numbers, it added to the strength of the document. She did refrain from listing hobbies or other types of distracting information and phrases such as "References Upon Request," etc. I think the revised document, which follows, is a good improvement and one that produced results.

DIANNE M. KEEPERS
1000 Pleasant View Avenue
Brookfield, Wisconsin 53005
(414) 555-1010
keepers.dm@worldnet.att.net

Summary of Experience

Eighteen (18) years of diversified experience in transactional legal matters. Areas of concentration include secured transactions, finance, strategic contracts and financial services regulatory compliance matters. Geographic areas served: North and South America, Europe, and Australia.

1987 to   **ANC Global, N.V.,** Brookfield, Wisconsin
2001   A global manufacturer and distributor of agricultural and construction equipment with sales of $10 billion and receivable portfolio of $12 billion.

> **Senior Counsel, ANC Global N.V. and Vice President and Finance Counsel,**
> **ANC Capital Corporation:** Responsible for global legal affairs of financial services subsidiaries, and for supporting procurement activity of manufacturing company. Supervised three (3) attorneys, two (2) paralegals and two (2) clerical employees.
>
> - Closed funding transactions including syndicated bank loans, medium term note and commercial paper programs and asset-backed securitizations in US, Canada and Australia raising funds in excess of $12 billion. **Net Result**: Diversified sources of funding, reduced cost of funds and received 1995 Chairman's Award.
>
> - Drafted, reviewed and negotiated contracts including software licensing, logistics, procurement agreements for raw materials, components, service parts, wholegoods, equipment and services and real estate leasing and mortgage agreements. **Net Result**: Reduced corporate risks while maximizing corporate return.
>
> - Led legal team that established bank in Ireland in 2000. **Net Result**: Created ability to "passport" the banking license to other European financial countries.
>
> - Negotiated and drafted Exit Agreement from European financial services joint venture. **Net Result**: Established organized transition from joint venture to other affiliated finance companies.
>
> - Designed US and Canadian retail and wholesale credit documentation. **Net Result**: Streamlined forms with e-commerce implementation in 2001.
>
> - Redesigned New Central Credit and Arca Credit suite of retail loan forms into one set of forms for both brands. **Net Result**: Promoted consistency in financing terms and conditions, with annual originations of $2.5 billion.
>
> - Implemented revolving account program in US and Canada, which enabled customers to finance parts and labor. **Net Result**: Generated receivable balance of $93,000,000.
>
> - Converted New Central Credit open account program to Arca Credit open account program. **Net Result**: Enhanced ANC's ownership rights in receivables and reduced administrative costs by eliminating one program.
>
> - Structured Arca Credit's newly created commercial lending, marine and motor vehicle finance programs. **Net Result**: Generated marine portfolio balance of $100,000,000 and received 1997 Chairman's Award.

- Launched "Soris Financial," a private label financing program. **Net Result**: Expanded product offerings to 800 new customers, accounted for 29% of 1998 originations and received 1998 Chairman's Award.

- Supervised over 1,000 retail and wholesale bankruptcy, replevin and other collection actions in US and Canada and restructured US process by utilizing regional counsel. **Net Result**: Projected to reduce recovery time and improve efficiencies.

- Restructured collection process in US by performing additional services internally. **Net Result**: Projected minimum cost savings of $225,000 in first year.

- Counseled business clients on advisability of terminating wholesale credit lines extended to dealers based upon state laws affecting agricultural and construction equipment dealers. **Net Result**: Minimized risk of wrongful termination lawsuits.

- Counseled business clients on wholesale pricing programs to dealer network. **Net Result:** Minimized risk of discriminatory pricing actions.

- Supervised regulatory compliance activity, including the maintenance and procurement of relevant state sales finance licenses as well as advising clients of state lending restrictions, including maximum interest rates. **Net Result**: Avoided adverse regulatory actions and customer compliance lawsuits.

1986 to   **White & Herschel**, Milwaukee, Wisconsin
1987   A general practice law firm with 100 attorneys.

        <u>Associate</u>: Responsible for bankruptcy, real estate matters and preparation of loan documents.

1985 to   **Harter & Black**, Dallas, Texas
1986   A general practice law firm with 380 attorneys.

        <u>Associate</u>: Responsible for bankruptcy matters.

1982 to   **Goodman, Udale, Varner, Melton & Anderson**, Dallas, Texas
1985   A small boutique law firm specializing in collection and bankruptcy matters.

        <u>Associate</u>: Responsible for bankruptcy matters and preparation of loan documents. Represented Unsecured Creditors Committee in Chapter 11 bankruptcy proceedings of Braniff Airways, Inc.

Education: JD Degree, Hamline University School of Law, St. Paul, Minnesota, 1982
Rank: 3 of 141, Silver Gavel Honor Society, American Jurisprudence Awards: Torts, Corporations, Family Law and Creditor-Debtor Rights, Moot Court, Primary Editor of Law Review.

               BA Degree, International Relations, University of Wisconsin, Milwaukee, Wisconsin, 1977

Admissions: State Bar of Wisconsin
State Bar of Texas (inactive)

1500 Springbrook Ln.
Naperville, IL 60564

630-555-2222 (H) 630-444-5555 (cell)
sweepersp@aol.com

Paul Sweepers

Summary of Experience   Executive with fifteen (15) years experience in industrial based operations. Diverse management background including new product & process development, quality and reliability engineering, product safety/regulatory support, and manufacturing
operations. Extensive background in concurrent product/process development process, continuous improvement, robust design, systematic problem solving, and applied statistics.

Experience   1998-2001   ABC Global Corp.   Burr Ridge, IL
Director-Engineering Process Organization
Member of Corporate Product Development Board Reporting to VP-Function Engineering, Corporate Technical Center. Responsible for Testing, Engineering Process, Reliability Engineering, Advanced Quality Methods, Systems Engineering and Corp. Product Safety/Regulatory/Homologation operations worldwide.

- Led the ABC global development team for integration of industry best practices to define the DFSS (Design-For-Six-Sigma) approach for new product development. Launched DFSS process documentation and website, trained in excess of 600 leaders and initiated project consultation worldwide. Received executive endorsement from CEO and divisional presidents, vice presidents. **Net Results**: Projected reduction of prototype phases from 4 to 2 (40 to 50% reduction in product development cost), projected time to market improvement of between 6 to 8 months (20% improvement), projected improvement of product launch quality from 2σ to 6σ (300,000 to 3 defects per mil. opportunity).
- Provided testing support for all product development activity world wide involving engine/trans. dynamometer, full vehicle vibration and temperature extremes, structural stress analysis, electrical component durability, and full vehicle field verification testing. **Net Results**: On time launch for 6 major product programs in 2 years.
- Led the development of improved operational efficiency through development of Test Information Management System, testing procedures/standardization, and material efficiencies. **Net Results**: Improved operational efficiency by $1.5 million annually.
- Developed and standardized methods, training, and implementation process for *System Engineering*. Over 150 engineers trained, reduction of product development time of over 6 months on major planter development program. **Net Results**: Generated $1.25 million savings in product development expense.
- Introduced systematic methodologies to facilitate *Root-cause Problem Solving & Corrective Action Verification*, and *Design FMEA*, on flagship tractor program. **Net Results**: 50% failure rate reduction.
- Developed and championed new product development implementation of the Six-Sigma initiative. Created management alignment for selection of Black Belt candidates and financial support for initial project development. **Net Results**: Initiated (6) Black Belt projects formulated to prevent 99% anticipated failures and generate warranty related cost savings in excess of $1 million.

1992-1998   Michigan Motor Co., Power train Quality & Reliability   Livonia, MI
Section Supv., Reliability/Robustness Implementation (and New Methods Development)
Development of leadership strategy for pilot implementation of the Ford Product Development System/Robust Engineering Process (FDS/REP) in new transmission development programs.
- Managed the pilot implementation of FPDS/REP for the AX4S and 5R100 transmission programs. Project team received Chairman's Award for Parking Brake Robustness Project. **Net Results**: Reduced defects per milion from 66,000 to 200 (3σ to 5σ).
- Developed key sections of *Robust Engineering Process* as part of worldwide team working on Power train Breakthrough Initiative for new product/process development. Primary architect for *Concept Selection, Robust Design, Design Verification, Process Control* phases. **Net Result**: Precursor to DFSS process currently implemented.
- Initiated effort to integrate reliability and robust design methodologies. First *International Conference on Integration of Reliability and Robustness (Nov. 1994)*. **Net Results**: Senior executive approval for integrated methods approach, policy deployment for Breakthrough Initiative on robustness.
- Project manager for the completion of over 30 Robust Design case studies within Power train product development. **Net Results**: Reduced process defect per million (opportunities) from 300,000 to 200 (2σ to 5σ) with total cost reduction net effect in excess of $5 million per year.
- Administration of graduate research and co-op programs in the area of Industrial Engineering and Applied Statistics. Participating institutions include Univ. of Michigan, Wayne State Univ., and Oakland Univ. **Net Results**: Annual improvement between $900k and $2 million (for combined manufacturing process and product development project for engine and transmission development)

Experience (continued)

1989-1992   Michigan Motor Co., EFHD (currently Vericom)   Ypsilanti, MI
Manufacturing Operations Superintendent (and Engr. Specialist)
Responsible for the scheduling, production, quality, and cost performance of the DIS (Distributorless Ignition Syst.) and e-Core ignition coil operations involving the supervision of 102 hourly and 6 salaried personnel (3 production shifts, 19 separate end-items).

- Provided technical leadership to resolve new operation launch problem (DIS thermal shock failure mode) enabling ISIR approval and Job-1 commitments for the Alba Plant in Hungary through application of statistical problem solving and Taguchi methods. **Net Results**: Improved component B_{10} reliability from less than 100 hrs. to over 100 hrs. (accelerated test results)
- Provided process and technical leadership for EFHD;s first implementation of Ford's Continuous Process Improvement system (project: 'DIS Continuous Process Improvement Study')/ **Net Results**: Improved operations performance from 90 jobs/hr., 68^ 1st run capability…to 320 jobs/hr., 90% 1st run capability, and $13 CPU net savings.
- Managed the successful implementation of a TQM system in coil operations. **Net Results**: Successfully petitioned for Michigan Q1 award (Ypsi Plant) with the DIS operations serving as showcase quality system example for the Ypsilanti plant.
- Managed the successful launch of the first DIS coil operation at BIC quality level.
- Annual improvements to E-Core ignition coil quality, productivity, and customer satisfaction. **Net Results**: Extended the profitable life of product by 4 years (incremental revenue in excess of $14 mil.).

1985-1989   Michigan Motor Co., EFHD (currently Vericon)   Ypsilanti, MI
Manufacturing/Process Engineer, Ignition Engineering Dept.
Development of advanced processing material and testing technologies for this production of DIS coil (Ignition system components) as a key member of multi-function team.

- Successfully transferred epoxy processing, wire termination, robotics, and injection molding technologies from benchmark competitor Nippondenso.
- Transferred benchmark DIS technologies into functional specifications for manufacturing and assembly, material development, and equipment development.
- Provided technical leadership for reverse engineering and optimization of the epoxy and injection molded sub-component designs using Taguchi methods. **Net Results**: Reduced process defects per million from 300,000 to 200 (2σ to 5σ)
- Directed the development and installation of fully automated epoxy vacuum processing, coil preheat, epoxy/coil during processes with annual capacity of 2.1 million units and cross-product loading flexibility. **Net Results**: Demonstrated specified process capability and capacity at start-up. On-time launch, Best in class product quality at launch.

Education

1987-Present   Michigan Motor Co./ABC Global sponsored
- Six Sigma Black Belt (ASQ, March 2001)
- Six Sigma Champion Certification (ASQ, 2000)
- Taguchi Methods Expert Cert. (1996, Dr. Genichi Taguchi, American Supplier Institute)
- Credits toward MSE, Industrial Engineering – Wayne St. Univ.
- TRIZ (Theory of Inventive Problem Solving)
- Principles of Axiomatic Design (Prof. Nam P. Suh, MIT)
- Workplace Diversity (Michigan Motor Co. Facilitator and Trainer)
- Communispond (executive communications and presentations)
- Michigan Motor Co.'s Cont. Process improvement methodology (leadership trng.)
- Michigan Motors Co.'s BD-Team Oriented Problem Solving (leadership trng.)
- Design-of-Experiments I & II, SPC I & II (Eastern Michigan Univ.)

1997   Central Michigan University
- MSA, Master's Degree, Science of Administration, concentrating on Leadership and Change in a business environment, and implementation Strategies for a Integrated Product Development Process.

1995   University of Michigan-Dbn.
- BSME, Bachelors Degree, Mechanical Engineering, concentrations on use of statistical methods in design of mechanical systms, and composite material design & testing.

ANALYSIS OF MR. PAUL SWEEPERS' RESUME

A quick look at page one will indicate the immediate problem with Mr. Sweepers' resume. It is difficult at best, if not impossible, to read because of the small font style. There are no spaces between bullet points and this makes skimming the document very fatiguing. The font style of his name suggests that he may have an ego problem when compared with the size of the rest of the fonts on this resume. His name and personal information, including E-mail address, were centered for ease of reading and reference.

In this particular resume, we were able to keep it at two pages, but with a format that allowed for easier reading or skimming. Bullet points or accomplishments citing net results were double-spaced also for ease of reading, along with the actual numeric results of his work activities. The revised document looks exceptionally well and did very well in his actual campaign.

PAUL SWEEPERS
1500 Springbrook Lane
Naperville, Illinois 60564
(630) 555-2222
sweepersp@aol.com

Summary of Experience

Executive with fifteen (15) years experience in industrial based operations including new product and process development, quality and reliability engineering, product safety/regulatory support, and manufacturing operations. Extensive background in concurrent product/process development, continuous improvement, robust design, systematic problem solving, and applied statistics.

1998 to **ABC Global,** Racine, Wisconsin
2001   A global $11 billion designer, manufacturer and distributor of agricultural, construction equipment and financial services, with over 35,000 employees and 10,000 dealers and distributors.

Director Engineering Process Organization: responsible to Vice President-Functional Engineering. Member of Corporate Product Development Board as leader for product testing, engineering process, reliability engineering, advanced quality methods, systems engineering, and product safety. Supervised 6 engineering managers and 230 personnel worldwide.

- Led development team and launched Design-For-Six-Sigma (DFSS) approach in new product development. **Net Result**: Projected reduction in product development costs of 50% and quality improvement from 2σ to 6σ (300,000 to 3 defects per 1,000,000).

- Initiated six (6) Black Belt projects formulated to prevent 99% of anticipated failures. **Net Result**: Generated warranty related cost savings in excess of $1,000,000.

- Directed laboratory and field test support for all product development activity worldwide. **Net Result**: Launched, on time, six (6) major product programs in two (2) years.

- Developed Test Information Management System for procedures/standardization and material efficiencies. **Net Result**: Improved operational efficiency by $1,500,000 annually.

- Established methods, training and implementation process for Systems Engineering. **Net Result**: Trained over 150 engineers, reduced product development cycle by 6 months, and generated savings of $1,250,000.

- Introduced systematic methodologies to facilitate Root-Cause Problem Solving & Corrective Action Verification, and Design FMEA. **Net Result**: Reduced failure rates 50% in 1st year.

1985 to **Michigan Motor Co.**, Dearborn, Michigan
1988   A global $162 billion automotive/truck engineering and manufacturing company with over 350,000 employees and worldwide product development and distribution.

1992 **Section Supervisor, Reliability/Robustness Implementation and New Methods Development**:
to   Responsible for pilot implementation of the Michigan Motor Co. Product Development
1998   System/Robust Engineering Process (FPDS/REP) in new transmission development programs.

- Initiated pilot implementation of FRDS/REP for AX4S and 5R100 transmission programs. **Net Result**: Received **Chairman's Award for Parking Brake Robustness Project** and reduced defects per 1,000,000 from 66,000 to 200 (3σ to 5σ).

- Developed key sections of Robust Engineering Process as part of worldwide team working on Power train Breakthrough Initiative for new product/process development. Served as primary architect for Concept Selection, Robust Design, Design Verification, Process Control phases. **Net Result**: Implemented as precursor to DFSS process.

- Led effort to integrate reliability and robust design methods. Produced first International Conference on Integration of Reliability and Robustness. **Net Result**: Gained senior executive approval for policy deployment for Breakthrough Initiative on robustness.

- Completed over 30 Robust Design case studies within Power train product development. **Net Result**: Reduced defect opportunities per 1,000,000 from 300,000 to 200 (2σ to 5σ) with total cost reduction in excess of $5,000,000 per year.

- Administered graduate research and co-op programs in Industrial Engineering. **Net Result**: Reduced annual process and product development costs by more than $900,000.

1989 to 1992   **Manufacturing Operations Superintendent (and Engineering Specialist)**: Responsible for scheduling, production, quality, and cost performance of the Distributorless Ignition System (DIS) and E-Core Ignition coil operations. Supervised 108 hourly and salary personnel.

- Resolved new DIS operation launch problem enabling ISIR approval and Job-1 commitments for Alba (Hungary) plant through application of statistical problem solving and Taguchi methods. **Net Result**: Improved component B_{10} reliability from 100 hrs. to over 1,200 hrs.

- Provided process and technical leadership for EFHD's first implementation of Michigan's Continuous Process Improvement system (Lean Engineering). **Net Result**: Improved DIS Coil operations performance at Ypsilanti from 90 jobs/hour, 68% 1st run capability to 320 jobs/hour, 90%1st run capability, and net savings of $13 CPU.

- Managed the successful implementation of a TQM system in coil operations. **Net Result**: Successfully petitioned for Michigan Motor's Q1 aware, Ypsilanti Plant with the DIS operations serving as showcase quality system example.

- Launched E-Core Ignition coil design and quality initiatives. **Net Result**: Extended profitable product life by four (4) years generating incremental revenue of $14,000,000.

- Promoted to Section Supervisor. Reliability/Robustness Implementation and New Methods Development.

1985 to 1989   **Manufacturing/Process Engineer, Ignition Engineering Department**: Responsible for development of advanced processing material and testing technologies for the production of DIS coil (ignition system components) as key member of multi-function team.

- Provided technical leadership for reverse engineering and optimization of the epoxy and injection molded sub-component designs using Taguchi methods. **Net Result**: Reduced process defects per million from 300,000 to 200 (2σ to 5σ).

- Directed development and installation of automated epoxy vacuum processing, coil preheat, epoxy/coil curing processes with annual capacity of 2,100,000 units and cross-product loading flexibility. **Net Result**: Achieved on-time launch, best-in-class product quality.

- Promoted to Manufacturing Operations Superintendent (and Engineering Specialist).

Education: MSA, Science of Administration, Central Michigan University, 1997
BSME, Mechanical Engineering, University of Michigan-DBN, 1985

Additional Training   Six Sigma Master Black Belt (American Supplier Inst., Price Waterhouse Coopers, Feb. 2001)
Six Sigma Champion Certification (ASQ, 2000)
Taguchi Methods Expert Certification (American Supplier Institute 1996)
Credits toward MSE, Industrial Engineering, Wayne State University
TRIZ (Theory of Inventive Problem Solving)
Principles of Axiomatic Design (Professor Nam P. Suh)
Workplace Diversity (Ford Facilitator and Trainer
Communispond (executive communications and presentations)
Michigan Motor's Continuous Process Improvement Methodology (leadership training)
Michigan Motor's *D-Team Oriented Problem Solving (leadership training
Design-of-Experiments I & II, SPC I & II (Eastern Michigan University)

UTILIZING THE INTERNET IN YOUR JOB CAMPAIGN
HOW TO GET YOUR RESUME ON THE INTERNET

Traveling the Information Highway – no longer the road less traveled

Electronic communication has become a way of life in this age of the Information Highway. The use by job seekers of the Internet with its instant access to information is a necessity just to be competitive in the employment market. With more and more companies and recruiters turning to the World Wide Web to post job listings and source candidates for positions, the ability to respond electronically is essential.

This section will guide you through the process of developing a plain-text version of your resume that will be compatible with any word processing software and will allow E-mail response to Internet job listings as well as the posting of your resume to Internet databases.

Specifically this section addresses:

- Developing an Internet-Friendly Resume: Converting to Electronic Format

- Sending Your Resume via E-mail

- Posting Your Resume on the Internet

- Where to Post

- How to Post

DEVELOPING AN INTERNET-FRIENDLY RESUME

With a few adaptations, the resume that you developed using Lawrence & Allen's **Guidelines for Preparing an Action-Oriented Resume** can be used for electronic application. This document already includes the information that paints a verbal picture of your work history and selected achievements using keywords and phrases. The content will remain the same; however, the manner in which the content is presented must be altered for retrieval by a variety of software packages operating on various computer platforms. It is necessary to put the resume into a commonly understood text language for electronic reply or Internet posting. The "American Standard Code for Information Interchange," better known as ASCII (pronounced "askee"), is a plain-text format that is universally accessible and can be retrieved into any E-mail or word-processing package.

CONVERTING YOUR RESUME TO ELECTRONIC FORMAT

To create your ASCII resume, simply type your resume in any word-processing software, keeping the following in mind:

- **FONTS AND ATTENTION-GETTERS**: ASCII is very basic and does not recognize certain word-processing formatting commands. Bolding, underlining, italics and size will not translate into ASCII. Do not try to incorporate these features into your resume. Substitutes you may wish to consider to call attention to certain areas within your electronic resume include: capital letters instead of bolding; asterisks (*) or plus signs (+) instead of bullets; quotation marks instead of italics. Use these sparingly so that you call attention where intended but do not create difficulty in reading. Be aware that specialty characters such as mathematical symbols will not transfer to ASCII.

- **TABS**: Use the spacebar instead of tabs to indent. ASCII does not recognize tabs.

- **ALIGNMENT**: ASCII defaults to left justified. The line of text should be sixty to sixty-five characters with hard breaks used at the end of the line. Word wrap will create awkward breaks in text on different sized monitors and can throw your resume into a jumbled mess. Remember to use the spacebar instead of tabs.

When you have completed your plain text resume, be sure to spell check your document and then proofread. Lastly, E-mail a copy to yourself to check appearance and, if possible, to a friend or acquaintance for further proofing. Save the resume as a text-only document, not as a replacement for the resume you send "snail mail," but as an electronically acceptable resume to transmit via the Internet. A sample plain-text resume for Robert T. Thomas is included in this section for your review.

ELECTRONIC RESPONSE VIA E-MAIL

Many classified ads as well as Internet job postings will specify electronic response. Should you wish to respond via E-mail, simply compose your E-mail cover letter, just as you would if responding to an ad in the local newspaper, and attach your plain-text resume document. As always, read the posting in its entirety and follow directions.

It is strongly recommended that you first send the E-mail to yourself for proofing before forwarding to the specified address.

POSTING YOUR RESUME ON THE INTERNET

Once you have prepared your electronic resume, the decision on whether or not to post on the Internet will have to be made. There are some factors to consider when making this determination:

- Once posted, the resume becomes a public document over which you have little control. The private resume posting Web sites do not always allow you to dictate who sees your resume. With this in mind, make sure that you are comfortable with anyone and everyone having access to your resume.

- Is there a cost to posting your resume? Is there a charge for updating the information on the resume? Some Internet resume databases allow you to post with no fee but charge for updating. Some charge a fee to post, but allow a specified number of free updates. Read the information on the Web site carefully.

- How long will your resume stay on the Internet? Some Internet services retain resumes for a specified period of time, such as three to six months, then delete if the document is not updated within the time period. Others retain the resume until you remove it from the database. If your resume is posted, remember to remove it from the Internet when you have accepted your new position. Otherwise, should your new employer become aware that you have a resume posted on the Internet, you could face an embarrassing situation.

WHERE TO POST

There are numerous resume databases on the Internet, both public and private. Some of these databases are sponsored by search firms to identify assignment candidates, while others are in business to sell corporate memberships to facilitate recruiting efforts.

"Public" means that anyone can search through the database, whereas private indicates that only specified companies or individuals can access the information. Both can charge fees for posting or accessing resumes. In some cases, Internet resume databases will require you to register a name and password. Keep track of this information if you decide to post your resume to one of these databases.

The universe of Internet resume databases changes daily. Web sites for Internet job listings and resume postings can be found in directories, newspapers, telephone books and magazines. The public library reference department has directories of Internet addresses categorized by subject in which you can find numerous general resume databases as well as a variety of specialized resume databases. With little effort, you can find more than you will ever need. Just be sure to read all the information contained on the Web page so that you will know exactly what to expect.

Listed below are some of the larger and better-known Internet career Web sites:

Career Mosaic www.careermosaic.com: Offers extensive database of job listings in general, accounting, healthcare, human resources, insurance and technical areas for entry level up to professional positions. Resume posting and editing.

Career Web, Inc. www.cweb.com: Job database of almost 40,000 online listings. Post resume and review affiliate sites specializing in positions for healthcare professionals and transitioning military personnel.

HeadHunter.net www.headhunter.net: Database exceeding 160,000 job openings no more than one month old listed with recruiters nationwide. Resume posting.

Monster.Com www.monster.com: Job database listing more than 255,000 employment opportunities. Research companies and relocation information including salary calculator to determine cost of living variance.

America's Job Bank www.ajb.dni.us: More than 1,400,000 job listings across the country. Site incorporates job opportunities listed with states' Job Service offices. Search by occupation, keyword, military code or job number. Post resumes and track job search information.

Career Builder Network www.careerbuilder.com: Links with several Web sites to develop job database exceeding 1,000,000 opportunities. Allows for receipt of E-mail listings of jobs meeting your specified criteria.

Additional career Web sites are listed at the end of this section for your review. Please note that this is only a partial listing of available sites. Additions, deletions and changes in Web sites occur continuously. You may want to consult reference directories periodically to identify new listings or search for new Web sites by using various Search Engines to identify previously unknown sites. A list of search engines is included to assist you in this effort.

HOW TO POST

Find the Internet resume database service(s) in which you are interested. The service will give specific instructions for posting your plain-text resume to their database. Just follow the directions.

Some of the services may ask you to fill in the blanks with your specific resume information on a preformatted screen. Others may ask you to separate your summary of experience into technical and non-technical skills. Use keywords from your summary so that company representatives and recruiters scanning resumes in the database will notice yours. Above all, follow the directions for posting your resume to the specific database.

THE HARD FACTS ABOUT USING THE INTERNET IN YOUR JOB CAMPAIGN

Just remember that the Internet is a tool to be used in conjunction with other tools in your job search. It provides information on published employment opportunities and allows your resume to be viewed by some interested parties. It is not a substitute for proactively pursuing the unpublished market.

The Internet may no longer be the road less traveled by job seekers. It is, however, simply another road on the job campaign trail.

Basically there are two ways to use the Internet. You may post your resume electronically on a specific Web site and hope that a potential search firm or employer will take the time to surf the Net and read or skim your resume. Obviously, posting is a very passive activity with minimal results to be expected. The other way is to respond to a specific posting where the resume and cover letter (and remember a cover letter should be sent along with a resume) is sent to a specific employer or location. This is a preferable alternative, but the downside means you have many Web sites to surf and peruse, and only a few will respond.

Our own research suggests that most corporate management personnel do not have the time to peruse all the resumes that are E-mailed to their location or to peruse all the resumes that are posted on various bulletin boards. My own estimate is that there are approximately 100,000,000 resumes on various Web sites, and no one has determined how many of these are duplicates or triplicates of earlier editions that job seekers have elected to post.

Hard fact number one is that less than 5 percent of the positions that are filled today through private search firms/recruiters or corporate management human resource recruiters come from interviews secured from responses to Internet postings. The Internet has a long way to go. It is definitely not the current method of choice for corporate recruiters. While I encourage people to use the Internet, in the same breath, I also encourage them to use it efficiently.

Earlier in this book, I have listed a number of ways by which an individual can enroll his or her co-captain, i.e. spouse, in the job campaign process. One of these ways is to have the spouse, assuming he or she is not gainfully employed outside the home, do the surfing and research to locate positions that have been posted on the Internet, and also to prepare appropriate cover letters for response.

For the individual who does not have a co-captain on the team, I would advise people to surf the Net only after 7 p.m. The reason I suggest this time frame is twofold. Number one, daylight hours should be spent trying to contact decision-makers and individuals to whom previous correspondence, either electronic or snail mail, has been addressed. This is a time when you know where the decision-makers are. They are at their desks. When they leave in the evening, I would use this non-personal search time for the Internet. Second, sooner or later, one of the problems all job hunters have is that everyone is faced with periods of inactivity. The campaign is simply not moving along.

I have seen too many of my own clients spend the whole day in front of the monitor searching for positions, responding, and then continuing to search for more positions. At the end of the day, they feel very satisfied since they have accomplished something. They have been busy – yes, productive – no. They have responded to twenty or thirty different positions. They feel it was a good day. Unfortunately, what happens is that while they may get a response, very, very few individuals receive invitations for interviews. There is just too much competition on the Net.

Again, less than 5 percent of the people hired today are hired directly through or over the Internet. This can be verified by simply asking friends and neighbors who have been unemployed in the past what method they used to gain re-employment? What successes have they gained by posting their resume on the Internet or responding to specific job postings at specific Web sites? One needs to be keenly aware of how he or she is using their time. This is definitely an activity for the evening. The key operative word here is "balance." Balance campaign tactics! Don't overload one particular tactic or strategy to the detriment of others.

SAMPLE E-MAIL RESUME

ROBERT T. THOMAS
1234 Main Street
Anywhere, State 99999
(765) 555-1212

SUMMARY OF EXPERIENCE

Twenty (20) years of diversified manufacturing experience in both heavy equipment and light appliance operations. Extensive background in materials management, production planning, production management, and inventory control. Work environments have included both union and non-union manufacturing operations.

1980 to Present - MONROE MANUFACTURING CORPORATION, Plantville, U.S.A.
A publicly held $140,000,000 corporation producing a diversified line of kitchen appliances.

1983 to Present

MANAGER OF MANUFACTURING OPERATIONS. Responsible to the General Manager for all manufacturing operations including metal fabrication, machine shop, plastic fabrication, assembly, painting and finishing, packing, warehousing, and receiving and shipping departments.

*Directly supervised a management staff of one (1) general foreman, nine (9) department foremen, plus 145 hourly, union, and clerical employees.

*Redesigned and modernized the layout of three (3) departments in a 150,000 square-foot plant increasing the flow of raw materials, subassemblies, and finished goods. Net Result: Increased production in the first year without additional equipment or manpower by 9.9% or $3,600,000.

*Proposed, developed, and implemented the introduction of numeric control (NC and CNC) machining equipment. Net Result: Achieved first year labor savings of $250,000.

*Reduced material scrap and defective workmanship by developing a new Quality Assurance Program. Net Result: Generated $138,000 savings first year.

*Established first Company and Union Safety Committee. Net Result: Reduced accidents by 55% and saved $54,600 in workmen's compensation claims.

1982 to 1983

PRODUCTION CONTROL SUPERVISOR. Responsible for scheduling of all production for all product lines. Introduced an "ABC" Inventory Control System. Net Result: Reduced purchasing requirements the first year by $68,000.

*Established first Materials Management Committee which integrated the functions of production, sales, purchasing, and inventory control. Net Result: Eliminated all parts and subassembly shortages while more closely tying production requirements to anticipated customer demands.

1980 to 1982

GENERAL FOREMAN. Responsible for the supervision, selection, and training of nine (9) department foremen.

*Installed new plating process for finished goods. Net Result: Trimmed processing time 50%.

*Developed new packing process. Net Result: Eliminated all returned or damaged goods and generated a first year savings of $31,000.

1970 to 1980 - BURRO CRANE, INCORPORATED, Hometown, U.S.A.
A privately held $20,000,000 company producing 15-ton industrial railroad cranes.

1974 to 1980

GENERAL FOREMAN. Responsible for four (4) departments (Structural Shop, Machine Shop, Subassembly Department, and Final Assembly Department) supervising 110 people with a budget of $4,000,000.

*Increased production rate by 50% from two (2) cranes per month to three (3) cranes per month by improved production management techniques.

*Combined limited second shift operation with first shift. Net Result: Reduced shift premiums by $125,000.

1971 to 1974

FOREMAN, MACHINE SHOP.
Promoted to General Foreman.

1970 to 1971

LEAD MACHINIST. Operated a variety of machines, set up equipment, and instructed other operators.
Promoted to Foreman.

EDUCATION:

B.S. Degree - Industrial Management, U.S.A. University, 1975, (Evening Program).

Currently pursuing M.B.A. Degree, Eastern Western University, (Evening Program).

KEY WORDS FOR SCANNING: Manufacturing, operations, management, heavy equipment, light appliance, materials management, production planning, production management, inventory control, union, non-union, B.S. Degree, industrial management.

INTERNET SEARCH ENGINES

Search Engines can assist the user in finding information by topic and linking to previously unknown Web sites. Listed below are several that can be beneficial to the job seeker in identifying career Web sites that may prove helpful during the job campaign. These are certainly not all the search engines available on the Internet. You may want to consult Internet address directories for additional ones.

Advanced Software Search www.ftpsearch.ntnu.no Lycos Home, Site Map, My Lycos Search Computers: Location: Lycos computers > Free Downloads > Software Search, Advanced FTP Search, Search Parameters, Search for Search Type: Case insensitive substring search, Case sensitive substring.

All-in-One Search Page. www.albany.net/allinone All-in-One is the Internet's original metasearch page. Over 500 of the best engines, indexes, directories and catalogs in one place. If you can't find it here, it doesn't exist!

AllTheWeb.com www.alltheweb.com Search all the Web, all the time: help, customize, advanced search language: African, Albanian, Arabic, Basque, Byelorussian, Bulgarian, Catalan, Chinese (trad), Chinese (simp), Croatian, Czech, Danish, Dutch, English, Estonian, Faeroese, Finnish, French.

Alta Vista – The Search Company. www.altavista.digital.com Alta Vista provides the most comprehensive search experience on the Web.

Alta Vista www.altavista.com Search engine linking to a multitude of career sites offering job databases on a variety of industries and functions and resume posting, as well as advice on career topics.

AOL www.aol.com Large search engine with links to various career Web site. Point and click on area of interest or search on specific listing shown in menu.

CNET-Search.com www.search.com Search more than 700 engines by keyword, or do a metasearch using channels and specialized engines.

Dogpile www.dogpile.com An unusually named search engine with the ability to connect to many career Web sites containing databases and resume posting opportunities. Search on "Jobs" or "Career" for linkage, and then make selection from menu.

Fast Search www.alltheweb.com Offers a large database for fulfilling search requests on the desktop. Real company history and strategy and FAQ.

Google www.google.com Search engine returns keyword search results based on relevance of content and the number of links to a particular URL from other sites.

Job Search Engine www.job-search-engine.com Search engine that scans the top USA and Canadian job boards for employment opportunities that match the criteria specified.

Lycos www.lycos.com Search engine that allows access to career information and job databases. Search for "Jobs" and follow leads given.

MSN Search www.search.msn.com Microsoft's Internet search service features the LookSmart Web directory, international search sites, special features and links.

Netscape Search www.home.netscape.com Netscape search combines the Open Directory Project with Google to deliver an exceptional Internet search-engine experience.

Northern Light www.northernlight.com Search the Web and a sizeable number of sources including WSJ abstracts, newswires and periodicals. Includes tools for customized searches.

Search Bug www.searchbug.com Search engine that can connect to job database and resource information.

Search-It-All www.searchitall.net: Search engine with linkage to eleven career Web sites offering ability to search job databases as well as post resumes.

Search Engine Watch www.searchenginewatch.com Informs users and Web developers of all aspects of search engines and directories. Get the latest news on the search-engine industry.

W3 Search Engines www.cuiwww.unige.ch Check out this collection of search-engine links. Find general search crawlers and Web directories along with specialized search tools.

Yahoo www.yahoo.com: Search engine that can connect to job database Web sites as well as to other sites providing useful career information.

CAREER WEB SITES

www.4work.com

4Work: Lists job, internships, volunteer positions, part time positions; uses "Job Alert," asking for E-mail address, then requests personal information. NO resume posting.

www.accountingjobs.net

AccountingJobs: Site of Accents on Achievement, a recruiting firm, specializing in accounting and finance positions in lower Southeast Michigan.

www.ajb.org

America'sJobBank: Job seekers can post resumes and search by state, occupation and key word.

www.associationjobs.org

Association Jobs: Association employers and recruiters can post jobs and/or search the resume bank.

www.bayarea.com

Bay Area-San Francisco: Joint effort of *The Mercury News* and the *Contra Costa Times* which features jobs in Silicon Valley.

www.bestjobsusa.com

Best Jobs USA: For job seekers and employers. Can post resume. Features articles and relocation guide, as well as "best" choices.

www.bio.com

BioOnline: Focuses on science professionals. Offers employment positions and one search firm specializing in pharmaceutical and biotech industries. Has online resume form to post resume; lists jobs.

www.blackenterprises.com

Black Enterprises: Career Channel link for African-American executives, managers and professionals. Selection of jobs uploaded daily. Confidential resume posting.

www.blackvoices.com

Black Voices: A wide variety of jobs from the premier online community for African-American professionals.

www.blackworld.com

BlackWorld: For African-American professionals. Searches jobs as well as posts for employers. Will post a resume.

www.bloomberg.com

Bloomberg: Career opportunities in the financial industry. New jobs uploaded daily. Confidential resume posting.

www.bradenton.com

Bradenton (Tampa/Bradenton): Jobs in Manatee County from the *Bradenton Herald*.

www.brassring.com

BrassRing: Search technical jobs nationally, post resume and obtain technology information.

Career Web Sites (cont'd.)

www.brilliantpeople.com   **BrilliantPeople:** Management recruiters international site, listing open positions for which candidates are being recruited.

www.career.com   **Career.com:** Lists jobs by company and location. Can post a resume. Employers can post jobs and candidates may search jobs by company, level, international, etc.

www.careerbuilder.com   **CareerBuilder:** Lists jobs, locations. Has a specific feature whereby a search agent will E-mail you jobs that match your interest. Offers career help including interview questions, information on companies. Has question and answer section on career issues.

www.careercast.com   **CareerCast:** For job seekers and employers. May post a resume. Offers resume data information and offers related Web links.

www.careercity.com   **CareerCity:** Offers job listings in hi-tech, healthcare, bio/pharma, government, and education careers. Also offers salary surveys and recruiters, plus information on companies.

www.careermag.com   **CareerMagazine:** Has job openings for employees, employers, articles. Can post resume; has place just for college students. Features employers of day and articles on today's "hot topics," regarding jobs, entrepreneurs, etc.

www.careershop.com   **CareerShop:** Specialty is computer technology. Offers virtual job fairs. Can post resume.

www.careersingovernment.com   **CareersInGovernment:** A free site. Government and public-sector positions database. No posting of resumes.

www.careersite.com   **CareerSite:** Requires registration using login and password to use. CAN post resume. Offers recruiter services and profiles company information.

www.careerweb.com   **CareerWeb:** Both national and international; Can post resumes and Link to sites for healthcare professional and transitioning military personnel. Job posting site offered.

www.charlotte.com   **Charlotte:** Jobs in the Charlotte metro area from *The Charlotte Observer.*

www.chicagotribune.com   **Chicago Tribune:** Jobs in the greater Chicago area from Chicago's leading newspaper.

Career Web Sites (cont'd.)

www.collegeclub.com   **College Club**: A wide variety of jobs from the world's largest college community.

www.columbiatoday.com   **Columbia Today**: Jobs in Columbia and the Midlands of South Carolina from *The State* newspaper.

www.computerjobs.com   **ComputerJobs**: Specializing in information technology positions nationwide.

www.computerwork.com   **ComputerWork**: For computer and contractor professionals. Can post resume.

www.ceweekly.com   **ContractEmploymentWeekly**: Has jobs for engineering, IT/IS & technical personnel; offers recruiters; no resume posting.

www.cjhunter.com   **Contract Job Hunter**: Contractors and consultants jobsite postings. Charges membership fee.

www.coolworks.com   **Cool Works**: Thousands of jobs in national parks, ski resorts, ranches, and cruise ships, plus spotlights on those hiring now.

www.ctnow.com   **ctnow (Hartford Metro/New Haven)**: Jobs in Connecticut from *The Hartford Courant*, Connecticut's largest newspaper.

www.dailypress.com   **Daily Press (Hampton Roads/Norfolk)**: Jobs in Southeastern Virginia from the *Hampton Roads Daily Press*.

www.dallasnews.com
www.wfaa.com   **Dallas News (Dallas/Fort Worth)**: Career opportunities in the Dallas metro area from *The Dallas Morning News*.

www.dfw.com   **DFW (Dallas/Fort Worth)**: Jobs in the Dallas/Ft. Worth area from the *Star Telegram*.

www.dice.com   **Dice**: Offers hi-tech jobs. Register login and password to use. Offers resume posting and job listings in several languages. Offers other Hi-tech web services.

www.duluthsuperior.com   **Duluth Superior**: Jobs in the Duluth, Superior, Northeast Minnesota and Northwest Wisconsin areas from the *Duluth News Tribune*.

www.e-insite.net   **e-inSITE**: Jobs for EOEM professionals from the electronics industries premier knowledge network. Jobs posted by actual employers and uploaded daily. Confidential resume posting.

www.engineeringjobs.com **Engineering Jobs**: Offers engineering positions, recruiters and job databases. Can post resume.

www.classifieds2000.com **Excite Classifieds**: Has very small section related to employment, job searches and companies. Can post resume.

www.execunet.com **Exec-U-Net**: Solely for the $100K + executive. Fee to utilize resource database links. Offers money back guarantee. Offers recruiters.

www.experience.com **Experience**: Job center for "twentysomethings" new to the marketplace. Can post resume.

www.fedjobs.com **Federal Jobs Central**: Offers federal government jobs; offers job application kits online. No posting of resumes.

www.fedworld.gov **FedWorld**: A giant database of federal government jobs.

www.jobs.findlaw.com **Findlaw Jobs and Resumes**: Legal job postings and resume database for attorneys, law library clerks, secretaries, assistants and paralegals.

www.flipdog.com **FlipDog**: Job-hunting, employee-seeking database with 620,000 job listings. Can customize search by profession, city, or keyword. Can enter resume and cover letter online for immediate application of viewed job. E-mail confirmation of application. User friendly.

www.gojobzone.com **GoJobZone (Riverside/San Bernardino)**: Jobs in Riverside and San Bernardino Counties from *The Press Enterprise*.

www.grandforks.com **Grand Forks**: Jobs in North Dakota from the *Grand Forks Herald*.

www.headhunter.net **HeadHunter**: Offers recruiters, job lists. Can post resume. Can receive jobs list by E-mail. Offers nationwide and international job searches.

www.healthjobsite.com **HealthJobSite**: Career opportunities for healthcare professionals. New jobs uploaded daily. Can submit resume via E-mail.

www.hirediversity.com **HireDiversity**: Popular Web site for multicultural professionals. Positions posted and removed by employers and uploaded regularly. Confidential resume submission process.

Career Web Sites (cont'd.)

www.hire.com

Hire Online: Lists jobs by company. Posts profile for automatic notification of available jobs meeting specific criteria.

www.hotjobs.com

Hot Jobs: Offers job search (general); no recruiters; company listings, career fairs. Can post resume. Has jobs posted in Canada and Australia.

www.hrsjobs.com

HRS: Offers federal job search. They will E-mail federal vacancies DAILY to your E-mail address for a FEE. No posting of resumes.

www.iccjobs.com

International Computer Consultants, Inc. Charges fee to both job bank and post resume. Offers table of contents. Has government jobs too. Contract-to-hire.

www.infospace.com

InfoSpace: A regular search engine like Yahoo. Has business section on jobs, industry specific, international, and misc.; when you hit "Classifieds," links you directly to careerpath.com.

www.infoworksusa.com

InfoWorksUSA: Career resources Website; posts jobs; posts resumes. Offers special recruiting tool, for IT, medical, and sales and marketing professionals.

www.inkpad.com

IncPad: A technology jobsite. Can post resume. Searches jobs and articles about careers, companies, etc. Must register with login and password.

www.operationIT.com

ITCareerCenter: For professionals in information technology. Can post resume.

www.it-ta.com

The ITTA Connection: For IT professionals only. Must register to search list of jobs. Free; find jobs by questions and answers re software usage and application.

www.ivillage.com

iVillage: Jobs from the leading online women's network. Wide variety of positions posted daily. Quick and confidential submission process.

www.jobbankusa.com

Job Bank USA: Offers list of jobs, recruiters. Can post resume. Offers career fairs, news groups, and assessment tools. Also offers instant reference checking for jobseekers and employers.

www.joblink-usa.com

Job Link USA: Offers interview tips; may view job listing; can post resume.

www.joblynx.com	**Job Lynx:** Headhunters search for qualified candidates. Can post resume.
www.jobnet.com	**Job Net**: Offers news/info in addition to job search. Must register with login and password. For the Delaware Valley/Philadelphia area only. Can post resumes.
www.joboptions.com	**Job Options**: Offers salary comparison; has an E-mail "job alert" notification of jobs fitting your search criteria. Must register login/password. Can post resume.
www.jobs.com	**Jobs.Com**: Formerly www.jobs98.com; CAN post resumes; offers student job search; offers free download of Resume software called Resumail.
www.jobs4it.com	**Jobs4IT**: Broad range of jobs in the IT field. All positions may be applied for online.
www.jobsonline.com	**Jobs On Line**: Offers free job postings as well as salary information.
www.thejobresource.com	**The Job Resource**: Entry-level jobs or jobs requiring little experience. Contact information is provided for most positions, but registration is required for online application.
www.jobweb.org	**JobWeb**: National Association of Colleges and Employers career centers site. Offers job listings, employer profiles and resume postings for recent graduates and college students.
www.kansas.com	**Kansas-Wichita**: Jobs in Wichita and the South Central Kansas area from the *Wichita Eagle*.
www.kansascity.com	**Kansas City/Overland Park**: Jobs in the Kansas City metro area from *The Kansas City Star*.
www.kentucky.com	**Kentucky/Lexington**: Jobs in Kentucky from the *Lexington-Herald Leader*.
www.latimes.com	**LA Times-Los Angeles Metro Area**: Jobs in Southern California from the *Los Angeles Times*.
www.latpro.com	**TheLatProProfessionalNetwork**: For Spanish & Portuguese speaking professionals. Offers recruiters and "Green Card" information. Has many links, can post resume.

Career Web Sites (cont'd.)

www.leadersonline.com	**LeadersOnLine:** Heidrick & Struggles Executive Search. Free membership access to open search assignments for management professionals in the $75,000 - $180,000 salary range.
www.localcareers.com	**LocalCareers:** Offers articles for college graduates on obtaining jobs and managing career; may sign up for job E-mail alerts; offers online career consulting on how to get job or start business. Allows forwarding of resumes to recruiters.
www.macon.com	**Macon:** Jobs in Middle Georgia from *The Macon Telegraph*.
www.marketingjobs.com	**MarketingJobs:** An employment Web site specializing in marketing and sales jobs across the nation. Can post resume, free. (Expanding into Canada).
www.medhunters.com	**MedHunters:** Lists current featured Medical employers. VERY SLOW to load. Must register login/password. Can post resume. Offers links to other jobsites.
www.miami.com www.broward.com	**Miami/Broward:** Jobs in Miami and Broward County from *The Miami Herald*.
www.miningco.com www.about.com	**Mining Company:** Provides general job search and career-management information for people with technical skills, people looking for science and not-for-profit jobs, and members of the U.S. military.
www.mississippicoast.com	**Mississippi Coast – Biloxi/Gulfport:** Jobs in the Mississippi Gulf Coast region from *The Biloxi Sun Herald*.
www.mondojobs.com	**Mondo Jobs – St. Petersburg/Tampa:** Jobs in the Tampa Bay/St. Petersburg area from the *St. Petersburg Times*.
www.medsearch.com	**MonsterHealthcare:** Can post resume; offers chat room and message boards, interview tips, newsletter, career advice to medical professionals.
www.monster.com	**MonsterBoard:** Can post resumes; offers help locating international jobs, chat rooms, newsletter. It is a general, all professions site.
www.monstertrak.com	**MonsterTrak:** Offers resume posting. Register login/password to use. Offers job search tips, scholarship TRAK, and online career fairs.
www.montereyca.com	**Monterey/Salinas:** Jobs in the Monterey, CA, area from *The Monterey Herald*.

www.mcall.com   **Morning Call – Allentown/Bethlehem/Easton**: Jobs from *The Morning Call* of Allentown, PA.

www.myrtlebeachonline.com   **Myrtle Beach**: Jobs in the Grand Strand area of South Carolina from the *Myrtle Beach Sun News*.

www.ntes.com   **NationalTechnicalEmploymentSociety**: Offers links to many companies. Can post resume.

www.nationjob.com   **NationJobNetwork**: Offers career advice, company and industry reports; aids entrepreneurs in obtaining information on obtaining capital. Can post resume.

www.netshare.com   **NetShare:** A members-only site for executives with salary range of $100,000 plus.

www.net-temps.com   **Net-Temps**: Temporary, contract and direct hire jobs in all fields, national. Can post resume. Offers recruiter services.

www.newsday.com   **Newsday – Long Island/Queens**: Jobs from the leading news site for Long Island and Queens.

www.ohio.com   **Ohio – Akron/Cleveland**: Jobs in Northeast Ohio from *The Beacon Journal*.

www.orlandosentinel.com   **Orlando Sentinel – Orlando**: Jobs in Orlando and Central Florida from the *Orlando Sentinel*.

www.passportaccess.com   **PassportAccess**: Offers search companies. Must register with login and password. Create resumes online. For all fields.

www.philly.com   **Philly – Philadelphia**: Joint effort of *The Philadelphia Inquirer* and *Philadelphia Daily News* offers job opportunities in Southeastern Pennsylvania.

www.preferredjobs.com   **Preferred Jobs**: Job listings primarily for sales, management and information-technology positions. Resume builder and links to jobs newsgroups and job fairs.

www.projo.com   **ProJo – Providence**: Jobs in Rhode Island from *The Providence Journal*.

www.dpjobs.com   **Provident Search Group, Inc.**: Strictly a search firm's site; offers relocation information. No resume posting. Exclusively for technical, data-processing professionals.

Career Web Sites (Cont'd.)

www.questlink.com   **QuestLink (Career Circuit)**: Targeted job database specializing in engineering positions. Positions posted and removed by employers and uploaded daily. Confidential resume submission.

www.realcolumbus.com   **RealColumbus**: Jobs in the Columbus, Georgia, area from the *Columbus Ledger-Enquirer*.

www.realstatecollege.com   **RealStateCollege – Altoona/State College**: Jobs in Central Pennsylvania from the *Centre Daily Times*, State College, Pennsylvania's news source.

www.recruitersonline.com   **RecruitersOnlineNetwork**: Works through recruiters only. Can post resumes.

www.rileyguide.com   **The Riley Guide**: Provides resources with links to job-listing sites for various occupations, salary surveys for job titles and industries; opportunities for women and minorities.

www.sacbee.com   **Sacbee – Sacramento**: Jobs in Northern California from *The Sacramento Bee*.

www.sanluisobispo.com   **San Luis Obispo**: Jobs in San Luis Obispo County from *The Tribune News*.

www.sciencemag.org   **ScienceOnline**: Offers links to scientific resources on Web, essays, material data to augment reports. May "ebate" colleagues online. Register with login/password, no resume posting.

www.j-robert-scott.com   **J.RobertScott**: A Fidelity Investment company site. Offers compensation evaluation; capital finding for entrepreneurs; jobs on line. No resume posting.

www.selectjobs.com   **SelectJobs**: For computer professionals only. Browse jobs; build and can post resume. Offers chat room.

www.siliconvalley.com   **SiliconValley**: Jobs for technology professional from the Internet's most timely and in-depth technology news site.

www.6FigureJobs.com   **SixFigureJobs**: User friendly, free site for experienced business, finance and information technology executives. Can submit resume. Offers career resources.

www.state.sc.us/jobs   **SouthCarolinaStateJobs**: Search by title, location, salary or agency.

www.southdakota.com   **South Dakota – Aberdeen**: Jobs in the greater South Dakota area from the *Aberdeen American News*.

www.stamfordadvocate.com
www.greenwichtime.com

Stamford Advocate/Greenwich Time: Joint effort of *The Advocate* and *Greenwich Time* and their Web sites to feature jobs in Fairfield County, Connecticut.

www.starpoint.com

StarpointSolutions: Offers recruiters, full-time and contract staffing in the IT field.

www.stepstone.com

Stepstone: Lists positions in the United Kingdom and Europe.

www.stlouismetro.com

St. Louis Metro – Belleville: Jobs in the St. Louis metro area from the *Belleville News Democrat*.

www.sun-sentinel.com

Sun-Sentinel – Ft. Lauderdale: Jobs in South Florida, including Dade, Broward and Palm Beach counties, from the *Sun Sentinel*.

www.sunspot.net

SunSpot – Baltimore: Jobs in the Baltimore metro area from *The Baltimore Sun*.

www.tallahassee.com

Tallahassee: Jobs in the Tallahassee area from the *Tallahassee Democrat*.

www.telecomweb.com

TelecomWeb (Career Center): Features positions in the telecommunications industry. Positions are posted and removed by employers and uploaded daily. Confidential resume submission process.

www.timesdispatch.com

Times Dispatch – Richmond: Jobs in Virginia from the *Richmond Times Dispatch*.

www.timesunion.com

Times Union – Albany/Schenectady/Troy: Jobs in New York's capital region from the *Albany Times Union*.

www.tristatejobs.com

Tri-StateJobs: Posts resumes and reviews jobs in New York, New Jersey, Connecticut, and Pennsylvania.

www.twincities.com

Twin Cities – Minneapolis/St. Paul: Jobs in the Twin Cities area of *St. Paul Pioneer Press*.

www.usatoday.com

USA Today (Career Center): Extensive database of jobs from the popular news site. Positions are posted and removed by the employers and new jobs uploaded daily. Confidential resume submission process.

www.vaultreports.com

Vault Reports: Provides detailed insider company profiles on more than 100 big firms plus short reports on more than 700 firms. Can receive free job listings via E-mail.

Career Web Sites (cont'd.)

www.weta.com **WETA (Career Center)**: Targeted site featuring jobs in the Washington, DC, metro region. Positions posted and removed by the employers and new jobs uploaded daily. Confidential resume submission process.

www.careerjournal.com **Wall Street Journal Career Journal**: Professional and managerial job listings, salary surveys. Can post resume.

www.wantedjobs.com **WantedJobs**: Searches more than 100 online job sites. No resume posting. US, UK, and Quebec, Canada.

www.wilkesbarrescranton.com **Wilkes-Barre/Scranton**: Jobs in Northeastern Pennsylvania from *Wilkes-Barre Times Leader*.

www.workopolis.com **Workopolis**: Canada's biggest job site. Provides E-mail alert. Can post resume. Website designed for English and French languages.

www.zoomjobs.com **ZoomJobs**: Offers free access to hundreds of thousands of employer direct and recruiter job openings in all fields for salaries $30,000 to $750,000.

Most states have Web site listings of open positions posted with job services as well as sites highlighting open positions within the state government. Call your local Job Service or Employment Security Commission for specific Web addresses.

ASSOCIATIONS
Additional Resources for Researching Job Postings

The Internet provides many links to job listings and information resources that are useful for the job search through the Web pages of associations, societies and institutes. The resources listed have been selected from a vast pool available on the Internet. This list is just the tip of the iceberg. You may wish to use various search engines to identify additional trade organizations. Follow directions within each Web site to efficiently weave your way to the desired destination.

Acting:

American Association of Producers, www.tvproducers.com

Accounting and Finance:

American Institute of Certified Public Accountants, www.aicpa.org
American Association of Hispanic CPAs, www.aahcpa.org
International Federation of Accountants, www.ifac.org

American Association of Finance and Accounting, www.aafa.com
American Women's Society of CPA, www.awscpa.org
Treasury Management Association, www.tma-net.org

Banking and Securities:

National Banking Network, www.banking-financejobs.com
National Association of Securities Dealers, www.nasd.com

Chemistry:

American Association for Clinical Chemistry, www.aacc.org
American Association of Textile Chemists & Colorists, www.aatcc.org
Chemical Manufacturers Association, www.cmahq.com

Computer and Technology:

Computer Society, www.computer.org
Techies.com, www.techies.com
Telecom Executive Group, www.clec.com/careersclec.cfm

Entrepreneurial:

U.S. Small Business Administration, www.sba.gov
SBA: Financing Your Business, www.sba.gov/financing

Education:

American Association of School Administrators, www.aasa.org
American Association for Employment in Education, www.aaee.org

Engineering:

Society of Petroleum Engineers, www.spe.org
American Society of Mechanical Engineers, www.asme.org
American Society of Engineering Education, www.asee.org
American Institute of Chemical Engineers, www.aiche.org
American Society of Civil Engineers, www.asce.org
American Consulting Engineers Council, www.acecorg

Healthcare:

American Medical Association, www.ama-assn.org
American Association for Respiratory Care, www.aarc.org
American Physical Therapy Association, www.apta.org

Library:

Association for Research Libraries, www.arl.org

Legal:

American Bar Association, www.abanet.org
Bar Association, www.barassoc.org

Manufacturing:

American Production and Inventory Control Society, www.apics.org
National Association of Manufacturers, www.nam.org
Motor and Equipment Manufacturers Association, www.mema.org
Association for Manufacturing Excellence, www.ame.org
Fabricators and Manufacturers Association, International, www.fmametalfab.org

Pilots:

Aircraft Owners and Pilots Association, www.aopa.org
International Air Transport Association, www.iata.org

Purchasing:

National Association of Purchasing Management, www.napm.org

Sales and Marketing:

Direct Marketing Association, www.the-dma.org
Sales and Marketing Executives International, www.sell.org

BUSINESS CARDS

A Professional Approach

Having personal business cards printed is a professional approach to a job campaign. Carrying your cards with you at all times is an added benefit to your networking campaign. If you run into a personal or business acquaintance while out and about, giving him or her your personal business card (with your name, address, telephone number, fax number, pager, and/or car phone, and E-mail address) will offer the individual an easy way to contact you if a potential position arises.

It also adds a professional touch to your campaign and shows that you are well organized and prepared. A sample card may look like this:

Phone: 555-555-5555　　　　　　　**Fax:** 555-555-5550

Robert M. Smith
1234 Main Street
Anywhere, State 01234

Rsmith@aol.com
Pager: 555-555-7777

NOTE: All data should reflect home or personal communication numbers – never use an old or former employer's business card!

This way all the pertinent information for an individual to contact you is readily available to him or her and less likely to get lost. An additional advantage is that you can also mail out your business card with any personal correspondence for networking, search firms, etc.

FOCUS TIME

Please **STOP**. Do not go any further until you have written your resume. As you write your resume, keep in mind that you will probably spend a minimum of eight to ten hours carefully constructing, revising, and finalizing this document. If you struggle with the construction of your resume, consider yourself normal, average and healthy!

From my experience, I find that in about one of every forty resumes, the writer has forgotten to include a telephone number or has transposed a digit, producing an incorrect phone number. Undoubtedly, you will probably have proofed your resume, *but proof it again*. If you use spell check, make sure that the words are not only spelled correctly but are the words you actually intended. For example, is it "read" or "red"? Don't forget to include your E-mail address if you have a home computer system with E-mail service.

Delete any reference to objective. Let the reader of your document assume for him or herself what you are looking for in light of what you have done as expressed in the last two to five years on your resume. The subject of indicating to a prospective employer what you are looking for can best be handled in the cover letter. This will be covered in subsequent pages.

The "Summary of Experience" section, I believe, is a much stronger opening than indicating what your career or immediate job objective is simply because it tells the reader what you are bringing to his or her company and what you can offer in terms of skill sets. Remember, the resume is a selling document.

What really sells is your track record of quantified accomplishments.

CHAPTER III.

GUIDELINES

FOR

WRITING COVER LETTERS

These Are Not Postcards.

N

ADVENTURES IN THE LAND OF COVER LETTERS

Cover letters are a significant and integral part of the job seeker's campaign. Therefore, it is crucial to define the purposes of a cover letter. They are as follows:

1. A cover letter highlights something that you feel would be of interest to the reader, i.e., perhaps your prior experience was in an industry similar to the reader's.

2. A cover letter acts as a "framing" or "focusing" document to prepare the reader for what is to follow, i.e., your resume.

3. Finally, a cover letter is the place, when appropriate or requested, where you indicate your most recent compensation. Compensation is defined as salary plus applicable bonus. **Not** included are the following: cash value of other perks, stock options, car allowances, benefits, club memberships, etc.

The purpose of sending a cover letter and resume to a company is to get an interview. A letter is written when you have heard about a company or a job opening through a friend, an acquaintance, a newspaper article, or research. A letter that is well written and interesting is an essential **part** of the well-conducted search for employment. Remember it is a "part." A cover letter alone will not get you a job. The letter may accomplish certain purposes, but few letters ever secure for the writers a job "on the spot." Almost all employers insist on a personal interview. This "job letter" can pave the way for a personal interview and make a favorable impression on your prospective employer. The rest is up to **you – in person**.

In order to insure the successful construction of cover letters, I have compiled the following review:

- The designation "cover letter" is derived from the fact that it lies on top or "covers" the resume. It is never stapled to the resume.
- A typed cover letter is always more effective than a handwritten cover letter.
- A handwritten cover letter is always more effective than no cover letter.
- There are four basic types of cover letters. Samples of each are included in the corresponding sections of the guide.

    1. Samples 7, 8, and 9 – Cover letters for contacting corporations.
    2. Samples 10, 11, 12, 13, 14, 15, 16, 17, 18, and 19 – Cover letters to search firms.
    3. Samples 20, 21, 22, and 23 – Cover letters for networking purposes.
    4. Samples 24, 25, and 26 – Cover letters for responding to advertisements.

As you begin drafting your own cover letter, remember that the above four types of cover letters are slightly different and should be adjusted for each targeted prospect. Too many applicants make the mistake of coming up with one "whiz-bang, sure-fire, all-purpose" cover letter. There are subtle differences in each letter, so you should study this section carefully.

Parts of the Letter

I.   Date block or heading.
II.   The inside address.
III.   The salutation.
IV.   The body of the letter.
V.   The complimentary closing – "Sincerely" is predominantly used in business letter correspondence.
VI.   The signature.
VII.   Below your signature, type "Enclosure," which indicates to the reader that there is an enclosure, i.e., your resume.

Points of a Good Letter

You will need to exercise great care to ensure that your letter achieves worthwhile results. Your letter must stand out in a *positive* manner from the many other letters your prospective employer will receive. It must reflect, as far as possible, your own personality. It must show that you are a solid and dependable type of person. It must excite the employer's interest – at least to the point where he or she will want to meet you. *In short, it must "sell" you.*

1.   Be neat. Use a typewriter or computer, if possible. When writing a letter, use *black* ink and always sign a letter in blue ink. Blue is a power color; it has stronger psychological impact than black ink.
2.   Use standard 8 ½ X 11" personal, white bond stationery. Do not use your former or current company letterhead.
3.   Be as brief as possible. The letter should be no more than one page long. Do not write on the backside of the page. Usually three or four paragraphs is sufficient.
4.   Always write to a specific individual. Slant the letter to the employer's needs and interests. Do not write to "The Employment Manager," etc.
5.   State a definite area of interest and skills. For example, consider the following sentence: "Possibly you may have an interest in an individual with fifteen (15) years of progressive experience in production control, inventory control, and materials management." Do not say that you want any kind of a job.
6.   Be yourself and be sincere. "Target" your correspondence – do not use the same letter over and over again. Form letters are seldom productive when generating interviews.
7.   State facts and accomplishments, using numbers when possible.
8.   Reflect personal confidence to do the job in question.
9.   Ask for an interview, but make arranging an interview as easy as possible for your prospective employer. See the following examples of closing paragraphs.
10.   Make certain that you have your name, address, and telephone number (with area code) at the top of your letter along with your home E-mail address.
11.   Write several drafts of the letter before you decide on the final one.
12.   Keep a copy of your letter so that you can refresh your memory at a later date as to what was written and when.

13.   Try to make your letter arrive on a Tuesday, as that is generally the lightest mail day of the week. The heaviest mail day is Monday.

Why Letters to Explore Employment Opportunities Are Discarded

There are many reasons why letters to explore employment opportunities are discarded. The most probable reasons are:

1.   Illegible, untidy, and uninviting presentation.
2.   Written on dirty or wrinkled paper.
3.   Written on lined paper or on a postcard. Yes, people do this!
4.   Written in pencil.
5.   Written in any other color than black. (For example red, green, etc.)
6.   Written on business stationery with the letterhead crossed out.
7.   Written on hotel stationery.
8.   Written on unusual sized stationery.
9.   Written on any other paper than white bond paper.
10.   Written on perfumed or scented stationery.

CONTACTING COMPANIES DIRECTLY

(After All – Where Do Paychecks Come From?)

Most individuals rely on two methods when launching a career campaign: responding to advertisements and registering with employment agencies or search firms. While these methods should be pursued, you should not rely solely on them. You will enjoy a higher degree of success in your career campaign if you contact companies directly.

FACT: Only 5 percent of all positions are located through search firms or employment agencies. Advertisements account for only 10 percent of new positions.

FACT: Forty-five percent of all open positions are filled from an individual's direct contact with a company.

FACT: Eighty-five percent of all positions are unadvertised.

Consequently, by directly contacting companies, you have the opportunity to discover these unadvertised positions. In addition, companies are always on the lookout for good talent. Even if a position is not currently open at the time of contact, there may be future openings for which you will be considered. Your direct contact will demonstrate initiative, aggressiveness, confidence, and interest.

Considering the high cost of using search firms, some companies have a policy against using these organizations. Additionally, if a company can hire a person without using either a search firm or running an expensive display ad in the local Sunday paper, the savings can be very significant.

While there is an economic incentive for the company to avoid using these recruitment tools, there is also an incentive for the applicant. Specifically, if an individual can secure employment directly, thus having the company avoid one or both of the above hiring costs, the greater the opportunity for an increased hiring salary and/or hiring bonus.

To whom should you direct your resume and how should you contact that hiring professional? You may either:

Call the company and ask for the name and title of the individual that you wish to contact.

OR

Write to the chief operating officer or highest ranking individual in the business unit that you are interested in joining.

There are five significant reasons why people who wish to change positions or those people who are unemployed should forward their resumes to the chief operating officer or the highest-ranking officer of each organizational unit:

1. The larger the organization, the tougher it is for an outsider to identify the appropriate person to send their material to. The task of sorting out the hierarchy, divisions, and sectors of multimillion/billion dollar corporations is very difficult. For example, if you were interested in working for General Motors or Motorola Corporation, the task of determining who your boss would be, considering all levels, divisions, sectors, North American or European Operations, etc., is overwhelming.

2. Forwarding your materials to the chief operating officer will avoid the majority of your competition, who generally route their materials to the Human Resources area. Human Resource people usually know of positions that have been approved for recruitment and subsequent hiring but, by and large, they are not aware of contemplated or new positions that exist in the minds of various line managers, etc. (These people are the real decision-makers!)

3. The objective of sending your resume to your potential manager – even if this person could be identified – poses the problem that if the resume is too strong, it may represent a threat to the potential manager. For every ten individuals who say theywould like to hire their successor, at least nine of them, in practice, will not make that hire – particularly in today's environment.

4. Routing your correspondence and resume to the chief operating officer has the distinct advantage of using him/her as a "switching or directing" mechanism. Materials that are directed to these individuals are not discarded but are forwarded down to the appropriate individual. The key point is anything coming from the "top" – whether it be the chief operating officer, president, or executive officer – is read, not skimmed, and is acted upon immediately. Compare this to the flood of resumes going into the recruiting or Human Resources office. Would you not read material sent to you by your president?

5. Not only is getting your resume in the right hands very important, but it also shows that you have done your homework in finding who the appropriate individual is. It shows that you took the time to find out what type of

business it is, who the highest-ranking officer is, and to address an appropriate cover letter directly to that individual stating your qualifications. By doing this, you exhibit your seriousness about securing a new position as well as your attention to detail.

This represents:

"Out-of-the-Box Thinking!"

- It's doing what most people don't do.

- It gives you a competitive edge.

- It reduces your competition.

And Most Important

- It increases your visibility, which increases your chances of securing more interviews.

Basically, the issue is determining what direction you want to go when contacting companies directly. Do you want to go upstream or downstream. The trickle down approach is much more effective. Attempting to go upstream is not nearly as productive simply because you are trusting that your resume will be forwarded "upstairs" and will be forwarded to the "right" person and, finally, will be acted upon because it came from a subordinate downstairs. Contacting the gentleman or lady in the paneled corner office has a higher sense of priority, which simply means "Action."

Research the organization to prepare an effective, targeted cover letter that is slanted to the organization's needs

1.   Make use of your local library. Most reference guides listed in this guide can be found there. Larger libraries have Business Librarians who can help you do research. Check industry periodicals, newspaper articles, library computer databases, and of course, the mighty Internet for further information.

2.   In addition to reference materials found at the library, you can also secure information directly from the company. Call and request an annual report, a quarterly report, 10K and 10Q reports, and product literature.

3.   Allow me to interject a slight word of caution at this point. I am not a strong believer in what I call a lot of "Front End" research during a job campaign. Researching broad industry growth patterns and emerging trends – yes, but researching voluminous numbers of companies for possible contact before you have

an actual interview scheduled is misplaced activity. Recognizing the fact that many companies will be contacted but only a few will respond with opportunities for interviews, it becomes readily apparent that the main body of research should take place just before an interview and once again after an offer has been extended, but before acceptance or rejection. This subject is discussed further in other sections.

WHAT TYPE AND SIZE COMPANIES SHOULD YOU TARGET?

An article in *Inc.* magazine (January 1993), which still has relevance today, discussed the likeliest path to true financial security in the future and cited the following statistics:

- "The stability of large companies is no longer what it once was. Going into the job market in 1953, you could place your bets on working for a long time in a large company and do it with a pretty safe feeling. The pace has moved so quickly since then that now it is much harder to do."
- Relentless downsizing undertaken by corporations drives this point home. One group in particular is vulnerable. "Middle management jobs are being eliminated far out of proportion to their numbers," says Eric Greenburg of the American Management Association (AMA). Each year the AMA conducts a downsizing survey of its 7,000 members. **While middle managers account for 5 percent to 8 percent of the total work force, they represented 19 percent of the layoffs over the past four years**. At present, this trend appears to be holding into the new millennium.
- Sixty-three percent of AMA sample companies that downsized reported that they had done so more than once.

The facts are clear: Fortune 500 companies are no longer a safe and stable place to hang your hat. The compensation in large companies may still be big, but working for a large corporation is riskier today than it was forty years ago. The area for growth and the ability to make an impact on business is more often available in smaller companies. Note the following statistics quoted in *Inc.* magazine (January 1993):

- Between 1988 and 1990, the country lost 974,000 manufacturing jobs. **But manufacturers employing fewer than twenty people mitigated the carnage by adding 220,000 jobs.**
- Eight percent of Americans work for companies with 100 or fewer employees.

While many people believe that small businesses are too risky to work for, *Inc.* magazine argues that small business survival rates are higher than commonly perceived. In a recent study, *Inc.* followed 812,000 small businesses (with fewer than 100 employees) over an eight-year period. While 28 percent ostensibly survived, *Inc.*'s research revealed that each year 3 percent of the sample changed ownership or type of ownership "at random or at the whim of the owner." That means that over the eight years, 24 percent of the sample appeared to disappear but, in fact, did not. Thus, 52 percent of the companies survived, not 28 percent as the data had first shown.

In addition, the number of small companies is increasing at a rapid rate. In 1954 about 117,000 businesses were founded. In 1992 that number approached 700,000. *Inc.* says there are currently 500,000 small U.S. companies growing at 20 percent a year. Meanwhile, Fortune 500 companies now lay off 400,000 people a year on average, and one-third of Fortune 500 companies fall off the list every five years. This trend shows no sign of abatement.

Consequently, as you plan and conduct your job campaign, I suggest that you seriously consider targeting small companies, as your chances for **career** security are at least as high as with the giant organizations.

IDENTIFYING GROWTH VS. DECLINING INDUSTRIES

In order to continue ensuring career security, you should target industries that are growing. Make use of sources to identify these industries: Use newspapers, magazines, industry publications, the Internet, specialty reports, analyst and economic reports. In addition, use your network of contacts as sources for information. At some point in your search, you may want to conduct informational interviews to secure information on a particular industry. If your spouse is not employed outside the home, this is an excellent task for him/her to assist you on your campaign.

FURTHER SUGGESTIONS ON TARGETING COMPANIES FOR DIRECT CONTACT

1. Do not be afraid to contact companies whom you have not heard of previously, don't know anything about, or are not publicly held. Everyone else contacts companies with recognizable brand names like IBM, Kraft, and Xerox. If you know the name of a company, chances are that your competition will know it as well. Contact companies you are unfamiliar with.

"OUT-OF-THE-BOX THINKING"

2. **Play the alphabet game!**

    Over the last five years our firm has conducted primary research on <u>why</u> individuals contact the companies they do. It should be clearly differentiated that understanding why individuals contact certain companies is not the same as why individuals accept offers of employment.

    With this point noted, over 5,000 individuals were surveyed. Every participant had just lost a job or would shortly be losing one for a host of different reasons. None had actually commenced their job campaigns, but were in the active planning stage, updating their resumes. Salaries ranged from $25,000 to $180,000 per year. They came from diverse geographic areas and industries.

124

Each person surveyed was asked to list at least twenty companies that they would "seriously consider" interviewing with. These companies could be located anywhere in the country. Tabulation of the results proved most interesting.

- People tended to consider the industry from which they came, regardless of the growth potential or how depressed the industry was, even when entrance requirements or previous industry experience were not a prerequisite.

- Lower salaried, non-exempt individuals focused more on the geographic location of potential employers. This is not unusual.

- Higher salaried, exempt personnel were much more receptive to relocation, with preferences given to the locations of existing family members. This is to be expected.

Further research indicated that companies whose names began with the letters A-M were contacted twice as frequently by job seekers as those beginning with the letters N - Z.

Even a smaller sampling of the Fortune 500 list in October of 1999 found that over 60 percent of the companies listed had names that began with a letter falling in the first half of the alphabet.

Bottom Line –   You can reduce your competition by half if you commence contacting potential employers with names starting at the end of the alphabet and work your way forward.

GETTING STARTED

Many times, the most difficult challenges in writing a quality cover letter are those of writing the first sentence and the closing paragraph. In order to help you in this area, I have prepared the following opening and closing paragraph samples.

Sample opening paragraphs for
cover letters contacting companies directly

Dear _____: (Insert contact's name)

Possibly your company has need of a _____ with _____ years of diversified experience in _____, _____, and _____.

OR

If your corporation requires a mature, operations-oriented generalist, I would appreciate your consideration of the enclosed data.

OR

I would like to explore career opportunities with your company. Consequently, I have enclosed a copy of my credentials for your review.

OR

Upon the suggestion of _____, please find an enclosed copy of my credentials.

REMEMBER

Letters addressed to a specific person by name and title have a higher rate of response than letters addressed to "Personnel Department," "Hiring Official," or "Employment Manager" or with no name.

Sample closing paragraphs
for cover letters contacting corporations directly

Perhaps you might be interested in talking about an opportunity.

Sincerely,

OR

I am seeking a challenging opportunity where the rewards, both professionally and financially, are based on one's ability to produce. Should you have an interest in my background, I would be pleased to hear from you.

Sincerely,

OR

From a distance, neither one of us can ascertain if what I can offer would be an enhancement for your operation. Therefore, if you have an interest, I would be pleased to hear from you.

Sincerely,

OR

Presently, I am exploring other career alternatives with an organization – large or small – where I can continue to be an integral part of an executive management team. If your schedule permits, possibly we could meet and explore areas of mutual interest.

Sincerely,

OR

To date, my career has included a number of progressively more challenging and responsible positions. Should your company have an interest, I would be pleased to hear from you.

Sincerely,

ROBERT T. THOMAS
1234 Main Street
Anywhere, State 99999
(765) 555-1212

SAMPLE "COVER LETTER"

Note: For contacting a company with a resume enclosure!

January XX, 20XX

Name
Title
Company
Address
City, State Zip

Dear _____: (Insert contact's name)

Good opening!
Soft sell – NOT desperate.

Perhaps your organization is in need of a manufacturing and operations management professional who has successfully reduced costs in both heavy equipment and light appliance operations by over $4,000,000 during the past twenty (20) years.

Cites key accomplishments.

Excellent use of numbers!

As Manager of Manufacturing Operations for Monroe Manufacturing Corporation, I have directed the redesign and modernization of a 150,000 square foot plant that directly resulted in increasing plant output by 9.9%, from $36,400,000 to $40,000,000, without the necessity of additional equipment or manpower. Under my leadership, production increased 50%.

Great use of #s!

Prior to Monroe Manufacturing Corporation, I successfully completed assignments for Burro Crane, Incorporated, as General Foreman, Foreman, and Lead Machinist, with supervision responsibilities for 110 employees and a budget of $4,000,000.

With a B. S. in Industrial Management and currently working on an M.B.A., I am interested in joining an organization – large or small – where my diverse manufacturing management expertise could be utilized. If you have an interest, I would be pleased to hear from you.

Sincerely,

Nice, simple closure.

Robert T. Thomas

Enclosure

Indicates that this is a cover letter.

SAMUEL A. SMITH
536 Longmeadow Circle
Anywhere, State 60174
(312) 555-1732

SAMPLE "COVER LETTER"

Note: For contacting a company with a resume enclosure!

January XX, 20XX

Name
Title
Company
Address
City, State Zip

Dear _____: (Insert contact's name)

> *Very strong opening sentence. Simple, but effective.*

Perhaps your company has a need for a sales and marketing professional that has increased sales by 75%, or $5,000,000, in the last four (4) years.

As a National Account Executive with Nationwide Cards, Inc., I had responsibility for two (2) national accounts with sales in excess of $12,000,000. I managed the national account activities of 95 Sales Representatives in 30 states. In the first eight (8) months of 1999, my sales were 16% ahead of the previous year, or almost $8,000,000.

In a previous position, I established and executed master distribution plans, developed contact with shopping center developers, created pro forma operating and cash flow statements, selected store owners and operators, and directed the openings of new stores. While in this position, I increased market penetration significantly by generating $900,000 in new business.

I am looking for an organization that will utilize my more than 19 years of diversified experience in sales and marketing. If you have an interest in my background, I would be pleased to meet you at a mutually convenient time.

Sincerely,

Samuel A. Smith

Enclosure

ROSIE M. SHANNON
1424 Washington Avenue
Anywhere, State 99999
(765) 555-5429

SAMPLE "COVER LETTER"

Note: For contacting a company with a resume enclosure!

January XX, 20XX

Name _____
Title
Company
Address
City, State Zip

Dear _____: (Insert contact's name)

   Possibly your organization may have a need for a Senior Secretary with over nine (9) years of diversified secretarial experience in the marketing and service departments of a major corporation.

   I have a full range of secretarial skills including typing at 90 wpm, shorthand at 120 wpm, operation of a computer for word processing, filing and spreadsheets, and am proficient in the use of electronic dictating equipment, copiers, fax, and telex machines.

   With a degree in Secretarial Science from the Institute of Business and currently working towards an Associate of Applied Arts degree in Business Administration, I am searching for an organization that will employ me in a responsible secretarial position.

   Enclosed is a copy of my credentials for your review and consideration. If you have an interest in my background, I would be pleased to hear from you.

Sincerely,

Rosie M. Shannon

Enclosure

STOP THE BUS!!
STOP THE ACTION!

We are missing some of the members of our guides!

What has happened to Harold Corona, Norma Panetella, and Jacob Robusto? Where are their examples of cover letters to corporations? Have they quit their job campaigns? Won the Lotto?

These three guides have decided to use a different strategy to market themselves. While they have developed resumes and will use them when contacting network contacts and search firms, they have decided not to use their resumes when contacting companies.

Read on to page 212 to see how Harold, Norma and Jacob market themselves without resumes, utilizing "Out-of-the-Box Thinking."

IDENTIFY AND CONTACT CORPORATIONS TO EXPLORE EMPLOYMENT OPPORTUNITIES

If you plan to execute a successful job campaign, you will need to obtain sources for the names of individuals and corporations to contact for employment possibilities. There are a wide variety of "types of information" within these sources. These resources are generally called manufacturing and services directories and a guide to the use of these directories has been included for your convenience.

You can find these directories in the business section of most public and private libraries, and I recommend that you utilize these free resources rather than purchasing the directories with your own money. These libraries, as well as the libraries of any undergraduate or graduate school of business, will typically have reference sources for directory descriptions and a collection of the most widely use directories. Additionally, most libraries provide Internet access for on-line research.

Another helpful guide is the *Directory of Special Libraries & Information Centers*. This guide provides information about more than 13,000 special libraries operated by businesses, educational institutions, government agencies, trade associations and professional societies, many of which are open to you. Ask your local librarian to arrange special permission for you to visit these libraries, as they are normally closed to the general public.

Your local chamber of commerce is another organization that frequently publishes a list of local companies. You should endeavor to contact your local Chamber of Commerce as you conduct your job campaign. It will also be aware of firms that are new to the area or have recently expanded and require extra staffing. The address can be found in you local telephone directory or by checking the *Thomas Register*, which contains a listing of all U.S. chambers of commerce.

The reference works listed below will enable you to identify the title and publisher of several sources.

Directories In Print
Contains complete information on over 15,000 directories printed worldwide. The content of each directory is briefly described as well as its cost and the name and address of the publisher. Gale Group, 27500 Drake Road, Farmington Hills, MI. 48331. (800) 877-4253. www.galegroup.com.

Directory of Corporate Affiliations
Lists over 4,100 parent companies and their subsidiaries, affiliates, and divisions. Information included on each parent company: name, address, telephone number, chief officers, number of employees, and approximate sales volume. In addition, the chief operating officer is listed for each subsidiary with appropriate address information and line of business. There is also an index listing 39,000 divisions in order to cross-reference the parent company. Reed Elsevier, Inc., 121 Chanlon Rd., New Providence, NJ 07974-9903. (800) 521-8110. www.reedref.com.

International Directory of Corporate Affiliations
Provides several different ways for users to locate detailed information on 24,000 companies doing business worldwide. You can look up 52,000 corporate subsidiaries, divisions, or

affiliates. The alphabetical index directs you to the listing for the parent company where you learn that organization's reporting hierarchy. Reed Elsevier, Inc., 121 Chanlon Rd, New Providence, NJ 07974-9903. (800) 521-8110. www.reedref.com.

Directory of Leading Private Companies
Lists 8,800 leading private companies including 12,000 corporate affiliations. This format allows you to determine at a glance how each subsidiary reports to the parent company – whether directly or through another subsidiary. Reed Elsevier, Inc., 121 Chanlon Rd, New Providence, NJ 07974-9903. (800) 521-8110. www.reedref.com.

Standard and Poor's Register of Corporations, Directors & Executives
Lists approximately 85,000 companies cross-referenced by product and company location. Includes approximately 500,000 key business executives and their business telephone numbers and more than 70,000 biographical sketches. Standard & Poor's Subsidiary of McGraw Hill, 55 Water Street, New York, NY 10041. (212)438-2000. www.standardpoor.com.

Encyclopedia of Associations
Furnishes details on nearly 23,000 national and 20,600 international nonprofit trade and professional associations; social welfare associations and public affairs organizations, religious, sports, and hobby groups; and other types of groups that are headquartered in the U.S. Entries are arranged by subject and provide complete contact information and a description of activities, including publications, computerized services, and convention schedules. Gale Group, 27500 Drake Road, Farmington Hills, MI 48331. (800) 877-4253. www.galegroup.com.

Thomas Register
Principally geared for buyers who are looking for suppliers. It contains over 156,000 manufacturers, listed by product and location. Information includes: company name, address, telephone number, and business line. Thomas Register, 5 Penn Plaza, 12th Floor, New York, NY 10001. (212) 290-7277. www.thomasregister.com.

Hoover's On-Line
Internet access to a variety of information on public and some private firms. (800) 486-8666 or (512) 374-4500. www.hoovers.com.

Dun & Bradstreet Million Dollar Directory
Lists about 160,000 companies covering all industries. Businesses are referenced alphabetically, geographically, and by product classification. Information includes: name, address, telephone number, annual sales volume, number of employees, line of business, S.I.C. code(s), officers, and directors. The *Million Dollar Directory* lists the name and location of some subsidiaries or divisions if the subsidiary meets the selection criteria.

Basic qualification for listing in this directory is an indicated net worth of $500,000 or more, or 250 or more employees, or $25 million in annual sales. Dun & Bradstreet, Austin, Texas 78731. (800) 234-3867. www.dnb.com.

America's Corporate Families

Includes detailed information on 11,000 U.S. ultimate parent companies and their 80,000 U.S. subsidiaries, divisions, and major branches. In order to be included, each ultimate parent company must meet the following criteria: net worth of a least $500,000, or net annual sales of $25 million, or 250+ employees, and maintain a controlling interest in one or more subsidiary companies. Dun & Bradstreet, 99 Church Street, New York, NY 10007. (800) 526-0651. www.dnb.com.

State Manufacturers Directories

Lists manufacturers and processors located in the particular identified state. The directories are typically divided into seven sections: buyers guide, alphabetical, geographical, S.I.C. index, computer index, zip code, and county marketing breakdown. Included in the description of each company is the following: name, address (including zip code), telephone number (with area code), date established, area of sales distribution (local, regional, national, or international), name and title of key executive(s), product description, S.I.C. codes, number of employees, annual sales, type of computer system, and location of plants or home offices. Manufacturers News, Inc., 1633 Central Street, Evanston, IL 60201. (847) 864-7000, (888) 752-5200. www.mninfo.com.

Dun & Bradstreet Reference Book of Corporate Management

Provides 52,000 professional histories of the men and women who serve as officers and directors of more than 12,000 U.S. companies. Dun & Bradstreet, 99 Church Street, New York, NY 10007. (800) 526-0651. www.dnb.com.

Dun's Industrial Guide – The Metalworking Directory

Contains data on more than 80,000 companies, including manufacturers as well as metal and machine tool distributors. Dun & Bradstreet, 99 Church Street, New York, NY 10007. (800) 526-0651. www.dnb.com.

For "industry-specific" research information, you may use the following directories:

ADVERTISING

Standard Directory of Advertisers: Reed Elsevier, Inc., Corporate Offices, 121 Chanlon Rd., New Providence, NJ 07974. (800) 521-8110. www.reedref.com

Standard Directory of Advertising Agencies: Lists 4,000 leading advertising agencies in the U.S. with key executives, major accounts, geographic index. Reed Elservier, Inc. Publishing Company, P.O. Box 31, New Providence, NJ 07974-9903. (800) 621-9669. www.reedref.com

APPAREL

American Apparel Manufacturers Association Directory: Lists member firms and executives. American Apparel and Footwear Association, 1601 N. Kent Street, Suite 1200, Arlington, VA 22209. (800) 520-2262. www.americanapparel.org

BANKING

American Bank Directory: Lists more than 93,000 banks, savings & loans and credit unions with officers and directors. Thomson Financial Publishing, 4709 Golf Road, Suite 600, Skokie, IL 60076, (800) 321-3373. E-mail: customerserviceetfp.com, www.tfp.com

CANADA

Canadian Trade Index: The CTI contains detailed information on over 30,000 Canadian companies, featuring over 100,000 product listings under 25,000 headings classified by product and location. Contains executive names. Nexport Media Inc., 333 Adelaide Street West, Second Floor, Toronto, Ontario Canada M5V1R5, (416) 595-1818 or (877) 463-6284 (Canada Only). E-mail: info@nexport.com, www.ctidirectory.com

CHEMICALS

The Rauch Guide to the U.S. Paint Industry: Rauch Group, Inc., P.O. Box 6802, Bridgewater, NJ 08807. (732) 940-1334.

CONSTRUCTION

A.G.C. Directory: Lists 33,000 major contracting firms by state with key executives. Associated General Contractors of America, 333 John Carlyle St., Suite 200, Alexandria, VA 22314. (703) 548-3118. www.agc.org

CONSULTANTS

The Directory of Management Consultants: Profiles 2,400 firms in North America, indicates where 4,300 principles work, and provides key data on each firm. Kennedy Information, Inc., One Kennedy Place, Fitzwilliam, NH 03447. (603) 585-6544 or (800) 531-0007. www.kennedyinfo.com

CONTAINER

Official Container Directory: Lists more than 4,000 container manufacturers. Advanstar Communications, 131 West First Street, Duluth, MN 55802 (800) 598-6008. www.advanstar.com

COSMETICS

Who's Who – The Cosmetic Toiletry and Fragrance Association Membership Directory: Lists 600 manufacturers of cosmetics, toiletries and fragrances in the U.S., 1101 17th Street, Suite 300, N.W. Washington, D.C. 20036-4702. (202) 331-1770, fax (202) 331-1969. www.ctfa.org

EDP

Data Sources – The Complete Product Directory: Lists 14,000 producers and vendors of 75,000 software, hardware, and data communication products. Gale Group, Inc., World Headquarters, 27500 Drake Road, Farmington Hills, MI 48831. (800) 877-4253. E-mail: galeord@galegroup.com, www.galegroup.com.

EDUCATION

Accredited Institutions of Post Secondary Education Directory: Lists colleges and universities with names of presidents. Greenwood Publishing Group, 88 Post Rd., West, Westport, CT 06881. www.greenwood.com

ELECTRONICS

U.S. Electronics Manufacturers Directory: Lists over 3,700 companies. Harris Publishing Company, 2057 E. Aurora Road, Twinsburg, OH 44087-1999. (800) 888-5900. www.harrisinfo.com

EIA (Electronic Industries Association) Trade Directory and Membership List: Electronic Industries Association, 2001 Pennsylvania Avenue N.W., Washington D.C. 20006. (202) 457-4900.

ENGINEERING – TEACHING/RESEARCH

Directory of Engineering Education Leaders: Lists names of 10,000 college and university engineering department chairpersons and research directors. American Society for Engineering Education, 1818 N Street N.W., Suite 600, Washington, D.C. 20036-2479. (202) 331-3500. E-mail: pubsinfo@asee.org, www.asee.org.

FINANCE

Corporate Finance Source Book: Reed Elsevier, Inc., 121 Chanlon Rd., New Providence, NJ 07974. (800) 521-8110. www.reedref.com

Who's Who In Finance & Industry: Reed Elsevier, Inc., 121 Chanlon Rd., New Providence, NJ 07974. (800)521-8110. E-mail: info@marguiswhoswho.com, www.marquiswhoswho.com,

FOOD

Association of Sales and Marketing Companies Directory of Members: Member firms with executive names. ASMC, 1010 Wisconsin Ave., NW, Ninth Floor, Washington, D.C. 20007. E-mail: info@asmc.org, . www.asmc.org.

Frozen Food Digest: *Frozen Food Digest*, 271 Madison Avenue, Suite 1107, New York, NY 10016. (212) 557-8600. No Website

AFIA (American Feed Industry Association) Membership Directory: AFIA, Attn: Publications Department, 1501 Wilson Blvd., Suite 1100, Arlington, VA 22209. (703) 524-0810. E-mail: afia@afia.org, www.afia.org

Candy Buyers Directory: The Manufacturing Confectioner. MC Publishing Co., 175 Rock Road, Glen Rock, NJ 07452. (201) 652-2655. E-mail: themc@gomc.com, www.gomc.com.

GAS UTILITY

Brown's Directory of North American Gas Companies: Executives of American and Canadian Gas utilities: Advanstar Communications, 131 West First Street, Duluth, MN 55802. (800) 598-6008. www.advanstar.com

GLASS

The Glass Factory Directory: Published each year, lists each of the glass manufacturing locations in Canada, Mexico and the U.S. Each listing gives the plant address, telephone number, fax number, the name of a contact person and a brief list provided to us by the company of the products they make. P.O. Box 2267, Hempstead, NY 11551-2267. (516) 481-2188. www.glassfactorydir.com

HEALTHCARE

The AHA Guide (American Hospital Association): American Hospital Association, Order Services, One North Franklin, Chicago, IL 60606. (800) 242-2626. www.aha.org

IMPORTS

Directory of United States Importers: 55,000 companies classified by location and type of product imported. Includes names of owners and key executives. *The Journal of Commerce*, 445 Marshall Street, Phillipsburg, NJ 08865. (908) 859-1300. www.joc.com

INTERNATIONAL COMPANIES

Directory of American Firms Operating in Foreign Countries: Lists over 2,600 American companies plus 34,500 of their foreign subsidiaries, affiliates, or branches. Classified by product and country. Contains name of U.S. executive in charge. Uniworld Business Publications, Inc., 257 Central Park West, New York, NY 10024. (212) 496-2448. www.uniworldbp.com

MANUFACTURING

National Printed Directory of Manufacturers: Lists over 52,000 U.S. manufacturers having at least 100 employees, classified by state and industry with executive names. Harris Publishing Company, 2057 E. Aurora Road, Twinsburg, OH 44087-1999. (800) 888-5900. www.harrisinfo.com

OIL

Worldwide Refining & Gas Processing Directory: Pennwell, Inc., P.O. Box 21288, Tulsa, OK 74121. (918) 835-3161. www.pennwell.com

PAPER

PIMA (Paper Industry Management Association) Membership Directory: Pulp and paper mill executives. Paper Industry Management Association, 1699 Wall Street, Suite 212, Mount Prospect, IL 60056. (847) 956-0250. www.pima-online.org

PUBLISHING

For directories in the publishing field, write to Reed Reference Publishing Co., P.O. Box 31, New Providence, NJ 07974-9903. (800) 521-8110. www.bowker.com

RECRUITERS

Directory of Executive Recruiters: Kennedy Information, Attn: Bookstore, 1 Kennedy Place, Route 12 South, Fitzwilliam, NH 03447. (603) 585-6544. www.kennedyinfo.com

Directory of Legal Recruiters: 800 recruiters in 320 firms – indexed by thirty-three legal specialties and geographic locations. Kennedy Information, Attn: Bookstore, 1 Kennedy Place, Route 12 South, Fitzwilliam, NH 03447. (603) 585-6544. www.kennedyinfo.com

RESEARCH

Research Centers Directory: 14,200 Research centers in all fields. Includes names of research directors. Gale Group, 27500 Drake Road, Farmington Hills, MI 48331. (800) 877-4253. www.galegroup.com

SCIENCE

American Men and Women of Science: Reed Reference Publishing Company, P.O. Box 31, New Providence, NJ 07974-9903 (800) 521-8110. www.reed-elsevier.com

SPORTS

NSGA (National Sporting Goods Association) Buying Guide: 1699 Wall Street, Suite 700, Mount Prospect, IL 60056. (847) 439-4000. www.nsga.org

TELECOMMUNICATIONS

Telecommunications Directory: Contact information for more than 3,400 national and international communications systems services. Gale Group, 27500 Drake Road, Farmington Hills, MI 48331. (800) 877-4253. www.galegroup.com

TEXTILES

Davison's Textile Blue Book: Textile mills and dyers with executives' names. Davison's Publishing Company, P.O. Box 1289, Concord, NC   28026.   (704) 785-8700. www.davisonbluebook.com

VENTURE CAPITAL

Gold Book of Venture Capital Firms: Lists 869 firms with full contact data. Kennedy Information, Attn: Bookstore, 1 Kennedy Place, Route 12 South, Fitzwilliam, NH   03447. (603) 585-6544. www.kennedyinfo.com

WASTE MANAGEMENT

Waterworld Municipal Directory: Pennwell Inc., P.O. Box 21288, Tulsa, OK   74121. (918) 835-3161. www.pennwell.com

A GUIDE TO THE USE OF MANUFACTURING AND SERVICES REGISTER DIRECTORIES

Information found in directories may be presented in a number of different ways. It can be classified alphabetically, geographically, by product or process (Buyer's Guide), or by Standard Industrial Classification Code. Many directories also offer computer type (brand) and major metropolitan zip-code listings.

Not all states or areas have both a Manufacturers and Services Directory, but most have at least a manufacturers register. Some directories may offer all six selections. Others may offer a combination of these. Not all directories will categorize the information in each of these ways. And not all directories will classify each section the way our examples are illustrated. In other words, information is not always displayed the same way in all directories.

STANDARD LISTING ELEMENTS

1. BUYERS GUIDE:

This section is an alphabetical breakdown of finished goods and processes.

Companies are listed in alphabetical order within each product or service group.

Since little detailed information is given in this section, you must reference the Geographical Section for a complete listing (see Section 3).

DRILL HEADS – Multiple Spindle

Automation Associates, Inc.
Telephone: (312) 255-4500
416 Campus Dr., Arlington Heights 60004
(See our ad under MACHINERY – Drilling & tapping, Combined)

Johnson Drill Head Division
Div. of Master Machine Tools, Inc.
602 Scott Blvd., Box 1627,
Hutchinson, KS 67505
(See our ad on the following page)

DRILL & TOOL GRINDERS

Jerico, Inc.
Telephone: (312) 286-3366
5510 N. Elston Ave., Chicago, IL 60630
----

2. ALPHABETICAL INDEX:

This section continues an A to Z listing of all companies within the area covered by the directory. This section is useful if you wish to locate a particular firm, but you may not be aware of the location(s) of facilities within the state or geographic area being researched. This listing provides only the name of the company and the city or cities in which those plants or offices are located.

Once the locations have been determined, you can reference detailed information in the Geographical Section (see Section 3).

Stenson Service Products	North Aurora
Stenzel Graphic Services	Rosemont
Step Products , Inc.	Elk Grove Village
Step Products , Inc.	McHenry
Step Up Performance	Roselle
Stepen Company	Elmwood
Stepen Company	Northfield
Stepco Corporation	Arlington Heights
Stephanie's Interiors	Elmwood Park
Stephen Construction Services	Joliet
Stephen & Wolff Foundry	Rockford
Stephens Printing	Lake Bluff
Stephenson-Carroll Publishers	Lena
Stereo Optical Company, Inc.	Chicago
Stereo Sentry Mfg. Company	Downers Grove
Stereotype Equipment Company	Chicago
Stericon, Inc.	Broadview
Sterling Mfg. Corp.	Chicago

3. GEOGRAPHICAL SECTION:

This section contains all of the information for a company. Part of the information may be repeated in the other sections of the book. The information is given as received from reporting companies and the amount of detail will vary from listing to listing. However, the following is an example of what can be found in this section.

Study the following example. It will be a useful guide when selecting information about various companies:

Company Name	**BELVIDERE**	City or Town
	(Boone County – N.E. Population 15,176)	
Address	APACHE BUILDING PRODUCTS CO.	County
	Div. of Millmaster Onyx Corp.	
	1005 McKinely Ave. (61008)	
Telephone Number	Telephone – (815) 544-3193	Population
	Est. 1963: Distrib. – International	
	V. P. Opers. – William Whitchurch	
Date Company was founded	GM – Fred Coglianese	Zip Code
	Plt. Mgr. –Larry Voiles	
	Pur. Agt. – Richard Sheridan	
	Off. Mgr. – Frank Zimmerman	SIC Code(s)
Executive Names/Titles	*Urethane Panels* (3296)	
	Employs – 45	Type of Business
	50,000 sq. ft.	
	Parent Co. – Millmaster Onyx Corp.	
	99 Park Ave., New York, NY (10016)	Number of Employees

Note: In some cases, annual sales and/or other information may be listed as "0." This does not indicate lack of sales, but merely the fact that the company or division is privately held and the management does not wish to provide this information.

4. STANDARD INDUSTRIAL CLASSIFICATION (SIC) SECTION:

An SIC Code is a group of numbers prepared by the Technical Committee on Standard Industrial Classification under the sponsorship and supervision of the Office of Statistical Standards of the Bureau of the Budget, Executive Office of the President. The SIC Code indicates the function or type of operation and the line. A business that produces more than one type of product will have more than one SIC Code number. Up to six classifications may be shown for each business. If a business carries several code numbers, it will be listed under each of those numbers:

A. A numeric index of the classification codes may appear in the first few pages of a directory.

The index is broken down by industry, and then by specific products.

The first two digits of the code describe the general industry classification. The third and fourth digits indicate the specific segment of that industry.

B. SIC Codes may appear in numerical order together with the industry title to which each refers.

Listings are shown alphabetically by state, then cities within states, and then alphabetically by business name.

3324	Steel investment foundries
Precision Unlimited Inc.	Rosemont

3325	Steel foundries, not elsewhere classified
Acme Ind. Co. Inc.	Carpentersville
Alou Steel Casting Co. Inc.	Chicago
Cast Rite Steel Casting Corp.	Chicago
Goltra Foundries, Inc.	Barrington
Hellstrom Corp.	Franklin Park
Marengo Stell Products Inc.	Marengo
Midland Industries, Inc.	Chicago
Rockford Fabricating	Chicago
Sterling Steel Foundry	Sauget

3331	Primary smelting and refining of copper
Chemetco Inc.	Hartford
Ruben Metal Co.	Chicago
Sipi Metals Corp.	Chicago

3332	Primary smelting and refining of lead
Babbitting Service, Inc.	Chicago
United American Metal Corp.	Chicago

3333	Primary smelting and refining of zinc
Amax Plating, Inc.	Elgin
Amax Zinc Co.	Sauget
Asarco Inc.	Hillsboro
Circle Smelting	Beckemeyer
Clearing Alloys Corp.	Chicago

3334	Primary production of aluminum
G. M. Scrap Metal	Cottage Hills
General Aluminum Corp.	Montgomery
Seigman Co.	Lincolnwood

A listing of the basic SIC Codes is as follows:

STANDARD INDUSTRIAL CLASSIFICATION CODES

Standard Industrial Classification (SIC) Codes were established in the 1930s by the United States Government for statistical purposes only. They have since become the basis for nationwide business classifications. Some companies list more than one SIC Code because they are involved in more than one primary activity.

[First Two (2) Digits – General Industry]

0100 to 0999 Agriculture, Forestry and Fishing
- 01 Agricultural Production – Crops
- 07 Agricultural Services
- 08 Forestry
- 09 Fishing, Hunting and Trapping

1000 to 1499 Mining
- 10 Metal Mining
- 12 Coal Mining
- 13 Oil and Gas Extraction
- 14 Nonmetallic Minerals, except Fuels

1500 to 1799 Construction
- 15 General Building Contractors
- 16 Heavy Construction, except Building
- 17 Special Trade Contractors

2000 to 3999 Manufacturing
- 20 Food and Kindred Products
- 21 Tobacco Products
- 22 Textile Mill Products
- 23 Apparel/Other Textile Products
- 24 Lumber and Wood Products
- 25 Furniture and Fixtures
- 26 Paper and Allied Products
- 27 Printing and Publishing
- 28 Chemicals and Allied Products
- 29 Petroleum and Miscellaneous Plastics
- 30 Rubber and Miscellaneous Plastics
- 31 Leather and Leather Products
- 32 Stone, Clay and Glass Products
- 33 Primary Metal Industries

34 Fabricated Metal Products

35 Industrial Machinery and Equipment

36 Electronic and Electric Equipment

37 Transportation Equipment

38 Instruments and Related Products

39 Miscellaneous Manufacturing Industries

4000 to 4999 Transportation, Communications, Utilities

40 Railroad Transportation

41 Local and Interurban Transit

42 Trucking and Warehousing

43 U.S. Postal Service

44 Water Transportation

45 Transportation by Air

46 Pipelines, except Natural Gas

47 Transportation Services

48 Communication

49 Electric, Gas, and Sanitary Services

5000 to 5199 Wholesale Trade

50 Wholesale Trade-Durable Goods

51 Wholesale Trade-Nondurable Goods

5200 to 5999 Retail Trade

52 Building Materials and Garden Supplies

53 General Merchandise Stores

54 Food Stores

55 Automotive Dealers and Service Stations

56 Apparel and Accessory Stores

57 Furniture and Home Furnishings

58 Eating and Drinking Places

59 Miscellaneous Retail

6000 to 6799 Finance, Insurance and Real Estate

60 Depository Institutions

61 Nondepository Institutions

62 Security and Commodity Brokers

63 Insurance Carriers

64 Insurance Agents/Brokers Services

65 Real Estate

67 Holding and Investment Offices

7000 to 8999 Services

70 Hotels and Other Lodging Places

72 Personal Services

73 Business Services

75 Auto Repair, Services, and Parking

76 Miscellaneous Repair Services

78 Motion Pictures
79 Amusement and Recreation Services
80 Health Services
81 Legal Services
82 Education Services
83 Social Services
84 Museums, Botanicals, and Zoos
86 Membership Organizations
87 Engineering and Management Services
88 Private Households
89 Services

9000 to 9721 Public Administration
91 Executive, Legislative and General
92 Justice, Public Order, and Safety
93 Finance, Taxation, and Monetary
94 Administration of Human Resources
95 Environmental Quality and Housing
96 Administration of Economic Programs
97 National Security and International Affairs

5. COMPUTER INDEX:

This section is a list of computers currently owned and operated by the companies listed in the directory.

The computers are arranged alphabetically by brand name. Under each category is the name and city of the companies possessing that computer. They are also in alphabetical order by company name. This section may be useful if your background is in systems or data processing and you wish to contact companies with systems that match your technical expertise.

IBM

A-1 Shock Absorber Co.	Chicago
A A A Instant Printing	Libertyville
A A Coil Products	Steger
A A R Corp., Aeronautics Div. .	Carol Stream
A B Seals, Inc.	Sullivan
A & B Tool & Mfg., Inc.	Franklin Park
A & B Wire	Addison
A E N Industries	Bensonville
A & E Plastics	Elk Grove Village
A F Industries	Carol Stream
S-Flex Label Corp.	Willowbrook
A Frame Boutique	Skokie
A G Communications Systems Corp. . .	Genoa
Algiers Industries	Chicago
Anderson Wire	Addison

144

FOCUS TIME

Stop now and draft your cover letter to corporations. As you write, keep the following points in mind:

- Your cover letter should sell your skills and experiences. Keep it to the point and quantify your accomplishments in terms that will be meaningful to the reader.

- If you have a degree, you should mention the type of degree you hold and where you earned the degree. The best place to include this information is in the final paragraph. (For example, refer to Robert Thomas' cover letter to corporations on page 128.)

- Remember to indicate your interest in joining an organization where your skills and experience can be fully utilized.

- I suggest that your salary or compensation figures **not** be included in your cover letter to corporations.

- Regardless of whether you are contacting a corporation by U.S. Mail or through E-mail, your resume should always be accompanied by a cover letter with the resume serving as an attachment.

THE MECHANICS OF PRODUCING A LARGE MAILING

After you have selected companies for contact and drafted your cover letter, you will need to consider "the mechanics of mailing." If you have a home computer and letter-quality printer, I suggest that you keep your resume and letters on file. This convenience will allow you to print a large quantity of resumes and letters or individual letters as needed.

If you do not have access to a computer, I suggest that you utilize a local word processing or mass-mailing service. These services are listed in the yellow pages of your local telephone directory, often under the heading of "Letter Services." (Secretarial services are frequently not set up to do large mailings.) Do not be afraid to purchase these services.

Typically these services will type and print your resume, letters, and envelopes. Most services will keep your documents on file for a period of six months, or will allow you to purchase a disk for a minimal charge, and will keep the disk on file for an undetermined period of time. Costs vary, and we advise you to do some comparison-shopping before selecting a service. Some questions you may want to ask are:

1. **What software package do these services most frequently use?** One of the most commonly used software packages is Microsoft Word.

2. **Do they use laser printers or letter-quality printer?** Laser printers produce the highest quality printing, dot matrix the least.

3. **Do they charge by the page, by the hour, by document, by the typed line, etc.?** Our research indicates that many services have a flat fee for resume and cover letter typing and proofing as well as a rate for printing per resume/cover letter combination. In addition, there is typically a small charge for envelope printing. These services provide paper and envelopes but are generally willing to print on paper that is supplied by the individual.

4. **If you have access to a computer, can you supply your documents already on disk?** In this case, you should only be charged for printing costs, unless editorial changes need to be made.

5. **What are their charges for typing individual letters?** This will be especially pertinent when you are drafting customized ad-response letters and interview follow-up letters. Our research indicates that most secretarial services charge by the hour or piece for individual letters.

6. **What level of turnaround time can you expect?** Our research indicates that most services require three to four days to turn around a large mailing. (i.e., over 400 letters and resumes).

7. **If the above points seem like a lot of hassle and effort,** and you decide to buy your own computer system, consider purchasing the following:

- **Microsoft Office 2000** software – an updated version of Microsoft Word, which includes a mail-merge function, as well as PowerPoint, Excel, and Money.
- **Envelope Feeder** – really a must.
- It might be worth considering an upgrade for speed.

To save the expense of a secretarial service, I recommend that you explore the capabilities of your local library and/or the computer lab at the local community college. Most public libraries have computers and laser-quality printers available for your use. In this case, you simply supply your own disk and paper. Community colleges also have computer facilities available for a nominal fee.

A FEW WORDS ON MASS MAILINGS

While they have never been easier to produce, this technique of contacting potential employers still remains largely ignored.

Clients with whom I have worked universally assume that their campaigns and therefore their re-employment will always occur faster than what actually happens in real life. This possibly explains people's reluctance to invest time in the collection of names and addresses required to build a database for contact.

Combine the above with the ever-increasing use of electronic posting of resume on the Internet, and we again return to the question, are mass mailings necessary or worth the effort? Certainly, some people feel if they mail 400 - 500 pieces of correspondence, they will simply be deluged with requests for interviews. What a problem to have! Unfortunately, this seldom occurs.

Response to a typical mass mailing, defined as a resume and a cover letter, adjusted for compensation level and size of the marketing, is usually around 1 percent. This assumes well-drafted materials and a correctly targeted audience of recipients.

A review of the Internet as a resource for the job hunter is reserved for later discussion in this guide.

In closing, I would recommend using mass mailing simply because it is the best and quickest way for an individual to penetrate the market with any depth.

"Out-of-the-Box Thinking"

Never underestimate the power of a letter. It has staying power!

An E-mailed resume is only one stroke of the "delete" key away from erasure!

Perhaps the recruiting manager of an engineering firm said it best when, regarding the "abundance" of resumes on the Internet, she said, ***"There's just too much out there!"***

EMPLOYMENT SEARCH FIRMS AND AGENCIES

Employment search firms and agencies are additional sources for locating employment opportunities and should be a part of any job campaign. However, it is wise to exercise as much caution and good judgment using their services as you would with any organization that derives its income from the sale of services.

Should you use search firms and employment agencies? YES!

How to Use Search Firms and Employment Agencies Effectively

Search firms and employment agencies play a role in your job search, but this role should not be the "star" of the show. Today two to five percent of the job opportunities are generated through search firms and employment agencies. Most people find this number surprisingly low. When one considers the relatively high cost of using a search firm, either retainer or contingency, the low utilization of search firms becomes very apparent. However, since you do not know where or when a job opportunity will materialize, I suggest that you do not leave this stone unturned.

To the uninitiated job hunter, the above statistic recounting that only two to five percent of jobs today are secured through an employment agency or search firm, may seem a surprising figure. Many individuals are under the mistaken impression that the majority of employment opportunities are satisfied through one of these service agencies or consulting firms. The truth of the matter is that using an executive search firm or employment agency is the most expensive way for a company to recruit personnel. Fee schedules are discussed later in this section. While I do not suggest avoiding the use of search firms and employment agencies, be sure to place their role in the employment process in proper perspective.

Many individuals have had negative experiences with search firms at some point in their past and consequently are reluctant to use employment agencies or "Headhunters" to assist them in conducting their job campaign. The term "Headhunter" is a common descriptive used for executive recruiters or search firms today. The term was generated by negative and sometimes impersonal experiences in the past. Remember that the use of the term is not complimentary. There are some employment agencies in every geographical area that do not deal with candidates professionally. Nevertheless, the search industry has continued to grow, and at the present time, the impact of headhunters on an individual's job campaign does not appear to be diminishing. Because of this growth, there have been a number of professional agencies that have earned outstanding reputations – both nationally and in your local area. When conducting a successful job campaign, you should use every avenue available to you. Employment agencies are **one** of those avenues, not the only avenue.

Develop a strategy to use the search firm avenue. Understanding the functions, differences, and philosophies of this avenue will aid you in utilizing this source.

148

THE STRATEGY: Contingency-Type vs. Retainer-Type Search Firms

1.   What is the difference?

How does an employment agency differ from an executive search firm?

There are two major distinctions: First, an employment agency represents the employer on a "contingency" basis, while the executive search firm always represents the employer on an exclusive "retained" basis.

Contingency agencies handle multiple job orders at one time with little or no exclusivity for the positions with any one company. This creates the high volume, high pressure, and sometimes-impersonal experiences found in utilizing agencies.

Retainer search firms are hired by companies to search out a qualified candidate for a specific open position. The company grants exclusive search rights to the search firm and thus reduces the need for the high volume, high-pressure atmosphere sometimes found with employment agencies.

Second, the methods of payment differ, even though the employer generally pays the fees in both cases. With employment agencies, the employer's payment is "contingent" upon the agency making a successful placement and the candidate reporting to work. With retainer search firms, the employer retains the services of the firm and pays a fee regardless of the outcome of the search – a retainer fee.

Third, employment agencies do little "qualifying" of their candidates while executive search firms are paid, in part, to provide this service.

"Qualifying" a candidate means different things to the contingency firm than the retainer firm. When an employer decides to release a position for search, the search firm (regardless of type) usually requests a job description and a job specification. The job description details the responsibilities and organizational interfaces with other individuals, departments of the company, or with outside dealers or customers, etc.

The job specifications, on the other hand, do not deal with the job or work assignments but rather detail the "specification" or background and experience that the company believes the successful candidate must have to do the job. Specifications would include such items as education, professional certification, advanced degrees, previous work experience, previous industry experience and, of course, track record of accomplishments.

Contingency-type employment agencies typically compare these documents to a candidate's resume, and if it appears to be a match, they may telephone the applicant for more information before trying to arrange an interview. It is important to note that the contingency recruiter, at this point, and the candidate may not have had an actual face-to-face meeting. It is a telephone relationship. Speed is everything! The employer may have contacted two or three contingency agencies to expedite the search process. Since the company is under no cost or fee obligation until the person is actually hired, contingency firms cannot afford to have an exhaustive "qualifying" process because other candidates may be already scheduled for interviews.

The retainer-type or executive search firms are paid in part not only for their "searching" effort but also for their "qualifying" efforts. A true retainer or executive search firm will always want to meet its candidate before referring him or her to their client. It will want to see how the individual looks, acts, speaks, and dresses. It will want to know more about career history, reasons for job changes, compensation, education, family background, work ethic, and the list goes on.

Sometimes the above data is collected by the search firm's researcher who will turn the information over to a partner of the firm. Sometimes the partner, depending on the level of the search, will do the preliminary screening telephone interview. Regardless of who does the telephone interview, the next step, if there appears to be a match, would be a face-to-face meeting with the search consultant – not the company.

The following chart will assist you in understanding the major differences between contingency and retainer firms and why you need to know that information before enlisting their assistance in your job campaign.

	CONTINGENCY FIRM	**RETAINER FIRM**
Most commonly called:	Employment Agency Personnel Agency Placement Agency/Firm Headhunter	Executive Search Firm Executive Recruiter Headhunter
Fee:	20 to 30% of First Year's Salary	30 to 33% of First Year's Total Annual Compensation, Plus Recruiting Expenses Incurred During the Search
When Is Fee Paid?	Upon Completion of Search Assignment	A Portion Is Paid Up Front (usually one-third), Progress Payment (one-third) After a Month, and the Final one-third of the Fee Upon Completion of the Search, Plus Expenses as Incurred
Who Pays the Fee?	Corporate Client (Employer)	Corporate Client (Employer)
Licensed by the State?	Yes	No
True Consulting Firm?	No	Yes
Typical Candidate Salary Range:	$40,000 to $75,000 and Below	$80,000 and Above

2. Where can I find search firms or agencies?

There are two major sources for employment agencies or search firms.

A. *The Directory of Management Consultants* is a comprehensive listing of over 2,000 contingency and retainer search firms. This directory is also known as "The Red Book" – so named because of its bright red cover. Several cross references are also given, arranged by the following categories:

- Functional (Job) Classifications
- Industry Classifications
- Geographical Index
- Key Principles Index (lists recruiters by name)
- Retainer Recruiting Firms, A to Z
- Contingency Recruiting Firms, A to Z

The alphabetical listings contain the detailed information on each firm. When referencing a firm or individual in any of the other sections, turn to the alphabetical listing for more detail.

The Directory of Management Consultants is published annually by:

The Directory of management Consultants
Kennedy Publications
Attn: Bookstore
Templeton Road
Fitzwilliam, NH 03447
(603) 585-6544
E-mail: bookstore@ kennedyinfo.com

B. You can supplement this information locally by looking in the Yellow Pages under the following headings:

- Management Consultants
- Executive Search Consultants
- Personnel Consultants

Remember, however, that the telephone company is not very discriminating in its policy of allowing businesses to select categories for listings. An "Executive Search" firm that is also listed under "Employment Agencies" is probably the latter. Check with the Better Business Bureau or Chamber of Commerce for reference.

3. How do I effectively contact a search firm or agency?

The most effective and efficient way to contact a search firm or agency is with a well-written letter and resume. This letter is a cover letter, since your resume is enclosed with the letter.

When writing your cover letter to search firms and employment agencies, always – repeat, always – include your last or current salary or compensation figure when requesting employment assistance from an agency or search firm. In actual practice, employment agencies and executive search firms give little or no attention to resumes that do not include current or most recent salary or compensation. Always include these figures in your cover letter. You will find additional tips on writing cover letters at the end of this section.

Compensation is expressed as follows: "My compensation is an annual salary of $240,000 plus bonus, stock ownership and stock options."

if applicable

4. Should I follow up or contact the search firm or agency to which I sent my resume?

No! Do not be a pest!

Executive search professionals appreciate receiving resumes, but telephone calls from unknown candidates are neither welcome nor necessary.

Most job seekers realize that recruiters cannot help them unless they have a suitable assignment. But some otherwise capable professionals are so traumatized by unemployment that they forget this reality. They call monthly, "just to check in," obviously not recognizing that this immediately puts them in the "never consider" file. People assume that recruiters are aware of all kinds of job openings. Not true. Recruiters only know about their current assignments and a few others they may have discussed with their clients.

Recruiters do not have the time to field telephone calls. Time is money to them, and they do not want to waste it. After all, they work for themselves. They are not career consultants!

The key to using a recruiter is in understanding that their time is valuable and worth money. If a recruiter is interested in you, he or she will call you without delay. NO CALL – NO INTEREST. Do not take it personally because tomorrow he or she may receive a job order from a company that matches with your background, and your telephone will ring.

5. How do I "work" with a recruiter without being "worked over"?

You do not. He or she works with you when he or she is ready and has a real search assignment. Do not expect search firms to be guidance counselors or Outplacement consultants.

A recruiter views you as an opportunity to generate income by placing you, as well as a source of information regarding your current or previous company, opportunities you are pursuing, and names, in the form of referrals.

Working with a recruiter can be advantageous for your campaign as long as you know how to deal with the persistence of an aggressive recruiter. The following tips and suggestions are provided for you to consider when investigating or working with a contingency recruiter.

A. Who is responsible for the fees? How does the agency or search firm derive its fees? Are the fees paid by the job hunter, the employer, or split between both the job hunter and the employer? Ask!

- What happens if I am separated or leave voluntarily during the first six months to one year of employment; will I be liable for any or all of the original search fee?

- Are there any circumstances where I might become liable for your fee?

B. Is the search firm a contingency agency or retainer search firm?

- A contingency firm receives its fees from the corporate client only upon completing the assignment.

- A retainer search firm receives a percentage of its fees from the corporate client in order to initiate the search. The balance is received during and at the end of the search.

- Additionally, retainer search firms are reimbursed for documented search expenses incurred by the search consultant on behalf of the engaging client company. Such expenses include postage, parking charges, travel – either by the consultant or the applicant – lodging, business meals, fax charges and telephone charges. Never offer to pick up a meal check when dining with a search consultant. Contingency firms have no expense reimbursement.

C. Is there a fee for any other services offered by the agency? Agencies may offer additional services such as assessments, consultations, and outplacement.

D. Do not sign anything except the application form. If you are asked to sign any other document, be sure to read **all** the fine print.

E. Beware of high-pressure tactics. An agency may try to pressure you into accepting a position to quickly complete the assignment and, of course, to collect its fee.

F. Advertisements for glamorous or "perfect" jobs should be treated with skepticism. Very often, these advertisements are used to bait candidates.

G. Be cautious of agencies that suggest an immediate career change or ask if you have skills that are unrelated to your career or desired position. Chances are they are more interested in immediately filling a vacant position than they are in assisting your career (bait and switch tactics!).

H. Consultants who appear overly friendly (with invitations to lunch, drinks, etc.) may have a hidden agenda.

I. Do not tell the agency or consultants the names of the companies with whom you have interviewed or are pursuing. If you do, when a fee can be earned, you may find yourself competing with a fellow candidate from the same agency.

One of the most common means used by employment agencies – not executive retainer search firms – get this information is by asking the job candidate the following question: "So that we don't duplicate your efforts, would you share with me with whom you have interviewed or plan to interview?"

That sounds reasonable, but in practice the contingency employment agency won't send your resume to the companies you have contacted, but – and it's a BIG BUT – it can now send other resumes to "your" companies since you have told it who else is actively seeking people with your background. Loose lips not only sink ships but can sink additional prospects for interviews.

J. Avoid agencies that display any evidence of discrimination pertaining to race, religion, ethnic background, or politics.

K. Carefully interview the agency. How long has it been in business? How successful has it been in placing candidates similar to you? Will it provide references?

L. Make your initial contact with agencies on Wednesdays or Thursdays.

- This not only avoids the rush of responses to the Sunday advertisements, but it also makes you appear less desperate.

- Fridays force you to vie with the weekend for the agency's attention.

M. Contact as many agencies or executive search firms as you can. Do not think that an agency will work exclusively on your behalf unless the right match has been made.

N. Periodically place a follow-up call to the agency (note: not to a retainer search firm) to check on recent developments once you have had contact with the agency. However, again, do not be a pest.

O. Do not state the amount of compensation you will be willing to accept. If asked, indicate that you are "open."

- It is important to use the word "open" when employment agencies ask what salary you are seeking. The reason I recommend using the word "open" is that it simply means that you are open to listening to any offer a company might make to you. When saying "open," you will not eliminate yourself from being sent to interviews for any positions because you are too high or too low on your salary requirements. The agencies will have a good indication of the range of compensation you are seeking based upon your last or current salary. Using the word "open" when asked to discuss what type of compensation you are willing to accept is always the safest and best response.

P.   However, never be reluctant to tell an employment agency or search firm your current or most recent salary and bonus. Be exact! This figure will probably be verified.

Q.   Employment agencies generally have a fee structure averaging 20 to 30 percent of the successfully placed candidate's first year of compensation. For this fee, ask yourself, "What has the agency really done to help me in the interview?" The point is, do not be afraid to ask questions that will help you prepare for the interview. Ask the search consultant to provide you with as much background information as possible on the company, hiring officer, and position:

- Ask for quarterly, annual, and 10K reports.

- Ask for product literature.

- Has the consultant conducted any successful search assignments for this company?

- What is the company looking for in the successful candidate? What types of candidates have succeeded in the past?

- Probe for what you should stress and what you should avoid.

- What are the decision-maker's hot and cold buttons?

- Interview the search consultant – ask penetrating questions.

R.   Some agencies or consultants will suggest that you are overpaid or may have to accept a pay cut. Remember that regardless of location or identity, the greatest demand is for the best.

S.   Many firms are using temporary agencies and/or contract firms as a way to pre-screen potential employees. Therefore, you may want to consider using this option during your career search.

6. **How does a recruiter get to know me? Can he/she help me in my search efforts if he/she does not meet with me in person?**

> Recruiters make quick evaluations based on the quality of your resume and cover letter. This quality includes the mechanical correctness of your materials and, more importantly, your accomplishments within your experience as compared to their open positions.

> Today's recruiter will usually call for more information or send a "fact sheet" for you to complete.

> If a potential match is evident, you will probably receive a telephone interview/screening, which will vary in length of time from a few minutes to an hour. This telephone interview/screening is a "real" interview, so you will want to listen carefully and respond with specific accomplishments and results whenever possible. Have your resume ready – next to your telephone.

> Through these written communications and verbal discussion(s), the recruiter creates his or her "perception" of you. If everything fits, he or she presents "you" to the client company that has the open position.

> In the case of a retained search, you want to be, and most likely will be, invited to a face-to-face interview with the recruiter. Be prepared to handle both types of interviews and screenings. For more specific information regarding interviewing, refer to the Interviewing section on page 273.

7. **Remember, never leave a stone unturned in the search for your next opportunity – you never know where it will materialize.**

To help you draft an effective search firm/employment agency letter, we have included, beginning on page 159 a list of suggested opening paragraphs and sample letters.

EXECUTIVE SEARCH FIRMS – RETAINER TYPE

As indicated in the preceding pages, some search firms ask their corporate clients to engage them by placing them on retainer. This means that a portion, usually a third, of the agreed-upon search fee is paid up-front with commencement of the search. In other words, the firm is effectively retained with this partial payment. Executive search firms of the retainer type are generally compensated at 30 to 33 percent of the successful candidate's first-year compensation plus all expenses that can legitimately be passed on to the corporate client. These expenses may be travel expenses either for the search consultant to visit a candidate or a candidate to visit the search consultant, meals, faxing, postage, mileage expense and any identifiable expense that can be directly associated with conducting the search. The actual fee, if it is 33 percent of the individual's first year's total annual compensation, is typically paid in increments of one-third. The first one-third is the retainer, with another one-third paid after thirty days, and the final one-third (which is the hold back) is actually paid upon the hiring of the individual and ascertaining what his or her final compensation will be. This may be either higher or lower than the initial agreed-upon compensation that was discussed between the client company and the retained search consultant.

The easiest way to determine whether you are working with a retainer firm or a contingency firm is simply to ask, "Are you a contingency firm or are you on retainer?" Another simple test is that retainer firms always want to see the individuals they are going to refer to their client company. They want to see how the person looks, dresses and acts. Does he or she present the appropriate professional image? I estimate that at the present time there are between 1,300 and 1,500 retainer executive search firms, some specializing in particular functional areas of business for their searches. Others do what is commonly called "most" type searches. These firms are engaged to do two things: first, the actual searching or hunting for prospective clients, and second, qualifying the candidate. Does the person actually have the background that the client has indicated?

The initial contact by a retainer search firm may be from an individual who is generally referred to as a research assistant and who asks key questions and gathers additional information that may not be covered in a candidate's resume. The resume plus the additional information sourced in a telephone interview are then forwarded to the consultant or a partner in the search firm who will make decisions about whether a candidate is worthy of a face-to-face meeting. The individual who is contacted by a retainer search firm may be asked to travel to the search firm's place of business or to some other location, which may be on the search consultant's travel itinerary. The search firm, who is in turn reimbursed by the engaging client, always assumes expenses for such a trip.

If an individual is requested to travel to the search firm's office, it is always appropriate to pack an extra change of clothes in the event the person is asked to stay over an extra day because certain individuals' schedules now permit a face-to-face meeting. It does happen but not with a high degree of consistency.

Some search firms do perform preliminary psychological assessments. These assessments, although optional, are generally prerequisites to a face-to-face meeting with one or more of the client company's management team. If an individual is asked to take a psychological assessment, usually consisting of a number of different types of batteries to enhance reliability, it is usually followed by an in-depth interview with the company's psychologist. It is considered appropriate that before one agrees to take the various instruments and have the results shown to the client company, it be agreed the results will be shared with the interview candidate. Another good question to ask is, "What will happen to these results; how long will they remain on file with the company?"

In my own career, when I arrived at the headquarters of our corporate office, it had been a practice to have candidates at the executive level meet with our "shrink" who administered certain instruments and conducted a psychological interview. The results of the interview and the instruments were then submitted in written form. At our headquarters, these reports were filed and kept by the president's secretary, who had the annoying habit of never disposing of them but would read them to amuse herself during slow periods or at lunchtime and then leave them on her desk for anyone passing her desk to see.

Interview candidates are advised that these types of instruments are indeed confidential, and steps should be taken to ensure their confidentiality, as well as their disposal, after twelve months. Psychological instruments have a shelf life, and individuals are subject to life experiences that over the course of a career can change one's responses to certain questions on the instruments involved. Consequently, future management decisions regarding promotions and reorganizations should not be based on psychological instruments that are five years old, etc.

If I were to offer a critical appraisal of retained search firms, it would be the fact that they are very professional on the front end of a search when contacting an individual. But they lack a little professionalism on the tail end of the search when they should inform preliminary candidates that they might not be selected for a trip to the client company for successive interviews. Typically, the mode of this behavior is simply to refuse calls or to stop all communications with previously sourced candidates. The fact of the matter is that it only increases the candidate's frustration, and he or she becomes less tolerant of this type of activity.

If a retainer search firm is conducting a search for an individual with an anticipated base salary of $100,000 plus bonus, upon successful completion of the assignment the fee is generally going to exceed $33,000. Corporations recognizing that this is a significant amount of money usually require the search firm to surface at least three candidates in order to be able to make candidate comparisons. In other words, the attitude is "we are paying all this money; let's see more than one candidate." Consequently, the individual is well advised to keep in mind that the retainer search firm, like the contingency search firm, works and is paid by the client company and has the interest of the company and itself as a primary interest. It does not represent the individual job hunter.

After an interview has been arranged, the search consultants will always contact the candidate to ascertain levels of interest, impressions, etc. The candidate will be contacted first, and then the company will be contacted to provide feedback. After receiving feedback from the company, many search consultants will discontinue further communication with the candidate if the company has expressed no interest. Most search firms are reluctant to share any feedback with the candidate as to reasons why there would be no further interest upon the company's part in the candidate.

It has been my experience when working with senior management that the executive should maintain an open and candid dialogue with the search consultant. However, this openness and directness has a point of conclusion. If the individual candidate receives an offer and the offer is not what the candidate wishes to accept, and he or she is desirous of attempting to negotiate the offer, it is advisable to stop communicating through the search consultant regardless of whether he or she is a retainer or contingency recruiter. Simply because for negotiations to be highly successful, it requires both parties to effectively read the other side and to avoid communication that is inadvertently filtered or misread. Therefore, in summary, if one is going to attempt to negotiate an offer (and this section is amplified later in the manual), at some point the decision should be made to contact and communicate directly with one's potential employer/decision maker – not the search firm.

SAMPLE OPENING PARAGRAPHS FOR SEARCH-FIRM COVER LETTERS

Dear _____: (Insert contact's name)

Please review my experience and qualifications against your current client-search requirements.

OR

Dear _____: (Insert contact's name)

If in the course of your search assignments, you have a requirement for a high-powered sales executive, I would be interested in exploring any attractive opportunities.

OR

Dear _____: (Insert contact's name)

I am currently conducting a search for myself in the senior sales and marketing management area of the healthcare industry. Hoping that you may have a client search underway that might be a match with my talents and background, I have enclosed my resume for your review.

OR

Dear _____: (Insert contact's name)

If one of your clients is contemplating major business decisions for implementation, possibly my ten (10) years of extensive experience in capital equipment and computers may be of interest to you.

OR

Dear _____: (Insert contact's name)

When I joined my present company, sales were flat and earnings were declining. Recognizing that better direction and leadership were needed, I guided the turnaround of the company, increasing sales from $18 million to $45 million and increasing earnings 555 percent over the last ten years.

I am writing to you because you may have a client who is seeking a senior manager with experience directing the profitable growth of a manufacturing operation.

OR

Dear _____: (Insert contact's name)

I am pleased to enclose a copy of my credentials for your consideration regarding any search assignments you have undertaken recently in the field of information systems.

Therefore, if you have a client who requires management expertise in the mid-range for personal computing systems, including a strong background in software systems, I would be pleased to hear from you.

OR

Dear _____: (Insert contact's name)

Turning cost centers into profit centers for the group of a $150 million corporation was not an easy task. But it was accomplished!

Possibly one of your clients may be considering the need for such an individual to join their organization. As Regional Sales Manager, I refocused the market and sales efforts of the region to maximize market penetration by . . . .

SAMPLE 10

ROBERT T. THOMAS
1234 Main Street
Anywhere, State 99999
(765) 555-1212

SAMPLE COVER LETTER TO SEARCH FIRMS AND EMPLOYMENT AGENCIES

January XX, 20XX

Executive Search Agency
299 South River Road
New York, NY 20202

This salutation is only used when you can't identify the person to whom you are writing.

Dear Sir or Madam:

Perhaps one of your current clients is seeking a manufacturing and operations management professional who has successfully reduced costs in both heavy equipment and light appliance operations by over $4,000,000 during the past twenty (20) years. If so, the enclosed material may be of interest to you.

Use numerals to quantify accomplishments.

As Manager of Manufacturing Operations for Monroe Manufacturing Corporation, I directed the redesign and modernization of a 150,000 square foot plant which directly resulted in increasing plant output by 9.9% from $36,400,000 to $40,000,000 without the necessity of additional equipment or manpower. Additionally, I proposed, developed, and implemented the introduction of numeric controlling equipment, both NC and CNC, which resulted in savings of $250,000 in the first year alone.

Prior to Monroe Manufacturing Corporation, I successfully completed assignments for Burro Crane, Incorporated, as General Foreman, Foreman, and Lead Machinist, with supervision responsibilities for 110 employees and a budget of $4,000,000. Under my leadership, production increased by 50%.

Note excellent use of numbers!

With a B. S. degree in Industrial Management, I am interested in joining an organization – large or small – where my diverse manufacturing management expertise could be utilized. My current salary is $79,300. If you or your clients have an interest, I would be pleased to hear from you.

Never approximate or "round-off." This number will be verified.

Sincerely,

Robert T. Thomas

Enclosure

SAMUEL A. SMITH
536 Longmeadow Circle
Anywhere, State 60174
(312) 555-1732

SAMPLE COVER LETTER TO SEARCH FIRMS AND EMPLOYMENT AGENCIES

January XX, 20XX

Name
Title
Company
Address
City, State, Zip

Dear _____ : (Insert contact's name)

    One of your clients may have a need for a sales and marketing professional that has increased sales by 75%, or $5,000,000, in the last four (4) years. If so, the enclosed credentials may be of interest to you.

    As a National Account Executive with Nationwide Cards, Inc., I had responsibility for two (2) national accounts with sales in excess of $12,000,000. I managed the national account activities of 95 sales representatives in 30 states. In the first eight (8) months of 2000, my sales were 16% ahead of the previous year, or almost $8,000,000.

    In a previous position, I established and executed master distribution plans, developed contact with shopping center developers, and directed the opening of new stores. While in this position, I increased market penetration significantly by generating $900,000 in new business.

    I am looking for an organization that will utilize my more than 19 years of diversified experience in sales and marketing. My current salary is $67,400 plus bonus. If you or your clients have an interest in my background, I would be pleased to meet with you at a mutually convenient time.

Sincerely,

Samuel A. Smith

Enclosure

ROSIE M. SHANNON
1424 Washington Avenue
Anywhere, State 99999
(765) 555-5429

SAMPLE COVER LETTER TO SEARCH FIRMS AND EMPLOYMENT AGENCIES

January XX, 20XX

Name
Title
Company
Address
City, State Zip Code

Dear _____: (Insert contact's name)

Possibly you may have a search assignment for a Secretary with over nine (9) years of diversified secretarial experience.

I have a full range of secretarial skills and am proficient in the use of microcomputers, electronic dictating equipment, copiers, telecopiers, and telex machines.

With a degree in Secretarial Science and currently working towards an Associate of Applied Arts Degree in Business Administration, I am searching for an organization that will employ me in a responsible secretarial position.

Enclosed is a copy of my resume for your review. If you or one of your clients has an interest in my background, I would be pleased to meet with you at a mutually convenient time. My current salary is $_____.

Sincerely,

Rosie M. Shannon

Enclosure

SAMPLE 13

HAROLD J. CORONA
120 South Carol Street
Milwaukee, Wisconsin   53706
(414) 333-1111
HJCorona@execpc.com

SAMPLE COVER LETTER TO SEARCH FIRMS AND EMPLOYMENT AGENCIES

January XX, 20XX

Name
Title
Company
Address
City, State, Zip

Dear _____ : (Insert contact's name.)

Grab reader's attention!!!

If in the course of your search assignments you have a requirement for a senior financial executive/CFO, with eighteen (18) years of experience within the international consumer product businesses I would be interested in exploring any attractive opportunities. I have enclosed a copy of my credentials for your review.

Use numerals to quantify accomplishments.

As CFO/Senior Vice President-Finance, Strategy and Information Systems I directed the strategic analysis of major projects, including international distributorships, internal initiatives, brand and acquisitions which identified projected savings of over $9,000,000 annually. Additionally, I led two (2) transforming initiatives, with the help of investment bankers that examined two (2) separate international alliances each totaling over $1,000,000,000.

Earlier, I led the Information Systems & Financial Analysis Group as Vice President, where I provided the worldwide financial forecasting, budgeting, and P&L planning. I created a team orientated financial and budgeting process with each operating company and established a five (5) year telecommunications agreement with projected savings of over $200,000,000.

Summarizes career background.

With twenty (20) years of domestic & international consumer product experience, and background roles in leadership, finance, controllership, SEC reporting, information systems, corporate audit, and strategic planning, I am interested in joining an organization that could utilize my expertise in a senior financial position. My current salary is $251,898 plus annual and long-term incentive compensation. If you or your client has an interest in my background, I would be pleased to hear from you.

Sincerely,

Never approximate or "round-off."
This number will be verified.

Harold J. Corona

Enclosure

NORMA M. PANETELA
777 Career Drive
Hightown, State 99999
(555) 555-1234
Npanetela@dot.net

SAMPLE COVER LETTER TO SEARCH FIRMS AND EMPLOYMENT AGENCIES

January XX, 20XX

Name
Title
Company
Address
City, State, Zip

Dear _____ : (Insert contact's name)

Link an "attention getter" to business.

Please review the enclosed resume with respect to current client assignments that match my experience and qualifications.

Discusses recent work experience and accomplishments.

I have over 18 years of experience in various marketing, sales and finance positions in the consumer products industry, both domestically and internationally.

Recent accomplishments.

Most recently, as Vice President of Marketing for Millennium One, a $5,000,000,000 operating company of MLM, Inc., I reversed a five (5) year decline in flagship brand, and directed the launch of a multibrand line, which generated $386,000,000 in revenues and a 53% share of segment. I found that achieving multiple objectives, while deploying $900,000,000 in marketing investment across a 25-brand portfolio and directing a 171-member department requires a clear sense of business focus and priorities.

Earlier in my career with Unilever, General Foods, Pepsico and MLM, Inc., I earned my stripes and promotions to broader responsibilities in some of the most highly contested global consumer product categories.

Career goals.

My career aspirations are now focused on general management, including Division or Company President within the consumer products industry. My salary is $285,235 plus bonus. If you are interested in my background, I would be pleased to hear from you.

Sincerely,

Norma M. Panetela

Enclosure

JACOB J. ROBUSTO
3361 Innovation Lane
Tampa, Florida   33761
(813) 555-1212
JJrobusto@aol.com

SAMPLE COVER LETTER TO SEARCH FIRMS AND EMPLOYMENT AGENCIES

January XX, 20XX

Name
Title
Company
Address
City, State, Zip

Dear _____: (Insert contact's name)

Grab reader's attention.

One of your clients may have a need for an individual who took a calculated business risk and generated $50,000,000 in incremental sales since the launch of the commercial Electronic Fly Trap in 1988.

Business results from resume.

As Director of Technical Development for Better Products, Inc., a $5,000,000,000, privately held marketer of commercial and consumer products, I also launched a consumer model Electronic Fly Trap in five (5) months that will be mainstreamed into the ZAP product line. I have presented and closed the sale of the flytrap to McDonald's, Wal-Mart, K-Mart and Target, which resulted in incremental sales of over $4,000,000 and projected sales of over $12,000,000 within three (3) years.

Rethinking today's business was another way I generated profits for our division and largest client. I recaptured the $12,000,000 Wal-Mart account by taking a risky, but creative approach in presenting to executives the reason we were the only company that could succeed in profitably satisfying their needs.

With a Ph.D. in science and an MBA, I have positioned my career to bring together business, science, imagination, and have taken the risks to profitability. I am seeking to be part of an organization that wants to identify and market tomorrow's big opportunities ahead of the competition.

Indicate salary.

Enclosed is my resume for your review. My base salary is $119,700, plus bonus. If I can contribute to meeting your client's growth objectives, I would be pleased to hear from you.

Sincerely,

Jacob J. Robusto

Enclosure ← *Enclose resume.*

The following is an actual cover letter used to contact search firms. Over 900 of these search-firm letters were produced by this individual, leading to zero (0) contacts or replies. (Not by my firm, thank God!) Read the letter carefully and determine for yourself what and where the problems were in this letter.

On the following page, you will find a critique. The same letter was subsequently redone with an excellent level of response.

SAMPLE 16

January XX, 20XX

SAMPLE COVER LETTER TO A SEARCH FIRM

Ability Search, Inc.
1629 "K" Street, N. W.
Washington, DC 20006

Dear Sir or Madam:

I am seeking a worthwhile human resources or line management position in a medium to large size company. Twelve years of broad and diversified experience in Employment Relations, plus four (4) years of general management experience qualify me for such a position.

My accomplishments and expertise in Employee Relations led to my assuming in 1992 the new position of Director of Employee Relations for XYZ, Inc., a subsidiary of American Can Company.

After successfully organizing the Employee Relations Department in 1994, I became General Manager of the company's pharmaceutical division and was assigned the responsibility for solving the division's management and labor related problems. While in that capacity, I assembled and restructured a new management team, negotiated a new labor agreement with a continuous operation with 12-hour shifts on Saturday and Sunday at straight time pay and replaced an entire labor force with substantially reduced operating costs. The division became profitable and in 1998, I was elected Corporate Vice President.

I have enclosed a resume that describes in more detail my employment history. My current annual compensation is $ _____.

After you have reviewed my qualifications, please call me if they are appropriate any position you may have. I may be reached at the above number or discretely at work at _____.

Thank you for your consideration.

Sincerely,

Enclosure

SAMPLE 17

SAMPLE COVER LETTER TO A SEARCH FIRM

January XX, 20XX

Ability Search, Inc.
1629 "K" Street, N. W.
Washington, DC 20006

Not the strongest selection of vocabulary.

What the writer has done is to "split" his objective in the misplaced belief that this broadens his appeal. This is a major mistake! Why? It indicates the writer does not know what he wants to do! Human Resources is not the same as Line Management. Don't assume Search Firms are career counselors!

Dear Sir or Madam:

I am seeking a worthwhile human resources or line management position in a medium to large size company. Twelve years of broad and diversified experience in Employment Relations, plus four (4) years of general management experience qualify me for such a position.

My accomplishments and expertise in Employee Relations led to my assuming in 1992 the new position of Director of Employee Relations for XYZ, Inc., a subsidiary of American Can Company.

After successfully organizing the Employee Relations Department in 1994, I became General Manager of the company's pharmaceutical division and was assigned the responsibility for solving the division's management and labor related problems. While in that capacity, I assembled and restructured a new management team, negotiated a new labor agreement with a continuous operation with 12-hour shifts on Saturday and Sunday at straight time pay and replaced an entire labor force with substantially reduced operating costs. The division became profitable and in 1998, I was elected Corporate Vice President.

How much?

I have enclosed a resume that describes in more detail my employment history. My current annual compensation is $ _____.

Self-evident.

Sounds desperate!

After you have reviewed my qualifications, please call me if they are appropriate for any position you may have. I may be reached at the above number or discretely at work at

_____.

Thank you for your consideration.

Sincerely,

Enclosure

Three points here:

1. This information can be obtained from the resume.

2. Strongly suggests disloyalty, i.e., working on company time for personal gain.

3. Typo: "discreetly."

The following is another actual search-firm cover letter that was used in a job campaign. This letter is really more suitable for use as a direct mail piece of correspondence. The subject of direct mail letters will be discussed on subsequent pages.

The letter itself, although well written, is possibly a bit long. Review this letter and its rewritten "cousin" on the following pages.

SAMPLE 18

January XX, 20XX

SAMPLE COVER LETTER TO A SEARCH FIRM

Dear _____:

Perhaps one of your clients is seeking a management professional who, as a Senior Manager for two major financial institutions, has had the opportunity to dedicate management expertise to maximize profitability and increase operational efficiency. If so, the enclosed information may be of interest to you.

With 14 years of diverse management background, which includes mergers, acquisitions, data conversions, human resource reorganization, marketing, and product design and profitability, I am seeking a challenging opportunity to contribute my skills to a team-oriented management group.

For example, as Senior Vice President of Regency Savings Bank, a $325 million institution, my responsibilities encompassed the entire retail banking operation: corporate purchasing, building management, all back room deposit and transaction account operations, and product design. Under my direction, new programs were initiated eliminating 3,000 nonprofitable checking accounts and increasing fee income 43%, and reducing the monthly of outstanding uncollected checks by 38%. In addition, I developed a consumer loan application program and incentive plan that increased the average new loan volume from $955,000 to $1,435,000 monthly.

Previously, I served as Director of Human Resources and developed the employee policy manual, EEO compliance, and employee incentive plans, one of which resulted in teller shortages being reduced to $56.00 per teller annually.

Prior to my employment at Regency Savings Bank, I held the position of Vice President with American Heritage Savings. My responsibilities included special projects administration for the Board of Directors, human resources, brand coordination, deposit and retirement account administration. Also, I coordinated the operations transfer during the Household Bank acquisition of American Heritage from the FSLIC in which 35 key staff members remained and supported senior management.

My credentials include a Master's in Educational Administration and a B. S. in Communication from Northern Illinois University. My current compensation is $87,800 with incentives.

I am interested in joining an organization – large or small – where my management expertise could be utilized. If you or your client has an interest, I would be pleased to hear from you.

Sincerely,

Enclosure

SUGGESTED REVISION TO SEARCH FIRM LETTER ON PREVIOUS PAGE

January XX, 20XX

Dear _____ :

Please review the enclosed resume with respect to any current client assignments that match my experience and qualifications.

I have over fifteen (15) years of senior-level banking experience encompassing retail banking, marketing, product development, as well as operations management experience.

As Senior Vice President of Regency Savings Bank, a $325-million institution, I had total responsibility for the retail banking operation. Three of my most recent accomplishments have included: eliminating 3,000 unprofitable accounts while increasing income 43%, designing the Presidential Election Certificate Program, which generated $3,000,000 in deposits in ten (10) days, and developing a consumer-loan program which increased new loan volume from $955,000 to $1,435,000 monthly.

Earlier in my career, I spent eight (8) years as Vice President for Household Bank in Bloomingdale, Illinois. My current salary is $87,800 plus bonus. I would be pleased to talk with you about an appropriate opportunity.

Sincerely,

Enclosure

FOCUS TIME

Please stop now and write your cover letter to employment agencies. As you write the letter, keep in mind the following tips:

1. Be direct and quantify accomplishments as you did in your cover letter to corporations.

2. Do not attempt to be cute or drastically different in your letter. These individuals receive hundreds of letters a day, and they will know a straightforward, results-oriented cover letter when they see it.

3. Always indicate the **exact** amount of your most recent compensation in your letters to search firms or employment agencies. Refer to the preceding sample letters for an example of this.

4. Keep in mind that search consultants are not guidance counselors or career advisors. They are businessmen seeking to earn a fee upon successful placement of a candidate. I strongly recommend against using the "spray and pray" technique. This technique indicates that you are unfocused and really have no idea what you are looking for. "Spray and pray" typically involves a paragraph such as, "I am seeking a worthwhile human resources or line-management position in a medium-to large-sized company. Twelve years of broad and diversified experience in employee relations plus four years of general management experience qualify me for such a position." This actual opening paragraph in a cover letter to search firms indicates the person is "spraying" himself across different functions in the mistaken belief this will increase his chances for an interview. He doesn't know where he wants to go, and he is "praying" that the search firm will select the appropriate opportunities.

NETWORKING . . .

Who You Know Is as Important as What You Know

Hitting on everyone you know for a job or asking for favors is not networking. A casual meeting with a contact over lunch or handing out resumes does not qualify as networking either. If you approach people this way, friends will begin avoiding you, and professional acquaintances will simply ignore you.

Networking is a structured approach to building contacts. It requires research, preparation, and follow-up to be effective. The goal of networking is to get advice or suggestions from your contacts for the purpose of:

- Increasing personal visibility in the job market
- Gathering information on companies, industries, and trends
- Obtaining referrals to people with the authority to hire.

Through networking you will multiply your contacts. Like a daisy chain, one contact can link you to another, and you will never know who knows whom. While statistics vary, most people would agree that between 50 to 80 percent of all people working today found their jobs through networking contacts. Utilizing the following points will aid in maximizing your networking activity:

1. Develop a list of everyone you know. Do not hesitate to contact individuals who are not close friends or acquaintances you have not seen in years. If approached properly, they will be flattered to be asked for advice. The list that follows this section will provide a starting point to identify who you know.

2. Avoid making initial network contacts by telephone.

"OUT-OF-THE-BOX THINKING"

Contrary to what most people do – that is, to race to the phone to contact friends, colleagues, etc., seeking leads and information – I strongly recommend against this networking tactic. Why? Because it is slow, inefficient, cumbersome, and not nearly as productive as initially networking through the mail.

Communicating with networking contacts by mail ensures that the individual has your resume immediately. It helps avoid repeated telephone calls to the same contact and the "rehashing" of your story of why you are in the market.

The fact of the matter is, almost all networking contacts when hit on by an unexpected telephone call will generally get around to asking for a copy of your resume. Mailing first insures that your material is in the hands of your networking contact when you place the follow-up call.

Also, networking contacts are seldom helpful when caught cold by a telephone call. Carefully draft a cover letter to send with your resume. This will permit the contact person to think, reflect on your situation and your resume, and make a few telephone calls on your behalf.

3. Your networking cover letter should be positive and upbeat. In the first paragraph, mention why you are writing. There are several possible openings. (Review the samples that follow this section for direction.) In the next paragraph, ask for suggestions, advice, or assistance in your job search. Include one or more resumes with your letter. Finally, and most importantly, inform your contact that *you will follow-up shortly.*

4. Do not include your current salary or compensation in your cover letter. Do not be defensive about the reason for being in the market, nor allow self-pity to show in the tone of your cover letter. Keep the letter brief and upbeat.

5. Before your follow-up call, spend some time doing some research. Gather information on markets, industries, and companies to explore and develop questions to ask your contacts.

6. Organize and prioritize your contact list. Begin the process of letter contact and telephone follow-up with individuals you know fairly well in order to increase your comfort level. Complete a "Network Data Sheet" on each contact to ensure effective follow-up. (A sample is included at the end of this section.)

7. Script your telephone follow-up introduction. Make notes on questions to ask including information on companies or industries you are targeting. The goal of your conversation is to gather some market intelligence, get some advice on your job search, and obtain referrals to other contacts. A sample introduction will include the following:

Greeting and Personal Identification:	"Mr. or Ms. _____, (or use the person's first name) good morning/afternoon. This is _____."
Remind the Contact of Your Relationship:	"We met at the Purchasing and Inventory Control Meeting."
State the Reason for Your Call:	"I sent you a letter recently requesting some of your thoughts on my job search."
Offer Reassurance:	"I want you to know that I am not asking you for a job. I do not even have any reason to believe that you even know of any openings."

State Your Goal:

"The reason for my call is that I need some advice, information, and, if you feel comfortable, referrals to some other people who might be helpful."

8. Be prepared to tell the contact about yourself in a brief summary. Include your most recent position, experience and accomplishments, as well as a short career summary. Objectively state your reason for being in the market, and finally note your job search goals as they relate to the information or advice you are requesting. For example:

> I have a strong MRP-based purchasing background in steel, plastics, wire, and cable. Most recently I held the position of Materials Manager with a $60 million manufacturer of automotive cable assemblies. In my five years with the company, I implemented the conversion from manual to computerized resource planning, established a master-scheduling plan integrating three plants, and managed purchases of $30 million with a staff of two.

> In prior positions, I purchased up to $10 million in plastics, contract services, and machined metal parts as a buyer for two Fortune 100 lawn and garden equipment manufacturers.

> I am pursuing new career opportunities because Zena Technologies, my recent employer, consolidated its operations and in the restructuring eliminated several positions, including mine. *(Note: Keep your reason for being in the market brief, positive, and objective. If possible, do not discuss it at all.)*

> With my broad background in automotive and lawn and garden, those industries are my primary targets. I would appreciate any information or advice you can give me on those markets.

Another example for an executive secretary with word-processing experience might be:

> I have more than fifteen years of diverse executive secretarial, word processing, and administrative-support experience in manufacturing, legal, and health-service environments.

> In my most recent position as Secretary to the Vice President of a $25-million consumer-products manufacturer, I typed reports, correspondence, and statistical data using Microsoft Word and other Microsoft Office programs. I was also responsible for greeting visitors, managing the appointment calendar, scheduling travel, and arranging conference plans for three managers in the Sales and Marketing Department.

Before joining Troy, Inc., I was Office Manager and Typist for four years at a small corporate-law firm with five attorneys. I also had eight years of medical transcription experience in a large community hospital.

My software knowledge includes MultiMate, Microsoft Office 95, Lotus 123, DOS, dBase III, and PowerPoint.

I am seeking a new position because of a reorganization in my company, which eliminated my job. I would appreciate any direction you can give me on companies in the area that I should explore. *(Note: Be brief, objective, and positive if explaining why you are in the market.)*

9. Take notes on any information shared by the contact. If not useful now, you may need the information later. Thank the contact for any assistance and ask permission to stay in touch. The Network Data Sheet at the end of this section is an excellent tool for recording any contact information.

10. Write a follow-up letter expressing appreciation and the desire to stay in touch, as well as confirming any commitments made by the contact. Complete the "Networking Data Sheet" on your contact.

The networking contacts you develop in your job search can be beneficial throughout your career. When you have landed your next position, do not forget to share the good news with your contacts. Send them a letter thanking them for their assistance and telling them about your new position.

"OUT-OF-THE-BOX THINKING"

When preparing a networking mail campaign, start with your Rolodex of contacts. Hopefully you did not throw it out or leave it behind when you left your old office.

Next, send a letter to those people appearing on your Christmas card list. Remember, if you thought enough of people to send them a card at Christmas – send them your letter and resume after Christmas.

WHO DO YOU KNOW?

The first step in developing a network is to make a list of everyone you know.

Include even those individuals you see only infrequently or have not talked to in years. If approached properly, they will be flattered. The following list will get you started.

Who do I know from my family?
- Mother, Father
- In-Laws
- Sisters
- Brothers
- Others

Who do I know from my old job?
- Former employees/employers
- Fellow workers
- Customers/clients
- Former competitors
- Others

Who do I know from my church?
- Fellow members
- Church leaders
- Sunday school teachers
- Ushers
- Others

Who do I know from school(s) I attended?
- Sorority/fraternity friends
- Schoolmates
- Alumni associates
- Teachers, professors
- University officials
- Others

What kind of professionals do I know?
- Doctors
- Dentists
- Accountant
- Lawyer
- Banker
- Insurance agents
- Others

Who do I know from my past?
- Neighbors
- Friends
- Customers
- Armed forces
- Others

Who do I know from my hobbies?
- Club members
- Card groups
- Sports (bowling, golf, tennis)
- Athletic clubs
- Others

Who do I know because of my children?
- Teachers
- Parents of their playmates
- Coaches
- PTA
- Others

Who do I know through public service/charitable interests?
- Community fund
- Chamber of commerce
- Alderman
- Volunteer
- YMCA/YWCA
- Others

SAMPLE 20

ROBERT T. THOMAS
1234 Main Street
Anywhere, State 99999
(765) 555-1212

SAMPLE NETWORKING LETTER

Note: To be sent to friends and business acquaintances.

January XX, 20XX

Name
Title
Company
Address
City, State Zip

Start on a positive note.

Dear _____ : (Personal salutation, i.e., "Dear Mr. Jones" or "Dear George")

After 20 years of diversified manufacturing and operations management experience, I have made the decision to leave Monroe Manufacturing Corporation to explore other career opportunities. This decision was not made easily, since I found my association with Monroe both satisfying and challenging in many ways.

Ask for his or her help.

Therefore, I have taken the liberty of contacting you and a few other close friends and business acquaintances to seek your assistance in my job search. Enclosed is a copy of my resume to bring you up to date on my background.

This is the real purpose of your letter.

I will follow up shortly with a telephone call. If, in the meantime, you have any thoughts or suggestions, I would be pleased to hear from you.

Sincerely,

Remember, you can insert several copies of your resume.

This is most important! It keeps your networking contacts thinking!

Robert T. Thomas

Enclosure

Don't discuss the reasons why you are leaving or have left your last employer! This clouds the purpose of the letter.

177

SAMUEL L. SMITH
536 Longmeadow Circle
Anywhere, State 60167
(312) 555-1732

SAMPLE NETWORKING LETTER

Note: To be sent to friends and business acquaintances.

January XX, 20XX

Name
Title
Company
Address
City, State Zip

Dear _____: (Personal salutation, i.e., "Dear Mr. Jones" or "Dear George")

     I am currently exploring other career opportunities. Consequently, I have taken the liberty of enclosing a copy of my resume to bring you up to date on my career. If you have any thoughts or suggestion regarding my job search, I would be most receptive to hearing them.

     I will call you shortly and possibly we could discuss any ideas or suggestions you may have at that time.

Sincerely,

> *This letter is short and to the point. It leaves plenty of room to jot down a personal postscript.*

Samuel L. Smith

Enclosure

SAMPLE 22

ROSIE M. SHANNON
1424 Washington Avenue
Anywhere, State 55555
(765) 555-5432

<u>SAMPLE NETWORKING LETTER</u>

Note: To be sent to friends and business acquaintances

January XX, 20XX

Name
Title
Company
Address
City, State Zip

Dear _____: (Personal salutation, i.e., "Dear Mr. Jones" or "Dear George")

    With over nine (9) years of diversified secretarial experience and a degree in Secretarial Science, I have decided to explore other career opportunities. I would like to capitalize on my extensive background of secretarial skills to further enhance my career.

    I have taken the liberty of contacting you to solicit any ideas or suggestions you may have to assist me in my job search. Enclosed you will find a copy of my resume to familiarize you with my career to date.

    I will contact you shortly and would be pleased to discuss any thoughts you may have.

Sincerely,

Rosie M. Shannon

Enclosure

YOUR NAME
Your Address
City, State Zip
Telephone Number

SAMPLE NETWORKING FOLLOW UP LETTER

Note: To be sent to friends and business acquaintances.

January XX, 20XX

Name
Title
Company
Address
City, State Zip

Dear _____:

I appreciate the opportunity to have spoken with you about my job search.

Your advice concerning the type of manufacturing companies to contact in the local area will help me focus my search. Also, thank you for referring me to John Mack and Susan Brown. I will call them this week and follow up with you afterward.

Thanks again for your time and interest.

Sincerely,

Your Name

In networking, as in any other job campaign process, following up is the key to your success. To assist you in effective follow-up, we have included the "Network Data Sheet." I recommend that you make copies of this page to keep accurate records of your networking efforts.

NETWORK DATA SHEET

Name: _____   Salutation: Dear _____ : _____

Title: _____   Home Phone: ( ) _____

Address: _____   Work Phone: ( ) _____

_____

Zip: _____

Referred by: _____

Company Name: _____

Address: _____

_____

Position Held: _____

Prior Company Name: _____

Call Date	Follow-Up Action	Comments

FOCUS TIME

Please stop here to organize your networking activities.

1. List everyone you know, then prioritize the list for networking contacts.

2. Write your networking letter. As you write the letter, keep in mind that you should frame everything in a positive manner. You need not mention any events surrounding your recent separation or your compensation.

   A. Ask for your contact's assistance.
   B. Include two or more copies of your resume for your contact's review. This will be helpful as your contact begins to form his or her thoughts and suggestions regarding your career search. Including extra copies of your resume will encourage your contact to pass it on to other contacts.
   C. Inform your contact that **you will follow up shortly**.

3. Develop questions to ask your contact in the telephone follow-up. These should include information on your target companies, market intelligence, and the request for referrals to other contacts.

4. Draft your telephone follow-up introduction. Call your contact. Listen carefully and take notes.

5. Complete your "Network Data Sheet" immediately after the telephone call.

6. Send a follow-up letter thanking the contact, expressing the desire to stay in touch, and confirming any commitments.

THIS SECTION IS STRICTLY CLASSIFIED!

TO RESPOND . . OR NOT TO RESPOND? THAT IS THE QUESTION.
THE BASIC VALUE OF ADS IN A JOB SEARCH

It is Sunday morning. You pull out the unemployment classified advertisement section of your local newspaper. You see an ad. The ad has your name written all over it. It was customized for you. You mail out your cover letter and resume. You never get a response. What went wrong? Potentially, many things. This section of *From Here To There* will help you to present yourself professionally and greatly reduce chances of being eliminated from the process. Also, it will show you how ads can be used for other information aside from applying for the position named.

The "published" job market is very competitive because job applicants with little business exposure or limited networking contacts are part of your competition. They can go to the library or purchase newspapers or magazines and respond. Although advertisements represent less than 15 percent of employment opportunities, responses can yield good results if you follow some simple, yet significant steps. Just remember that, as in so many areas of your search . . .

It is the little things that matter!

You cannot be there in person to explain or point out details to the reader. Subjectivity is part of the process. If you can capture the screener's interest, use creativity, and most importantly, match your professional skills and results with the advertiser's needs, your chances will be greatly enhanced.

SUGGESTIONS TO MAXIMIZE YOUR ODDS

- **Evaluate the Qualifications.** Answer the ad **even if you do not have all of the listed qualifications**. An employer is often unable to find the ideal candidate and must consider individuals with different qualifications than originally requested. Sometimes the job does change to fit the qualifications available or to take advantage of unique skill sets from you or other applicants.

- **Let Ads Age.** When responding to ads, it is not "first come/first served."

REMEMBER - Your competition is putting its responses in the mail either the day the ad appears or first thing the following morning.

FACT: The employer receives 85 to 95 percent or more of the responses to an employment advertisement in the **first** week following its running. These resumes get less review time because of sheer volume and human nature. You are therefore eliminated for subjective reasons. Does it make sense to submit your material with all the others? Of course it doesn't. If your response arrives a few days later (seven or so) it will get a closer review, as will your cover letter. Why? Because there are fewer responses to command the attention of the individual screening the responses. Sometimes an additional fifteen to twenty seconds can make a huge difference. After all, the employer has already committed thousands of dollars in advertising costs. It doesn't make sense to hire one of the first people to respond. Most employers want to make sure that they receive the best return on their investment.

- **Read All Ads in the Classified Ad Section.** Sometimes ads are not placed under obvious headings. Often they are listed under industry or function. Also organizations have ads for a variety of positions. This is a strong signal that the company is in a growth mode. This should prompt you to research that company and contact the manager heading your potential area. Do not respond to the Human Resources department if

DON'T RESPOND TO ADS (RIGHT AWAY)! **WAIT!**

you can avoid it. A better alternative would be to send your response to the real decision-maker – not the gatekeeper. He or she is busy reviewing the responses to the ads. Have your resume hand-delivered by an employee if possible.

- **Read Publications Every Day.** Even though particular publications dominate circulation and carry the bulk of ads, others instruments should never be overlooked. They can be a great source of openings. Do not ignore local, neighborhood, ethnic and national newspapers, and trend magazines. Also, as you will see, cost prompts an employer to run ads on weekdays. The cost per ad is less expensive when compared to the Sunday edition of the same newspaper.

- **Advertisers Are Serious.** Advertising is not inexpensive for companies. The larger the organization placing the ad, or the larger the ad itself, will often determine the number of responses received. It is not unusual for the screening professional to receive 300 - 400 resumes during the first week following the ad.

Ads are also **very** expensive. The chart below shows example prices of a two-column, six-inch display, or approximately 4" by 6". These costs are for one insertion in the employment-classified section.

Newspaper	Weekday	Weekend	Blind Box Rental Time
Milwaukee Journal Sentinel [A]	$ 895.44	$1,868.16	30 Days
Chicago Tribune	$1,680.00	$5,308.00	14 Days
Los Angeles Times	$6,176.00	$6,176.00	30 Days
New York Times*	$2,730.00	$1,890.00	30 Days
Wall Street Journal**	$2,100.00	Not Applicable	90 Days

Atlanta Journal	$3,150.00[C]	$3,617.04[C]	14 Days
Dallas Morning News	$3,598.56[D]	$3,969.04[D]	30 Days
Denver Post	$2,733.12	$4,354.37	14 Days
St. Louis Post – Dispatch	$3,284.20[B]	$3,284.20[B]	14 Days

Internet Posting	Cost	Duration
Milwaukee Journal Sentinel	$250.00	4 weeks
Chicago Tribune	Included w/Sunday ad	1 week
Los Angeles Times	(See footnote "A")	14 days
New York Times	$250.00	2 weeks
Wall Street Journal	$250.00	60 days
Atlanta Journal	(see Footnote "C")	(see Footnote "C")
Dallas Morning News	(see Footnote "D")	(see Footnote "D")
Denver Post	Included w/Sunday ad	1 week
St. Louis Post – Dispatch	(see Footnote "B")	(see Footnote "B")

* National Circulation
** Regional Edition
[A] Includes Internet posting
[B] Additional $25 for Internet posting for the duration of ad.
[C] Additional $60 for Internet posting of 1 week.
[D] Additional $100 for Internet posting of 1 week.

- **Follow the Instructions.** Employers often ask that respondents include certain information when replying to advertisements, such as salary, references, or compensation requirements. If salary or salary history is requested, include **only** the **most recent salary or wage**. **If your salary is not addressed in the cover letter** as requested, **your resume may be eliminated**. Remember this basic truth, "If you cannot follow instructions when attempting to get a job, why should a potential employer believe you would follow instructions on the job?" Only a naïve job seeker would think that he or she could get his or her next job without revealing his or her current or most recent salary. Do not play games! Tell the employer, if asked, what your **exact** salary was. Don't "round off," which usually means round up. It can be verified!

- **Notice Subtle Differences.** One ad may ask for "salary history." This is asking for your last or current base salary. Another ad will ask for "salary requirements." That is not asking for your current or last base salary, so it is critical to say that you are "open" in terms of compensation, as this now includes base and possibly bonuses. **There is a difference. Do not ignore it.** "Salary requirements" are simply what you want on your next paycheck. It may not be what you get, so consider it as part of your wish list.

- **Don't Just Look Forward! Go Backwards.** Job hunters always look forward to getting the Sunday edition of their newspaper. After all, this one single edition has the majority of classified advertising.

  Respond to ads that have run in the past. Go backwards – your competition will be looking forward. Answer ads that ran up to two months ago. Don't assume that all jobs advertised fourm, five, six seven or eight weeks ago have been filled. They haven't!!!

- **Cover Letters.** Develop a well-writen cover letter to respond to the majority of your ads. To do this you must review ads, in your field over the past eight to ten weeks. After reviewing these ads you should be able to create a shell to open and close a cover letter. However, the substantive issues highlighted in the ad should be matched in a customized fashion. Otherwise, why would you be considered? You should always tailor your cover letter to an ad. As you will see, there are alternative cover letters and alternatives **to** cover letters.

- **Repeat Ads.** By waiting to respond, your competition is reduced. This is called "aging your response." Also, you can see if an ad may be repeated. If the same ad appears in the next edition (one week), use the same strategy previously mentioned (waiting seven to ten days). It is likely that it is being run as part of a package. If it appears three to four weeks later, never respond to the same bait. Use a direct mail letter (see Sample 29) or the comparison format (see Samples 25 and 26 in this section.) Both should include current salary if requested in the ad. What did not work the first time around definitely will not work the second time either.

- **Miscellaneous "Little Things."**

  - **Do not use a postage meter.** It will appear that you are spending your company's money to subsidize your search. After all, how many people have a postage meter at home?
  - **Use quality stationery for all correspondence** (all typed, of course.)
  - **Take time to reseach** and get a contact name whenever possible.
  - **Do not get cute;** it usually backfires.
  - **Do not forget the important associations, publications, and trade journals.** Classified ads appear in these also, which should be responded to as well. If you are a member of a trade association, highlight that in your letter.
  - **If a telephone number is listed in the ad – use it – and do not wait.** Even if it is Sunday.
  - **Follow-up and be persistent** but not a pest. (No telegrams please.)
  - **E-mail or fax your resume if requested** but always follow up the fax or E-mail with a hard copy of your response.
  - **Do not use ads to pick up random names and addresses.** There are better sources for this activity, such as networking contacts and reference books.

SALARY ISSUES MADE SIMPLE WHEN RESPONDING TO ADS

This is one of the most discussed issues regarding ads – and the question is – "Why?" When responding to ads, why do most people, not include their current or most recent salary or compensation when requested? **This is a mistake.** I recommend that the following rules be followed:

1. If requested to provide current or most recent salary or compensation figures in the ad, you should provide the information. Be exact. Do not give a range, as this may be verified. For a further description of salary history, see page 334.

2. If an ad requests salary history, recognize that what is really requested is not a complete year-by-year description of your salary increments but only your current or most recent salary compensation. In turn, this information should be provided. Salary means just your salary, no perks, fringe benefits, car allowance, etc. Compensation means salary plus bonus. Since bonuses vary from year to year, it is customary to express compensation as follows: "My compensation is a salary of $_____ plus bonus, or plus bonus that averaged $_____ over the past three years."

3. If the ad is silent as to whether to include or not include salary or compensation figures, do not provide this information.

4. Many people hold the belief that by refusing to include salary information that has been requested in an advertisement, they are avoiding early rejection of their candidacy. Typical thinking dictates that if you do not provide salary or compensation information, you cannot be excluded because your salary is too high or too low for the position. Such logic is unrealistic and faulty. Such conduct portrays the applicant as someone who is evasive and cannot or will not follow directions.

5. There is another school of thought on this issue. For that information see page 197, "Alternative Stategies."

Do not try to get fancy and give ranges. It is okay to say that you are "open" to the question "**What are your salary requirements?**", but not in lieu of giving the advertiser what he or she requested. Why eliminate yourself unnecessarily? "Open" means that you are "open to listening to a competitive offer."

Again, why be evasive or even what may be percieved as antagonistic? Be direct. Answer the question. If you cannot follow directions when **applying** for a job, why should a potential employer believe you can follow directions **on** the job? Salary information is and always has been a legal disqualifier. It is simply naivete to think that by dodging the salary question, recruiters or decision-makers will actually track you down to remind you that "you forgot to answer this issue, and could we discuss it?" Read the ad and answer the question or address the salary issue when needed. It is that simple. If you are disqualified because your salary was too high or too low – so be it. Better to be "cut" sooner than later.

ADS ARE NOT ALL THAT COMPLICATED, BUT READ ON

There are essentially two types of ads you will encounter, and each should be treated differently. They are:

Open Ads – You see who the company is in the ad, as the company openly identifies itself.

Blind Box Ads – You respond to a P. O. box, and no name is given.

Let us evaluate the differences, which are significant.

RESPONDING TO ADS – THE BEST STRATEGY

Remember that:

- Competition for ad-generated positions is fierce when the company name is used. The advertiser will receive 85 to 95 percent of responses to an ad during the week following placement of the ad.

- When researching ads that list a company name, go back eight to ten weeks. Many of the listed job openings remain unfilled for at least that amount of time. This is especially true in national publications.

- Wait seven to ten days to respond to an ad. By waiting, you decrease your competion, and you are able to see if the ad is run again the following week.

- Increase your chances to be favorably considered by sending your response midweek so that it arrives after the initial "crunch" but avoid having your ad response arrive on a Monday. Mondays are the heaviest mail delivery day of the week.

- Response to a typical ad can often total several hundred viable applicants. Make sure that you increase your chances of success by taking the time to find out the correct name and title of the individual if the ad only uses initials, or if his or her title is not listed in the ad call the company!

SAMPLE OPEN AD

DATA PROCESSING

Applications Programmer

XYZ Corporation, a growing, fast-paced North Shore company has an opening for a BASIC Programmer. Experienced new grads welcome to apply. Must be willing to help maintain operations. Knowledge of Data General AOS/VS a plus. Business programming experience a must. Our company offers a competitive compensation and benefits package, including a 401(k) plan. Send resume with salary history to:

Mary Smith
XYZ Corporation
123 Main Street
Northbrook, IL 60065

This "open" ad provides you with a golden opportunity. Now it is up to you to go that extra mile. What can you do? Try the following:

- Call XYZ Corporation and find out who Mary Smith is by getting her title. Use that title in the heading of your letter. When calling for information, ask if you can speak to Mary Smith.

- If you connect, ask her what she is looking for in the successful candidate and about other key ingedients *not* listed in the ad.

- Call the company, identify the decision-maker, and call the person to get additional information on the position and qualifications. For example, in the sample "Open" ad above, is Mary Smith the Manager of Employment, or is she the Manager of Programming? You will not know until you call.

- Ensure that your cover letter provides appropriate examples that paint you as the ideal candidate. Match as many of your qualifications as possible to the requirements stated in the ad. Many times requirements are listed in the order of importance, so match your qualifications in the order in which the requirements are listed.

- Research has shown that Human Resource professionals do not want faxes – unless requested. Faxes are often printed on poor quality paper and diminish the professional efforts and appearance of your printed documents.

- Have your cover letter and resume delivered in person by an employee of the company. This has a tremendous positive effect. Make sure it is delivered to the "decision-maker."

- On e-mail – Fast? Yes, but a word of caution. The format in which you send your e-mail response (cover letter and resume) may not be the format in which it is received. Always follow up e-mail messages with a hard copy.

- See Sample Letters 24 and 25 for suggested formats for responding to this ad.

- Most important – do not use the same cover letter for every ad response. Remember to target, target, and **target** your response.

SAMPLE OPENING PARAGRAPHS FOR RESPONDING TO AN AD

When responding to an open advertisement, always address the cover letter to the individual listed in the ad. If no name is listed, call the company and find out to whom you should direct the letter.

When responding to a blind ad, the proper salutation is "Dear Sir or Madam" or "Dear Hiring Official."

"In response to your recent newspaper advertisement for a (Insert Position Title), please accept the enclosed copy of my credentials."

OR

"The scope of responsibility cited in your recent ad for a (Insert Position Title) indicated that my background is well-suited to your needs. Therefore, I have enclosed my resume for your review."

OR

"In the recent edition of *CPA News*, your ad for a (Insert Position Title) piqued my interest, and I have therefore enclosed a copy of my resume for consideration."

OR

"I think you will agree that my background may be an ideal match for your need for a (Insert Position Title) as addressed in your recent ad in the (Insert Publication Name here)."

MARGARET JOHNSON
4321 Kennedy Street
Anywhere, State 99999
(708) 555-4321

SAMPLE OPEN AD RESPONSE LETTER

January XX, 20XX

Ms. Mary Smith
Manager of Employment
XYZ Corporation
123 Main Street
Northbrook, IL 60065

Dear Ms. Smith:

The scope of responsibility cited in your recent ad for an Applications Programmer indicated that my background is well suited to your needs.

I am a 1998 graduate of DeVry College, majoring in Applications Programming. In addition, I posess two years of hands-on experience doing BASIC programming in a software development consulting firm utilizing Data General AOS/VS. My primary responsibility was to head a team of programmers on a major conversion for a Fortune 500 client company.

My search is for an in-house position where my experience can be an ongoing contribution. My current base salary is $46,570. If you have an interest, I would be pleased to hear from you.

Sincerely,

Margaret Johnson

Enclosure

MARGARET JOHNSON
4321 Kennedy Street
Anywhere, State 99999
(708) 555-4321

SAMPLE AD RESPONSE LETTER
(Comparison Format)

January XX, 20XX

Ms. Mary Smith
Manager of Employment
XYZ Corporation
123 Main Street
Northbrook, IL 60065

Dear Ms. Smith:

I think you will agree that my background may be an ideal match for an Applications Programmer as described in your recent ad.

Outlined below is my rationale for this match.

Your Requirements	My Background
Experienced Recent Graduate	A 1998 Graduate of DeVry College in Applications Programming with two (2) years of business experience.
Knowledge of Data General AOS/VS and BASIC programmer.	Led a team of programmers using BASIC in a conversion to Data General AOS/VS.
Willing to help operations.	Worked in a Fortune 500 environment leading a special project team, contributing to my firm's daily operations as well.

The enclosed resume will further substantiate my qualifications. My current salary is $46,570.

I look forward to hearing from you.

Sincerely,

Margaret Johnson

Enclosure

SAMPLE "BLIND-BOX" AD

Financial Systems Analyst

A Fortune 500 consumer-products company headquartered in St. Louis has an excellent career opportunity for an experienced Financial professional to play a key role in developing and executing long-term financial-system plans.

The successful candidate will be a detail, results-oriented self-starter, MBA/CPA with 4-6 years accounting experience including the design and implementation of automated systems to improve internal controls and labor efficiency. Ability to analyze requirements/benefits and communicate with technical personnel and senior management is critical. Experience with client/server applications is a plus. Applicants must be interested in a financial accounting career and be willing to travel and relocate within the next two years.

We offer an excellent salary, generous benefits package, and an outstanding opportunity for career growth. For prompt consideration, send your resume and salary requirements in confidence to:

P. O. Box 411040
Dept. 416
St. Louis, MO 63141

Equal Opportunity Employer

BLIND-BOX ADS

- Blind box ads are set up as a depository for the responses received to a previously placed advertisement. The responses are handled in two fashions:

  - The advertising publication, usually a newspaper, will collect all responses and forward them to the advertising company. They go directly to the individual designated in the agreement. The "box" is rented for a period of time, sometimes up to three months in national publications. NOTE: Collected responses are mailed to the prospective employer – NOT delivered. This adds three to five more days until the "screening party" may actually see your information.

  This is important because if one considers the time it takes for the resume and cover letter to reach either the newspaper or designated post office box, the incoming mail time – the collection time at the blind-box address – and the ongoing mail time back to the advertising company, the result becomes obvious. Your response and cover letter will take at least seven to ten days before your documents will be actually received.

- There are several reasons why an employer might place a blind-box or "anonymous" ad:

  - The company wants to maintain anonymity and sets up a blind box for receiving the responses.

  - Eliminates the burden of acknowledging numerous responses.

  - Avoids needless disruption of the office workday by thoughtless job applicants who insist on telephoning or dropping in without an appointment.

  - Delays negative reaction from existing employees until the position is filled.

  - Provides confidentiality when an incumbent is being replaced.

  - Avoids communication of market intelligence to the competition. Other companies in the industry are unaware of your company's plans and/or needs.

  - Publishers will not divulge the source of blind-box advertisements.

- What is protocol for responding to a blind-box ad?

  - Call the newspaper that has printed the blind-box ad to verify the time length if the rental box. If it is only thirty days, you must respond within that time period for your resume to be forwarded to the company.

  - The salutation should read, "Dear Sir or Madam" or "Dear Hiring Official."

  - As alternatives to a traditional response, as in Sample Letter 24, use a direct mail letter as shown in Sample 29 or a comparison format illustrated by Samples 25 and 26. Samples 29, 30, and 31 are normally sent **without** enclosing a resume because they are direct-mail letters that are meant to pique interest, leading to a request for a resume. Direct mail is discussed starting on page 212.

  - Send the response addressed to the box number in care of the publication. For an example, see the following "Manufacturing Professional" ad.

  - Wait eight to ten days before responding to a blind-box ad.

  - Wait fourteen to twenty-one days before responding to a blind box ad if the ad is in the *Wall Street Journal.* (Consult the chart on pages 184 - 185 for the posted duration of a blind-box rental.)

A "TYPICAL" BLIND-BOX AD

<u>MANUFACTURING PROFESSIONAL</u>

A leading manufacturer of equipment for industrial markets is seeking a Director of Manufacturing to manage existing facilities and handle expansion and modernization in support of anticipated growth.

Qualifications include at least 8 years experience in automated machining processes and management of 100,000+ square foot manufacturing plant with at least 150 employees, preferably in a union setting. Position requires at least a B. S. degree in Management or a related field; M. B. A. preferred. Experience with plant restructuring and modernization and cost-reduction programs a plus.

We offer an excellent compensation package and benefits commensurate with your experience.

Interested applicants should forward a resume along with salary history to:

Box 100 B
The Wall Street Journal
400 Alexis Blvd.
Naperville, IL 60563

In responding to any ad
the key is always
linking qualifications with requirements.

<u>Ad Requirements</u>	<u>Robert Thomas' Qualifications</u>
At least eight years of experience in automated machining processes.	Twenty years of manufacturing and operations experience.
Management of a 100,000-sq. ft. plant.	Redesigned and modernized a 150,000-sq. ft. plant.
Experience in plant restructuring and cost-reduction programs.	Increased output by 9.9 percent and saved $250,000 in the first year.
B. S. in Management; M.B.A. preferred.	B. S. in Industrial Management and an M.B.A.

Remember...
Salary History is asking for what? *Your current or last salary base!*

ROBERT T. THOMAS
1234 Main Street
Anywhere, State 99999
(765) 555-1212

SAMPLE AD RESPONSE LETTER
(Comparison Format)

January XX, 20XX

Box 100 B
The Wall Street Journal
400 Alexis Boulevard
Naperville, IL 60563

Dear Sir or Madam:

It was with great interest that I read your recent ad for a Manufacturing Professional. I believe my background is an ideal match with your needs. I have outlined the critical areas below.

Your Ad	My Background
At least eight (8) years of experience in automated machining processes.	Twenty (20) years of manufacturing and operations experience.
Management of a 100,000+ square foot plant.	Redesigned and modernized a 150,000 square foot plant.
Experience in plant restructuring and cost-reduction programs.	Increased output by close to 10 percent and saved $250,000 in the first year.
B. S. in Management; M. B. A. preferred.	B. S. in Industrial Management and an M. B. A.

Enclosed is my resume, which expands further on my career highlights and accomplishments. I am interested in joining an organization where my diverse manufacturing management experience could be utilized.

My current base salary is $79,300. If you have an interest in my background, I would be pleased to hear from you.

Sincerely,

Robert T. Thomas

Enclosure

ALTERNATIVE STRATEGIES

There are some important issues that you need to be aware of when responding to ads:

- There are two schools of thought concerning salary disclosure in your cover letter. First, as previously presented, follow the directions and provide the information requested. Second, some feel that stating in your cover letter that you are "open" to discuss salary after getting an opportunity to learn more about the position is acceptable. However, you do need to be aware that you will probably not get that opportunity. My feeling is that the item is requested for a reason. The risks you take in addressing it on **your** terms are high and unnecessary.

- In addition, when a company identifies itself in an ad, send a cover letter and resume following the instructions in the ad. Also send a direct-mail-style letter to the president without salary information. The direct-mail concept is not the same thing as using a cover letter and a resume to get an interview. This concept and its advantages are explained in Chapter V. Read on! It greatly enhances your opportunity and shows creativity. Granted, this will take more effort, but employers know that if you work hard trying to get a job, you will work hard on the job.

- Whenever possible, find out who will make the hiring decision. Attempt to contact (call) this person to find out more about what he/she is looking for in the ideal candidate.

- Never include references either on the cover letter or on a separate page. Those will be requested only after the interview process has begun. This also holds true for letters of recommendation.

- When answering an ad that is rerun, after you have already responded to the first ad, do not send out the same bait. Send a direct mail letter – **WITHOUT A RESUME!** What did not work the first time will not work the second time either. Use a new approach.

- The comparison style letter (see Sample Letters 25 and 26) is extremely effective and pointed. It hits the nail on the head. Use it!

SUMMARY

"To Respond or Not to Respond?" is not a question with a cut-and-dried answer. My recommendation is to follow the guidelines I have set forth in the preceding pages. Do not expect a strong return on your responses to advertisements and, more importantly, remember that:

Ads represent less than 15% of the available positions in the marketplace.

This is not to say that ads should be disregarded. You should budget your time and efforts appropriately. Carefully balance answering ads relative to the time and effort put forth in more "productive" activities (i.e., networking, direct mailings, contacting search firms, etc.).

During your campaign, you will encounter people with varying opinions. A well-intentioned friend may hear you say, "I have responded to over fifty ads and have not gotten a single interview." His suggestion might be, "Shorten your resume from two pages to one page."

This is a strategy that is highly unlikely to correct this problem. Carefully review this entire section to ensure that you are using the professional and proven methods.

Do not let what you cannot do interfere with what you can do.

- John Wooden

AD-RESPONSE WORKSHEET

Date of Ad: _____ Source of Ad: _____

Open or Blind Ad: _____ Date to be Mailed: _____

Company Name and Address:

_____

_____

_____

Respond To:/Title: _____

Method of Response (Mail, E-Mail, Fax): _____

Job Title: _____

Include Salary?

         Yes _____ $_____

         No _____

REQUIREMENTS LISTED IN THE AD

1. _____

2. _____

3. _____

4. _____

5. _____

MATCHING QUALIFICATIONS IN MY BACKGROUND

1. _____

2. _____

3. _____

4. _____

5. _____

FOCUS TIME

Stop now and draft the shell of your ad-response letter. While each letter will differ according to the particular ad, the main body of the letter, stressing your accomplishments, will remain consistent. As you draft your individual ad-response letters, remember the following helpful hints:

1. Match your qualifications to those expressed in the ad. **Target, Target, Target!**

2. Follow the instructions in the ad. If an ad requests your most recent salary, include it. If you cannot follow instructions when responding to the ad, what will lead the potential employer to believe that you will follow instructions on the job?

3. Typically, the first person to receive the ad responses is an individual in the Human Resources department. This individual may or may not have written the actual ad, so to increase your chances of "making it through the first cut," use the exact words from the ad in the order that they appear.

4. My experience has shown that the comparative style of cover letter as discussed on pages 195 and 196 has a higher degree of success than other types of ad-response cover letters. The comparison format as displayed on page 192 versus its counterpart on page 191 indicates succinctness and directly addresses the requirements the company is looking for.

CHAPTER IV.

DEVELOPING YOUR OWN AGGRESSIVE JOB CAMPAIGN
BY
TELEPHONE

Calling Collect Is Not An Option.

N

UTILIZING THE TELEPHONE IN YOUR JOB CAMPAIGN

Time is a precious commodity these days – especially if you are unemployed. Therefore, you must make effective use of Alexander Graham Bell's marvelous invention – **the telephone**.

The telephone is a quick and effective means of developing and following up on contacts. To assist you in effective use of the telephone during your job campaign, I have put together the following guidelines.

THE CAR VS. THE TELEPHONE
(You Can't Beat the Odds)

Americans love their automobiles. This statement is also true for the job hunter. There seems to be an almost compelling urge to jump into one's car and go visit an office, see a plant, a facility, or an industrial park and actually visit the site where one hopes to get an employment interview. In a study involving countless non-exempt personnel, when asked how many sites they visited in a day – driving around visiting various industrial parks, office buildings, manufacturing plants, warehouses, etc., the typical answer ranged from four to six locations. Many believed that they could actually visit more.

When it was explained that once they walked into a particular office, they would probably be asked to fill out an application form and, recognizing that the two-to-four-page application would generally take between thirty to fifth minutes to complete, it became readily apparent that if an individual could actually visit six locations in one day, it would take an entire day. Since an individual never knows when a person might say, "Please take a minute to step into my office. I'd like to talk to you about an opening that we have," an individual must always be ready for an interview by being dressed appropriately. Interview dress is discussed on page 276.

Individuals that were diligent, organized, and had planned their day with a telephone book and a quiet place to make telephone calls found it easy to maintain a calling average of sixty companies per day. Some of these calls, obviously, were very short in duration. Others were longer. It became readily apparent to participants in this study that using the telephone instead of the automobile to develop sources for employment leads was easily ten times more effective: sixty contacts via phone versus six contacts by using an automobile.

The question then is raised, if this is such a more effective means to develop opportunity leads and potential interviews, why don't more people use the telephone? There is a possible double explanation. First, many individuals are apprehensive about contacting an individual they have never met or spoken with to tell he/she that they are seeking employment. The second reason is that very little thought goes into the telephone call. Typically, the job hunter asks something such as, "Is your company hiring?" When the response is, "No," the conversation is quickly over. The frustration of making fifty or sixty of these types of call per day increases one's anxiety level.

Another key point to consider is that when an individual drives around a particular location, there is strong evidence that he or she looks for large facilities – assuming that large facilities mean lots of employees and good job opportunity potential. If one were going to drive around the countryside looking at plants, one should never consider the size of the plant as an indicator of employment opportunities. Some of the largest plants are process-operated facilities such as chemical plants or warehouse/distribution centers. Both are excellent examples of large square-foot facilities with small employment levels. If one were actually going to make a visual inspection of the facility, it is easier to look at the size of the parking lot, number of cars, and whether the parking lot has a number of weeds and cracks, indicating low usage. Expressed simply, the more weeds, the fewer employees; hence employment opportunities would appear limited.

DIALING FOR DOLLARS

Remember that it is always advisable to cold-call by telephone rather than in person. Walking into a prospective employer's place of business seldom produces an interview. Using the telephone saves time, saves money, and permits the job candidate to contact many more prospective employers than if he/she cold-called in person. Keep in mind that attempting to contact business people **without** a prior telephone call or letter requesting an appointment is **not** considered an acceptable business practice.

The best time to place a telephone call is **fifteen minutes** before normal starting times or **fifteen minutes** after normal quitting time. This usually allows you to bypass the secretary and make direct contact with the decision-maker. If you happen to reach the secretary, ask the secretary what is the best time to reach the individual you are trying to contact.

DEALING WITH THE GATEKEEPER

Often you will encounter a receptionist or secretary who screens the calls. This person is called the "Gatekeeper," as she/he determines which calls get through. Obviously, the higher the person is in the organization, and the larger the corporation, the better defined the screening process will be. The best strategy for handling a third party who stands between you and your target contact is to level with them. The following is a suggested script:

Secretary: *"May I ask what this is in reference to?"*

You: (Pleasantly) *"I sent her a package last week and promised to call her at this time. Is she in?* (Your "package" was your resume and your cover letter.)

Even if the person is not in, the fact that you called when you said you would and properly left a message will score you points. **The probability of the target calling back increases when he or she is handed a message that says you called exactly when you said you would.** Ask the gatekeeper if he or she could suggest the best time for you to call back. If given a time, thank him or her and request the message be conveyed that you will be calling again at X o'clock (the time suggested.) Then, of course, do so.

If the secretary cannot suggest a time to call back, then offer one. If you are calling in the morning, choose a time during the afternoon. If you are calling in the afternoon, choose a time the next morning.

If the secretary is uncooperative, remain pleasant but professional. "She is very busy right now and will not be available for several days. May I take your name and number? I will see that she gets it." If you are confronted with this type of response or one that is even less informative, you have several options:

First, you can use the techniques of a super salesperson: state your business, using such words as, "I have a message of importance." Then, issue a polite order: "Kindly put me through to her." Or you can inform the gatekeeper that you will be calling back on such-and-such a day, at such-and-such a time. The day and time you select should be one day after the "busy" period. Or inform the secretary that you will send a follow-up letter. In essence, the letter will say, "When I called you last week, I learned that it was a very busy period for you. I will give you a call next Wednesday at 11:30 a.m."

Whatever you do, **DO NOT** make an enemy of the secretary. Secretaries are paid to do what they do and may frequently be confronted by overly aggressive, rude, or otherwise unprofessional callers. Stand your ground, remain unflustered and professional, and convey your intentions. Your professional demeanor does get back to the target person and will pay off in the long run.

Successful executives can tell by the way a caller treats their receptionists or secretaries whether or not they will want to get in touch with the caller. Callers, who behave as blowhards to the secretary and sugar and spice to the target, are revealing their true natures and will rarely receive respect from the targeted contact.

If the above strategy still does not get you through to the hiring or decision-making party, we suggest the following: First, call the switchboard of the company and ask for the normal office hours of the facility you are trying to contact. Second, if the office hours are for example, from 8 a.m. - 4:30 p.m., try calling at 7:45 a.m. In most cases, the person you are trying to reach is a manager, and most managers, assuming those at the Director/Vice President level, do not keep strict office hours. However, very few secretaries are at their desks at 7:45 a.m. While they may be in the building having a cup of coffee, their employers in upper-management are at their desks working.

When you contact the office switchboard to identify the normal office hours, take initiative and ask for the direct-dial number of the person with whom you wish to speak. Most corporations are switching to direct-dial systems, which is an excellent facility for the job seeker.

"OUT-OF-THE-BOX THINKING"

We have reviewed the calling patterns of thousands of job hunters. They fall into very distinct patterns. Specifically, most calls to a corporation come between the hours of 8 a.m. – 10 a.m. Therefore, if you are unsuccessful, we suggest that you look at your calling frequency and patterns of success. Consider putting in a call at 4:45 p.m. or later – even after 6 p.m. when the clerical and secretarial forces have generally left the building, leaving your targeted contact individual unprotected. The most frequent rate of success, in terms of calling patterns, generally comes in the last two hours of the day. We have also found that this is the period of time when most other people are suffering from the frustrations of engaging in the job search and have knocked off for the day. These two calling times, 7:45 a.m. to 8 a.m., as well as after 4:30 p.m., or the last two hours of the day, should enhance your rate of "connects" significantly.

TELEPHONE DOS AND DON'TS

Following is a list of telephone dos and don'ts. If you follow these tips, you will easily surpass 95 to 98 percent of all other job seekers in effective use of the telephone.

Dos	Don'ts
Come to the point	Ramble
Ask questions	Assume you know the answer
Accept the target's point of view	Argue
Compliment the competition	Knock the competition
Talk with them	Talk at them
Talk about the listener	Talk about yourself
Visualize the listener	Daydream
Sit erect (move around or even stand if it helps you)	Slouch in your seat
Control your emotions	Reach to their negativity
Smile while conversing (Why? Because it imparts a warmer tone to your voice. Try it!)	
Sell solutions	Sell hardware and techniques
Thank them	Hang up first
Talk from a location where there is no ambient noise, i.e., radio, stereo, little children, etc.	Talk with the speakerphone turned on
Have your resume next to the telephone	
Don't be afraid to "ask for the order," i.e., for an opportunity to meet	
Stay focused – prepare a telephone script if you have to (See the following page.)	

COLD CALLING USING
A TELEPHONE SCRIPT

Since most people are nervous about calling a stranger or an individual with whom they have never before spoken, I recommend that you prepare a script to assist you in getting over your initial nervousness. In addition to calming your nerves, having a script beside you when placing telephone calls will help keep your mind focused and attentive to the specific points about your background that you would like the individual to know. The following script is only a guideline, and each individual should prepare his or her own script according to his or her skills and background. **While you do not have to recite the script verbatim, it should be left by the telephone to help keep your mind focused when placing or receiving calls.**

Remember the principles of *"IDS"*

Identify: "Good morning, Mr./Ms. _____. My name is
_____."

Define: "I am calling to check on employment opportunities with your company."

Specify: "Specifically, I have _____ years of _____
experience with _____ in the areas of
_____ and _____." *(This is where you tell the person you are calling what it is that you are selling. Include as many accomplishments, skills, tools, and equipment as possible. It should come directly off of your resume.)* "I would like the opportunity to discuss my background with you or a member of your staff."

Using the principles of IDS reinforces your career accomplishments. Remember that this script should only be approximately fifteen seconds in length. Rehearse it so that your delivery flows smoothly and naturally.

At the end of your telephone conversation, ask for an appointment to be interviewed. Give yourself at least three days so that you can research the company.

UTILIZING THE TELEPHONE SUCCESSFULLY

Be Energetic: An energetic voice sets the tone of any conversation and shows you have good communication skills.

Be Natural: Use simple language. Avoid slang and highly technical terms.

Be Expressive: Speak at a moderate rate and volume but vary the tone of your voice to add vitality and emphasis to what you say.

Be Distinct: Pronounce your words clearly and carefully. Always speak directly into the telephone transmitter. If your telephone has a speakerphone feature, don't use it. Pick up the receiver.

Be Pleasant: Personalize your conversation by using the person's name.

Be Courteous: Good telephone habits are nothing more than good manners.

* REMEMBER *

Always have a copy of your resume by the telephone. Being prepared will assure that key facts, dates, and quantified accomplishments are never forgotten!

VOICE MAIL

The Scourge of Job Seekers

Of all the challenges that accompany a job search, one of the most frustrating is placing a business call to a specific individual only to have a recorded message tell you to leave your name and telephone number. This communication roadblock is so common that most callers are amazed when the living, breathing person to whom the call was placed actually answers.

In theory, companies installed **Voice Mail** to promote greater employee efficiency through more effective time management. The reality is, however, that voice mail has been used to screen calls, often preventing the receipt of information beneficial to the company. It has, therefore, become the job seeker's responsibility to find a way to complete the two-way communication circuit for the benefit of both parties. After all, your value could be of great interest to the organization.

STORMING THE BASTION

Just leaving a message does not ensure that a return phone call will be forthcoming. Moreover, leaving multiple messages does little to improve the odds. So then, how does one overcome the roadblock known as voice mail? The following will provide suggestions for doing just that.

- **CALL THE RECEPTIONIST AND ASK IF THE PERSON IS IN THE OFFICE:** If not, find out when he or she is expected back and call at that time. If yes, place your call(s) at more strategic times such as between 7:30 and 8:30 a.m., or during the lunch break, or after 5 p.m. Try calling on Saturday morning when executives may be in the office.

- **CALL THE DEPARTMENT AND SPEAK WITH THE DESIRED PERSON'S ASSISTANT:** Indicate that your calls have been answered by voice mail, and you understand that Mr./Ms. Doe is in the office today and wondered when would be a good time to call the person again. Place another call based on the assistant's recommendation. Start building rapport. The assistant could be very helpful in your quest.

- **ASK FOR THE PERSON'S EXTENSION OR DIRECT OFFICE NUMBER:** Having this information will allow you to call after the switchboard closes and greatly increase your chances of making the connection. In some cases, the call will go to a telephone that bypasses voice mail. Additionally, smaller companies sometimes install voice mail only on the department's main telephone number – the one that the receptionist normally answers.

- **CALL ANOTHER DEPARTMENT.** If the receptionist and/or assistant refuses to share the extension or direct-dial telephone number with you, call a different department. For example, if you want an individual in Finance, call Purchasing or Sales. Tell the person who answers that you were trying to reach Mr./Ms. Doe and could the person please share the correct number with you so that you won't be a bother again. Often individuals whose primary function is other than answering telephones, or who are not a part of the department you are trying to reach, will provide you the information you seek.

If none of the above suggestions enables you to reach the individual you seek, leave a carefully worded message. State your name and telephone number at the beginning. You may also increase your odds for receiving a return telephone call by allowing curiosity to work in your favor. How do you do that? In a pleasant but business voice, leave your name and telephone number with, "Please call me," and nothing else. Not knowing you or the purpose of the call will sometimes work magic.

> **THE KEY TO SUCCESS:** If you cannot reach your objective directly, go over, go under, or go around the obstacle. Giving up at the first roadblock is unacceptable.

ORGANIZING YOUR HOME OFFICE

Before you begin your job search, you should select a work area in which you feel comfortable and organize that area of your home in which you will place and receive business calls. It should be a quiet location, supplied with paper, pen/pencil, resume, calendar, telephone message pads, a listing of companies you have contacted by telephone or mail and newspaper ads you have responded to, as well as any network contacts you have made.

Organization is the key to effective follow-up. And effective follow-up on all correspondence and telephone contacts made in your job search is very important to a successful job campaign. If you are not organized and do not keep accurate records of companies and individuals you have contacted, or do not keep track of follow-up dates in your calendar, you will have so much information to keep track of that effective follow-up will not be possible.

Even though working out of your home is totally acceptable in today's world, when using the telephone from your home office, there should be no background noises such as a dishwasher, television, radio, children, etc.

ANSWERING MACHINES

Your first investment in your job campaign should be an answering machine. This equipment allows your telephone to be answered professionally at all times and gives you the ability to check your messages from a remote location. The message on your machine should be professional. This is not the time to be cute.

CALLER ID

With today's advancements in technology, caller ID has become a popular device. You come home one day to find on your caller ID the name and phone number of a company that you have sent your resume, but there is no message on your answering machine or a voice mail. What should you do? One suggestion is to look up the information that you sent to the company to find out the contact's name. Then pick up the phone and call him or her! It shows that you are assertive and outgoing. Explain that you saw the name and phone number on the caller ID and wondered if you might be of assistance. Ask for an interview. There was a reason why he or she called you in the first place.

HOW SOMEONE IN YOUR HOUSE ANSWERS THE TELEPHONE MAY COST YOU A JOB OFFER!

If you do not possess an answering machine or if other members of your household will be taking messages for you, you must instruct them on the importance of taking detailed and accurate messages. To help you, we have designed the following message sheet with prompts for the message-taker. Make copies of this sheet and leave them by your telephone to ensure that pleasant, professional messages are taken.

TELEPHONE MESSAGE

TO_____ DATE_____ TIME_____
("May I tell him/her who called, please?")

MR/MS_____ TITLE_____
    ("Would you spell your name, please? Thank you.")

COMPANY_____
    ("Would you spell your company name, please? . . . . Thank you.")

Please Call Back:__ Returning Call:__ URGENT:__ No Message:__ Will Call Back:__

"Would you like to leave a message?"

_____

_____

_____

_____

TELEPHONE NUMBER: (_____) - _____ - _____

"What is the best time to return this call?"   _____ _____
                                     (Anytime)   (Specified)
"Thank you very much."

MESSAGE TAKEN BY: _____

FOCUS TIME

     Take a moment to write your own personalized telephone script. Remember the principle of **Identify, Define, and Specify.** This is the key to successful telephone contact.

     You want to avoid sounding like you are reading from a script when you are making the telephone call, so be sure to make the script **sound** like you speak. The script will serve as a guideline and after making five or ten telephone calls, you will have automatically memorized it.

     Even after you have memorized the script, you should always keep it in a handy place to refer to during those unexpected or returned telephone calls.

CHAPTER V.

DEVELOPING EMPLOYMENT OPPORTUNITIES

THROUGH

A TARGETED DIRECT MAIL CAMPAIGN

The Road Less Traveled.

DIRECT MAIL
A BOLD AND DIFFERENT APPROACH

OF MICE AND PEN

It is often repeated that the pen is mightier than the sword. But the question today is, is the pen mightier than the mouse? Considering the number of pens in the world vs. the number of mice (plural of mouse), it would seem the lowly mouse would have a distinct advantage.

The world appears to be taken over by E-mail and the almighty mouse. A click here and communication becomes instantaneous. Throughout this guide, there are a couple of consistent themes that are reproduced in different variations. Marketing yourself in the same manner that everyone else markets himself or herself certainly allows you to be a prime candidate to be trampled on. On the other hand, I do not like individuals to stand out but to appear to blend in, to be part of a prospective team. So where do you draw the line? Considering the number of E-mails that businessmen and women are getting every day and the abuse of E-mail, it appears that job-hunting communication is just a mouse click away from being sent into oblivion.

Letters are unique. They are personalized. Sometimes I wonder if anybody really writes letters to anyone these days. Regardless of the truth of the foregoing statement, it is obvious that letters, not E-mail, have staying power. An open envelope with the letter withdrawn has the unique ability to reside on somebody's desk a lot longer than reports, resumes, and other documentation printed from an E-mail or certainly an E-mail display.

The problem with the electronic revolution is that anything has the potential of being just a mouse click away from dissolution. While I believe E-mail has a very important place in commerce and our society, I have always advised clients that if you use E-mail for your communication, you have no way of knowing whether your E-mail can be opened and therefore whether it was received. Coincidentally, it is always good business practice to put a hard copy in the mail as well. Letters have been, and still remain today, a very powerful form of personal communication. Their impact on today's commerce and society is greatly underestimated by people who are just joining the ever-soaring ranks of business today.

Bottom line – using hard – copy mail results in doubling your campaign efforts, once with E-mail, second with hard copy.

"OUT-OF-THE-BOX THINKING"

A direct mail letter is a targeted, convincing, one-page marketing letter that describes your major accomplishments and how these accomplishments might be of service to a potential employer. The difference between a direct mail letter and a cover letter is that **the direct mail letter does not include a resume**. The direct mail letter is longer, normally a full page that stands alone. A cover letter normally is only three or four paragraphs and "covers" or lies on top of an enclosed resume. A direct mail letter will typically be read while a resume with a cover letter will be skimmed! While this approach may seem new to you, I have found this method to be quite successful.

Direct mail is a technique based upon the premise that less is more. The average "read time" that a resume receives in the hands of a potential employer is twenty seconds or less. Knowing that only twenty seconds will be devoted to skimming the information contained in a resume and a cover letter, it is safe to assume that the key data and accomplishments covered in a resume will not be noticed in great detail. In a nutshell, resumes are skimmed. Letters are read!

It takes the reader an average of less than thirty seconds to read a one-page letter. There is another subtle point to be made here. When the recipient of the correspondence opens the envelope and a cover letter with resume falls out, the recipient immediately knows, without reading the correspondence, what the purpose of the communication is. Simply stated, someone is looking for a position. This is instantly known because why else are resumes sent? This early and immediate indication of the purpose of the correspondence is a key fact to generating the response to skim the resume. Conversely, a one-page letter does not by itself, when unaccompanied by a resume, "telegraph" its purpose. What happens next is that a strong motivating force takes over. The recipient's sense of curiosity says, "I can find out what this is all about in less than half a minute. All I have to do is simply read the letter." Therefore, the letter is read.

The strongest yet simplest means of separating these two approaches – direct mail, which is simply a one-page letter and a cover letter with resume – is that one document is usually skimmed (cover letter and resume) while the other is read (one-page letter). The bottom line is what type of input mechanism do you wish give to the recipient of your marketing communications? Do you want it skimmed, or do you want it read? If you vote for reading, then the direct mail method, if done properly, can generally develop more interviews than a cover letter with resume when sent together.

WHAT IS THE OBJECTIVE OF DIRECT MAIL?

The main objective of a direct mail letter is to get an interview by piquing the curiosity of the reader. In essence, the objective of the direct mail approach is the same objective as sending out resumes and cover letters: to get the all-important interview. The use of a one-page direct mail letter rather than the cover letter and resume approach is considered more effective simply because it gets the attention of the targeted reader.

It should be clearly understood that a follow-up response to using direct mail might be a request for further information (i.e., "We would like to have you send us your resume."). In a period of recession, when there is a great proliferation of resumes, this marks a creative and yet simplistic alternative to marketing oneself in a very positive manner. Additionally, it communicates the ability of an individual to write and express his or her thoughts in a coherent manner as indicated by the crafting of a well-written direct mail letter. Because of this latter point, this also becomes a powerful tool for those who may be changing career directions or the recent graduate who is looking for his or her first full-time job.

WHY IS DIRECT MAIL EFFECTIVE?

Direct mail is effective for a number of reasons. The primary reason that direct mail works so well is that it allows you to avoid the competition that exists in the published job market – those openings identified through ads.

Direct mail also affords you the opportunity to project your best image. Direct mail does not account for your entire work history like a resume does. The use of direct mail allows you, the writer, to selectively choose significant accomplishments from your background and communicate those accomplishments to the reader. The resume, by nature of its format, does not allow as much flexibility in communicating key accomplishments as a direct mail letter.

Direct mail also offers the best potential for you to obtain a position at a significant increase in earnings. The reason for this is that with a direct mail letter, you will be contacting individuals at the executive level, and these individuals have the authority to offer attractive compensation.

Direct mail is effective for individuals who are seeking to go into a new field. If you are looking to change careers or go into a new field, a resume will quickly highlight the fact that you have little or no experience in the new chosen field. However, the direct mail letter allows you to select the experiences and accomplishments that you want to communicate to the reader. It also allows you to highlight those experiences in your past that you feel will pertain or "translate" to your new chosen field.

WHY IS DIRECT MAIL NOT UTILIZED BY MOST JOB SEEKERS?

"IN-THE-BOX THINKING"   **VS.**   **"OUT-OF-THE-BOX THINKING"**

Most people do not use direct mail for several reasons. First, many are reluctant to put forth the extra effort necessary to write a strong, well-written direct mail letter. Admittedly, this *is* going to take extra time and effort. Second, many individuals have been trained to believe that the "almighty resume" is the best way to get an interview. Expressed simply, they have never heard of this concept. It is totally alien to most job hunters. Third, since direct mail letters are individually produced and resumes are mass-produced, the "easiest" way for people to market themselves is with a resume. However, along with networking, direct mail is one of the most effective methods to uncover employment opportunities. Finally, launching an effective direct mail campaign takes time, energy, and money. Most job seekers are unwilling to put in the time and energy necessary to write an effective direct mail letter and launch a direct mail campaign. Research indicates that the average unemployed individual spends less than two hours a day on his job campaign!

Direct mail can be an effective source of job opportunities if correctly executed. As a result of our firm's extensive experience in consulting on direct mail campaigns, I have established the following guidelines regarding the technique.

1. Targeting your direct mail letter to the highest-ranking officer at a particular site will always generate more results than mailing to any other individual in the company. (This could be a president, CEO, general manager, plant manager, etc.) For further information on reasons for contacting the senior-level executives, please refer to page 120, regarding Contacting Companies Directly. A mailing to the highest-ranking officer will always generate more results than a mailing to any other individual for the following reasons:

    A. Fewer people will actually write to a high-ranking officer. Most job seekers believe that writing to a president or vice president will not be an effective use of their time. Consequently, your chances of getting a response through the use of direct mail to a senior-level executive will increase significantly due to less competition. **DON'T DO WHAT YOUR COMPETITION DOES! YOU WILL BE TRAMPELED IN THE CROWD!**

    B. Even if the senior-level executive does not read the letter, he or she will route it to the appropriate department head for further action.

    C. Letters or memos received by subordinates from senior-level executives are acted upon with expediency. And equally important, they are read, not skimmed.

2. A mailing to individuals by name will always be more effective than a mailing to individuals addressed by title alone. Consequently, you will need to do the proper research to identify the name and title of the person you will be targeting with the direct mail letter. Remember that the highest-ranking officer at a particular location could be the Plant Manager, Division General Manager, or Vice President, etc.

3. A mailing consisting of a one-page letter by itself (i.e., a direct mail letter) will almost always produce higher results than a mailing, which consists of a cover letter and a resume. Direct mail letters should be limited to one page. However, if you choose to use monarch or executive-size stationery (7¼ x 10½") in your direct mail campaign, the direct mail letter could be a page and a half.

4. Mailings using a white or light shade of stationery, such as buff, seem to produce slightly better results than the same materials printed on other light-colored stationery. In addition, the use of bold, dark, or other strong colors will always lower your response.

5. When sending a direct mail letter, do **not** include your current compensation or salary in the letter.

RULES OF THUMB FOR MAXIMIZING DIRECT MAIL EFFECTIVENESS

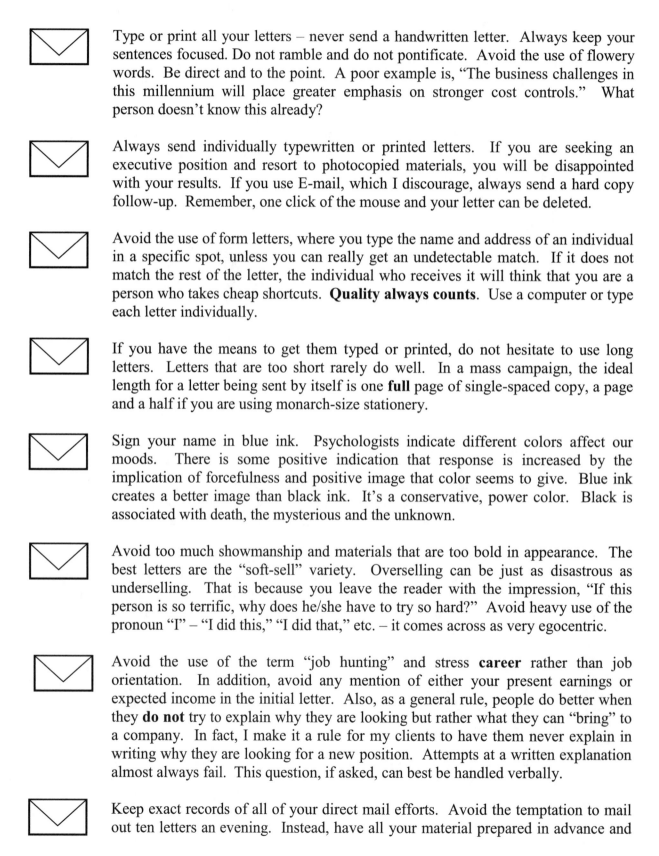

Type or print all your letters – never send a handwritten letter. Always keep your sentences focused. Do not ramble and do not pontificate. Avoid the use of flowery words. Be direct and to the point. A poor example is, "The business challenges in this millennium will place greater emphasis on stronger cost controls." What person doesn't know this already?

Always send individually typewritten or printed letters. If you are seeking an executive position and resort to photocopied materials, you will be disappointed with your results. If you use E-mail, which I discourage, always send a hard copy follow-up. Remember, one click of the mouse and your letter can be deleted.

Avoid the use of form letters, where you type the name and address of an individual in a specific spot, unless you can really get an undetectable match. If it does not match the rest of the letter, the individual who receives it will think that you are a person who takes cheap shortcuts. **Quality always counts**. Use a computer or type each letter individually.

If you have the means to get them typed or printed, do not hesitate to use long letters. Letters that are too short rarely do well. In a mass campaign, the ideal length for a letter being sent by itself is one **full** page of single-spaced copy, a page and a half if you are using monarch-size stationery.

Sign your name in blue ink. Psychologists indicate different colors affect our moods. There is some positive indication that response is increased by the implication of forcefulness and positive image that color seems to give. Blue ink creates a better image than black ink. It's a conservative, power color. Black is associated with death, the mysterious and the unknown.

Avoid too much showmanship and materials that are too bold in appearance. The best letters are the "soft-sell" variety. Overselling can be just as disastrous as underselling. That is because you leave the reader with the impression, "If this person is so terrific, why does he/she have to try so hard?" Avoid heavy use of the pronoun "I" – "I did this," "I did that," etc. – it comes across as very egocentric.

Avoid the use of the term "job hunting" and stress **career** rather than job orientation. In addition, avoid any mention of either your present earnings or expected income in the initial letter. Also, as a general rule, people do better when they **do not** try to explain why they are looking but rather what they can "bring" to a company. In fact, I make it a rule for my clients to have them never explain in writing why they are looking for a new position. Attempts at a written explanation almost always fail. This question, if asked, can best be handled verbally.

Keep exact records of all of your direct mail efforts. Avoid the temptation to mail out ten letters an evening. Instead, have all your material prepared in advance and mailed at the same time. With the exception of holiday weekends, the best day to mail is Tuesday. This way your letters will normally reach the contact on Wednesday or Thursday, which is the time when they are most likely to be at their desks and have the time to read your letter. Avoid mailing on a Friday – those items tend to arrive on a Monday. Monday is the heaviest mail-delivery day in the United States.

 While there is no single way to write a letter, you should outline your letters before you write them. The most communicative and persuasive letters are the ones that are alive, cheerful, and enthusiastic, as well as personal, warm, and human. They "read" like people speak. They sound like they were "individually written" for just one person. Materials that are detached or cold never seem to do as well, even though you may think they are professional.

 Based on our experience, there are certain times of the year when a direct mail campaign is most effective. These campaigns definitely have a seasonal nature. Their success rate apparently does not relate to the published job market or the amount of help-wanted advertising that appears each month. Our experiences show that January is the best month to launch a job campaign and June and July are the worst. A mailing in June will bring about half the response of the same mailing done in January. The chart below illustrates a direct mailing success-rate average by month using January as a 100 percent successful campaign month:

Month	Rate	Month	Rate
January	100	July	40
February	95	August	50
March	90	September	80
April	75	October	90
May	70	November	80
June	50	December	70

THE IMPORTANCE OF A FOLLOW-UP

If you do not hear from a firm in which you have particular interest, it might be worth it to you to have, depending on the size of the mailing, a selective telephone follow-up after three weeks. In your follow-up, you should restate your interest in the company and be sure to mention a contribution you feel you could make. A good follow-up plan sometimes brings results. In fact, you may wish to duplicate an entire mailing. For example, let's say that you sent a direct letter to the President of 1,000 consumer-product companies. If three months later you were to send a resume and a cover letter to the same people, you would normally get about 80 percent of the number of interviews generated by your first mailing. Remember, if the fish are not biting, do not change lakes or the boat – change the bait!

The following letter was actually drafted to be used in a direct mail campaign. It was the individual's first attempt at construction of a direct mail letter. Read it over and study it. What do you think?

MARK A. PAUL
1340 N. Park Road
Suite 183
Chicago, Illinois 60613
(312) 111-2222 ◄——— *Note:* This number was his work telephone number!

DRAFT – DIRECT MAIL LETTER

Date

Name
Title
Company
Address
City, State Zip

Dear _____ : (Insert contact's name)

This is really obvious!

A little too much pontification here.

"Education" has always, and will continue to be, an integral part of shaping our future. "Electronic Superhighway" is a new term for the infrastructure that will deliver information to our homes and offices well into the future. Both of these infrastructures are merging.

For the past five (5) years, I have successfully driven sales and intellectual property acquisitions for Prentice Hall's Higher Education Group. Working with internal editorial staff and key authors, I have identified, contacted, and signed in excess of twenty (20) textbooks and related instructional materials. The net result is anticipated sales of $2,000,000 over the next five (5) years.

Through a consultative approach to selling, I have successfully developed relations at multiple levels of the publishing process. I have identified and increased sales in new markets, as well as further penetrating strategic accounts. Over a five (5) year period, I increased sales by greater than 20% per year while industry growth was less than 5% a year during the same time span.

Prior to Prentice Hall, I successfully completed assignments with Burdines Department Stores as an Operations Manager and a Department Manager in a $20,000,000 store. I supervised eight (8) full time and three (3) part time seasonal employees and generated a 15% or $600,000 sales increase.

With an MBA in Marketing and over nine (9) years of diversified business experience, I am looking to be part of a dynamic team where my analytical skills and creative abilities will be maximized. I am also seeking a company position to take advantage of opportunities using technology to facilitate education and training. My research indicates that your organization may fit these criteria. I would be pleased to talk with you or a member of your staff regarding how my background and talents can complement your corporate goals.

Sincerely,

OK, but this sentence is not really necessary as the thought is implied since the recipient is reading the letter.

Mark A. Paul

On this page, you will find the same letter, edited and reduced. It still contains all the significant quantification of accomplishments and highlights Mark's career in a very succinct manner. Keep in mind that although direct mail letters are difficult for the "rookie" or the uninitiated to draft, they are well worth the commitment of time. The brevity of this letter ensures its readability by the intended recipient.

SAMPLE 28

MARK A. PAUL
1340 N. Park Road
Suite 183
Chicago, Illinois 60613
(312) 555-2452

> *The telephone number was changed to his home number to avoid the impression of a conflict of interest.*

Date

DRAFT – DIRECT MAIL LETTER

Name
Title
Company
Address
City, State Zip

Dear _____ : (Insert contact's name)

> *Short but hard hitting.*

The Print and Publishing media are no longer the "frontier" areas of education and training I seek.

I have committed myself to the following task for which I ask your assistance. I am seeking to explore career opportunities with a company positioned to take advantage of existing, as well as developing technology, to advance the process of education and training to new levels of performance and profit.

For the past five (5) years, I have successfully driven sales and intellectual property acquisitions for Prentice Hall's Higher Education Group. Working with internal editorial staff and key authors, I have identified, contacted, and signed in excess of twenty (20) textbooks and related instructional materials. The net result is anticipated sales of $2,000,000 over the next five (5) years.

> *These numbers say it all.*

Expressed succinctly, over a five (5) year period, I increased sales by greater than 20% per year while industry growth was less than 5% a year.

Prior to Prentice Hall, I completed four (4) years of direct sales experience, three (3) of which were in highly visible sales management positions. At 32 years of age, I am currently employed and have completed an MBA in Marketing.

May we talk?

Sincerely,

Mark A. Paul

SUMMARY COMMENTS ON DIRECT MAIL

When you design your direct mail campaign, you should try not to plan every possible detail of your work career. In fact, as you progress in your campaign, you should be ready to make adjustments if your response is not as expected. It is very important to keep in mind the following:

Only change your marketing materials in response to hard feedback, i.e., "I didn't understand that you actually had experience in the areas of _____, _____, and _____."

Otherwise, to change your marketing materials in the face of what you perceive as a poor response is really only shooting in the dark. Only change materials or adjust your materials in the face of hard feedback. Hard feedback does not mean changing margins one or two spaces, or putting the dates on your resume on the right side rather than on the left side.

There are some major risks in using direct mail. Over time I have found that it is not uncommon for professionals and managers at all levels to conduct mail campaigns that fail. When this happens, they typically lose confidence in their marketability.

Subsequent analysis usually determines that their failure stemmed from improper assessment of their target selection and inadequate quality or quantity of their materials.

Because I know of the time and care needed to create an attention-getting direct mail letter, I have included nine samples in this guide. All of these examples are excellent and had high response rates.

SAMPLE OPENING PARAGRAPHS FOR
DIRECT MAIL LETTERS

Dear _____: (Insert contact's name)

Seldom does a Regional Sales Manager have the opportunity to turn around a depressed market to the point where the region is 56 percent ahead of order budget and 35 percent ahead of shipments.

OR

Dear _____: (Insert contact's name)

Seldom does a company in a depressed market have a region that is running 56 percent ahead of order budget and 35 percent ahead of shipment budget.

OR

Dear _____: (Insert contact's name)

In one of the most competitive fields of them all – capital equipment sales – I have increased product sales and developed new products amounting to more than $30 million in the past twelve months.

OR

Dear _____: (Insert contact's name)

After ten (10) years of diversified line, staff, and management experience with IBM and the Construction Equipment Group of the FMC Corporation, I have decided to capitalize on my background and seek an executive management growth opportunity in the _____ industry.

OR

Dear _____: (Insert contact's name)

The Print and Publishing media are no longer the "frontier" areas of education I am seeking.

OR

Dear _____: (Insert contact's name)

Turning cost centers into profit centers for the Construction Equipment Group of a $150 million corporation was not an easy task. But it was accomplished!

Possibly you are considering the need for such an individual for your own organization. As Regional Sales Manager, I refocused the marketing and sales efforts of the region to maximize market penetration by . . . .

OR

Dear _____: (Insert contact's name)

During the past ten (10) years as a Sales and Marketing executive, I have generated millions of dollars in profitable sales of two (2) different Fortune 500 companies.

To do this, I have had to find new effective marketing strategies, create new selling techniques, and train and develop new and existing company and distribution personnel. Here are four (4) of my accomplishments, which required me to reorder priorities, develop new markets, and refine existing selling practices.

OR

Dear _____: (Insert contact's name)

If your organization is contemplating major business decisions for implementation in the coming year, possibly my ten (10) years of extensive experience in capital equipment and computers may be of assistance to you.

OR

Dear _____: (Insert contact's name)

As Regional Sales Manager for the Construction Equipment Group of FMC Corporation, I have successfully identified and subsequently introduced new capital equipment to new and existing markets in the eastern half of the United States and Canada. Possibly my background might be of interest to your firm.

SAMPLE CLOSING PARAGRAPHS FOR
DIRECT MAIL LETTERS

Perhaps you might be interested in talking about an opportunity.

Sincerely,

OR

At thirty-three, I am seeking a challenging opportunity where the rewards, both professionally and financially, are based on one's ability to produce. Should you have an interest, I would be pleased to hear from you.

Sincerely,

OR

From a distance, neither one of us can ascertain if what I can offer would be an enhancement to your operation. Therefore, if you have an interest, I would be pleased to hear from you.

Sincerely,

OR

Presently I am exploring career alternatives with an organization – large or small – where I can continue to be an integral part of an executive management team. If your schedule permits, possibly we could meet and explore areas of mutual interest.

Sincerely,

OR

To date, my career has included a number of progressively more challenging and responsible positions. If your organization has an interest in a highly motivated, profit-oriented sales and marketing professional, I would be pleased to hear from you.

Sincerely,

ROBERT T. THOMAS
1424 Main Street
Anywhere, State 99999
(765) 555-1212

SAMPLE DIRECT MAIL LETTER

Note: This letter is intended to be sent *without* a resume.

January XX, 20XX

Name
Title
Company
Address
City, State Zip

Dear _____: (Insert contact's name)

During the past twenty (20) years as a manufacturing and operations management professional, I have reduced costs by $4,000,000 for two (2) manufacturing companies. To accomplish this, I have had to identify and attack key productivity problems by building solid management teams and applying innovative problem-solving techniques.

As a Manager of Manufacturing Operations for Monroe Manufacturing Corporation, a $140,000,000 manufacturer of a diverse line of kitchen appliances, I have directed the redesign and modernization of a 150,000 square foot plant. To do this, I implemented a computerized process planning and standards system and put online NC and CNC machine tools, which resulted in a labor savings is $250,000 in the first year.

The redesign and modernization has resulted directly in increasing plant output by 9.9%, from $36,400,000 to $40,000,000, without the necessity of additional manpower. Furthermore, I reduced material scrap and defective workmanship by developing a new Quality Assurance program that saved the company $138,000 annually. Under my leadership, production increased by 50%.

Prior to Monroe Manufacturing Corporation, I successfully completed assignments for Burro Crane, Incorporated, as General Foreman, Foreman, and Lead Machinist, with supervision responsibilities for 110 employees and a budget of $4,000,000.

With a BS in Industrial Management and currently completing an MBA, I am interested in joining an organization – large or small - where my diverse manufacturing management expertise could be utilized. If you have an interest, I would be pleased to hear from you.

Sincerely,

Robert T. Thomas

SAMUEL A. SMITH
536 Longmeadow Circle
Anywhere, State 60174
(312) 555-1732

<u>SAMPLE DIRECT MAIL LETTER</u>

Note: This letter is intended to be sent *without* a resume.

January XX, 20XX

Name
Title
Company
Address
City, State Zip

Dear _____: (Insert contact's name)

In one of the most competitive fields of consumer products, I have increased product sales by 75% in four (4) years. I have developed merchandising programs that have generated incremental sales of $7,980,000 over the same period.

As a National Account Executive with Nationwide Cards, Inc., I had responsibility for two (2) national accounts with sales in excess of $12,000,000. I managed the national account activities of 95 Sales Representatives in 30 states. In the first eight (8) months of 1999, my sales were 16% ahead of the previous year, or almost $8,000,000. In addition, I directed the merchandising and installation of 38 new accounts in a three (3) month period. These accounts generated $1,100,000 in additional sales.

In previous positions, I established and executed master distribution plans, developed contact with shopping center developers, created pro forma operating and cash flow statements, selected store owners and operators, and directed the opening of new stores. While in this position, I increased market penetration significantly by generating $900,000 in new business.

I am seeking a challenging opportunity where the professional and financial rewards are based upon one's ability to produce. From a distance, neither one of us can ascertain if what I offer would be an enhancement to your operation. Perhaps we should meet and explore the possibilities of joining forces.

Sincerely,

Samuel A. Smith

ROSIE M. SHANNON
1424 Washington Avenue
Anywhere, State 99999
(765) 555-5429

SAMPLE DIRECT MAIL LETTER

Note: This letter is intended to be sent *without* a resume.

January XX, 20XX

Name
Title
Company
Address
City, State Zip

Dear _____: (Insert contact's name)

Your organization may have a need for a Senior Secretary with nine (9) years of diversified secretarial experience in the marketing and service departments of a major corporation.

I have a full range of secretarial skills including typing at 90 wpm, shorthand at 120 wpm, operation of software systems utilizing Word Perfect 6.0, Lotus 1-2-3, and dBase III, spreadsheets, and filing and am proficient in the use of electronic dictating equipment, copiers, fax, and telex machines. My excellent organizational skills are supported by the ability to work well against short deadlines. I also work well individually and as a member of a team.

In my recent position, I revised a division-wide cross reference master index and reduced the time necessary to research information by six (6) hours. In addition, I negotiated special rates with hotels and car rental services, reducing our department's travel expenses by 20% in 1999.

With a degree in Secretarial Science from the Institute of Business and currently working towards an Associate of Applied Arts degree in Business Administration, I am searching for an organization where I can make significant contributions to the operation, if given the opportunity. Perhaps we should meet and discuss mutual possibilities.

Sincerely,

Rosie M. Shannon

HAROLD J. CORONA
120 South Carol Street
Milwaukee, Wisconsin   53706
(414) 333-1111
HJCorona@execpc.com

SAMPLE DIRECT MAIL LETTER

Note: This letter is intended to be sent *without* a resume.

January XX, 20XX

Name
Title
Company
Address
City, State Zip

Dear _____ : (Insert contact's name.)

> *An overall good letter, but the opening sentence is not a grabber! Who does not know this? The opening sentence should impart information to get attention.*

Creativity, quality, and focus on the fundamentals are the essence of outstanding business performance. Over the last 10 years as a senior financial executive within the $80 billion worldwide consumer products businesses of UBR, Inc., I have:

> *Highlight accomplishments.*

- Directed both international and domestic acquisitions/divestitures as well as due-diligence teams ($5 million to over $4 billion).
- Led business turnaround situations including rationalizing manufacturing facilities and the establishment of a first-class management team.
- Developed strategic business plans for Ubermacher, a $7 billion wholly owned operating company of UBR, Inc.
- Established a worldwide corporate audit organization of over 150 professionals with 4 offices in Europe, 4 in the United States and 2 in Asia. Resulting in annual savings in excess of $13 million per year and the leveraging of best business practices.
- Solved accounting and finance issues including working capital and cash flow management improvement, capital expenditure forecasting and analysis, SEC filings (10K and 10Q), and the streamlining of costs.

> *Highlight prior experience.*

As CFO/Senior Vice President - Finance, Strategy and Information Systems with Ubermacher, I directed worldwide business building initiatives, (acquisitions, divestitures, J.V.'s, etc.) as well as the total finance, accounting, and IS functions. Earlier in my career, I led UBR's Worldwide Information Systems and Financial Analysis group as its Vice President.

> *Summary of Background.*

With 20 years of domestic & international consumer products experience and with a background in leadership roles in the functional areas of Finance, Controllership, Information Systems, Corporate Audit, and Strategic Planning, I am interested in joining a progressive organization that could utilize my expertise at a senior level financial position. If you have an interest in my background, I would be pleased to hear from you.

Sincerely,

Harold J. Corona

NORMA M. PANETELA
777 Career Drive
Hightown, State 99999
(555) 555-1234
Npanetela@dot.net

SAMPLE DIRECT MAIL LETTER

Note: This letter is intended to be sent *without* a resume.

January XX, 20XX

Name
Title
Company
Address
City, State Zip

Dear _____ : *(Insert contact's name)*

Link an "attention getter" to business.

Discusses recent work experience and accomplishments.

Teaching a $1.5 billion elephant to dance again is a rewarding experience, especially when one sees the bottom-line results. In the case of Millennium Melts, I got the elephant back up on its toes by galvanizing the organization behind a new business strategy and a completely overhauled marketing bundle.

As Vice President of Marketing for Millennium One, a $5 billion operating company of MLM, Inc., I not only reversed a five (5) year decline in the flagship brand, but also directed the launch of a multibrand line, which generated $386,000,000 in revenues, and a 53% share of segment. I have found that achieving multiple objectives while deploying $900,000,000 in marketing investment across a 25-brand portfolio and directing a 171-member department requires a clear sense of business focus and priorities.

Indicates broad perspective and prior experience.

With over 18 years of experience in various Marketing, Sales, and Finance positions, both domestically and internationally, my career has progressed with major companies including Unilever, General Foods, PepsiCo and MLM, Inc. I have earned my stripes and promotions to broader responsibilities in some of the most highly contested global consumer products categories, where sophisticated competitors with deep pockets demanded clear long-term strategies as much as short-term tactics.

Defines goals.

My career aspirations are now focused on general management, including Division or Company President, within the consumer products industry. If you have any elephants in need of a choreographer, I would be pleased to hear from you.

Sincerely,

Links back to statement in first paragraph.

Norma M. Panetela

JACOB J. ROBUSTO
3361 Innovation Lane
Tampa, Florida   33761
(813) 555-1212
JJrobusto@aol.com

SAMPLE DIRECT MAIL LETTER

Note: This letter is intended to be sent *without* a resume.

January XX, 20XX

Name
Title
Company
Address
City, State, Zip

Grab the reader's attention!!!

Grab reader's attention.

Dear _____: (Insert contact's name)

Build a better mousetrap and they will beat a path to your door! I built a better flytrap and the path has generated $50,000,000 in sales since 1988.

Emphasize business results.

As Director of Technical Development for Better Products, Inc., a privately held marketer of commercial and consumer products, I also launched a consumer model Electronic Fly Trap in five (5) months that will be mainstreamed into the ZAP product line. I have presented and closed the sale of the flytrap to McDonald's Corporation, Wal-Mart, K-Mart, and Target, with incremental sales of $4,000,000 and projected sales of over $12,000,000 within three (3) years.

Prior experience and recognized names.

Rethinking today's business was another way I generated profits for our division and largest client. I recaptured the $12,000,000 Wal-Mart account by taking a risky, but creative approach in presenting to Wal-Mart executives why we were the only company that could succeed in satisfying their needs profitably.

Ties close to opening of letter.

With a Ph.D. in Science and an MBA, I have positioned my career to bring together business, science, and imagination and have taken the risks to profitability. I am seeking to be part of an organization that wants to identify and market tomorrow's big opportunities ahead of the competition. If I can contribute to meeting your growth objectives, I would be pleased to hear from you.

Sincerely,

Jacob J. Robusto

The observant reader will note that examples of job campaign materials, specifically direct mail letters, from the "cigar trio" of Messrs. Corona and Robusto, and Ms. Panetela have now reappeared in this manual.

The reason for this is simple. These three cast members each enjoy a salary alone well in excess of $100,000. The decision was made in each of their respective campaigns to contact certain key corporations using the direct mail approach. Since no resume was sent to the companies in question, there was no need to draft a cover letter to corporations.

The other three members of our cast Robert Thomas, Samuel P. Smith and Rosie Shannon initially opted for the more traditional or "in-the-box thinking" approach of contacting companies with a resume and cover letter. Eventually, these three people were curious enough to try the direct mail approach; hence, copies of both types of materials have been included for your perusal.

Following are three more excellent examples of direct mail letters. Each of their authors took between two to four days to reach their final draft. If you should get writer's block, drop the project for a day and go back the following day. Let twenty-four hours clear the blockage!

SAMPLE DIRECT MAIL LETTER

Date

Name
Title
Company
Address
City, State Zip

Dear:

Grabs the reader's attention with a pop-culture image.

Captain Kirk of *Star Trek* fame once dared men *"to go where no man has gone before."* As a former Naval Officer aboard a "fast-attack" nuclear submarine, I have not only been under the Arctic ice, but I have also employed management skills on the battleground of consumer products marketing.

Nice transition.

Shows current position and results.

As an Assistant Brand Manager within the *Glade* division of SC Johnson Wax, a $4 billion privately held marketer of consumer and commercial products, I was instrumental in implementing a new marketing program for *Lasting Mist* air fresheners. It was one (1) of the company's newest products and technologies, which increased sales by 52% and market share by 38%. I accomplished this through supervising the production of improved package graphics, assisting with the evaluation/production of improved TV advertising, as well as analyzing and implementing a major price rollback.

Discusses prior position and results.

Prior to Johnson Wax, as a marketing manager intern within the American Chicle Group of the Warner-Lambert Company, I analyzed and identified large-scale sampling opportunities to build trial for the newly restaged *Clorets* brand of breath fresheners. In doing so, I also analyzed business opportunities with the potential to generate $500,000 of incremental sales for the Division from an under-utilized trade outlet.

Emphasizes advanced educational qualifications.

With an M.B.A. from the University of Michigan and a B.S.E.E. from the Navel Academy at Annapolis, I have positioned myself to take advantage of a very broad and diverse management background for success in business. I am seeking an organization that relishes creative and enthusiastic individuals who will move business forward. If you have an interest, I would be pleased to hear from you.

Sincerely,

Oh, no! This got past the "spell check," which is possible. Use the "Spell and Grammar" feature cautiously! In the final draft, this was spotted and corrected.

Name

SAMPLE DIRECT MAIL LETTER

Date

Name
Title
Company
Address
City, State Zip

Dear:

Uses an "attention-getter." Links career and accomplishment to opener.

Never before has death been so profitable. During the past eight (8) years as a consumer products research and development team leader, I directed the development of products that contributed to a $250,000,000 insecticide business. To accomplish this, I directed a multi-disciplined professional team of scientists, toxicologists, designers, engineers, and regulator affairs specialists.

Blockbuster number!

As a Research Associate and Worldwide Personal Repellent Team Leader for S. C. Johnson Wax, a $3,500,000,000 producer of consumer and professional products, I have directed development teams for RAID Fumigator, OFF!, and Deep Woods OFF! Skintastic product lines. To do this, I identified key technologies and developed reasonable timetables that allowed the critical path to product launch to be accurately followed. RAID Fumigator became a major profit center soon after its launch. OFF! Skintastic's demand exceeded supplies its first year of production. Under my direction, communications with marketing and upper management improved from previous team leaders and deadlines for product development were met or shortened.

Tells of current work and accomplishments.

Earlier in my career, I taught undergraduate chemistry at the University of North Dakota, Grand Forks. These courses included general chemistry, organic chemistry, and biochemistry for pre-medical students, engineers, nurses, and physical education majors.

Discusses earlier career.

With a Ph.D. in Organic Chemistry and extensive experience in team leadership, I am interested in joining an organization that will utilize my twenty (20) years of experience and where my technical, organizational, and people skills expertise could be utilized. Should you have an interest, I would be pleased to hear from you.

Repeats expertise to clarify career interests.

Sincerely,

Name

232

SAMPLE DIRECT MAIL LETTER

Date

Name
Title
Company
Address
City, State Zip

Dear:

"Attention-getters" generate interest!

Lambeau Field. Black Wolf Run. Augusta National. Pebble Beach. Only golfers and coaches knew the secret of greener grass until I successfully launched Seattle's recycled fertilizer to the multi-billion dollar retail market.

Discusses accomplishments, results, and how results were achieved.

As Market Development and Planning Manager for Seaorganite, I increased sales by 34%, making Milorganite the leading natural organic fertilizer. To accomplish this, I developed the strategic long-range plan that repositioned Seaorganite via a new packaging, brand development, target marketing, and an improved advertising message. To support the plan, I designed and directed market research that included focus groups, exit surveys, and phone questionnaires. Additionally, I nurtured relationships with garden writers and educators by designing a quarterly newsletter that increased media exposure by 44%.

Earlier in my career, I served as a business-planning analyst for Shopko/Super Valu Inc., conducting research and strategic marketing. In addition, I gained experience in sales with the Pillsbury Company.

Discusses accomplishments in prior positions.

With an MBA in Business, I am interested in joining a dynamic organization that will utilize my fifteen (15) years of diversified experience in strategic planning, market development, sales, advertising, promotion, market research, training, negotiations, and finance. If you have an interest, I would be pleased to hear from you.

Emphasizes credentials in this paragraph.

Sincerely,

Name

233

The following pages contain real examples of actual direct mail letters that were used in various job campaigns. As you review the letters, pay close attention to the following key points:

- The topic sentences in the first paragraphs of these letters are written in the form of a declarative sentence, not a question or interrogative statement. They tell the reader something he or she did not know previously. There are no "prying" types of rhetorical questions.

  When you initiate a direct mail letter with a question or a series of short questions, the writer is inviting the reader to respond with one or more "no's." Hence, the letter receives an early rejection.

- The topic sentences are "mind catching" – they make you think.

- The topic sentences do not pontificate or make a statement of one's philosophy. For example:

  > "The successful manufacturing company in the
  > new millennium will have put in place effective
  > cost controls."

  Who doesn't already know this? The above type of opening is a common mistake.

- The topic sentence should not be a joke or an attempt at broad humor but may provoke a "mental smile."

- The closing paragraphs are good examples of a "soft-sell closure."

- The text of each letter duplicates or uses excellent quantified accomplishments from each of the writer's resumes.

- The text of each letter uses the actual numbers as opposed to the alpha equivalent of the numbers to allow greater emphasis and visibility of the accomplishments described.

- Each letter is about five or six paragraphs and takes about half a page – not long! Direct and to the point.

The following twelve direct mail samples were selected because of their creativity and the fact that they came from a broad spectrum of business disciplines.

NAME
ADDRESS
CITY, STATE ZIP CODE
(AREA CODE) TELEPHONE NUMBER
E-MAIL ADDRESS

Date

Name   **SAMPLE DIRECT MAIL LETTER**
Title
Company
Address
City, State Zip

Simple but an effective opening letter.

Dear:

Managing 8,000,000 ounces can be a heavy job, especially if they are troy ounces of silver valued at $40,000,000.   As a cash manager, I did just that.

During the past three (3) years at ABC, Inc., I participated in the design, selection, and implementation of the U.S. domestic banking system that resulted in the annual savings of $250,000. This included implementing cash management services and cultivating banking relationships with Wachovia, Bank of America, Chase Bank of Texas, Wilmington Trust, and the Royal Bank of Canada. I also improved cash availability by facilitating repayment of $120,000,000 intercompany debt to the U.S. by providing the international holding company and foreign subsidiaries with monthly debt and interest expense schedules, including foreign withholding tax. Additionally, I monitored a $60,000,000 foreign currency-hedging portfolio, which eliminated the company's exposure to volatility.

Prior to ABC, I successfully participated in the management buy-out of BCD Inc. by providing extensive financial analysis for the public issuance of $110,000,000 senior notes. In addition, I was involved in all phases of transitioning the treasury function away from CDE Industries to independent activity under BCD, which produced annual cost savings of $100,000.

Being a Certified Public Accountant and a Certified Cash Manager, I am seeking a challenging opportunity that will utilize my ten (10) years of experience in corporate treasury and accounting. From a distance neither of us can determine if what I can offer would be of benefit to your organization. May I suggest meeting at your convenience to discuss possible opportunities?

Sincerely,

Name

NAME
ADDRESS
CITY, STATE ZIP CODE
(AREA CODE) TELEPHONE NUMBER
E-MAIL ADDRESS

Date

Name   <u>**SAMPLE DIRECT MAIL LETTER**</u>
Title
Company
Address
City, State Zip

Dear:

Nothing more straightforward than this!

I believe I can make more money for your company.

As a seasoned Sales and Marketing Professional with over 20 years of experience my accomplishments demonstrate that I have made money, cut costs, increased profit margins, increased market share and grew various product lines.

I grew my products from $0 to over $35,000,000 in three years. I reduced discounts and returns from an industry average of 12% to just over 1% during that time.

The marketing programs I have designed have taken advantage of opportunities to increase average system value while improving market share, leveraging the installed base and adding value through the exploitation of engineering excellence. These programs have encompassed both products and services.

My experiences have been both domestic and international, developing my abilities to function across ethnic and cultural boundaries. I have dealt with direct and indirect sales organizations and within marketing organizations. In a matrix environment, I developed abilities to work across organizations using problem solving and consensus building skills.

From a distance, neither of us can determine if what I can offer may be of benefit to your organization. If gaining an unfair share of your market intrigues you, may I suggest we explore possible opportunities in a meeting at your convenience?

Sincerely,

Name

NAME
ADDRESS
CITY, STATE ZIP CODE
(AREA CODE) TELEPHONE NUMBER
E-MAIL ADDRESS

Date

Name   **SAMPLE DIRECT MAIL LETTER**
Title
Company
Address
City, State Zip

Dear:

Tim Taylor of *Tool Time* always said *"**more power**"* would solve any problem. As Vice President of an engine division that produced lawn mower tractor engines, I directed the development and launch of a tractor engine that produced **25 HP**. This engine contributed $130,000,000 in sales and $35,000,000 in profits to the engine business. To accomplish this I directed a multi-disciplined group of manufacturing engineers, quality engineers, product managers, product engineers and bunch of talented folks on the shop floor.

As Vice President and General Manager of the Large Engine Division of ABC Corporation, a $1,400,000,000 producer of air cooled engines, I directed new engine product launches, warranty reduction projects that saved $10,500,000, scrap reduction initiatives that reduced rates by 20%, Kaizen workshops, employee involvement programs, supply chain cost reduction projects as well as ISO 9000 quality programs. All of these activities were accomplished through clear communication and solid leadership with the goal always being an improved bottom line for the two (2) plants I managed in Georgia and Alabama.

Prior to my last assignment, I successfully launched as Plant Manager a green field plant start-up for ABC. My job was to initiate operations that ranged from aluminum diecasting to the assembly and shipment of the final product with some stops in machining and plating along the way. Doing this in a small midwestern community with no industrial base made it even more challenging. The plant, however, was profitable in just eight (8) months.

With an MBA and 15 years of ever increasing P&L experience in the manufacturing world, I am interested in joining an organization that will allow me to do what I do best: lead a team to world class manufacturing status and make a lot of money for the company doing it. Should you have an interest in my background, I would be pleased to hear from you.

Sincerely,

Name

NAME
ADDRESS
CITY, STATE ZIP CODE
(AREA CODE) TELEPHONE NUMBER
E-MAIL ADDRESS

Date

Name   **SAMPLE DIRECT MAIL LETTER**
Title
Company
Address
City, State Zip

Dear:

Thus far in my career, I have contributed more than $300,000,000 in new business to my employers while exceeding profitability goals by 125 basis points. If your organization has a need for a management professional with a demonstrated record of achievement in strategic planning, business development, product/program development, marketing and project management, you may be interested in reviewing the following information.

As a Business Manager with ABC Corporation, the capital leasing and financial services division of a Fortune 500 Corporation, I developed new products and implemented new programs that generated over $100,000,000 annually in new business. While in this position, I created a long-term modeling and forecasting process, then initiated the first-ever, five-year P&L business plan for the $1,200,000,000 lease business group.   Additionally, my plan for a Syndication/Participation business initiative has been projected to increase receivables another $100,000,000 annually while providing business diversification and risk management.

Previously, in roles as an officer for financial institutions, including BCD Service subsidiary to the world's largest bank, BCD Bank, my strategic planning and business development skills were utilized in the development of $60,000,000 in capital lease opportunities. My talent for developing commercial leasing capabilities and incorporating the product line into the national sales focus provided for more than $50,000,000 in business opportunities and asset growth.

While in the role of Manager, Finance, with P&L responsibility and a $2,500,000 budget for the start-up CDE Credit, I led multiple projects designed to develop "best in class" products, systems, and operations processes. Through implementation of these competitive products, company receivables grew from $200,000 to $4,200,000,000 in just four (4) years.

With a degree in Finance and Law, extensive experience in commercial and consumer leasing and the finance industry, as well as professional certification, I am exploring opportunities that will allow me to contribute to an organization's profitability. If you have an interest in my background, I would be pleased to hear from you.

Sincerely,

Name

NAME
ADDRESS
CITY, STATE ZIP CODE
(AREA CODE) TELEPHONE NUMBER
E-MAIL ADDRESS

Date

Name   **SAMPLE DIRECT MAIL LETTER**
Title
Company
Street
City, State Zip

Dear:

    In today's competitive market, creating shareholder value is a primary mission of management. My 20 years of broad-based business experience in public companies has been focused on achieving this goal.

    At ABC Corporation, I created and led the Investor Relations function after its spinoff from XYZ in 1994. Under my direction, the Company established a strong reputation on Wall Street. More than 20 sell side analysts regularly published earnings estimates on the company and rated the stock buy. The stock appreciated from an IPO price of $19 to a high of $72.

    Prior to ABC, I was for 14 years with BCD Corporation, a telecommunications company. As corporate Vice President, Finance, I was responsible for $750 million of Wall Street financing, directing a subsidiary IPO, and leading Investor Relations during contentious merger with Sprint.

    At BCD, I directed corporate/strategic development activities and executed 25 mergers, acquisitions and joint ventures in high-growth communications businesses. In addition, I was a successful profit center manager, doubling operating earnings within a two (2) year time period.

    My record of achievement is supported with an MBA from the University of Chicago and a CPA certification.

    I am interested in applying my extensive senior level experience in a leadership role with a progressive organization. If you have an interest in my background, I would be pleased to hear from you.

Sincerely,

Name

NAME
ADDRESS
CITY, STATE ZIP CODE
(AREA CODE) TELEPHONE NUMBER
E-MAIL ADDRESS

Date

Name   **SAMPLE DIRECT MAIL LETTER**
Title
Company
Address
City, State Zip

Dear:

> *The art of progress is to preserve order amid change and to preserve change amid order.*
> Alfred North Whitehead, 1957

Effective organizational change is no different. Progress for any company as measured by reduced costs and improved profitability requires a strong business partner in its Human Resources function that will guide change while sustaining growth.

As the head of Human Resources for a $120,000,000 service organization with 2,100 employees, I developed strategies that enabled the organization to achieve the strategic objectives. This included reengineering, which identified $1,700,000 in cost reductions, an initiative that relied mainly on employee participation. By implementing gainsharing and management bonus programs, I aligned the compensation systems with this initiative.

A major focus of my role for the past five (5) years has been mergers, acquisitions, and joint ventures. I ensured that Human Resources facilitated these ventures that resulted in revenues increasing by $28,000,000. I assessed cultural differences of the organization, the impact on employees, and costs associated with benefits and compensation – both financial and emotional – and created solutions that were viewed positively by employees and cost effective for the organizations involved.

With over 14 years experience as a Human Resources professional with service and manufacturing organizations, I have led initiatives that directly impacted the bottom line.

If you have an interest in a senior level Human Resources professional who will drive results, I would be pleased to hear from you.

Sincerely,

Name

```
┌─────────────────┐
│   SAMPLE 44     │
└─────────────────┘
```

NAME
ADDRESS
CITY, STATE ZIP CODE
(AREA CODE) TELEPHONE NUMBER
E-MAIL ADDRESS

Date

Name   **SAMPLE DIRECT MAIL LETTER**
Title
Company
Address
City, State Zip

Dear:

If only Frank Lloyd Wright were here to experience it … new state-of-the-art computer-controlled comfort in his historical 1930s ABC corporate headquarters. During the past five (5) years, I directed this project and over $3.5 million in similar capital improvements for over 40 diverse buildings while cutting $1.5 million, or 30%, from my $5 million budget.

As a Manager of facilities for ABC, a $5 billion consumer products company, I strategically directed and budgeted over 188 mechanical related facilities improvements on time and 3% below budget. These improvements cut $500,000 in operating costs while improving comfort and reversing the corporate campus's rising energy consumption to a steady decline. For this, I received a company-wide team WOW award for innovating and implementing environmentally friendly solutions.

Previously, I successfully managed and engineered hundreds of projects as a consultant for BCD, and CDE Engineering, with cuts in capital and operating costs exceeding $1.5 million.

With a BSME and extensive experience in facilities innovative solutions, I am interested in joining an organization where my passion for helping and improving the lives of others will continue to make an impact. If you have an interest, I would be pleased to hear from you.

Sincerely,

Name

SAMPLE 45

NAME
ADDRESS
CITY, STATE ZIP CODE
(AREA CODE) TELEPHONE NUMBER
E-MAIL ADDRESS

Date

Name   **SAMPLE DIRECT MAIL LETTER**
Title
Company
Address
City, State Zip

                                        Clever!

Dear:

Delivering a COW to the Wisconsin State Fair sounds like a normal occurrence. Not when it's a 50 foot tall **C**ellsite **O**n **W**heels! As Regional Vice President for ABC, I directed sales and marketing efforts that contributed to a 400% increase in sales revenue in only 3 years.

At ABC, I directed all wireless operations in Wisconsin, the BCDComm paging operation in Minnesota, and the start-up of the Cleveland PCS market. With full P&L responsibility for annual sales revenue of over $140,000,000, I supervised more than 250 employees. Additionally, I grew market share in Wisconsin from 35% to 50% within 5 years while maintaining higher than industry average margins, growing the customer base from 40,000 to 360,000.

Currently, as Vice President-Sales for a start-up PCS "C" Block wireless telecommunications company, I established sales and customer care operations from scratch. In addition, I negotiated roaming agreements with over 25 carriers in North America and negotiated Clearinghouse agreements for processing roaming revenue.

Earlier in my career, I completed assignments for a 92-store national consumer electronics retailer. As Vice President-Merchandising, I oversaw over $200,000,000 in purchasing and merchandising/advertising of audio and mobile products representing 30% of the hard-goods retail chain operating in 10 states.

With a recent B.S. degree in Business Management, I am interested in joining a dynamic organization that will utilize my more than 20 years of wireless telecommunications and retail experience. If you have an interest, I would be pleased to hear from you.

Sincerely,

Name

NAME
ADDRESS
CITY, STATE ZIP CODE
(AREA CODE) TELEPHONE NUMBER
E-MAIL ADDRESS

Date
Name   **SAMPLE DIRECT MAIL LETTER**
Title
Company   ┌──────────────────────────┐
Address   │ *As you may recall, this*   │
City, State Zip   │ *oversight/error caused the* │
                                             │ *probe to crash on the*   │
                                             │ *surface of Mars.*   │
                                             └──────────────────────────┘

Dear:

 While NASA engineers could not make up their minds whether to calibrate the recent Mars probe in feet or meters, my group never has that problem; we always calibrate in dollars.

 Most recently as Vice President for ABC Corp. and previously at BCD Company, I directed the full technical support and Research & Development effort for a 900 person, $300,000,000 manufacturing facility, including 100+ technical professionals, 23% of which were Ph.D.'s, and managed a $20,000,000 annual budget. Practicing performance, not just promises, the following was accomplished:

- Developed or enhanced 10 products to improve market share from 27% to 29% of the $400,000,000 U.S. x-ray film market. This 2% market gain is worth $8,000,000 annually in new revenues.

- Nurtured, in partnership with another company, the invention of a new imaging system resulting in 3 U.S. Patents issued, with 6 still pending. Most importantly, this will bring in revenues, in its first full year, of $13,000,000.

- Successfully implemented product technology enhancements, yield improvements, process recycling programs, and improved product quality and consistency. **Net Results:** Reduced raw material costs by over $10,000,000 annually and reduced customer complaints by 60%.

- Increased capacity of polyester film manufacturing by 15% via reduction of downtime losses and increased throughput, without capital investment.

- Exceeded regulatory requirements by reducing volatile organic compound emissions by 54% and OSHA recordable injury rate from 1.6 to 0.6 per 200,000 exposure hours.

 From a distance, neither one of us can determine if what I can offer would be an enhancement to your business. Therefore, if you have an interest in exploring areas where I might contribute to your profitability, I would be pleased to hear from you.

Sincerely,

Name

```
┌─────────────────┐
│   SAMPLE 47     │
└─────────────────┘
```

NAME
ADDRESS
CITY, STATE ZIP CODE
(AREA CODE) TELEPHONE NUMBER
E-MAIL ADDRESS

Date

Name   **SAMPLE DIRECT MAIL LETTER**
Title
Company
Address
City, State Zip

Dear:

Convincing companies including 3-M, General Mills, Pepsi, and Sony to throw out their packaging line inkjet systems was a tough sell … considering that capital outlay for laser coder technology is four (4) times greater. During the past three (3) years, however, I have successfully displaced 400 competitive systems.

As a marketing and product management professional with an engineering background, I have extensive experience in business-to-business sales of technology based products and capital equipment, strategic planning, and introduction of new products for companies such as ABC subsidiary of BCD Corporation, and CDE, Inc.

In my most recent position as Product Manager, I successfully directed the marketing effort for a technology-based machine that is integrated into high-speed packaging lines. With 25% annual growth, my initiative catapulted the company to be recognized as the world's leader in the manufacture and sale of laser coders, capturing 45% of the global market share.

My degree in Mechanical Engineering, coupled with marketing and business development experience, provides me with a unique background not readily found in the packaging industry. I am currently exploring career opportunities that will allow me to contribute to an organization's profitability. Should you have an interest in my background, I would be pleased to hear from you.

Sincerely,

Name

NAME
ADDRESS
CITY, STATE ZIP CODE
(AREA CODE) TELEPHONE NUMBER
E-MAIL ADDRESS

Date

SAMPLE DIRECT MAIL LETTER

Name
Title
Company
Address
City, State Zip

Dear:

    Embarrassing household odors can be very profitable, especially when you can gain market share leadership of the fast growing domestic scented candle market. That was the result when I directed the $120,000,000 XYZ Candle brand and launched the #1 and #2 selling candles in the United States.

    As a Senior Brand Manager with ABC Corporation, a privately held $6 billion worldwide consumer products manufacturer, I directed the $210,000,000 WYX business, growing the brand to a 63% market leader share and delivering profit growth. To accomplish this, I directed a marketing strategy focused on extending product use, leading cross-functional teams to launch new products, and developed equity-building advertising.

    Previously, with BCD Company, an $8.3 billion international consumer product marketer, I developed strategies to grow the sales and profit of market share leaders in the food industry, including EFG Candy and FGH Nuts. Additionally, I directed the $100,000,000 GHI Gum brand, including budget and P&L, and increased profitability by 240%.

    With over 14 years of marketing and sales leadership with Fortune 500 companies, my career interests are now focussed on joining an organization that shares my passion for growing brands in a senior marketing leadership role. If you have an interest, I would be pleased to hear from you.

Sincerely,

Name

NAME
ADDRESS
CITY, STATE ZIP CODE
(AREA CODE) TELEPHONE NUMBER
E-MAIL ADDRESS

Date

Name   **SAMPLE DIRECT MAIL LETTER**
Title
Company
Address
City, State Zip

Dear:

      Alfred Korzybski was right – "either-or" thinking limits success. At ABC Corporation the paradigm that creative, original new products could only be developed internally was *"King"* – until I led the Personal Care product development team that created 22 men's grooming products for the Trim® line in less than 8 months by creatively combining internal leaders with outside technical resources to form a strong development partnership. Today, more than three-fourths of total Trim® sales depend on technology developed by this partnership.

      As a senior technical executive, I have delivered new products to global businesses in seven (7) ABC Corporation categories. Previously, after returning from the Shanghai joint venture where I integrated 11 separate sections at 3 sites into a single R&D division, I formed and led an executive team to the successful conclusion of a $2,000,000 study of a new product development process. We – the R&D executive committee – implemented these results to develop a renewed and more vital R&D organization, which is now more strategically focused and faster to market by 15%.

      My career with ABC Corporation, and earlier with BDC Clinic, has been challenging and fulfilling. I have developed and led executive teams, leading as many as 142 scientists and engineers with R&D budgets of over $20,000,000. As the senior technical member of U.S. and International business teams, I have brought a broad technical understanding of R&D to the development of an integrated business and technology strategy, an appreciation of the need for speed, focus, and accountability in the R&D process – and an ability to develop an organization that can deliver those critical attributes.

      I am seeking a senior technical executive position that takes advantage of my technical breadth and strong business management expertise. From a distance, neither of us can discern whether my background would be of value to your organization. If you are interested in exploring that probability further, I would be pleased to hear from you.

Sincerely,

Name

SAMPLE 50

NAME
ADDRESS
CITY, STATE ZIP CODE
(AREA CODE) TELEPHONE NUMBER
E-MAIL ADDRESS

Date

Name   **SAMPLE DIRECT MAIL LETTER**
Title
Company
Address
City, State Zip

Dear:

Traveling up the Amazon in search of a supply source and negotiating with 60 non-English speaking Czech dairy farmers were just two (2) of the challenges I faced in order to deliver savings of $65,000,000 to national and international corporations. If results such as this could be beneficial to your organization, you may be interested in reviewing the following information.

Most recently, as Senior Vice President of Manufacturing with ABC USA Inc., I implemented manufacturing and supply chain strategies that identified operating savings of $30,000,000 and inventory reduction potential of $18,000,000. Additionally, my implementation of integrated manufacturing strategy and performance measurement increased output by an average of 30%.

In a previous position with MNO Consumer Division, as Global Vice President of Manufacturing and Product Supply, I introduced a global purchasing strategy that saved $10,000,000 in the first year. I also re-structured the organization to focus on the supply chain; introduced consolidated demand planning and scheduling; and achieved customer service levels in excess of 98% across the board. Essentially, the company changed from a production driven to a customer service driven organization.

As Operations Director in Central and Eastern Europe for XYZ, Inc., I led the re-structuring of manufacturing operations, integrated the regional supply chain and implemented a manufacturing acquisition strategy. Among other improvements, this produced initial purchasing savings of $1,000,000 from the dairy farmers and reduced total overall operating costs by 9 percentage points.

My goals throughout have been to exceed customer expectations, achieve significant supply chain performance improvement and low cost operating status. I would welcome the opportunity to discuss with you how my skills and experience might assist you in improving product margins and bottom line performance.

Sincerely,

Name

247

NAME
ADDRESS
CITY, STATE ZIP CODE
(AREA CODE) TELEPHONE NUMBER
E-MAIL ADDRESS

Date

Name   **SAMPLE DIRECT MAIL LETTER**
Title
Company
Address
City, State Zip

Dear:

I had a drug problem. Actually I had hundreds of them. As the Senior Supply Chain Executive for both ABC Corporation and earlier with XYZ Corporation's international consumer business, costs were too high due to the lack of purchasing, production and distribution synergies. Here are some examples that highlighted my success in solving these problems.

In my position with ABC Consumer Division, as Global Vice President of Manufacturing and Product Supply, I introduced a global purchasing strategy that saved $10,000,000 in the first year. I also re-structured the organization to focus on the supply chain; introduced consolidated demand planning and scheduling; and achieved customer service levels in excess of 98% across the board. Essentially, the company changed from a production driven to a customer service driven organization.

As Head of International Operations Services with the Consumer Brands Division of XYZ, I combined specific consumer and pharmaceutical operations, saving $7,000,000. A global redesign of operational strategy led to manufacturing consolidation, business process reengineering and performance improvements. These collectively ensured divisional profit growth in excess of 15%. Additionally, I also implemented operational support and supply chain integration initiatives with Australian licensees which provided the reduced operational cost basis that secured a $10,000,000 re-investment program.

My goals throughout have been to exceed customer expectations, achieve significant supply chain performance improvement and low cost operating status. I would welcome the opportunity to discuss with you how my skills and experience might assist you in improving product margins and bottom line performance.

Sincerely,

Name

When I present the concept of direct mail versus the mailing of a cover letter and a resume, almost all my clients are intrigued and recognize the strength of using this strategy of direct mail versus the resume approach. This, of course, does not mean that you won't need a resume, as many times the direct mail letter sparks great interest, and the prospective employer will require a copy before an actual interview is established. But, the door has been opened.

Those who have elected this strategy almost universally encounter the problem of getting past the first paragraph. Specifically, more time is spent being creative without being comical to develop an interesting, eye-catching, mind-grabbing first paragraph. Because this is the most difficult part of constructing a direct mail letter, listed are some additional opening paragraphs. These paragraphs are presented to show how people from a variety of professions in the business have expressed their mind-grabbing opening paragraphs. They are presented only as examples and you, of course, should develop your own paragraph.

I was told, "don't drive like a woman" when I climbed aboard Volvo's 40-ton, 350 hp, 6-speed, and largest articulated hauler for a little test drive. That was just one of the things I did to bridge the cultural gap when I became the first female Vice President of Human Resource for Volvo Construction Equipment North America, a $700,000,000 NAFTA business unit of AB Volvo Group.

*****

Creating a cherry red, turbo-charged, 440-horsepower, four-wheel drive (4wd), quadtrac tractor from a vision is not impossible; it's profitable. During the past four years, as the Director of Information Services (IS), Strategic Planning, I reengineered a global product-change process, which contributed to a $10 billion Agricultural and Construction Equipment business. To accelerate the new reengineered process, I directed the collaboration of a cross-functional, cross-continental team that is implementing an Enterprise Product Data Management (ePDM) system.

*****

To paraphrase Peter Drucker, management guru, "Instead of trying to optimize the future by looking at the trends of yesterday, planning should aim to exploit the new and different opportunities of tomorrow." This philosophy has been the foundation of the planning processes that I have used to produce significant growth.

*****

The sound of Customer Inertia: "We Never Did That Before," or "We Have Always Done It This Way." By leveraging rather than fighting it, I have successfully grown sales channels to achieve rapid bottom-line results.

*****

Forecasting smooth sailing for business in Latin America during hurricanes, presidential elections, and currency devaluation is no easy task. As challenging as that was, setting the course and reaching the destination with sales of $150,000,000 made it worth the trip.

To be successful in a highly competitive business environment, mountains need to be moved and landscapes need to be changed. With Engineering and Operations responsibility for a $1.5 billion product line, I have done just that.

*****

The bottom line, increase wallet share! Who would have thought that financing a competitor's product would be growth opportunity? Yet I found this to be worth $868,000,000.

*****

When *CFO Magazine* recognized our shared services center with its prestigious REACH Award for excellence in process reengineering, it was the capstone of a strategic finance initiative that saved $25,000,000 annually for Call Corporation.

*****

Wouldn't it be great if all of the problems encountered during product launch and use by the customer could be anticipated and prevented? For the last 15 years, I have been doing just this by incorporating the teachings of Dr. Genichi Taguchi on Robust Design.

*****

The task of propelling the world's fourth largest navy at Disney World in Orlando brings tough reliability and performance demands. With a new innovative strategy, I integrated commercial engine requirements and improvements with Disney's world-famous preoccupation for service. This new program displaced competitive makes and helped the first American "environmentally green" marine engine become the industry benchmark for durability.

*****

Seldom does an 83-year-old company increase its gross bookings from one year to the next by over 60%, but it's even more uncommon in a mature, depressed industrial market. Yet, that's exactly what I accomplished at Green Bay Gear Company.

*****

To win long-term customer loyalty through improved product quality and reduced costs, I've had to go beyond typical off-the-shelf programs. Implementing a responsive "customer-first" mentality has brought about a culture change both on the shop floor and in management that has delivered bottom-line savings of over $15,000,000.

*****

In one of the most intensely competitive markets of all, Metropolitan Detroit, I initiated and implemented strategic account business plans focused on consultative, relationship-based selling that resulted in a sales increase of 157%, or $3,000,000, in 3 years.

*****

Convincing an established staff in a profitable plant of 500 people to create new business units and adopt lean manufacturing was not easy. Yet, I implemented a team-based strategy that increased market share by 5% and reduced total manufacturing costs by $14,500,000.

Beverages and shower cleaners have a lot in common. Both need to be easy to use and deliver results. By applying the joint principles of convenience and performance, I led the cleaning products R&D organization to deliver $70,000 in new products in one (1) year. To accomplish this, I applied my experience as beverage and food R&D executive to lead the Home Cleaning R&D organization.

*****

Seldom does a transactional attorney have the opportunity to spinoff its company, develop four (4) new financial products, integrate the company subsequent to acquisition, and raise funding in excess of $12 billion in a six (6)-year span.

*****

Over the past 20 years, I have led the development of 85 new medical diagnostic products. By focusing on reliability, process efficiency, and speed-to-market, I have balanced the objectives of quality, cost, and timing to generate substantial revenue and profits.

*****

It has been said that to be successful in sales requires thick skin. Nowhere is it more evident than in the leather industry. Selling to such diverse end users as Harley-Davidson, Nike, Ping, Jansport, and Wells Lamont requires persistence and creative sales strategies.

*****

When I was asked to start a research library at Johann's Service Company in 1973, I could not have foreseen what it would become 27 years later. From a small conference room with a hundred books and journals for a handful of scientists and engineers, it grew to include four networked libraries in Wisconsin and Michigan serving more than 100,000 worldwide employees of the now $12 billion Johann's Controls Inc.

"BAITING THE HOOK"

When to Use a Direct Mail Letter
vs.
a Cover Letter With Resume

In developing your personal job-search marketing strategy, you will need to decide when to use a targeted direct mail letter or when to send a cover letter with a resume in contacting prospective employers. This is known as how to select the right "bait for your hook."

A direct mail letter is written to get the attention of a prospective employer. It is sent **without** a resume, since a letter is read while a resume is skimmed. Your intent is for a prospective employer to read your letter and contact you to learn more.

A cover letter is written to be sent **with** a resume. It "covers" the resume, serving as an introduction to your employment history and accomplishments.

The following are considerations to help you decide which letter strategy is right for you.

1. **Define Your Purpose:** What is your objective when you send correspondence to a perspective employer? Is it to inform the reader that you are seeking a new position, or is your real purpose to generate a response from that employer? Your objective should always be to create action, not simply to provide data to be filed.

   With an action as your goal, you must use a strategy that will ensure that your correspondence, first and foremost, is read. Individuals will read an organized, to-the-point, one-page direct mail letter but will likely skim or place to the side correspondence of three or more pages (cover letter with resume).

   A direct mail letter in most cases is an effective means to get the response you desire – a request for an interview. It gives enough information to pique interest in you, but not enough to answer all the questions about your employment history. Therefore, it leads to a call and an interview.

2. **Attract Attention:** Think of your accomplishments and your area(s) of expertise. If you have skills and results that will help solve common business problems or create innovations in an industry, you can develop a direct mail letter that will create resonance with your reader. This is a type of "bait" or "lure" that will catch the eye and result in a call or request for more information about you.

   Case Sample: In the previous direct mail example, a product manager wanted to attract attention to his accomplishments in the successful marketing of an insect spray. His direct mail letter began, "Death has never been so profitable . . . ." He attracted attention and received calls as a result.

3. **Career Focus:** A direct mail letter can be used to emphasize certain aspects of your career.

> Case Sample: A Sales Coordinator had varied experience in customer service, inside sales-support training, and direct sales. His most recent job had been in training sales people. However, he now wanted to pursue a career in sales. His strategy was to write a letter that accentuated his sales achievements and ability to develop customers. His other experience (training and sales support) was mentioned only as a foundation for his selling skills. As a result, he received calls and requests for interviews. Had he sent his resume with a cover letter, he would have diluted his message.

Use the direct mail letter when you want to zero in on one part of your career.

In another case, a Quality Assurance engineer had extensive background in computer applications to improve production systems. His direct mail letter highlighted his computer expertise and accomplishments versus his quality and inspection positions.

4. **Career Shift:** If you would like to build on your experience from one part of your career history, use a direct mail letter.

> Case Sample: A Production Supervisor had some experience in Total Quality Management (TQM) and Statistical Process Control (SPC) training but never had a job title that reflected these responsibilities. Her strategy was to write a direct mail letter to embellish this part of her work history. Again, her resume would not have the strength or focus that she created in the letter.

5. **Create a Common Theme:** If you have had several jobs that are seemingly unrelated, your strategy in a direct mail letter would be to create a common theme.

> Case Sample: A Purchasing Manager had experience in banking as a credit analyst, had installed commercial alarms, had performed personnel duties, and had been responsible for packaging and purchasing functions. His strategy was to create a consistent thread by pulling his experience together into a set of diversified business expertise targeted at small, growing companies. He appealed to the entrepreneurial owner of a business who needed assistance in managing the internal operation of her business.

6. **Limit Your Liabilities:** Use a direct mail letter to minimize perceived liabilities in your background. Certain readers may perceive gaps in employment, a short tenure at a company, an unrelated career deviation, demotions, or indicators of age as liabilities. A direct mail letter can be written to "accentuate the positive and eliminate the negative." A cover letter with resume provides a full front photo of you; a direct mail letter is your best profile.

7. **Dare to be Different:** Sending a direct mail letter will be different than what 99 percent of your competition will think of doing. That alone makes direct mail a strategy to consider as part of your marketing campaign.

8. **Don't Put a Return Address on Your Envelopes:** Regardless of the type of mailing you use – direct mail or resume with a cover letter – omit your return address.

It is almost impossible to have a large, 100 percent accurate database of correct names and titles to contact. If the person you sent your marketing materials to is no longer at the addressed company, (possibly because of retirement, reassignment, transfer, death, voluntary separation, etc.) you want the person who has taken his/her place to open your correspondence.

Placing a return address on an envelope ensures that the letter will be returned to you, but what good will that do? You will only throw it away. Most business people routinely read the mail of their predecessor if not marked confidential or forward it on to his/her new location if he/she has remained with the company.

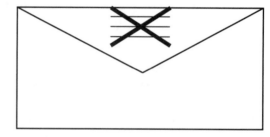

When Should You Consider Using a Cover Letter with a Resume as Your Strategy?

If You . . .

Are a Technical Wizard: If you are a highly skilled technical professional with extensive experience in specific technologies, use a cover letter with a resume. A computer software developer or a hardware specialist would fall into this category. Your reader will want to know the details only your resume can communicate.

Have Secretarial Expertise: You have solid secretarial experience in several organizations. However, your responsibilities were very similar in each position. The cover letter with a resume approach may be best for you. The reader will want to know the "what," "when," and "where" of your career history, which is clearly outlined in your resume. The cover letter should highlight your word-processing skills and a number of your accomplishments. The resume will give the details.

Are a Production Pro: If your experience is in production or assembly manufacturing, consider the cover letter with a resume approach. Highlight your summary of experience in your cover letter and enclose the resume with your production background.

Want to Change Your Bait: If you have sent a direct mail letter and have not heard from some of your prospects in three months, consider rewriting your letter to generate interest or send a cover letter with a resume. **If the fish did not bite with one lure, change the bait.** A low response from direct mailings does not mean that these are the wrong target companies, or that they may not need a person with your skills. It simply means that you did not get their attention with your first approach. So, cast again! Persistence pays off in both fishing and employment.

These considerations will help you determine the right approach for you.

ORGANIZING YOUR MAIL CAMPAIGN

In order to help you remember which letters include resumes and/or salary in your mailing efforts, please refer to the following chart:

TYPE OF LETTER	RESUME INCLUDED	SALARY INFORMATION INCLUDED
Direct Mail or Broadcast Letter	No	No
Employment Agency or Search Firm Cover Letter	Yes	Yes
Ad-Response Cover Letter	Yes – If requested	Yes – If requested
Network Cover Letter	Yes	No
Cover Letter to Corporations	Yes	No

FOCUS TIME

Please stop and write your direct mail letter to corporations. As you write this letter, keep in mind the following tips:

1. This letter will require extra effort. Take the necessary time to compose it well because it is one of the most effective methods of uncovering employment opportunities.

2. The ideal length of this letter is one full page of single-spaced copy on standard-sized stationery.

3. Avoid using the term "job hunting." Stress career rather than job orientation.

4. Avoid any mention of either your present earnings or expected income in your initial direct mail letter to an organization.

5. Do not attempt to explain "why" you are looking.

6. Most importantly, quantify your accomplishments – use numbers, numbers, and **more numbers**. Remember that **results count**.

7. Direct mail letters work. They are different, they inspire curiosity, and they are read while resumes are only skimmed. Plus there is one additional interesting fact that cannot be disputed. A well-written and targeted direct mail letter will have staying power. It will reside longer on an executive's desk than a three-page resume and cover letter that will have the tendency to be moved off the executive's desk faster.

IMPORTANT
A Special Note From the Author

During the first week of October 2001, several individuals and organizations within the United States started receiving mysterious envelopes with threatening letters, which also contained various amounts of the disease Anthrax. Besides infecting a limited number of individuals with this disease, a further repercussion was the response by the United States Post Office. This response included an admonishment to individuals to review their mail with a certain degree of caution. The general public was advised to treat with suspicion envelopes that did not carry return addresses or whose postmark did not match the city of the return address.

The preceding pages in this chapter advised people not to put a return address on correspondence simply because if the intended recipient has moved on, retired, or is no longer at that company, we wanted the correspondence to be opened by the intended recipient's successor. In light of the recent tragic events and until these events have been successfully resolved, such strategy would not be deemed appropriate. Therefore, I am suggesting that all correspondence carry a return address and home telephone number with area code and that said correspondence should be mailed from the same city as the residence of the sender.

CHAPTER VI.

WHEN
YOUR JOB SEARCH
LACKS RESULTS,
ARE YOU POINTING
YOURSELF IN
THE
RIGHT DIRECTION?

**Maybe It's Time
To Check Your Bearing.**

N

WHAT IS YOUR ETA?

I think every one of us, at one time or another, has taken a trip to an unfamiliar destination and experienced a certain amount of doubt as to whether we are going in the right direction. This is especially true, if the route we have selected to reach our destination is lacking in highway legends, markers or signposts. The longer we travel without those reassuring guideposts to indicate just how far our destination is, the greater our doubt is that we are on the correct path. And so it is with job hunting. Each job hunter has his/her unofficial estimated time of arrival (ETA), that is, the individual's *own* estimate of how long it will take to find his or her next position. If the actual time it takes to reach the final destination is taking longer than the ETA, then we must be doing something wrong. Doubt begins to creep into our minds. Why haven't I gotten there by now? Maybe I should take a different tack, do something different, etc.

Every client that I have worked with has experienced two phenomenons without fail. First, every individual goes through certain dry periods during his or her campaign. Not only are there no interviews scheduled, but they also have no idea when an interview opportunity might develop. When this happens, it becomes a very dry period, and particularly if the person is unemployed, the time seems excruciatingly long. Second every individual whether employed or unemployed who is seeking to find new employment is the recipient of well-meaning, well-intentioned advice from friends, relatives, colleagues, professional acquaintances, and even the milk man. Everyone seems willing to give you advice. Even those individuals who lack expertise on job hunting want to give you their thoughts.

Addressing the second phenomenon first, most people when they receive this advice are thankful for the thoughts the individual has communicated. However, as the campaign continues over any duration of time, the more advice a person receives, the greater the probability of hearing conflicting theories and thoughts on how to find your next employer. Consequently, what I would do to separate the good advice from the bad is to give greater weight or credibility to the advice given by people who derive their entire income from helping people find employment. This does not necessarily include search consultants unless, of course, you are seeking advice on how search firms operate, etc. Outplacement consultants are a much better choice simply because they are paid to help people find employment. Search consultants are paid by companies to find individuals to fill known vacancies, not to plan and execute marketing campaigns for people seeking to find their next employer.

Placing emphasis on Corporate Recruiting Managers gets the job partially done, but most companies who have full-time internal recruiting staff like to recruit certain types of individuals in terms of experience, education, and background. Advice and information from these types of people may or may not have relevance to your particular situation.

In summary, talk to many people but always ask yourself these questions, "How does this person make his/her income? What is his or her field of expertise? Is the advice supported by professional experience?"

Returning to the first concern, dry periods in one's campaign, obviously, lack of job campaign activity, interview opportunities, or opportunities for second or even third interviews are discouraging. A key point, which is difficult to remember, is that all people go through very slow periods in their campaign. The slower or the drier the periods between interviews forces some people to want to change their campaign, tweak their resumes, change their letters, and change their strategy. All these changes are necessitated by one's feeling that "I should be doing something different." Only change your strategy and campaign, only tweak letters or change resumes when you have hard evidence that people are not aware that you have particular skill sets, background, accomplishments, etc. Unless someone specifically indicates to you, "I didn't know you had this type of background," stay with your materials because all campaigns have multiple dry periods and if the individual keeps changing the materials, it leads to a hopeless morass of confusion and frustration.

WHEN YOUR JOB-SEARCH RESULTS SAY, "CHANGE THE BAIT!"

If you are not catching fish, you do not sink the boat. You change your position on the lake, change the bait, or spend more time casting.

Managing a job campaign is a lot like fishing. There may be periods when you don't net anything. This can be a time when self-esteem slips, the job search seems hopeless, and you are ready to abandon the search. Well-meaning but uninformed friends may blame your lack of "bites" on age, job history, education, or a downturn in the economy. You may consider changing careers, going back to school to retool skills, or accepting the next offer that comes along.

Do not quit quite yet! Job searches, like fishing, require patience and perseverance. There is no right length of time for finding the right match. Changing directions for the sake of change is not beneficial to a successful job search. After all, what are you going to change? How are your changes going to help you? Do you know that the answer to the preceding question is a fact or a hoped-for result?

I frequently find that job seekers underestimate the amount of time and effort that must go into an effective search. The letters, telephone calls, and networking activity build a momentum that if sustained with consistency and persistency, will result in job offers.

If your campaign is faltering, review the following Action Plan to improve your performance in the market. Remember:

- Only interviews with a decision-maker will get you the next right position.

- The more interviews you generate, the greater the chance of getting more than one offer. With more than one offer, your bargaining position improves.

- The greater the level of job-search activity, the more contacts you will develop. The more contacts you develop, the greater the opportunity for an interview with a decision-maker.

- Establish weekly job-search-plan goals. Log the amount of time you are committing to your job search. Identify as clearly as possible target contacts, companies, industries, agencies, and publications for the following week. Covering all four avenues of the job search is a full-time job – networking, direct company contact, employment agencies, and ads.

Many times when a corporation is orchestrating a significant downsizing or reduction in staff, our firm will have the opportunity to provide group workshop programs on re-employment techniques. Typically, over the course of these programs, I ask the attendees the following question: "If you were going to start your job campaign today, how long do you think it would take you to find your next position?" I ask people to express their answer in terms of a number of weeks. I ask them to write it down on a tablet or piece of paper, place a circle around that number, and put their initials under the circle. Then, I ask them to draw a box under their initials and place my estimate of how long it will take them to find their next position inside the box. My estimate is their estimate multiplied by three. Then I tell them to put my initials underneath the box. Of course, I am high, and their estimate is low. However, in almost every analysis, my estimate is much closer to the truth than theirs. Everyone has a very optimistic time frame in which they think they will be able to locate and secure new employment.

This is a rather sobering exercise. However, once you are advised up-front that the time to find new employment is longer than your original estimate, you are better prepared to face the "dry" periods.

Part of the problem with dry periods in a job campaign is that corporations tend to move at what I call "glacial speed." Glaciers do not wish to be stopped, turned, or accelerated. It is very difficult for an individual as a non-employee of a corporation to try to accelerate the decision-making pace of that corporation. Consider for a moment. How were you able to able to turn or accelerate the decision-making pace of your former employer? Corporations, like glaciers, move at their own pace.

JOB-SEARCH PLAN WORKSHEET

1. TIME COMMITMENT: DATE: _____

Networking   _____   Hours per week
Company Contacts   _____   Hours per week
Employment Agencies   _____   Hours per week
Answering Ads   _____   Hours per week
Surfing the Net   _____   Hours per week
Spouse's Activities   _____   Hours per week
Interviews this Week   _____   Hours per week
Telephone Activities   _____   Hours per week
Business/Industry Research   _____   Hours per week
Written Communications   _____   Hours per week

2. NETWORKING CONTACT LIST:

_____   _____
_____   _____
_____   _____
_____   _____

3. COMPANIES OR INDUSTRIES TO EXPLORE THROUGH DIRECT MAIL:

_____   _____
_____   _____
_____   _____
_____   _____

4. EMPLOYMENT AGENCIES TO BE CONTACTED:

_____   _____
_____   _____
_____   _____
_____   _____

5. PUBLICATIONS TO READ THAT MAY CONTAIN APPROPRIATE ADS:

_____   _____
_____   _____
_____   _____
_____   _____

6. SPOUSE'S ACTIVITIES/RESEARCH ACTIVITIES

_____   _____
_____   _____
_____   _____
_____   _____

At the end of each week, carefully review that week's activity and answer the following questions: Did you meet your time goals? If not, how will you improve in the upcoming week? What contacts did you make, and what information on target companies or industries did gather? How will that information aid your search? Did you get any referrals? Have you contacted them? How many direct mail letters did you send? Did you follow up by telephone with any of these companies? How many employment agencies or executive search firms did you contact? How many ads did you answer? Did the week's activity indicate the need for more research, and, if so, in what areas?

JOB SEARCH PLAN REVIEW

ACTUAL TIME SPENT:

Networking	___Hours per week	Spouse's Activities	___Hours per week
Company Contacts	___Hours per week	Interviews	___Hours per week
Employment Agencies	___Hours per week	Telephone Activities	___Hours per week
Answering Ads	___Hours per week	Business/Industry Research	___Hours per week
Surfing the Net	___Hours per week	Written Communications	___Hours per week

CONTACTS MADE:

Name	Telephone	Key Information & Follow Up
_____	_____	_____
_____	_____	_____
_____	_____	_____

COMPANIES CONTACTED BY DIRECT MAIL:

Company	Follow Up
_____	_____
_____	_____
_____	_____
_____	_____

EMPLOYMENT AGENCIES/EXECUTIVE SEARCH FIRMS CONTACTED:

Name	Telephone
_____	_____
_____	_____
_____	_____
_____	_____

E-MAILS/RESUMES SENT:

Name	E-Mail Address
_____	_____
_____	_____
_____	_____
_____	_____

By setting realistic goals and reviewing each week's level of activity, you will be able to identify the areas of your job search that require more time and effort. A balanced search incorporates all avenues, with the higher percentage devoted to networking. Over 50 percent of all people working today found their jobs through networking, partly because 99 percent of all job hunters don't use direct mail or correct search firm strategies.

If the time and effort you are putting into your campaign is the equivalent of a full-time job, and you are not generating results, then consider changing lakes and/or varying the bait.

1   Target companies of all sizes. The greatest growth is not in corporate giants, but in organizations with fewer than 100 employees. Eighty percent of people working today work for companies in this category. This is a market greatly overlooked!

2   Expand your geographic preference. On a map, extend a line outward to a maximum desirable driving distance from your home. Continue in a circle around your home location. Contact all organizations in the cities within the circled area that may have a need for your skills, background, and experience.

3   Consider contacting other industries to which your skills and experience would easily transfer. For example, if you have a background in customer service with a long-haul carrier, you might also consider customer service positions in other transportation service and manufacturing areas.

4   If most of your telephone calls to hiring officials have been between 8 a.m. and 10 a.m., try calling between 4:30 p.m. and 6:30 p.m. or try calling between 7:30 a.m. and 8 a.m. Many decision-makers arrive early and stay late. Typically the best time to reach them is before they are involved in meetings and when the secretarial staff is not in place.

5   Follow up on referrals, direct mail letters, and meetings in a timely manner. If a telephone call is required, initiate contact within five working days. If a letter is needed, draft and mail it within three days of meeting.

6   Be prepared for all information gathering and hiring interviews. Spend time at the local library researching the organization; use the Internet and, if possible, research the individual with whom you are meeting. Poor preparation makes a poor impression. There is the story of the top-notch sales person who did not prepare for an interview with IBM. She was certain that her experience alone would get her the job. The interviewer's first question was, "What does IBM stand for?" She did not know the answer. Her lack of preparation cost her the position.

7   Draft responses to the common interview questions found in this guide and practice saying them aloud. Know your resume information thoroughly. Be prepared to talk about your background and experience in terms of skills, actions you took in response to problems or situations, and the results of your actions as they benefited the organization. Remember that numbers sell, so bring them up. Don't let your numbers "rest" on your resume. A significant number of interview candidates really don't know their own resume.

8   Spend more time doing informational interviews to gather background on target companies and industries, and gain referrals to other contacts that may know a hiring authority in an organization you have targeted.

9   Only change your marketing letters and resume in light of hard feedback. Lack of an interview for several weeks is not by itself sufficient reason to change your marketing materials. Besides, without new market intelligence and constructive feedback on which to base your decision, what are you going to change?

10   Job hunters **always** get lots of well-meaning advice on their resumes, job campaigns, and career directions from friends, neighbors, and relatives, especially when there has not been a "nibble" for a long time. Give the greatest credence to the most credible sources. People whose entire careers are focused on the employment process are better qualified to offer direction on your employment search than Uncle Harry, who got his job in 1964, or the neighbor who knows "this really good headhunter."

11   One rule of thumb for measuring weekly interview activity is based on a comparison of salary range with the number of interviews.

One Interview Per Week at an Annual Salary of:	Indicates an Activity Level That Is:
Under $30,000	Poor
$31,000 - $50,000	Fair
$51,000 - $75,000	Good
$76,000 - $125,000	Very Good
Over $125,000	Excellent

12   Remember the three P's – **p**erseverance, **p**ersistence, and **p**ositive attitude. A job search takes time, but if you follow the advice in this guide, you will "net" the right position.

FOCUS TIME

Please check any of the following statements that apply to you and your job campaign.

☐   I feel totally frustrated.

☐   My campaign is stalled.

☐   I cannot see my next interview coming anytime soon.

☐   I am getting too few interviews.

☐   I am getting so much "good" advice that I am confused.

☐   I do not know whether it is time to change my campaign strategy and my campaign materials.

☐   I do not know whether it is time to stick with my campaign strategy but change or redo my campaign materials.

☐   I am lost!

If one or more of the above statements describes what you are feeling, or your current state of mind, I would suggest that you are quite average and normal. In fact, if the serious job hunter does not, from time to time, feel that his/her campaign has stalled, feels totally frustrated, or is not getting enough interviews, then I truly believe he/she is not applying himself/herself diligently to the task at hand. All of the above feelings are quite normal. The time to worry is when these feelings do not dissipate and the individual continues to feel totally lost and frustrated all of the time; then it's time to regroup and toughen up the mental capacity and attack the problem again.

I am not a big believer in taking two weeks for a trip to the mountains or a month at the beach to clear one's head. Those types of activities do not produce anything except more debts to be paid. What I do recommend, if the above conditions appear, is for the individual to take a break from campaigning for a day or two. Begin the morning with a brisk walk. An hour to one-and-a-half hour walk has the benefit of clearing one's head to focus on the day's schedule of activities. Hopefully, the exercise period can be shared with the co-captain on the marriage team or a significant other, so that a healthy exchange of ideas can manifest itself without interruption.

In my own life, I have found that doing chores around my farm, such as mowing pastures, etc., allows me to be completely isolated and focused on the tasks coming up in the next day or week.

All campaigns stall, and all individuals feel they are not getting enough interviews. In recessionary economies, things are even slower. The one universal truth is that companies never move fast enough. Days between interviews are never short enough. Advice usually comes from individuals who are employed. After all, advice (particularly if it's good advice) coming from people who are unemployed would suggest that if they followed their own advice, why aren't they employed?

The majority of people who suffer these effects of their campaign don't become paralyzed for life. It happens, and will pass. Do not allow yourself to wallow in self-pity longer than forty-eight hours. Do not seek people to cry on their shoulders. But if asked, tell them your story factually in two minutes or less and move on.

Re-examine your contacts. Get rid of the losers, the downers. You're known by the company you keep. Try to make new contacts with people who understand what it means to be unemployed. Don't retreat into a shell or withdraw from groups and social activities. These are the times when you need to be around others.

Most of us go to work to fulfill our need for self-satisfaction, esteem, or ego or need to work for the income to satisfy our lifestyle needs. The feeling of inactivity, emptiness, or voids goes counter to what we have done most of our lives. Taken in its entirety, negative feelings are not only normal but should be expected. They go with the territory.

In summary, don't measure lack of results as failure; rather, measure success in terms of perspiration and effort and resolve not to be denied a winning campaign quest.

CHAPTER VII.

GUIDELINES

FOR

PREPARING FOR
THE JOB INTERVIEW

**It's Not The Final Destination,
But You're Getting Close.**

FILLING OUT APPLICATION FORMS – UGH!!!

Companies will ask you to complete an application form at some point for many reasons. The information in the application will help the Human Resources department and the interviewer judge you as a prospective employee and your ability to handle a specific job for which they may have an opening. An interviewer may frequently go over all the information in your application before inviting you for a face-to-face interview. In addition, an application form gives the employer reference information to check your records, your past employment, your credit standing, and anything else that might be important to the prospective employer. It also gives him or her a record to keep if he or she cannot hire you now but would like to call you at some future date.

The interviewer or Human Resources Manager will judge you not only on the information you include but also on **HOW** you fill out the form. **BE NEAT.** Unless you are instructed otherwise, **PRINT** neatly or **TYPE** all the information requested. Avoid crossing out information to make a correction. Enter it correctly the first time. Avoid erasures. If you must erase, do it as neatly as possible. Keep the entire form clean and free of smudges. Be positive and honest in all your information. Remember that it is possible in many cases to check the information you give an employer, and an employer who is really interested in hiring may do so.

Remember, the bigger the company, the more applicants applying for each position. If your application is as complete as possible; if it is neat and legible and honest in the facts; if it shows that you are a careful, conscientious person—the kind the employer is looking for – then you stand a better chance of being hired. When filling out applications for employment, keep in mind the following rules.

TWENTY RULES FOR COMPLETING THE
JOB APPLICATION FORM

1. Read the application from top to bottom before beginning and then, and only then, start to follow instructions carefully. Remember, if you cannot follow instructions when you are trying to get a job, why then should an employer believe you could follow instructions if you were hired?

2. Be complete. Answer every question.

3. Be accurate. Read everything on the application carefully before you start to fill out the blanks. This will keep you from making mistakes.

4. List all types of education, experience, and on-the-job training that have given you skills for any type of work.

5. Describe your previous experience accurately and completely.

6. If the application form does not tell you whether to write or print, then print neatly using blue ink rather than black ink.

7. Do not use nicknames.

8. Do not give incomplete names.

9. Make sure the words you use are **spelled correctly.**

10. Do not use unclear abbreviations or acronyms specific to your past employer. If in doubt, do not abbreviate. For example, if you have experience using SAP, what does SAP stand for?

11. If the form does not tell you whether to circle, check, underline, or place an "X," follow these rules:

    A. If there is a small line, box, or circle, use an "X."
    B. If there is no line, box, or circle, you may either circle or underline.

12. When requested to provide your current or most recent wages or salary, be exact. **DO not "round off."** Compensation is the most frequent item verified in a reference check.

13. Be careful when completing questions dealing with, "Why did you leave your previous or most recent employer?" Be sure to answer this question in a positive manner. Avoid phrases such as "Quit," "Left for more money," or "Personality conflict." Rather use positive statements such as: "Left for more responsibility or career advancement."

14. Try to avoid using the phrase "laid off," as this term implies "recall rights." Employers are reluctant to hire any individual if they believe the individual could be recalled. If, in fact, you have been "laid off," use "department/plant reduction" or "total company reorganization."

15. When confronted with questions such as "wage or salary desired or expected," use the word "Open." Do not say "negotiable" or indicate an exact dollar amount. The word "Open" means that you are open to listening to a competitive offer.

16. Never fill out an application form in a company's waiting room **unless** you know that upon completion of the application, you will be seeing an interviewer. When receiving an application, ask the following question: "Upon completing the application, will I have an opportunity to see someone to discuss employment opportunities?" If the individual handing out the application indicates there are no positions available right now or that all the interviewers are busy, accept the application and request a return envelope. That evening, fill out the application form and return it by mail. Remember, try to avoid wasting time by filling out employment applications at a company when there is no opportunity to see a hiring official. Get the application but go on to your next company or appointment. Completed applications can be returned by mail, and you may follow up with a telephone call. Use your job-hunting time wisely!

17. Unless specifically requested otherwise, references should always be business references or former employers, not friends or neighbors who are not fully acquainted with your work history.

18. Do not fill out applications with a friend. It only increases your competition for the job.

19. If an application is unclear or confusing, do not hesitate to ask for clarification.

20. Once an application is on file, do not be shy about calling back every two to three weeks to determine your employment status. Employers know that if you work hard getting a job, you will probably work hard on the job.

TEN RULES FOR REFERENCES

1. Ask permission in advance. **Do not assume** that someone will be willing to be used as a reference.

2. Have two or three references that can legitimately comment on your professional abilities. Make sure they have a copy of your resume.

3. Ask your references **where** and **how** they wish to be contacted and include the necessary information (address and/or telephone number).

Where?	--	Office or Home
How?	--	Telephone or Mail (If by mail only, do not include a telephone number; also indicate, "Contact by mail only.")

4. Have references typed on a separate sheet of paper with your name and address information at the top. Only give references when requested. Never volunteer references. Why? Because you never can be absolutely sure what your references will really say.

5. Do not attach a reference list to any of your letters or your resume.

6. When asked to provide references after an interview, call each individual and alert him or her so that he or she will be in a position to provide specific information that will assist you. Give your references as much information as you can regarding how your experience and background fit the requirements of the position. In this way, they can tailor their responses to individual questions.

7. Never give more than three references.

8. If the company wants more, they will ask for more.

9. Give only business references, not personal references.

10. Don't give your former President as a reference unless he/she really knows your work accomplishments and background. Remarks of your references only count if they really know your work contributions.

SAMPLE REFERENCE LIST

REFERENCES

Mr. Bob Smith
President
XYZ Corporation
8000 Centerview Parkway, Suite 300
Cordova, Tennessee 38018   (Contact by mail only)

Mr. William Jones
Vice President, Operations
ABC Corporation
3241 Spring Grove Avenue
Cincinnati, Ohio 45225
(444) 444-4444   (Work telephone number)

Mr. Tom Jones
General Manager
LMN Corporation
401 Eagle Drive
Claryville, Kentucky 41001
(333) 333-3333   (Work telephone number.
                              Although Tom does travel
                              heavily, he does return
                              telephone calls.)

HANDLING THE INTERVIEW PROCESS

Oftentimes, "the interview" is the most intimidating component of the job campaign. This is unfortunate because if you are properly prepared, the interview can be the easiest, most enjoyable part of the process. **WHY?** Because the topic of discussion during an interview is you. **No one is more qualified to discuss you than you are!**

Why, then, is interviewing seldom the easiest part of the search?

Because people lack experience in interviewing. We have been conditioned not to brag or boast. And while this may be true at dinner parties, we must realize that the goal of the interview is to convince the interviewer that you have the ability, experience, personality, and other characteristics required to do a good job and to enlist the interviewer's help in getting you that job.

What follows is a wealth of information to help encourage and prepare you for the exciting opportunity that faces you in an interview.

CLEARING THE DECK

Let's clear the deck and get a simple but sound foundation underway. Unfortunately, at least in my opinion, most interviewers are not good interviewers simply because they have had no training. Members of management may think they are good interviewers because they do a lot of it. However, it appears to me, after countless debriefings with our clients, both in the matter of presentation and the questions asked, that many interviewers are making the same mistakes over and over again. It is very difficult to find people who interview at the professional level today who have had training on becoming a good interviewer. Again, because of the lack of training, there is a repetition of errors and mistakes. Most people who conduct interviews do so for the wrong reasons – they look for reasons why they should not hire an individual candidate. When an interviewer looks for reasons not to hire a person, he or she will never be disappointed. In contrast, a good interviewer will look for what the person can bring to the organization that fulfills the needs and helps solve the problems of the organization.

When an individual is called to establish an interview meeting, before the candidate and interviewer actually meet and exchange the right hand of friendship, the candidate can safely assume the interviewer really does believe that he or she can satisfy the requirements of the position. This is not an invalid assumption because if the interviewer believed the candidate could not fill the requirements of the position, he or she would not have made the call in the first instance. Therefore, the candidate's task, very simply, is to avoid talking oneself out of the position, not talking oneself into the position. The resume, assuming it was the major source of stimulation to the interviewer to make the call, must have satisfied more than a majority of the position's requirements. Otherwise, the prospective candidate would not have been called at all.

I am still amazed at the number of individuals who are searching for a new employer and actually turn down the opportunity to interview. The most commonly cited reasons are: geographic, "It doesn't seem commutable," "The company has a bad reputation," "The position responsibilities are beneath me," or "The salary is insufficient to meet my current needs."

It's my opinion that even if these points are absolutely correct, the individual should go for the interview. I do not believe it is good procedure to take interviews just for the "practice." Too many individuals have done that only to find out halfway through the interview that the position really is interesting, but because of the lack of sensitivity or intensity – after all, this is only "practice" – an invitation to further interview with the company was lost.

Nevertheless, even if the position is not geographically attractive or within acceptable commuting distance, how does the candidate know that the actual job will be at the same site where the interview is scheduled to take place? Even if a company is saddled with a bad reputation, unless the candidate interviews with the company, he or she will never know if, for example, there is new management in place that is seriously trying to reshape the company and its reputation.

Unless the candidate has an actual interview and finds out that the job is not suitable for his or her career (or pays a salary that is not acceptable) the candidate will never know if there might be another job at a higher salary for which he or she could be considered. All this leads to a general conclusion, which is very sound. **Take the interview.** Go for it! Determine for yourself if the listed points of reservation are valid or not. These points can only be resolved from going inside the organization, not listening from outside the organization.

Now that you have the opportunity to schedule an interview, plan your strategy so that you have the advantage. Try to ascertain how long the organization will be conducting interviews. You may want to say to the interviewer on the telephone, "Could you share with me how long you will be interviewing for this position?" Try to schedule yourself towards the end of the process. "First in does not usually win." The first person interviewed usually sets the standard. Others are compared against the first. While a company is interviewing, sometimes the company changes its requirements. Generally, Mondays are better than Fridays and morning is better than afternoon. Friday at 4 p.m. is your worst time! However, Monday at 8 a.m. is not a good time if you are first. Assuming you are not the very first person being interviewed, Monday mornings are excellent. You will be getting your interviewer in his/her most receptive listening posture. The workweek has not really begun, there is little distraction, and the interviewer is refreshed, coming off a two-day weekend. Once you have scheduled the appointment, make sure to ask the exact directions, location of the office, building and room numbers. Always get the telephone number of your interviewer in case of unexpected delays or a need to reschedule the interview appointment.

Before you conclude the conversation, be sure to ask the following:

"Mr./Ms. Interviewer, in order that I may prepare for this interview, would you share with me what your organization is looking for in the successful candidate?"

Do not sell yourself at this point . . . take notes!! Save your selling for the face-to-face interview. You already have the appointment.

If there are three working days between the call establishing the interview appointment and the interview, ask the company official to send you information on the company, i.e., annual report, last quarterly report, 10Q report, 10K report, and product literature. Show that you are an interested and a prepared professional. If less than three days remains before the interview, arrange for the material to be picked up or sent to you via overnight mail.

Don't overlook researching this information via the Internet. The best techniques for searching the Internet is simply to ask the person setting up the interview if the company has a Web site and what is its address. "Could you share with me your web site address so I may look up your 10K, 10Q, annual report, and quarterly report, etc.? Also, do you put product specifications and information on your web site?" In this manner, you are showing your interviewer that you are not only doing your homework, but you are computer literate, as well.

Research the Organization: Immediately after scheduling the appointment, commence your research on the organization. Do not wait for the mail. Start to dig for facts, figures, news articles, and product information. Go to the interview well prepared. Check out the Internet and the company's Web page if it has one.

It is very important to find out as much information as possible about a potential employer. This information will help you to appear knowledgeable during an interview and can also help you to make a better career decision when considering job offers. The following points are some of the items to research prior to the interview. You obviously may not be able to find answers to all of these questions, particularly if the company is privately held.

a. Relative size of the industry, relative size of the firm.
b. Potential growth for the industry.
c. Percent of annual sales growth during the last five years. Percent of annual growth in earnings per share.
d. Array of product lines and/or services.
e. Potential new markets, products, or services.
f. Various price points in product or service line.
g. Who is the competition?
h. Age of top management?
i. Organizational structure – produce line, function, etc.
j. Geographical locations.
k. Number of plants, stores, or sales outlets.
l. Short-term profit picture – last nine months. (You can find this information in the last three quarterly reports.)
m. Structured or unstructured training.
n. Average time spent per project or position. Admittedly, this might be very difficult to ascertain.
o. E-commerce activities or plans.
p. Who has employment contracts? This is found in the company's 10K report.
q. Pending lawsuits. Who is the defendant/plaintiff? Why? Also found in the 10K report.
r. Recent items in the news.
s. Structure of assets. Is the company liquid, cash poor, selling off assets, etc.?
t. Who owns the company?
u. Significant fluctuations in the price of the company's stock.
v. People you know in the firm.
w. Formal versus on-the-job training – depends on level of position.
x. Typical career path in your field.
y. Home-office location.
z. Name of recruiter/contact.

aa. Who makes the final hiring decision?
bb. Share of market.
cc. Current problems.

For information on how and where to research companies, refer to pages 132–144.

Dress for Success: As far as dress is concerned, a blue suit with a white or blue long-sleeved shirt is still the best compromise in view of all the types of people you will meet. Worn suits, frayed shirts, and shoes with holes in them will not help you. Women should not wear heavy makeup and trendy clothing. A solid blue or white blouse is still the best bet. Slacks or pantsuits are not a good idea. Most of all, wear clothes that fit – clothes that really fit. Also, do not forget the obvious: use a mouthwash and deodorant, and avoid heavy aftershave or perfume. In general, most people do their best by dressing conservatively and trying to appear as relaxed, neatly groomed, and successful as possible. Remember, your clothes talk for you before you open your mouth. In short, make sure you look and act like a winner. Dress for success.

With the advent of "business casual" attire with many corporations, the focus becomes one of not appearing to be overdressed or underdressed. What's appropriate? To handle this perplexing issue, simply ask the individual who is establishing the interview appointment the following question, "Is the attire for our meeting business or business casual?" Dress to blend in, not stand out. When in doubt, remember the following: "How you dress today is how I will remember you tomorrow."

One last comment on dress – specifically on the almighty briefcase – never leave home without it! Place extra copies of your resume in your briefcase along with the following:

- A list of business references
- The company's annual report or other documentation
- A list of prepared questions to ask. Leave nothing to chance!

Note: Jotting down a few pertinent questions in the margins of the company's annual report is a good way to show that you have done your homework.

Always Be on Time for an Interview: There is no excuse for being late! Try to avoid arriving too early for an interview. This makes people seem overanxious and too available. Or, even worse, that they cannot follow instructions. Five minutes before the actual interview is sufficient time.

Upon arriving at the interviewer's office five minutes early, announce yourself to the receptionist and have a seat. If you are kept waiting for thirty minutes, ask whether it would be more appropriate to schedule another appointment and, if need be, excuse yourself.

Do not fumble with a heavy coat. Ask the receptionist to put it in a closet for you.

At no point during the interview process should you smoke or drink coffee – even if offered! Coffee adds pressure to small intestines! If you accept coffee, where do you rest the coffee cup? Certainly not on the interviewer's desk.

You will need to be socially gregarious and aggressive – without being obnoxious. You will also want to appear learned, charming, and diplomatic. It is recommended that when one meets the interviewer, the candidate **gives a firm and enthusiastic handshake,** whether it is a man or woman, and then wait for the other person to initiate the discussion.

If a man is meeting a woman, always extend the right hand of friendship; grasp the lady's hand, but apply all the pressure with the thumb. Reserve the "Hulk Hogan" handshake for Jesse Ventura!

Use the chair in the interviewer's office for your competitive edge. Positive body language is most important. Position the chair so that when seated, you will establish good eye contact. If need be, do not hesitate to move your chair so that you are sitting directly across from your interviewer. Sit on the chair, leaning slightly forward. Position your hands on your knees. Do not touch the interviewer's desk, as this would be violating the interviewer's private space. When the interview is completed, return the chair to its previous position.

In this instance, normal body position would have your "line of sight" right past your interviewer.

Typical Interview Setting

Note: In the illustration, the arrangement of the chairs forces the interview candidate, when in his or her most comfortable posture, to look past the interviewer. Even when the candidate's head is turned toward the interviewer, the head will gradually turn back to its least stressful or most relaxed posture. That is, the head will again be focused away from the interviewer as shown by the vectors above.

When the interview candidate fails to look at his/her interviewer, two things happen. First, the more "eye-to-eye" contact that is lost – the more of the interviewer's questions/comments will be lost. They simply will not be heard. They are lost!

Second, avoiding eye-to-eye contact means the candidate is "avoiding" the interviewer or engaging in evasive behavior. Both are interpreted as negatives. So, reposition the chairs as shown in the illustration:

Move the chair to directly in front of the interviewer for good eye contact.

Line of sight.

Keep this area clear – no coffee cups or briefcases.

Always wait for your host to be seated first.

The illustrated position ensures direct eye contact, excellent listening posture and positive body language. After the interview, return the chair to its original position.

Never volunteer your resume until it is requested. However, be certain to take several copies of it to the interview so that it is available if requested.

Never apologize for any of your liabilities. We all have them.

When you are asked questions, you should be brief – but positive. Watch your speech, articulate as clearly as possible, and avoid "and . . . ah's" or other verbal slips. Keep your answers fifteen to twenty seconds in length. Prolonged or extended replies to questions do not reflect a focused or disciplined mind.

It's always wise to take a full, but not exaggerated, breath before answering any questions. This will enable your mind a couple of extra seconds to think and organize your reply.

Before replying to an interviewer's questions, there are steps that can be taken. For example: Ask for a definition of vocabulary used in the question. To the question, "What are your short/long – term objectives?" it would be wise to ask what the interviewer means by "long or short."

If the interviewer is nervous or is not articulate (it does happen) and his/her questions are poorly constructed, vague, or confusing – simply ask for an example of what the interviewer is referring to.

When I interview candidates for our firm, I expect them to have most, but not all of the answers to my questions. I think an answer like "I don't know" or "I'll have to think about that one" is much stronger than making up an answer the candidate thinks I would like to hear or "winging it."

Let me go back and ask the reader to reflect a moment on my earlier suggestion to keep responses to about twenty seconds. Sounds easy, doesn't it? But, in fact, too many candidates talk too much, possibly due to nervousness. They tend to not fully listen to the questions being asked. Consequently, answers are given to questions the candidate thought were being asked, not what was actually being asked. My experience holds this to be true. Think first, and only when the interviewer has finished his or her inquiry should you take a breath, focus on the question, then deliver a succinct twenty-second response. Then be quiet and await further instructions.

Absolute quiet is unnerving to the candidate. Why? Because the candidate comes into each interview with the assumption that he or she is expected to talk.

When confronted with silence, almost all candidates resume talking because they assume that the interviewer wants more information or that he/she did not understand the initial answer. Both assumptions are mistakes!

In reality the interviewer may be thinking about your response, grouping his or her thoughts for the next question, or have a momentary lapse of concentration. (It does happen to interviewers too!)

The key point is to know when to stop talking!
Answer the question; don't volunteer information that is not asked for!
Remember the Shakespeare quotation: *"Me thinks the lady doth protest too much!"*

Always underplay your need for a new job – remember you are looking for a career. And always use a soft-sell approach. You will be on your way to an offer when the firm starts recruiting you.

You should do your best to tell the truth and be as forthright and consistent as possible. If your background includes mental illness, bankruptcy, alcoholism, or having been in prison, do not volunteer the information. However, if you are asked, be sure to tell the truth without being defensive or feeling abnormal. If these things apply, you will need to develop your own personal approaches for handling them.

Years ago, I had the opportunity to interview an individual who had a noticeable gap of three years on his resume. When I asked what he was doing during that time, he replied, "When I was much younger, I got involved with the wrong crowd and made a terrible mistake. We took a car for a joy ride and got caught. As a result, I spent three years in a correctional institution to pay my debt to society – where, by the way, I finished my GED and nine semester hours toward my degree." What a solid answer!

Maintain your professionalism at all times. If your dignity is abused, simply stand up and close out the interview and go on to better things. If you are a woman and get what I call "funny questions," close out the interview. Go with your "gut" feelings.

If asked out for lunch, do not select sloppy or hard-to-manage foods. Take your cue on drinks from the interviewer and let him or her pick up the tab. Remember that nobody ever lost a job offer for failing to order a cocktail.

Since most applicants park in the visitor's parking area, there is the temptation to offer to drive since your car is closer to the front door. But don't volunteer to drive! The liability for the injury of one to three company managers or officers could be tremendous.

Be careful about posing as a threat to your prospective boss's position. People will say that they want to hire people who are better than themselves – but most of the time they don't mean it.

Never read the mail on your interviewer's desk, nervously drum your fingers, look at your watch, or exhibit other signs of nervousness or boredom.

At all times, you should project enthusiasm, confidence, and ambition. However, you will need to control your ambition in line with your estimation of each situation. Before you go to an interview, you should plan on projecting an image of yourself that is tailored to the specific position. In addition to the general qualities related to your occupational field, you would usually be wise to convey three important image qualities: sincerity, a dedication to achievement, and a high energy level.

Wherever possible, you should gear your comments to stress your accomplishments – sales, profit, cost reduction, and growth. Remember those great numbers on your resume. You should have questions prepared about the field of interest for which you have answers. The object in doing this is to create an opportunity that will enable you to demonstrate your knowledge of the firm and the position requirements. If you have identified some of the organization's problems, you can also relate your discussion to them. In this case, you would want to highlight your past experiences that are relevant to the potential solution to the company's problem. **This point is important – read it again!**

In today's job market, most interviewees are judged not only by the manner in which they answer questions but also by the questions they pose to the interviewer. Sample questions that you may want to ask during your interview are included in the next section for your review. I recommend that you keep in mind to ask those questions that will give you an opportunity to continue selling yourself.

For example, questions such as, "What are some of the long-term objectives that you would like completed?" and, "In what ways were you most pleased with what the past holder of this job did?" and, "In what ways do you see me having the biggest impact on this position?" are all good questions to ask. The answers to these questions will allow you to continue selling yourself by citing specific examples of what you may have done for past companies.

Always protect the confidence of your present employer. Any breach in this area will quickly close out your opportunity. This is because the potential employers will assume that someday you will do the same thing to them.

Always be prepared to say something that will indicate admiration for certain achievements of the organization or its top management. In the interview situation, flattery will not get you everywhere, but it will surely help.

Make sure you are extremely observant and that you learn something about your interviewer's interests and background. You may wish to use this information in your letter, which will follow up the interview.

Be a good listener, but remember that one of the easiest ways to impress people is to ask intelligent and penetrating questions about the firm and the position. We call these the "selling questions" because knowing the answers to these questions will allow you to frame further comments and correspondence in a manner that is meaningful to the listener. Simply put, they help "sell" you. Knowing these answers will be your "Recipe to Success!"

Areas for possible exploration include the following:

- Always find out what happened to the last person in the job, and if possible, get his or her name.

- Identify how many people have had the same position and where they have gone. The tip-off to many really bad jobs is in heavy turnover. This will also indicate how visible the position is – a key factor for promotions.

- Most individuals have a keen interest to see if the position they are interviewing for has potential for advancement or continued career progression. So very often, I have found that people try to ascertain potential for further advancement with a question such as, "Are there opportunities for advancement?" My thought on this type of question is simply that you know the answer even before asking. I have never heard in my career of a recruiter, employer, or search firm replying to this question with a succinct "No," or "No, there are no opportunities for promotion or advancement, and the people in this particular department are a bunch of empty helmets." The fact is the question is always answered in a positive manner. "Yes, of course; the sky's the limit." In actuality this may or may not be true.

  A much better and succinct way to ascertain how visible this position is would be to simply rephrase the question in the following manner: "How many people have held this position in the last five years, and where have they gone?" This will not only give you a good indication of promotability and visibility but also turnover.

- Find out about the company's method of handling budgets and purchase orders. If it makes it difficult for people to get paper clips and pens, chances are it will not delegate much authority or give an opportunity to succeed or fail.

- Discover as much as you can about the Chief Executive Officer of the company. Many companies directly reflect the personality of the top officer, and most presidents like to promote the people who are most like themselves.

- Ask your interviewer what he or she feels are the negative aspects of the organization. Find out how long he or she has been there and see what he or she says about his or her own experience.

- Does the company hire friends and relatives for key positions? Are they qualified? (If not, remember that nepotism can be a real monster.)

- When the interviewer has briefly covered a subject of interest, you should never hesitate to ask him or her to further expand, describe, or define.

- What are your priorities, and what is most pressing?

- Where or how can the next individual in this position have the greatest impact?

- What would you like done differently by the next person who holds this position?

- What do the terms "above average" or "excellent" performance mean to you?

- If a situation begins to stall, you can always raise questions about any subject by merely asking **who**, **what**, **when**, **where**, **how**, and/or **why**. However, never feel that you must keep the conversation going at all times. Sometimes it is best to just keep quiet.

- Ask some of the same three or four questions of each individual interviewing you. This will help you ascertain how well "The Team" communicates. Do you get the same answers to the same question? Such questions as, "What are the three most pressing problems facing the individual you hire for this position?" or "What's the number one priority?" will give a quick idea if everybody is on the same page! If their answers do not match up, chances are good that they have not truly defined what the company is looking for in a successful candidate.

Prepare your own list of interview questions before you go to the interview. Beginning on page 316, you will find a sample list of questions that you may want to ask during your interview. Don't be shy about actually producing a list of questions to ask. Don't trust your memory to ask all of the right questions. Producing a prepared list of questions not only reduces your nervousness and stress, but also shows the interviewer that you came to the meeting prepared.

Always ask for the interviewer's business card before leaving the interview. This will be helpful when you write your interview follow-up letter.

How do you spot an "easy" interviewer? Generally, the higher the organization level or the rank of the individual doing the interview, the more the interview is based on general chemistry over the correctness of the candidate's answers. Why? Simply because this type of individual is not really trained in interviewing. This individual believes that he or she is a good judge of whether the candidate will be able to work well with him or her. At higher levels, these managers, with noted exceptions, spend their days managing the business. They plan, execute, give directions, follow up, and study the progress of the organization against objectives and directives. Only the really good managers take the precious time to really listen to others. Technical questions about the candidate's field of expertise are rare. This may possibly be because "managers" assume that these questions have already been ferreted out (screened) by others – subordinates.

Another easy type of interview is with the interviewer who likes to talk (and talk, and talk). It is always a mistake to try to interrupt and take control of any interview! Recognize that the talkative interviewers are demonstrating a style of interviewing with which they are most comfortable. Some people like to pontificate, and some interviewers are revealing their nervousness by continuing to talk.

To interrupt only interjects an element of discord if not disrespect. The key is to maintain good eye contact and continue to listen intently. When appropriate, you may want to spice up the conversation with key phrases such as, "Yes," "Right," "Good," or "That's very interesting," but don't try to change the interviewer's thought.

Many times these talkative interviewers ask questions and provide their own answers. For example, I have heard an interviewer ask the question, "Tell me how you have solved these types of problems, etc. – because we are experiencing similar problems – and this is how we have gone about solving it …." Silence sometimes carries the day!

When I was the head of Human Resources for a large corporation, I arranged interviews for key senior management candidates. These interviews were conducted with several management personnel whom I "debriefed" as soon as the candidate was passed on to the next manager. One manager whom I got to know very well, when I asked him his opinion regarding a candidate, would invariably reply, "I liked him – I didn't hear anything that I disagreed with." Why? Because this manager would conduct his own talk-a-thon and not let the candidate speak.

PREPARING YOURSELF TO HANDLE
THE DIFFICULT QUESTIONS

The following interview questions are very similar to the ones you can expect during the interview process. These questions may or may not be a part of your upcoming interviews, but in order to prepare, read through this section and try to formulate your own answers. Preparation will enable you to think on your feet during an interview. Well-thought-out answers now will prepare you for a "worst-case" scenario later.

Many individuals have the ability to develop interviews but subsequently lose out because of a hesitancy and lack of poise in handling these very questions. Spend whatever time is needed to develop answers to these questions. Verbalize the answers aloud. Even if you think you are an accomplished speaker, you will be amazed at how much you will gain through such an exercise.

Every interview is an individual experience, and the answers that you must be prepared to give will depend on your goals and situation. The following answers have been prepared as suggested replies to these frequently asked questions.

The following suggested replies to interview questions are obviously not intended to provide the applicant with the "one correct answer." Rather, they are an attempt to expand your thinking to understand the nature of the questions and to suggest several different approaches to various questions. As you peruse this section, you will note that you are often prompted to refer to your resume. You should always carry an extra copy of your resume to an interview just in case your interviewer might need one. You should have your resume committed to memory, making it unnecessary for you to look at it during the interview process. Again, these answers should reflect the frame of reference of each applicant, based on his/her motives, goals, work skills, and aspirations. These suggested replies are examples that are intended to stimulate thinking, not necessarily to be memorized and parroted back.

1. Tell us about yourself.

This is the perfect opportunity to respond in fifteen-twenty seconds by reciting back the summary of experience paragraph at the top of your resume. Literally, this is the best approach. Many people have difficulty with this question because it seems so broad and too difficult to get one's hands on the meat of the question. Many individuals wonder what the interviewer is looking for; thinking this is a trick question. It is a difficult question because it appears so all encompassing. Tell us about yourself. Do you talk about your personality, work skills, hobbies, family goals, or outside activities? Where do you start?

It is important to keep in mind that you are in the interview to discuss business – and only business – unless otherwise directed. All answers should be given in a business-like manner. Therefore, the Summary of Experience from your resume is the perfect response for this answer. This question is probably the single most-asked question in interviews; therefore, it is necessary to develop a good, polished response. The thrust of the question is designed to get you to talk. When you start talking and opening up, the interview becomes less stressful, and you become more relaxed. The reason this question is selected is to accomplish this objective; who better to talk about this area where you are the world's greatest authority? Nevertheless, most people falter on this question because they have the tendency to be undisciplined, unfocused, and rambling. One individual, while participating in a practice interview in the office of Lawrence and Allen, actually took twenty-three minutes to answer this question, and then he had to be interrupted. Remember that a good response time is fifteen to twenty seconds.

2. What are your short-range objectives?

Questions 2 and 3 are interesting questions – what are your short-range objectives, what are your long-range objectives? Before attempting to answer, you would be extremely prudent to have a definition of the vocabulary. They seem so obvious, but what would be your response if you thought short-range objectives were one to two years and the manager or interviewer was looking for a response of three to five years? It is therefore strongly recommended that you ask for a definition of what is "short" and what is "long" so that the answer can reflect the proper time frame. Additionally, it never hurts to ask for clarification. Are we talking business or personal objectives? When in doubt, express your answer in business terms.

3. What are your long-range objectives?

See Question 2.

4. Describe the route you've chosen to get you to your ultimate career goal?

To gain maximum exposure and experience, I have chosen _____, etc.

5. What do you look for in a job?

Suggested answer: "I am looking for an opportunity to take my current skills and develop them into a career opportunity." Alternative answer: "I am not looking for a job; I am looking for a career." The implication here is that the term "job" implies short-term; "career" implies long-term. Using the summary of experience section of your resume, another appropriate answer might be, "I am looking for an opportunity to use my twenty-plus years in healthcare human resource administration. I am looking for an opportunity that allows me to use my extensive generalist background in employee relations, compensation, management development, recruiting, orientation and training, employee benefits, and security."

6. How did you decide on this type of work?

This is an interesting question. Many people decide upon a type of work after they are offered a position, in some instances, a position, which they did not expect; in other instances, a position for which they have planned and strategized. The employment situation is an interesting human game. In the process of finding employment, many potential employees run an aggressive job campaign and are offered positions that result from a direct mail letter or maybe from a network contact, reaching heights they never thought that they would achieve. Smaller companies may offer you a position that was not in your original game plan but is one where you wear many hats. So, if you are asked the question of how you decided on a type of work, a potential answer could be, "After considering the position, and considering the skills that would be required, as well as the opportunity for professional growth and the other pluses of the company, this position meets my goals and objectives."

7. What motivates you?

It is appropriate to pause and reflect on this question. A suggested answer after pausing and reflection might be as follows: "There just isn't one item that motivates me, many items and things provide motivation at different times in my life. The desire to excel and receive comparable recognition, remuneration or compensation for excellence is a strong motivator. I am motivated to provide a financially secure lifestyle for my family and myself. New challenges and market opportunities motivate me. I am motivated to excel in my career and to see that career advance to its highest possible potential or level. I am motivated by excellence, the desire to complete a job, task, project or assignment in the best possible manner, given the resources available. I believe in summary that depending upon the situation, environment and resources available, I am motivated by a number of stimuli."

8. Why did your business fail?

This is a commonly asked question. "Why is your business not doing well, why is your business slow, or why is your business downsizing?" These questions all indicate that your business is not doing well and imply you were part of the reason it is not doing well. In most instances, the majority of employees are not privy to the reasons behind why a business is not doing well. If you are a senior level individual and you are privy to that information, then you may want to provide the reason – market condition, lack of quality, lack of customer demand for product or service due to foreign competition, product development problems, etc. In many instances, though, due to the complexity of a corporation or organization, you, as the employee, really do not know why the business is not doing well. You may be given some information, but that may not be the whole story. A suggested answer is to say, "I really do not know all the facts surrounding our situation. It is an extremely complicated issue. However, the following information was given to me as to why the business is not doing well . . ." Drop it! Drop the question, keep the answer to twenty seconds, and go on to the next question. This is a good time for you as an applicant to ask a question yourself. Ask, "What is the status of your current business? According to my research I found . . . ." and give a few points of what you found out and ask the interviewer questions. Do not be afraid to interject questions.

9. Why are you leaving your present position?

Based upon the situation of why you are leaving your position, you may elect to respond, "I am not leaving my position; it left me," if, in fact you were separated due to a restructuring and downsizing force. This answer left by itself is probably too glib, so clarify briefly the circumstances surrounding your departure. If you were separated for another reason, there are several different strategies to use based upon the actual situation. If you were separated because you and your boss did not agree, take the bull by the horns and respond, "My boss and I agreed to disagree. He won and I am conducting a job search." You want to be up-front, straightforward, and honest with your answer. If, in fact, you were part of a reduction in force and it was a large reduction, then you could answer, "My position, along with 200 other positions was eliminated." If your company has had a series of reductions over the last year or two you may respond, "The organization has reduced staff for the last two years, and finally my position, along with 600 others, was eliminated and will not be replaced." Share the burden with others. Simply stating that you were "laid off" or downsized does not share with the interviewer if you were the only one let go or if there were other individuals involved.

10. How do you feel about leaving your present position?

"I have mixed emotions about leaving my present position. It was challenging and fun, and I enjoyed my colleagues and the people I worked with and the amount of work that we accomplished under sometimes very difficult situations and time parameters. I made a number of friends, colleagues and professional acquaintances that I know I will miss, but at the same time I am looking forward to moving on in my career to a new environment, new colleagues, new challenges, new opportunities. So, I feel a mixture of the sadness of looking back along with the excitement of looking forward."

11. Do you agree with the decision that was made to release you from employment?

This is a difficult question because an emotional factor is involved. Possibly one would be well advised to consider the following answers: "The decision to separate myself, I am sure, was not an easy one, and I admittedly have been baffled as I was not informed as to all the factors bearing on this decision. Therefore, it is difficult to agree or disagree." (This assumes, of course, that the reader is an individual separation.) If the reader is part of a larger group of downsizing, restructuring, or releases associated with a merger or acquisition, one can possibly be a little more philosophical without being flippant. For example: "As a result of the merger or acquisition, it was readily apparent there were significant areas of duplication. I happened to be in one of those areas that was duplicated, and I understand the decision to release me and the other individuals in the group."

12. What would you have done differently concerning the release?

"Immediately after my release, there were many items that were of concern, and the emotion of the moment made it difficult to think clearly. I think what I would have done was to take a couple of days to collect my thoughts and ask for a second meeting with my supervisor or a human resource representative. Then rather than trying to cover all these items at the separation meeting, which unfortunately I did not, I would have clearly understood what the company was providing in terms of separation benefits and their cost, outplacement assistance, or whether or not there was an opportunity to purchase my laptop, which I would have found very beneficial in my job campaign."

13. What can you do for us that someone else cannot do?

This question asks you to compare yourself with an unknown, and since you cannot address the unknown, you will need to remove the unknown from the answer. "Mr./Ms. Recruiter, I do not know who you have spoken to, but specifically I can do the following . . . ." What you should do is to reconsider the secret recipe question (What is the company looking for in the successful candidate?), find out what the company is looking for, and then resell yourself to its specific needs. Repeat your summary of experience from your resume because throughout the interview process, you want to sell, resell, and sell again. Constantly review your resume verbally because your potential interviewer may not be listening or may not have caught all of the information. Refer to the accomplishments and responsibilities listed on your resume, and do not be afraid to repeat your selling points – your significant accomplishments and your responsibilities.

14. Why should we hire you?

This is basically the same as the previous question. Here again, you repeat the secret recipe question, and sell yourself on those points the company is looking for in a successful candidate. (See and read page 318.) For instance, repeat your summary of experience from your resume, i.e., "Because I have fifteen years of experience in . . . ." Another alternative answer: "I think you should consider hiring me because I believe I am a capable manager of costs and profits. During the last fifteen years, I have consistently cut costs and increased revenue. Let me cite a couple of examples of these successful activities." Again, using your resume as your interview script, cite some of the key bullet quantitative points in terms of increasing revenue or activities that have, in fact, reduced cost. Every dollar of cost reduction, of course, falls directly to the bottom line.

15. Have you ever signed a non-compete agreement?

"Yes, upon my commencement of employment with XYZ Company," or possibly, "Yes, I did in order to facilitate receiving my separation benefits." Or, if you have not signed a non-compete agreement, simply say, "No, I have not."

16. Would you relocate? How does your family feel about relocation?

"Upon separation I sat down with my wife, first, and then my family (we have two children) to discuss the opportunities within our immediate geographic area versus those that may require relocation. I am open to listening to relocation, and we have not ruled out any particular area of the country. Because of prior discussions with my wife and family, we realize this might be a possibility, and we will consider it if and when it comes to that point."

17. How good is your health?

Your health is excellent. If you have had a health problem, or if your have missed work for more than two weeks in the last year, contact your Lawrence & Allen Consultant to discuss a strategy on exactly how to handle your health problem. A Human Resources hiring official or hiring manager is not a doctor, and it is not his or her role to interpret the status of your physical condition. If, in the interview process, the health question is probed further, and you have had a health problem, offer to take a company physical and let a doctor evaluate your health. Do not offer information about your health that could possibly be damaging to your career. Everyone has some type of a physical problem and if an applicant overplays physical problems, he or she could face significant detriments in the campaign.

18. Can you work under pressure, deadlines, etc.?

The answer is – "No problem." Pressure exists in an individual's head. You do not want to say that you thrive in a stressful environment because stress and pressure exist only in a person's head. A safe answer on this particular question is, "There is no problem." You may want to probe the interviewer on the workflow and planning of major projects, etc.

19. What is your philosophy or style of management?

If you were a manager, then you would want to expound upon how you feel individuals should be managed. Show flexibility and avoid the phrase "participative management." Participative management is interpreted by many as group decision-making. All employees are managed by somebody else, so from the "managee" perspective, you may want to share with the interviewer that your philosophy of management is to be managed in a fair manner, to be trained and supervised appropriately, to have your work criticized from an improvement standpoint, and to be acknowledged for a job well done. Far too many managers consider themselves truly participative managers when, in fact, they are not. This is a term that is woefully overworked in today's business scene.

After pausing and reflecting, consider the follow response, "I believe I am a situational manager. Specifically, my management style will vary depending upon the situation I am involved in. Possibly my role might be one of a coach with a subordinate. It may be one where I have ample opportunity to get a consensus of opinions from peers and subordinates, as well as superiors. Depending upon the time element involved, my management style may possess a greater sense of urgency where I direct my subordinates based on the information, facts, and sense of urgency at hand." Many people also respond to this question by saying they are a "hands-on manager" willing to take off their coat, roll up their sleeves, and pitch in. It is highly doubtful that people in executive levels of management are being paid for their hands-on talent. Lee Ioccoca, the former chairman of Chrysler Corporation, was initially trained as an engineer. Indeed, what a waste of time, energy, and creativity to have him roll up his sleeves and design a new fuel injection system. Executive management is paid to analyze, think, problem solve, and strategize, not to roll up their sleeves and actually perform the work.

I recently asked a vice president of operations what he thought his management style was and how he gets things done. He replied that when confronted with problems or issues, he would get the opinions of his direct reports and get them involved. While he never relinquished the responsibility of making the ultimate decision, he felt that sharing the problem with his staff and obtaining its constructive analysis consistently served him well.

When I pressed him to share with me how he would use this style of management if his phone rang and a voice on the other end of the line said in an excited tone, "There is a fire in shipping bay #2!" He replied, in that case, he would quickly assemble his direct reports and assess the situation. UGH!! The problem, as you might have determined, was that this gentleman was reluctant to make decisions. Consequently, no one would have pulled the fire alarm. Paralysis through analysis!

20. How do you promote both lateral and vertical communication within your area?

"I try to integrate a combination of written communication, both E-mail and formal reports, along with a balance of interpersonal communications, particularly on issues that require more immediate attention. The problem with E-mail, as I see it today, is that it can't be cross-examined, but it does allow everybody to be copied who might have bearing on the issue involved. Regarding communication with my immediate supervisor or superior, when I started to work for him, I took the time to sit down and specifically ask him what type of communication style does he appreciate from his subordinates and the frequency of those communications. That way, we started off on an excellent foot, which complemented his business style."

21. Do you prefer staff or line work? Why?

Before you can answer this question, you need to ask the interviewer how his/her organization defines "staff" and "line." Staff and line are not consistently structured in all companies and, based upon what position you are interviewing for, you would need to find out what the company's definition for each is.

22. What kind of salary are you worth?

In all salary questions, your first basic response should be that you are **open**. You want to avoid a number. The minute you start to discuss salary in terms of numbers, you start to close the sale. Pre-closure of a sale can destroy the sale. Many times the sale falls apart when an individual starts to discuss money up-front and has not finished selling himself or herself. Remember, with the reply, "**Open**," you are saying that you are open to listen to a competitive offer. This is the only answer you can share that will not blow you out of the water by suggesting a compensation that is too high for the immediate company to handle or, even worse, to leave money on the table because you were not assertive enough to ask for the appropriate amount. What are you looking for in terms of salary? "**I am open**. I am open to listen to a competitive offer."

23. What kind of manager was your former boss?

Psychologically, this may feel like a good time to vent any hostility you have and to really hammer your boss. A word of caution: an interview situation is not a suitable forum for this because you, as an applicant, will leave a negative impression in the interviewer's mind. The best thing to say is "My boss was an excellent manager because he/she allowed me to . . . ." and then list several of the accomplishments that you attained. As an applicant, you want to deviate from the point of discussing your boss to listing your accomplishments.

24. What are your five biggest accomplishments in your present or last job?
   Your career so far?

These questions should be answered from your resume. The reason you took time to prepare your resume in detail was to organize your thoughts. You want to reiterate the information on your resume. Your resume was good enough to get your foot in the door, and now it should become your interview script. You should use your resume as a resource to answer as many questions as you can. You want to reiterate in the same fashion and format the significant accomplishments and responsibilities that are on your resume. Do not tell the interviewer, "Well, here is my resume; look for yourself." Memorize your accomplishments so that you will be able to vocalize them.

It is most important when selling your accomplishments to be consistent and to quantify your answers. Most individuals, when they work on a resume with quantified accomplishments, have to spend a considerable amount of time digging and reconstructing these numbers. Do not let them remain on your resume. **Quantify, quantify, and quantify,** both in written form and in your verbal presentation. Do not forget to provide five accomplishments. If you do not follow directions during an interview, the employer will not have confidence that you can follow directions while on the job.

The answer, simply stated, should be the first five bullet points on your resume. Bullet points are nothing more than your accomplishments ranked in descending order of significance.

25. Why did you not do better in high school? College?

There are other questions in this section that are very similar to this – "Why have you not found a job so far," and, "Why are you not making more money at your age?" These types of questions are negative in orientation. They are basically saying that you, as an individual, have not done well and that you should have performed to the interviewer's expectations. The best way to answer the question is to turn it around and not be defensive or negative.

- "Why did you not do better in school? Why have you not found a job so far? Why are you not earning more at your age?"

  Simply say, "When I was in high school or college (based upon your situation) in addition to attending school, I did . . . and I feel that I did very well." Alternative answer: "I suppose I did not do better in high school or college because I was a lot younger then; my priorities were not as clear as they are now. Combined with a certain immaturity factor, I was not as disciplined at that time when compared to my current work ethic."

- "Why have you not found a job so far?" "Mr./Ms. Recruiter, respectfully, I am not looking for a job; I am looking for a new career assignment to continue to grow in my career path, and I am being very selective about the companies I am interviewing with. I am running a very methodical job search."

- "Why are you not earning more at your age?" This is a devastating question, basically saying that you are not earning as much as the interviewer expects. Although you may be earning a very fine salary, be careful how you handle compensation questions. If you were at a company where the salary increases have been minimal to none in the past years, use that as the reason. You may want to respond with, "At XYZ Manufacturing Company, there have not been a high number of increases in the last three or four years, but I am seeking to join an organization where my skills and accomplishments will be rewarded at a level commensurate with my contributions."

An interesting approach would be to softly challenge the interviewer's perspective on this question by implying something as follows: "In addition to my salary of $50,000 a year, I believe I have earned the respect and confidence, not only of my peers, but of my superior. I have earned the experience and discipline that comes with fifteen years of diversified and in-depth experience in _____. And I believe I have earned the confidence that accompanies the successes that I have enjoyed. So, in summary, I think I really have earned quite a bit for a person of my age." The key word in this question, of course, is "earned." You have very nicely taken this piece of vocabulary and given it a positive twist.

It is always important to remember that while some questions might be ego bruising, it is never appropriate to lose one's "cool." Try to maintain a straight, professional composure.

26. What is your biggest strength? Weakness?

When stating your biggest strengths, you should again refer to your resume and reiterate one or more of your most current significant accomplishments. Discussing areas of weakness can lead an applicant to talk too much, pontificate, and give information that could be devastating to his or her campaign. It is suggested that in the area of weakness, you should state that sometimes you are "too hardworking," pay "too much attention to detail," and are "too critical" of your work. Who would not want to hire someone who is hard working, pays attention to detail, or is critical of his or her work?

Choose positive qualities and attach the word "too." Avoid using words like "workaholic." A workaholic is not looked upon in a positive sense. An alternative response might be, "Sometimes I am too demanding of myself. Sometimes I am too quality oriented. Sometimes I am too concerned with broad-based concepts."

27. What business, character, and credit references can you give us?

Always be prepared to give a reference or list of references to a potential employer. It is suggested that you give the minimal amount of business references, which is at least two and no more than three. If asked to furnish character references, you should supply names of people who know you and your character. Credit references are tricky because companies are bordering on a fine line of asking information that may be illegal regarding your credit. If possible, during the job-search process, whether in the interview or on the job application, avoid giving your driver's license number. Your driver's license number allows a company, in most instances, to access any information it would like about you. Your credit is really not pertinent to the interview process unless the position requires you to handle money (i.e., work at a bank, handle petty cash, etc.). If this is a requirement of the position, then provide the information requested.

28. How long would it take you to make a contribution to our firm?

Be careful! This question could be your first step toward the door to exit the company. An employer will remember if you say that you will make a contribution immediately, within two to three weeks, or a month, etc. As an applicant, you do not know all the problems of the company, and you will not know for the first three to four months that you are there, so be very careful with this question. It is suggested that you would say something similar to the following: "I do not know exactly how long it will take me to make a significant contribution to the organization. Until I am privy to some of the company's goals and objectives that I would be asked to achieve, I could not make that assessment. Could you share with me some of the major goals of the organization and what you anticipate the successful candidate to achieve in the first three months, six months, or year?" Here again, ask another question. An individual who asks questions after he or she is given a question creates an excellent rapport with the hiring official. A nice and positive close for this question could be, "Based upon my past fifteen years of experience, I think I am a pretty fast learner and could make a contribution as quickly as I was able to grasp your problem with both the causes and the effects."

29. How long would you stay with us?

A simple response could be: "I would stay with the organization as long as I can continue to grow in my career." Be careful not to say, "until I retire" if you are in the fifty-or-older age category. Based upon your age, you will have to temper this answer. Statistically, you probably will not be with the company more than two or three years for a variety of reasons, but the suggested answer is, "As long as I have the opportunity to continue to grow in my career." An alternative answer would be: "I would stay with your organization as long as our goals are compatible."

30. How do you feel about people from minority groups?

The minority question could be death to an applicant in an interview. It is suggested that you not get into the discussion of what constitutes a minority group, etc. The question asks how you feel about people from minority groups, and it is suggested that you answer: "No problem." Questions that refer to race, religion, politics, or women in business should not be discussed during an interview because nine out of ten times, the applicant will lose, not knowing the biases of the hiring official(s). An alternative answer would be: "No problem, I work with minorities on a daily basis in my current position."

31. If you could start again, what would you do differently?

The applicant needs to be careful about the answer he or she gives to this question because a negative answer could hurt his or her chances as an applicant. If a negative comment about his or her previous employer is made such as, "I would not go to XYZ Manufacturing because they terminated me," this reinforces the negative, not the positive. It is suggested that you choose some event, career choice, decision, etc., that you made early in your career and focus on a minor mistake. Do not refer to your lack of education. Be careful about that issue. Suggested sample responses are: "I would have changed my major to business earlier in college," or possibly, "I would have returned to graduate school at an earlier age."

32. How do you rate yourself as a professional? As an executive?

Another question could be, "How do you rate yourself as an employee?" In any of these instances, always rate yourself at the top. For example, if you are given the question, "How would you rank yourself among your peers," you should say, "I rank myself number one." "How would you rate yourself as an employee?" "I rate myself at the top, at the very top." This is not bragging! If you are not number one, then the employer may continue to search for his/her number one-choice. Sometimes the question, "How do you rate yourself as a professional or as a business executive," is also couched with a third alternative: "How do you rate yourself as a husband/wife or family member? Possibly the following answer might be suitable: "On the universal '10' scale, "I would rate myself as a '10' as a professional, as a '9' as a business executive,' and as an '8' as a husband/wife or family member." Should you be asked to explain your rating you could simply say, "As a professional, I simply see myself as a flat number '10.' I am professional. As a business executive, I could support a score of '9' because I feel I have very strong qualifications and experience but realize that there are always more things to learn to increase my skill knowledge. As a family member or husband/wife, scoring myself with an '8' is based on the fact that I give a tremendous amount of my time to my job, my career, and my business. Sometimes this results in a sacrifice of personal time to my family and personal life; therefore, the scoring of an '8.'"

33. What new goals or objectives have you established recently?

This particular question can be looked at from two perspectives. First, if you had a recent significant accomplishment in your position, you could talk about these new goals and objectives. Second, your current goal and objective is to find a new career opportunity that will enable you to grow and take on more responsibilities.

34. Tell me about a business event occurring in a social setting in which you were working to enhance business relationships with customers or clients. How did you further your business objectives?

"Once a year, our company sponsors a golf outing where we invite key customers and suppliers with various members of our company. It is an excellent opportunity to further establish partnerships. It was at one of these golf outings that I picked up that one of our key suppliers was, in fact, anticipating a 3 percent price increase on its products, which naturally would affect our pricing to our key customers. This advance type of notification, while informal, gave us an opportunity to adequately prepare our customer for the inevitable price increase down the line. It softened the impact."

35. How have you changed the nature of your job?

Here again, you would refer to your significant accomplishments and responsibilities and show how you have made changes in your work area. Every quantitative bullet point in your resume, in effect, has changed the nature of your job. Again, without trying to be repetitive, use your resume as an interviewing script.

36. What position do you expect to have in five years?

Be careful. It is suggested that you do not use a specific title. Instead, use an area; for example, you should not answer with "Vice-President" or "Manager" of a certain area because that position may not exist. A better way to handle this would be to say, "After I am in my position, I hope that my accomplishments will be recognized, and I will be promoted upward to either a supervisor or management position," if that is in fact your career goal or objective. Alternative answer, "In five years I expect to be in a position (careful not to cite a specific title that could already be filled by an insecure manager) with the following types of responsibilities . . . ."

37. What do you think of your boss?

This is basically the same question as, "What type of manager was your boss?" See Question 23.

38. Why have you not obtained a job so far?

This was discussed in Question 25.

39. What is your feeling about women in business?

"No problem." See Question 30.

40. What features of your previous job have you disliked?

This question could be devastating to your career opportunity if you answer with a series of negatives. Every job has its downside and you do not want to harp on the negatives. If you were reduced in force, a good answer would be to say, "What I disliked about my previous job was that it went away from me. I was downsized out of my position," or whatever best describes your situation. If you are separated for other reasons, you may respond with a positive point instead of a negative; i.e., "The work flow varied so much that I could not give as much attention to quality or detail as I would have liked."

41. Would you describe a few situations in which your work has been criticized?

Cite situations from early in your career and not in your current work. We all make mistakes when we begin our world of work. Avoid using examples from your most recent experiences. For example: "When I started my first position, I did not realize the importance of deadlines. I did not realize to request an extension if I would not complete an item. I have conquered that problem!"

42. Would you object to working for a woman?

This is an issue just like women in business, minorities, etc.; the answer should be, "No problem."

43. How would you evaluate your present firm?

This is very similar to Questions 23 and 37. Be careful not to be negative about your most recent employer; get off the situation of the company, and get onto your accomplishments. For example, the answer could be, "The company was a great company because they allowed me to do . . . ." and list two or three of your significant accomplishments and responsibilities. These examples should fit the secret recipe question.

44. Do you generally speak to people before they speak to you?

However you choose to answer this question may indicate to the employer that you are brash and aggressive, or that you are very shy. A suggested answer would be, "It depends upon the situation." This type of answer shows that you are flexible, sensitive, and willing to be a team player.

45. How would you describe the essence of success?

This is an extremely interesting question because you are being asked to philosophize on your definition of success. Your answer should be centered on business activities. For example, it is suggested that you take one of the business activities or accomplishments that you have achieved and weave your definition of success around these types of accomplishments and activities in your work. If the interviewer asks, after you have defined success, if you consider yourself successful, you may want to hold back from being overzealous and saying, "Yes I am successful," by looking at the downside to your answer of "yes" because where are you going to go from there? If you consider yourself successful, are there no further objectives to obtain? No new mountains to climb? If asked the follow-up question ("Do you consider yourself successful?"), a suggested answer would be, "No, I am not successful because when I start to reach my goals and objectives, I push them up higher, and I continue to reach and stretch and grow." Alternative response: "Borrowing from the old toast: health, wealth, and time to enjoy both." Simple, but effective. Success is a journey, not an objective.

46. What was the last book you read? Movie you saw? Sporting event you attended?

These types of questions are good icebreakers, but they can also be questions that can get you into a series of distracting comments and conversation or can leave a negative thought about you with the interviewer. "What was the last book you read?" You should pick a business publication to discuss. Regarding the last book or magazine you have read, there is a lot to be said for the phrase, "readers are leaders." What is the last movie you saw? You should choose a non-controversial movie. If you have not attended a sporting event recently, then you may want to talk about one you watched on television. The interviewer may be looking to see if, in relation to sports, you are competitive in nature. People who participate in sports or attend sporting events have a tendency to be extremely competitive. Many people are reticent to go to theaters, movies, or sporting events because of fear of large crowds. These are not the types of persons that a company would want to send to a trade show or industry convention.

47. In your present situation, what problems have you identified that had previously been overlooked?

The answer to this question should be one or more of your significant accomplishments from your resume. For example: "In the last twelve months I . . . ."

48. What interests you most about the position we have? The least?

To answer what interests you most, it is suggested that you review the secret recipe question and the qualities and skills that the company is looking for in the successful applicant. For the last part, it is suggested that you say, "I do not know; could you share with me what you look at as the downside to this position or company," and let the interviewer talk. You may even want to ask the interviewer how long he/she has been with the company and how he or she has grown in his or her career and what have been some of the frustrations with the company. The more research you do on a company, the more likely you will discover mutual interests.

For example, an organization may be in a highly stimulating, competitive situation where they deal in high-tech products with a proactive corporate culture that matches your interests. Again, anytime that you can turn around and ask a question of your interviewer and get additional information, you are doing an excellent job of creating personal rapport. He or she will remember you in a positive sense as a well-prepared business professional.

49. Do you feel you might be better off in a different-sized company? Different type company?

If you answer "Yes," to this question, then why are you there for the interview? Whether your background is with a large company or small company you want to sell your skills and ability to that potential employment opportunity. If you are from a large company or Fortune 500 corporation, then you want to sell the fact that large companies are made up of smaller divisions and departments. If you are from a small company and you are talking to a large company, you want to sell the fact that within a large corporation, the departments and divisions are very similar to small companies. The answer is, "No, this is the type of company I want because. . . ."

50. Why are you not earning more at your age?

This was previously discussed in Question 25.

51. Will you be out to take your boss's job?

The keyword here is **take**; you are not really out to **take** your boss's job, but if the position became available, you would like to be considered. This shows that you, as an individual, have aspirations of moving upward. In fact, in many situations, that opportunity may never come to you, but you want to show that if it does, you would like to be considered. It shows that you are positive, cooperative, and that you are flexible. It is important to keep in mind who might ask this question. For example, "Will you be out to take your boss's job," might be answered differently if the person asking the question is the manager of recruitment or your potential immediate superior. In light of this comment, consider the following responses: "No, I would not be out to take my boss's job, but if his/her position became available, I would hope that my current and past performance would enable me to be one of the persons considered for the position." Or possibly, "My goal is to help my boss get promoted and become the best candidate for that position."

52. Are you creative? Give an example.

With all three questions (Questions 52, 53, and 54), the successful applicant should refer to his or her resume. "Are you creative?" "Yes," and go to your resume. "Are you analytical?" "Yes," and go to the resume with an example of significant accomplishments. "Are you a good manager?" If you are a manager, the answer is, "Yes," and then give an example from your resume. Stick to your resume. Your resume took a lot of time for you to prepare, and you want to continually quote the bullet points from it. Tell the interviewer once, tell him or her twice, and tell him or her three times. He or she is not listening that well to your qualifications. Reiterate your significant accomplishments and responsibilities. Remember: Commit your resume to memory and always have an extra copy or two with you during the interview.

53. Are you analytical? Give an example.

See Question 52.

54. Are you a good manager? Give an example.

See Question 52.

55. Are you a leader? Give an example.

See Question 52.

56. How would you describe your personality?

Since most of us are not psychologists, this could be a very difficult question. Over the years, I have seen many individuals basically destroy themselves when asked this question. A suggested answer is, "My personality is complex." If you are a manager, you may answer, "I try to be a very thorough individual, supportive of those that work for me." When you are in the role of a person directly managed by a supervisor, then you may want to say, "I try to be a very cooperative, flexible individual." Remember that you are not a psychologist, and it is not your role in the interview to give a technical definition of your personality.

57. Have you helped increase sales? Profits? How?

The answer to this question should come from your resume. Everybody in an organization should work on profits because when you reduce operating costs in a company, this has a direct relationship to making the company more profitable. Your work may indirectly affect sales and profits, but if you have direct examples in sales, then you would want to use this information from your resume. The same holds true with Question 58, "Have you helped reduce costs?" This answer is, "yes," and then give a definite example. "I made a suggestion, and I expedited a situation . . . ." or, "I cut time to do . . . ." or, "I improved quality, thus reducing the costs by _____ percent."

58. Have you helped reduce costs? How?

See Question 57.

59. What do your subordinates think of you?

This is a win-or-lose situation. Every supervisor always wants to think that their subordinates think that they are the best. Based upon your situation, you would want to say, "Sometimes my subordinates think I am a wonderful person because of . . . ." and give some reasons. "However, I am sure that sometimes they do not think I am so wonderful because I have to implement policies of which they do not approve, for example, . . ." Refer to your resume and show the results!

60. Have you fired people before?

If you have been in a position where you have fired employees, you would say, "Yes," and if you have not, you would say, "No." It is a simple "yes" or "no" question. When asked what time it is, do not tell them how to build the watch!

61. Have you hired people before? What do you look for?

This, too, would be a "yes" or "no" question. What do you look for! "I look for someone to . . . ." You want to communicate that you have a recipe to hire the best applicant. When many companies look to hire new employees, they really do not know what they are looking for. As they continue to talk to individuals, their thoughts on what it is they are looking for change and, in some instances, the boss's boss gets involved and the whole hiring queue gets changed around from the original target or goal. You want to show the potential interviewer that you are an organized, prepared individual and that before you begin to recruit for an employee, you know exactly what you are looking for in the successful candidate.

62. Why do you want to work for us?

It is suggested that your answer contain elements of the secret recipe question. Again, resell yourself. For example, "Mr./Ms. Recruiter, it was indicated to me that your company is looking for someone to . . . ." Share with him or her the skills that he or she is looking for and then use examples to reiterate what you have done in these areas. This is another opportunity for you, as the applicant, to resell yourself.

63. If you had your choice of jobs and companies, where would you go?

It is suggested that you as the applicant not describe a company exactly like the company you are talking with because such an answer would be rather transparent. A sample answer could be one that focuses on opportunity, such as, "I am looking for a company where I have the opportunity to do _____," or, "where I can capitalize on six years of _____."

64. What other types of jobs are you considering? What companies?

If you are early in your campaign, you would indicate to the interviewer, "I just started my search, and this is my first interview; I am being very selective with the companies with which I am interviewing." If you have had a series of interviews and no offers, be careful not to say, "I have interviewed with fifteen companies." Then the interviewer may ask if you have had an offer. If you answer, "No," then the interviewer might think, "Well, fifteen companies did not want him/her, why would I want him/her? There must be something wrong with him/her."

It is suggested that you develop a strategy that indicates that you have started a search, you have contacted several companies, you have had several preliminary interviews, and you are expecting secondary rounds with several companies. It is further suggested that you keep your job-search information confidential because it is a confidential matter. In some instances, you may be talking to a company where there is an incumbent who may be separated. Revealing certain information might also indicate that if you have loose lips about the confidential nature of your job search campaign, then you might have loose lips about the confidential matters of the company.

65. Why do you feel you have top-management potential?

"Do you feel you have top-management potential, or do you think you have top-supervisor potential, or do you think you have top-employee potential?" The answer is, "Yes," and then give examples from your resume to show why you have this potential. Nothing demonstrates top-management potential better than concrete, quantitative results of how you have either a) increased revenue, b) decreased operating expenses, or c) both a and b. There is nothing wrong with standing up and saying that you are a bottom-line-oriented individual. Business is not a spectator sport.

66. What do you look for in a job?

You are looking for a position that is similar to one that the company you are interviewing has, so here again, you want to indicate that you are looking for a position, that has the interviewing company's needed responsibilities and duties and requires the use of your acquired skills. For example, "Mr./Ms. Interviewer, you indicated your company is looking for someone to . . . . In my career to date, I have . . . ." Use examples of accomplishments from your resume.

67. What do you know about our company, business, or industry?

Before going into an interview, a successful applicant should thoroughly research the company. (Refer to sections in the interviewing chapter regarding preparing for the interview and researching companies.) Sometimes, however, if a company is privately held, you may be able to find very little, if any, information about the company. At this point, you would tell the interviewer, "Mr./Ms. Recruiter I checked the following research sources . . . and I could not find any information about your company. Could you share with me some information about your company?" If you have, on the other hand, researched the company and know the company very well, then you may want to have a list of questions prepared. It is advised that you have a list of questions prepared from your research about the company and ask questions about projects, products that were started several months ago, and the status on these projects and products, etc.

68. What do you expect from the company that hires you?

Employee's expectations of employers sometimes are extremely unrealistic. If an interviewer asks this type of question, you may want to consider the following answer: "I expect to have the opportunity to perform my job and to receive evaluations of whether or not I am doing my position well – not only the positive points but also the negative points so that I can improve in my position if there are deficiencies. I hope that my performance will be recognized, and I will be able to excel in my career."

69. What are some things you wish to avoid in the next job?

Based upon the situation, you may want to answer with one of the following: "I wish to avoid inconsistencies in my work load . . . ." or, "I wish to avoid having differences with my boss caused by poor or vague communication."

70. What has accounted for your progress (grades, awards, etc.)?

"Hard work, diligence, tenacity – these are all elements that have accounted for my progress." Be confident and sell yourself as a winner.

71. What would you do if your supervisor made a decision that you strongly disagreed with?

If you indicate that you would butt heads with your supervisor, you may be ruled out as a viable candidate. You may be considered too strong, too independent, or too argumentative, and you may not be seen as a person capable of making a contribution within the organization's operating structure. A suggested answer would be, "If the decision is not illegal, immoral, or damaging to people's health, safety, and welfare, I would agree with my supervisor, and at an appropriate time, I would request to discuss the situation."

If your supervisor makes a decision and you have information that your supervisor is unaware of, it is your duty to convey this to him or her before the decision is implemented. Be careful with this question. Based on the situation of the interview, you do not want to come across as overly strong, stubborn, and inflexible. You want to show that you are a well-learned business professional. Perhaps the following answer is more to the point: "I would close ranks and work hard to support the decision and to implement it."

72. What do you expect from the company that hires you? How can we meet your needs?

The reason people work is because they need (not necessarily in this order) security, money, benefits, intellectual stimulation, a place to go, structure in their lives, things to do, and socialization. Realistically, what your actual goals and desires are for your position should not be voiced in the interview. You should take this question and turn it around and say, "I expect to have the opportunity to work toward XYZ Company's goals."

73. What are two things you wish to avoid in your next job?

You may just say, "There is only one thing I wish to avoid in my next job, and that is seeing it disappear." Why give two potential negatives?

74. Are there any reasons why you cannot arrive on time and stay at work all day on a regular basis?

This question is a technique for an interviewer to ask questions that border on the illegal. This question could be asked to find out if the applicant is a mother and might have problems with children and therefore would not be able to be at work all the time. Also, if you are female, this is a way to probe to see if you might be planning a family. This is also a way to "force" applicants to identify any health problems or other types of extenuating circumstances that would prevent them from being on time and at work on a regular basis. Be careful with this question – just basically say, "No, there are no problems."

75. What is most important to you about your job? Why?

This question is asking what your values and feelings are about work. Here again, keep your answer directed toward work, stay away from benefits and the money/salary issue, and center your answer on what the required work skills are for the position and what are the requirements for the position. For example: "I feel that the responsibilities of . . . and the responsibilities of . . . . are important. Specifically I have . . . . [give examples]."

76. What kind of working environment do you prefer?

The successful applicant should describe a similar type of working environment as to that of the interviewing company. If you are interviewing at a 250-employee service organization, you may want to say, "I am seeking a medium-sized work environment where I can continue to . . . [use examples]."

77. How often were you late or absent in your last job?

It is difficult and virtually impossible for a company to verify this information because most companies today only verify the start date, the completion date, and salary with written request from previous employers. An employee's attendance is not normally a verifiable item. If you were **not** late or absent in your last job, you may indicate, "I have not had a problem with being late or absent."

78. What did you do to prepare for this interview?

As a general rule, first check the company's Web site. As a prepared applicant, you can share with the interviewer the process of research that you went through to prepare for this interview by saying, "I researched the company and reviewed . . . ." The interviewer may also ask how you sourced the company and, here again, you would discuss your research and how you developed your database of companies to contact. It is an excellent practice, when talking with a company representative or recruiter by phone to establish a mutually convenient time for the interview. At that point, ask or tell the interviewer that, in order to prepare for the interview, would they please send information on the company. Indicate you have checked the company's Web site and would like the following additional information. Specifically, you can ask your interviewer or potential supervisor before you arrive to send an annual report, a 10K report, a 10Q report, the last three quarterly reports, and/or recent product literature and information. After all, a picture is worth a thousand words. This will indicate to the interviewer that you are the type of person who is going into an important meeting well prepared. Remember that not all companies have Web sites and not all companies with Web sites offer the above information. These actions create a favorable first impression without the applicant and interviewer having had the opportunity for the first face-to-face meeting. If the company is privately held, there is little financial information that would be obtainable except for purchasing a D&B credit report. Such an action certainly would be advisable and a prudent investment of $89 before accepting an offer of employment from a privately held company.

79. Can you provide a list of your references?

In response to this question, the answer is, "Yes," and then provide a list of references. Provide no more than three references. If you can provide only two references that would be the safest. The fewer references you provide, the better because references are uncontrollable situations even though an individual will offer information about you in a positive sense. References sometimes talk too much, and they bring up points about you, your career, or your past that were not discussed in the interview – giving the interviewer a chance to delve into areas that are not necessarily pertinent to your campaign.

80. If you could change one thing about yourself, what would it be?

Looking at this realistically, if you are a free agent and unemployed, you would say, "If there was one thing that I could change, it would be to change my employment status. I do not like being a free agent." Use positive terms; instead of saying "unemployed," use the term "free agent." It will spark the interviewer to a positive sense indicating that you are a professional businessperson, and you are handling the situation in a positive manner. If you do have an area that you would like to change about yourself, make sure that it is a positive, not a negative. Do not say things like, "I wish I had completed my degree, or I wish I had more training in such and such or in a certain field." This shows a negative. Instead, take a positive approach and say, "If there was something I could change about myself, it would be that sometimes I have the tendency to be too quality oriented, and because of the work load it frustrates me." You want to go into a positive situation.

81. What did your last performance evaluation say about you?

This question is another opportunity to tell the interviewer about your positive strengths. However, the interviewer may say, "Ok, I understand that, but what about some areas of improvement; everybody needs improvement." You should be prepared to handle some of those areas of improvement – no one is perfect – but pick minor points and continue to highlight your positive points.

82. What would you do on the first day on the job?

Typically, people respond by indicating they would walk around and introduce themselves to their staff members or coworkers. In practice, if an individual can find the parking spot that has been assigned to him/her and the cafeteria, he/she is doing well for his/her first day on the job.

This is a key question because it can result in giving insight into a person's business acumen. Some people would answer, "I would make sure I had the latest revision of the company's policies and procedures manuals to get off on the right foot." This is a bland answer.

Consider an alternative approach. Because most people do not start working the day after they accept a position, there is a one-to two-week interval before the actual first day on the job. A smart applicant could respond to the above question by replying, "In the interval between acceptance of the position and reporting for the job, I would use that time to request the last six months' operating reports so that I could study how the company measures my unit's effectiveness.

"I would ask for internal operations and financial reports for the last six months. I certainly would want to ask the Human Resource department to select or make the personnel files of all staff members available for my review. I would dictate a letter to each staff member, indicating that I was looking forward to joining them on such and such date, and on that date, I would like to review the following items: a prepared memorandum outlining their major areas of responsibility, what areas they are having difficulty in, what areas they need assistance in, and what their specific career aspirations are within this organization. I would have those memorandums sent to my home where I could digest them in preparation for a meaningful first day on the job.

"I would request any additional corollary reports that would have a bearing on my unit's effectiveness, whether they come from the financial group, the marketing group, or the production group. I want to know how my unit is doing in the overall company schematic. I would have asked my supervisor before I started what areas were a major priority, what areas he/she would like me to work on first, what areas he/she would like me to change. I would also ask him/her in what areas was he/she most satisfied with the performance of the last person who held this job. Additionally, I would review the last performance reports of all individuals to indicate areas for continued improvement as well as noted areas of achievement, strength, and outstanding performance. In the afternoon, I would call a general staff meeting and outline my style of management so that everyone could understand my method of operation. I would review the department's objectives both annually and quarterly to assure that everyone is in tune with these same objectives."

83. What would you do if a disgruntled former employee of yours walked into the plant carrying a pistol?

See the answer to Question 84.

84. What was the toughest business decision you ever made, and why?

Obviously the answers to Questions 83 and 84 must be sought in one's own experience. No suggested answer can be crafted for an easy response.

85. Take about twenty seconds to define the position for which you are being interviewed.

86. Specify the action and results in your background that support your definition of this position.

Keep your answer succinct and focused on the definition of this position you feel will fit within the parameters as described.

87. Are you over-qualified or too experienced for the position we have to offer?

Short and simple is the best here. Your company will get a faster return on its investment because you have more experience than is apparently required. Besides, a strong company needs strong people!

88. What do you see as being the most difficult task in being a manager?

The broad answer that incorporates the scope of responsibility found in management positions may be the best answer here. Such as – the planning and accomplishment of objectives within budget.

89. What is your biggest weakness as a manager?

When answering this question, be honest and always end on a positive note. An example might be, "Reprimanding people is sometimes a problem, so I always begin the conversation by pointing out a positive aspect of their performance."

90. How do you feel about losing your benefits?

It is always a little disconcerting to realize that you and your family may not be covered by benefits such as health, retirement funds, and so forth. However, it is perfectly acceptable to be concerned although not panicky. Be confident in your ability to move into another position that will allow you to have the benefits again.

91. How do you evaluate your present firm?

It will not serve you well to make negative or discouraging remarks against the firm you left, even if you left at someone else's request as opposed to your own decision. Find something positive to say about the firm, perhaps that you had the opportunity to grow in scope of responsibility and to learn many new aspects of business.

92. Do you like working with figures more than words?

This is a personal preference question, and in questions such as these, you are better off being honest and up-front with your answer. Always be positive when answering questions that call for a definitive selection.

93. Have you thought about leaving your present position before? Why didn't you?

If you have not thought of leaving, say so – let the interviewer know that you have not entertained the thought of leaving your organization. If you have thought of leaving, you will want to answer that question on a positive note, such as: "I have thought of leaving in the past whenever the scope of responsibility or the challenges were not present to take advantage of my experience and drive. However, being dedicated to my position, I worked diligently to find ways to enhance the scope of ability and provide myself with challenges that assisted the company in driving profits."

The following questions are a bit more difficult and may only apply to individuals interviewing for the positions of Director, Vice President, General Manager, or any position with full profit-and-loss responsibility. Again these questions require some thoughtful consideration and can only be responded to in light of one's own experience.

INTERVIEW QUESTIONS FOR CANDIDATES WITH FULL P & L RESPONSIBILITY

1. Describe a complex problem you have worked on recently that required in-depth analysis. What factors or variables did you consider?

2. Describe a significant project or idea you have conceived within the last two years. How did you know it was needed and would work? Was it used? Did it work?

3. What sources of information did you use to keep aware of problems within your department? Can you tell me about a time you relied on those sources to inform you of a problem?

4. How often is your schedule upset by unforeseen circumstances? What have you done to improve the reliability of your schedule?

5. How have you stayed attuned to potential obstacles to achieving your goals or accomplishing your work?

6. How do you set your work plan for the year? What were your objectives for last year? How were they achieved?

7. What are your long- and short-term plans? Are they in writing? Describe how you use them. In this situation, make it for the last two years.

8. When beginning a new assignment, what steps do you take to plan how you will complete it?

9. When organizing a project, how have you determined which resources to use? Give an example of one project, describing the method and the result.

10. Describe a situation that required several things to be done at the same time. How did you handle it?

11. Tell me about a time when you reorganized your work group. What prompted you to do that, and what was the outcome?

12. Take me step by step through how you determined the budget for your unit or division. What information did you use in preparing the budget? What information was lacking?

13. Describe how you have estimated the costs of a project. What determines the priorities? Give an example.

14. How have you allowed for unexpected expenses when preparing a budget? How did you control your division's budget? What action did you take when expenses exceeded it?

15. What methods do you use to keep informed about what is going on in your area of expertise?

16. What have you done when you found that your techniques for monitoring activities were loosely adhered to by your subordinates? Give an example.

17. Describe a situation when you had to act quickly to correct a problem. Could closer monitoring have prevented it? What did you do? What was the result?

18. What difficulties do you have in establishing actions to take in your job? Give an example.

19. What was the most difficult decision you have made in the last two years? What made it difficult?

20. How have you gone about making an important decision related to your job?

21. What was a challenging business decision you have recently faced? How did you decide what to do?

22. When, if ever, have you delayed decisions to give yourself more time to think? Describe the situation and outcome.

23. What kinds of decisions do you make rapidly? Which ones do you take more time on? Give an example, please.

24. When have you declined to make work-related decisions? Why?

25. Describe a situation when you were faced with obstacles. How did you handle it?

26. Give me an example of the most practical decision you have made in the past two years. What were the alternatives? Why was it practical?

27. What are the most important business issues you have addressed in the last two years? Tell me what you did about them. What was the result?

28. What was the biggest risk you had to take while at your company? Why was it risky? Why did you take it? What was the outcome?

29. In your job, when did you have to use common sense? Tell me about the situation and the results of using common sense for that particular issue.

30. What other divisions or departments do you have to frequently deal with in your current job? How often and under what conditions?

31. Have you ever made a decision that affected departments or divisions other than your own? What was the situation, and what was the result?

32. How have events in your area of the organization affected other parts of the organization? Give examples.

33. What organizational resources or services do you most commonly use? What type of training or information about these resources do you give your subordinates?

34. With whom do you work to accomplish your objectives? How have you insured that you get cooperation? Give an example.

35. How did you keep your employees informed of what was going on in the organization?

36. How have you minimized undesired side effects from incorporated new procedures in your work unit? Give an example.

37. What was the biggest obstacle you had to overcome in order to incorporate a new idea or process in your area? Why was it an obstacle? How did you overcome it?

38. Describe a situation where you got the most mileage out of a procedure or policy change you had to introduce to your subordinates? How did you take advantage of the opportunity produced by the change?

39. Could you cite an example of when you were faced with delegating authority and/or responsibility? How did it work out?

40. When looking at applicants, how do you select the best person? Have you had any problems with this method? If yes, what were they?

41. Describe how you hired your last subordinate. How well is the person doing the job?

42. Have you oriented and trained your new employees?

43. How have you established work objectives with subordinates, and are they usually reached?

44. How have you used feedback to encourage good performance? Give a specific example.

45. How do you know if the feedback you give an employee is effective? Give a specific example.

46. How do you keep your employees informed of what is going on in the organization?

47. Describe how you handled the situation where a subordinate did an outstanding job, and what you did when a subordinate had a performance problem. What was the result of each situation?

48. How have you helped your subordinates develop themselves? Give specific examples.

49.   Tell me about a situation in which you dealt with a controversial topic at work.

50.   Tell me about the last time that you took a stand on an issue that others disagreed with. What were the merits in the others' viewpoints? Give a specific example.

51.   Tell me about a situation in which you became frustrated or impatient when dealing with customers, subordinates, boss, or coworkers. What did you do?

52.   Describe a situation at work when someone criticized you. How did you react?

53.   What is the most imaginative or innovative thing you have done in your present position?

54.   Can you think of a situation you had to handle in which old solutions didn't work? What did you do to handle it?

55.   Describe a problem in your organization that you handled in a different manner or different way. How was your approach different, and what were the results?

56.   How have you gotten your employees to come up with new ideas in the past? Give an example.

57.   Describe a new idea or suggestion.

58.   Tell me about a situation in which you had to adjust quickly to changes in the organizational priorities? What was the impact of the changes on you? Give a specific example.

59.   What was the highest-pressure situation in which you have been involved in recent years? How did you cope with it? Give a specific example.

60.   What situations do you find most frustrating? How have you dealt with them? Give a specific situation.

61.   How did you get your job at your present company?

62. What changes have you tried to implement in your area of responsibility? What have you done to get them underway?

63. How have you tried to influence events to achieve goals? Give a specific example.

64. In your position, how do you define doing a good job?

65. How do you measure success? Have you been successful at your present company? Explain.

66. Tell me about the time when you were not very pleased with your performance. What did you do about it? Give a specific example.

67. What competitive situations have you been in during your career? How did you handle the competition? Did you win?

68. Give an example of a project or task that needed an extra effort to complete. What did you do?

69. What was the biggest obstacle that you had to overcome to get where you are today? How did you overcome it?

70. How have you scheduled your time and set priorities?

71. In the past, what did you do when you became overloaded with work? Give an example of the situation.

72. What have you done recently to develop your knowledge or abilities? How have you applied that knowledge to your present position?

73. How does your current job relate to your career goals? What are your career goals?

74. What are your career goals for the next five years?

75. What magazines or newsletters have you recently read and gotten useful job-related information from?

76. What company-sponsored development courses have you taken? How did you get involved with those?

77. What was one of the worst communication problems you have experienced in your career? Give an example.

78. At one time or another, we have all had some problems getting our point across when talking on the telephone. Give me an example of when this happened to you.

79. What is the most complex topic you have had to explain to a group? How did you handle this?

80. How did you develop a rapport with your coworkers and people from other departments? Give an example.

81. Tell me about a situation when you felt you shared too much information or shared information with the wrong associate. Why? What was the result?

82. Tell me about some of the toughest groups that you have had to get cooperation from. Did you have any formal authority? What did you do? Give a specific example.

83. How frequently did you meet with your immediate subordinates as a group? Why? What did you do in preparation, at the meeting, and after the meeting?

84. What recent problem have you had in which you included your subordinates in arriving at a solution? What approach did you take to get them to accomplish the task?

85. How did you set the objectives for your unit last year?

86. What was one of the best ideas you ever sold to a supervisor? What was your approach in order to do that selling?

87. What was one of the best ideas you tried but failed to sell to a peer? What was your approach, and why did it fail?

88. How do you approach a negotiating situation? Describe a recent situation that required negotiating? What was the result?

89. Tell me about a situation when you had to work out a compromise solution. Did both sides compromise equally; if not, why?

90. What recent conflict have you had with a peer, subordinate, or supervisor? Did it interfere with getting the work done? How was it resolved?

91. Describe a situation when you had to help people with different viewpoints reach a constructive solution.

92. Did you have any subordinates who did not work well together? What did you do about it?

93. Have you, in your past career, perceived any problems you caused others? What are they? Could they have been avoided?

94. Tell me about a project you generated on your own because you saw a need for it. What did you do to set it up? Did others also see a need for the project?

95. Describe a change you have had to explain to other people. Did they understand your vision of the situation?

96. Describe a situation when you initiated a change that would affect many people. How did you involve those who would be affected with the change?

97. Tell me about some of the toughest groups that you have had to get working as a productive team. What did you do?

98. How often did you attend meetings with your peer? What role did you play in the meetings? Tell me about a meeting and how you participated in it.

99. How did you improve the decision-making process in any group meeting that you were a part of? Give me an example.

100. Sometimes we have to bend the truth a little when dealing with a particular customer or situation. Can you give me some examples of when you had to do this?

101. How have you become active in your community? What have been the results of your involvement?

102. We have all had to work with people who are difficult to get along with. Give me some examples of when this happened to you. Why was that person difficult? How did you handle that person?

103. When working with people, how do you determine when you are pushing too hard? How do you determine when you should back off?

104. How do you go about collecting information regarding your customers' likes, and dislikes, and priorities?

105. How far in advance do you usually know the details of a competitor's products? How do you learn about them? Give an example.

106. Tell me about how you forecast what the needs of your customers will be. Have your forecasts been successful? Why? Why not?

107. How do you keep up to date on key competition?

108. At your level, how have you maintained contact with your customers? What improvement do you notice in relationships with the organization because of your contact?

109. In your professional arena, how have you ensured that important details were not overlooked when planning a project? Be specific with an example.

110. We all have occasions when we were working on something that just "slipped through the cracks." Can you give me an example of when this happened to you?

111. Can you give me some examples of times when you found errors in your work? What were the causes? How did you handle the errors?

112. Do you have a system for controlling and checking errors in your own work? If so, describe that system for me.

113. Take me step by step through how you prepared the budget for your last project or your last budget.

114. How have you scheduled the timeline for a project and set priorities?

115. Can you think of some projects or ideas, not necessarily your own, that were implemented or carried out successfully primarily because of your efforts.

116. What kind of system do you have for keeping track of the progress workers are making on a particular project that you assigned them?

117. How have you prepared for meetings that you would be leading?

118. Tell me about a time when you were leading a meeting that the discussion got away from the agenda. How did you handle it?

119. Describe how you follow up a meeting to make sure that what was agreed to be done was completed.

120. Tell me about the three most important people in your education and career.

121. I would like you to think of the biggest challenge on the job where you succeeded and the biggest challenge you failed to meet.

WHAT TO ASK AND WHEN TO ASK IT!

On the following pages are sample questions you may want to ask during your interview. **DO NOT** take these sheets of questions with you to the interview. Instead, use them as a guideline in developing your own personal list of questions to ask as a result of your research.

I place quite a bit of emphasis on asking good questions. The reason for this emphasis is twofold. Asking good, well-thought-out questions shows sincere interest about the position and the company. It also demonstrates that you are coming into the interview well prepared. All too frequently, applicants focus on responding to the interviewers' questions and do not give adequate preparation time on questions to ask. Many individuals rely on the "old-standby" question, "Tell me about your benefits."

I have always found this question somewhat annoying because how important is it to know a company's benefits plans unless you actually work there. This means the company actually has extended you an offer. Who cares what the life-insurance coverage is at Apple Computer unless you actually work for Apple Computer? This subject is further discussed on page 319, "Questions *Not* to Ask During an Interview."

When asking questions, don't be afraid to ask some of the same questions to everybody you meet. In this manner, you will quickly determine not only if you get the same answers, but also if everybody is on the same page of the same game plan. Teamwork starts with clear communication.

The typical interview candidate will exhibit some degree of nervousness. This is natural. Admittedly, it is difficult to remember all of the questions to ask that I have listed. So don't try! Rewrite these or other questions on your own yellow note pad. When the interviewer asks the question, "What questions would you like to ask me?" Simply reach into your briefcase and reply, "Last night, when I was preparing for our meeting today, I took the liberty of writing a few questions that I'd like to share with you." Again, you demonstrate planning, thoroughness, and organization. No stress – just remember where you put your briefcase.

QUESTIONS TO *ASK* DURING AN INTERVIEW

There are two types of questions to ask during an interview: fact questions and selling questions. Fact questions simply give you an answer to a question, i.e., facts or data. Selling questions are designed to find out information from the interviewer that will allow you to continue to sell your accomplishments.

FACT QUESTIONS:

1. Why is this position open?

2. How often has this position been filled in the past five to ten years, and where have those people gone? (This is an excellent question for determining opportunities for advancement and career pathing.)

3. Does this position figure prominently in any succession planning? If so, why wasn't an internal candidate considered for this position?

4. What are the primary reasons for persons leaving the company?

5. Why did the person who most recently held this position leave?

6. What are some of the objectives that you would like accomplished in this job?

7. What freedom would I have in determining my work objectives, deadlines, and methods of measurement?

8. Is this position pivotal as an agent of change?

9. What kinds of support does this position receive in terms of people, finance, etc.?

10. Does your company support continual education and/or tuition reimbursement?

11. How would you describe your company's culture?

12. Is this the type of culture your company is striving for?

13. What is your company's growth plan for the next three to ten years?

14. How do you expect to accomplish these objectives?

15. How does your company growth compare with the growth of the industry?

16. Does your company have any plans for acquisitions or mergers?

17. Has your company ever gone through a reduction-in-force?

18. Who do you see as your company's toughest competitor, and why?

19. How would your describe your management style?

20. How does this compare with your boss or those above him or her, especially the chief executive?

21. In what ways has this organization been most successful in terms of products and services over the years? Particularly recently?

22. Share with me, within the span of the next three to five years, what will contribute the most to your growth: new products, acquisitions, increased market penetration, price increases, real market growth, etc.?

23. What is your e-commerce strategy? Is it working?

24. What e-commerce plans do you have?

25. Will I have budget responsibility? If so, how much?

26. What are the limits on my signature authority?

27. Will I have the authority to hire and fire individuals or to grant performance reviews and salary increases?

28. How will I know if my performance is good to average? Above average? Excellent?

29. How do these measures translate into salary increases? A year from now, if I do an excellent job for you, what type of increase can I expect? How does this differ from above average? From average? (Note: This is a very aggressive question.)

30. Have you ever given an above average or an excellent rating?

31. What does an "above average" or "excellent" job performance mean to you?

32. When appropriate, may I have an opportunity to talk with some of my peers?

33. In response to a request to meet the company's consulting psychologist for an interview and/or psychological testing:
  A. After I take the tests, will you share with me the results of the assessments?
  B. Who keeps the results of the tests, and how long are they kept?

34. What is the next step in this process?

35. When can I expect to hear from you?

36. May I have your business card?

37. When may I call you to follow up?

SELLING QUESTIONS:

1. What are you looking for in the successful candidate?

This, in my opinion, is absolutely one of the most important questions to ask! Basically, when an interviewer is asked this question, the applicant is really asking, "How will you recognize the person you want to hire from the runner-up?" This is the classical sales question, also referred to as the "secret recipe" question. It means, "What are you buying?" Once this question is answered, the applicant is well advised not to ask any other question but to take the answer and run with it!

For example, when politely pressed on this question, the answer generally is expressed in the following format:

> "We are looking for someone with ten to twelve years of experience in the areas of X, Y, and Z. Additionally, background in the areas of A, B, and C would be a strong asset."

Now, the secret recipe is out. Don't go on and ask about the company's life-insurance program where you have to be dead before your beneficiary gets three times your annual salary. The interviewer has just told you what he wants. Sell yourself! Match everything in your background that corresponds to the ingredients of the secret recipe. "Mr. Interviewer, while at El Paso Cigar Corporation, I had eleven years of experience in X, Y, and Z."

If you don't have any experience in function "Z," blow right past the point. Don't draw attention to what you don't have – sell what you have. Your experience in the functional areas of "X" and "Y" may be so strong that the company may decide to go with you and allow you to pick up experience or train you in the area "Z." The point here is job content, and requirements can and do change to reflect market and labor conditions.

Don't leave any interview without asking the "secret recipe" question!

2. In what ways were you most pleased with the performance of the last person who held this position?

3. Where is the greatest room for improvement?

4. What would you like done differently by the next person who fills the job?

5. What is most pressing? What would you like to have done within the next two or three months?

6. What are some of the long-term objectives that you would like completed?

7. What are the key or pivotal milestones you expect me to reach and within what period of time?

8. What are some of the more difficult problems that one would have to face in this position? How do you think these could be handled best?

9. What do you see as my strengths, shortcomings, and chances in this position?

10. Where could a person go who is successful in this position? Within what time frame?

11. What significant changes do you foresee in the near future?

12. In your view, how does my background fit with your requirements for this position?

13. What are the questions that I did not ask you but should have?

QUESTIONS *NOT* TO ASK DURING AN INTERVIEW

You should not ask the following questions until you have received a job offer. In most cases, the interviewer will cover these topics before the offer is made. If they are not offered, bide your time. You will appear to be concerned with trivial issues if you bring these subjects up during the interview.

1. What is the salary range of this position?

2. What are the fringe benefits?

3. How many sick days may I have?

4. How much vacation may I use in a year?

5. How many holidays are given?

6. Does this position carry an expense account?

7. How liberal is the expense policy of this company?

8. When can I expect my first raise? How much will it be?

9. Will I have to work overtime?

10. What is the relocation package?

Two reasons why you should not ask the above questions in an interview:

1. You are in the interview to sell yourself. If you do not sell yourself, who will? Selling means expounding upon the skills and experience that you have and can bring to the company to increase sales, cut costs, or both. You are there to talk about what you can contribute **on the job** – not what you want to enjoy off the job. Note: All of the above benefits are enjoyed away from work.

2. The only time you ask about the above items is **after** an offer has been extended but **before** you accept or reject the offer.

THE INTERVIEW . . . THINGS YOU SHOULD AVOID

Some of the things you should avoid doing in any interview include the following:

1. Avoid filling out applications in waiting rooms. See the person first, then, if you are interested, you can take your time and fill out the form carefully at home. Always use a **pen** with blue ink when filling out applications.

2. Try to avoid being interviewed by junior substitutes, or allowing yourself to be subjected to hasty interviews over the telephone. If these situations arise, be courteous and polite.

3. Try to avoid being subjected to an inquisition or tripartite interview, but be polite and courteous should such a situation arise.

4. You should generally avoid any discussions on race, religion, or politics. They only invite trouble.

5. Also, despite projecting confidence, you should never imply that you can do everything or that you are a miracle worker. People will not believe you.

6. Do not be a "yes-person." Do not interrupt. Do not lose your temper. And when you are selling yourself, do not brag. Also, do not name-drop unless you can be extremely smooth about it. Name-dropping usually backfires.

7. In general, try to avoid naming your references until the very end. If you give your references out too often, you will find that they will be less effective when you need them.

8. Do not permit yourself to get flustered by the presence of unusual décor, strange lighting, uncomfortable chairs, telephone interruptions, or an interviewer's nervous tapping.

9. Never bring or leave behind unsolicited samples of your work or give out confidential information about your past employer. While you may be requested to bring specific examples of your work (i.e., drawings, published articles, etc.), never let copies of your work be made. When you are finished with the interview, take your examples with you.

10. Avoid being too critical of your past organizations or specific people. Someday you might want to return or get other assistance from their executives.

11. Do not permit your time to be arbitrarily wasted by people who have the time to interview you but do not have a position available. Try to make sure that there is a job available or that a person with the authority to create a position is interviewing you.

12. You should always find out to whom the position specifically reports and try to ascertain both his or her skills and importance in the firm. Sometimes a look at the organizational chart will help in this direction.

13. Do not let an interview carry on too long. You should be able to sense when a discussion has peaked and then diplomatically lead to an end of the meeting. Also, do not linger after the interview is finished.

14. Never be pressured into accepting a job at a lower level than you seek. Inside of one month, you will regret it!

15. Never accept the offer of a job during the interview. Ask for some time to think over any offer, even if it seems like just what you want.

BEHAVIORS TO AVOID WHEN INTERVIEWING

1. Displaying a bad attitude or poor attitude toward your former employer is the main reason that people lose out on job opportunities.

2. Having a poor personal appearance.

3. Exhibiting an overbearing, overaggressive, conceited, superior, or know-it-all attitude.

4. Revealing an inability to express yourself clearly – poor voice, diction, grammar.

5. Frowning.

6. Showing nervousness by drumming your fingers on the desk or tapping your foot.

7. Squirming in your seat.

8. Playing with some object, i. e., briefcase, pencil, pen, clothing.

9. Checking your wristwatch frequently.

10. Looking out the window while the other person is speaking.

11. Displaying a lack of career planning – no purpose or goals.

12. Showing a lack of interest, vitality, and enthusiasm and appearing passive and indifferent.

13. Displaying a lack of confidence or poise by being nervous or ill at ease.

14. Being evasive, hedging, or making excuses on unfavorable factors in your record.

15. Revealing a lack of maturity.

16. Condemning past employers.

17. Failing to look interviewer in the eye.

18. Having a limp, fishy handshake.

19. Completing application in a sloppy manner.

20. Showing little interest by not having researched the company or industry prior to the interview.

21. Arriving late to the interview.

22. Failing to ask questions about the job or advancement opportunities.

23. Being a poor listener.

24. Overemphasizing money or being interested only in the best dollar offer.

25. Expecting too much too soon by being unwilling to start at the bottom.

26. Showing ill manners, lack of courtesy, or lack of tact.

27. Indicating a lack of social understanding.

28. Exhibiting a lack of a strong work ethic.

29. Giving indecisive or indefinite responses.

30. Failing to do anything constructive during leisure or vacation time.

31. Talking about an unhappy married life, divorce, problems with parents, or other personal problems.

32. Appearing to be a "window shopper" – not a serious candidate.

33. Wanting the job for a short duration.

34. Revealing little or no sense of humor.

35. Displaying a lack of knowledge in the field of specialization.

36. Allowing parents or spouse to make decisions for him/her.

37. Placing an overemphasis on whom you know.

38. Expressing unwillingness to go where company will send you.

39. Exhibiting a cynical or negative attitude.

40. Revealing low moral standards.

41. Appearing lazy.

42. Showing strong prejudices or intolerance.

43. Having few or narrow interests.

44. Complaining about paperwork, added workload, or overtime.

45. Giving an indication of poor personal financial handling.

46. Failing to participate in community or other activities.

47. Indicating an inability to take criticism.

48. Exhibiting a lack of appreciation of the value of experience.

49. Expressing radical ideas.

50. Chewing gum, smoking, or drinking coffee during the interview.

51. Failing to express appreciation for the interviewer's time.

THE FOLLOW-UP LETTER

The follow-up letter is the most misunderstood piece of correspondence in the job hunter's campaign. Expressed simply, the follow-up letter is not a thank-you note.

Immediately after you have an interview, it is most desirable to follow-up the interview with a well written, individually crafted follow-up letter. The follow-up letter is intended to do one, and only one, thing: to continue to sell yourself to a prospective employer. **It is not a thank-you note.**

Individuals who believe they should send thank-you notes to a prospective employer after an interview are naïve. What would you be thanking the interviewer for? His or her time? The possibility of making his or her life easier? Reducing costs? Increasing sales? Solving problems? Gaining a competitive advantage? No, of course not. So where does the thinking come that a thank-you note is appropriate? People who advocate sending thank-you notes do not have a clear idea of what the objective is of the correspondence. After all, when is the last time you ever heard of an employer writing to an applicant and thanking the person for his or her time or for gracing the employer's headquarters with his or her presence?

Stop, take a minute, and determine what you really want to do. A carefully prepared follow-up letter will provide you with the opportunity to sell yourself after the interview. Following up is just as important as doing well in the interview itself.

Place yourself for a moment in the chair of the interviewer. Possibly you have interviewed six to eight candidates for the position you are interested in. Perhaps the interview process has taken place over a period of five to ten working days or longer. After the last applicant has been seen, would you be able to distinctly recall the significant qualities of each individual, the particular skill sets that each person would bring to the position? Probably your memory becomes fuzzy with the passage of time, and outstanding skills, attributes, and qualities begin to be attributed to the wrong individual. Hence, it is most important to separate yourself from the competition, to seize the initiative and remind the interviewer who you are and what you are selling. The best way to do that is with a follow-up letter, **not a thank-you note.** It also shows attention to detail and good follow-up skills. There are a few key rules to remember when writing a follow-up letter.

"OUT-OF-THE-BOX THINKING"

1. The follow-up letter should be written as soon as possible after the interview. This way you will be able to carefully review all of the critical elements of the interview and be responsive to those issues the interviewer outlined in his/her comments as to what the interviewer is looking for in the successful candidate.
2. It is important that each follow-up letter be personalized. No standardized, computer-generated, fill-in-the-blank letter will do the job.
3. Extremely important is the fact that each individual who participated in the interviewing process receive an individually drafted follow-up letter. **NEVER, NEVER** send a carbon copy to other participants or send a form letter.

Perhaps the significant fact is that **not all** applicants take the time and thought to send a follow-up letter. The individuals who send follow-up letters always increase their chances of securing a position. However, a good follow-up letter, **and this point is key**, is predicated on the applicant during the interview asking the most important questions in the interview. Those question are the following: "Mr./Ms. Interviewer, would you share with me what you are looking for in the successful candidate? How will you recognize the person you want to hire?" By raising key issues, the applicant, if he or she is well prepared, will prompt the employer to describe those key skills and abilities, in other words, what he/she is "buying." After all, the applicant is there to sell himself/herself. He/she cannot do an effective job of selling if he/she does not know what the customer, the interviewer, is buying. The best way to find this out is to be straightforward and ask.

The above two questions are the best questions to determine what is of major importance to the employer. This simple step is of paramount importance because in the follow-up letter, you can refer to what is in many instances called "The Secret Recipe." The recipe being the ingredients that make up the successful candidate. It is only when all of the ingredients are known that the applicant can take an objective look and compare all the key "ingredients" (skill sets) that the employer is looking for to his/her background.

If the employer is requesting a set of skills that the applicant does not have, this point is simply omitted in the follow-up letter. Without this preparatory step of knowing what the interviewer is looking for, the follow-up letter is useless.

Keep in mind the following suggestions when you draft your interview follow-up:

- After the interview, in your car before you drive away, you should take the time to make some notes regarding key points of the interview. Specifically, what were the three to five key attributes that the employer said he/she wants in the person hired? Make notes now!

- Always send a follow-up letter to each individual you talked with after each interview, even if you have a second or third interview with the same individual. Obviously, during multiple interviews with the same individual, the same subjects will not be discussed.

- A handwritten follow-up letter after an interview is better than no follow-up letter; however, a professionally typed follow-up letter is most effective.

- Always mention that you appreciated the time and the opportunity but do not get carried away with this point. Obviously, an interview is a mutually agreed-upon meeting.

With a clear understanding that a follow-up letter is a strategic selling tool, the following key points are of major importance. When reviewing the sample letters on the following pages, keep in mind that the first paragraph can be designated as a thank-you paragraph. The second paragraph is far more important. This is the answer to the "recipe" paragraph. What did the interviewer say he/she was looking for in the successful candidate? In this paragraph, the writer simply states or reiterates everything that the interviewer stated that he/she was looking for in the successful applicant. The third paragraph is the most important because this is your "match and sell" paragraph. You match everything in your background, previous work experience, and education that corresponds to the "recipe" ingredients. This is when you start to sell yourself. Paragraph four is simply asking for the order. Many employers have no idea of the applicant's interest after they have concluded the interview. Be simple but direct. Tell them of your interest, and tell them of your desire to continue discussions.

The follow-up letter is also an excellent method of damage control. Specifically, if during the interview, you were asked a specific question for which you could not formulate a succinct answer, or had difficulty answering, this is a wonderful opportunity to enclose an additional paragraph to readdress and revisit the question or issue. This paragraph simply is an opportunity in a quiet moment to follow up on a point, which upon further reflection you wish to address. The manner in which you leave and follow up an interviewing opportunity is as important as how you enter the interview itself. There is no need to follow the follow-up letter with a telephone call. The next step is up to your potential employer. However, after two or three weeks without receiving any communication, positive or negative, call the interviewer and simply ask, "Would you share with me the status of my application?"

Remember, the follow-up letter is not a thank-you note!
It must continue to sell you!

FOLLOW-UP LETTER WORKSHEET

 The opener to the follow-up letter sets the scene for when you are interviewed, the title of the position, and the company name.

 Gives you the opportunity as the applicant to restate the secret-recipe question. In many interview situations, as the applicant, you will meet with multiple individuals. These individuals may be seeking different qualities in the successful candidate. Therefore, you should utilize this letter as a means to assist the decision-makers in focusing on the key requirements of the position. Expressed simply, take charge and lead the company to closure in their decision making by crystallizing the requirements for the position.

 Is your opportunity to address each of the requirements listed in paragraph 2 and resell yourself to the company by giving examples from your past experience which match the requirements stated in the secret-recipe question. To be logical and consistent, you want to address your examples in paragraph 3 to follow the same order as you listed them in paragraph 2. "A" in paragraph 2 is explained in the first sentence; "B" is illustrated in the second sentence, etc.

 Gives you the opportunity to ask for the next step, ask for the sale, ask for the position. This is the paragraph where you ask to keep the lines of communication open.

YOUR NAME
ADDRESS
CITY/STATE
TELEPHONE

Date

Mr./Ms.
Title
Company
Address
City/State/Zip

Dear Mr./Ms.

1 I appreciated the chance to meet with you yesterday to discuss opportunities at _____ and your requirements for _____ .

2 You indicated during our meeting that you are looking for someone with previous experience in **A**_____ ,**B**_____ , **C**_____ , and **D**_____ .

3 In my current assignment with _____ , I **A**_____ _____ **B** _____ _____ , **C**_____ , and **D**_____ .

4 Again, Mr./Ms._____ , it was a pleasure to talk with you. Please accept this letter as an indication of my interest in _____ and the position of _____ . I would be pleased to continue our discussions at your convenience.

Sincerely,

Name

ROBERT T. THOMAS
1424 Main Street
Anywhere, State 99999
(765) 555-1212

SAMPLE FORMAT FOR FOLLOW-UP LETTER

Note: To be used *after* an interview.

January XX, 20XX

Ms. Maria Torez
Director of Human Resources
ABC Manufacturing Company
890 State Street
Geneva, IL 60999

Dear Ms. Torez:

(1)   I appreciated the chance to meet with you yesterday to discuss opportunities at ABC Manufacturing Company and your requirements for a Director of Manufacturing.

(2)   You indicated during our meeting that you are looking for someone with previous experience in plant layout and material flow to ensure efficient departmental operations and someone who has had exposure to automated machining equipment.

(3)   In my current assignment with Monroe Manufacturing Corporation, I redesigned the flow of three (3) departments, which resulted in increased production the first year by 9.9%. Additionally, I successfully introduced numeric-control machining equipment that saved $250,000 in labor costs the first year.

(4)   Again, Ms. Torez, it was a pleasure to talk with you. Please accept this letter as an indication of my interest in ABC Manufacturing Company and the position of Director of Manufacturing. I would be pleased to continue our discussions at your convenience.

Sincerely,

Robert T. Thomas

SAMUEL A. SMITH
536 Longmeadow Circle
Anywhere, State 60174
(312) 555-1732

SAMPLE FORMAT FOR FOLLOW-UP LETTER

Note: To be used *after* an interview.

January XX, 20XX

Mr. Peter Desai
Vice President, Sales
Universal Marketing
1211 W. State Street
Anywhere, State 99999

Dear Mr. Desai:

(1)   I appreciated the chance to meet you yesterday to discuss opportunities at Universal Marketing and your requirements for a Director of North American Sales.

(2)   You indicated during our meeting that you are looking for someone with previous experience in senior level sales training and merchandising programs.

(3)   In my current role as National Account Executive with Nationwide Cards, I developed and delivered ongoing sales seminars to all fifty (50) Regional Account Executives. In addition, as a result of new merchandising concepts developed, overall sales in my area increased by 8%.

(4)   Again, Mr. Desai, it was a pleasure meeting you. Please accept this letter as an indication of my interest in Universal Marketing and the Sales Director position. I look forward to continuing our discussions.

Sincerely,

Samuel A. Smith

ROSIE M. SHANNON
1424 Washington Avenue
Anywhere, State 99999
(765) 555-5429

SAMPLE FORMAT FOR FOLLOW-UP LETTER

Note: To be used *after* an interview.

January XX, 20XX

Mr. Hermann Schmidt
Director of Human Resources
XYZ Corporation
1234 Main Street
Chicago, IL 60099

Dear Mr. Schmidt:

(1)   I appreciated the opportunity to meet with you today to discuss employment opportunities at XYZ Corporation and your requirements for a secretary.

(2)   You indicated during our meeting that you are looking for an individual with previous secretarial background, preferably in the corporate headquarters environment of a major corporation and who has experience with both word processing systems and dictating equipment.

(3)   While with the Quark Corporation, I was a key participant in the selection of the current word-processing system and had full responsibility for all word processing functions for the entire service department. In addition, I had the responsibility for taking dictation from the Service Manager as well as from the rest of the staff.

(4)   Again, Mr. Schmidt, it was a pleasure to talk with you. Please accept this letter as an indication of my interest in XYZ Corporation and the position as a secretary. I would be pleased to continue our discussion at your convenience.

Sincerely,

Rosie M. Shannon

FOCUS TIME

Now that you have prepared answers to the sample interview questions in this section, I suggest that you role-play a practice interview. Select different individuals in a variety of environments to choose a sampling of twenty interview questions, and let them interview you for an imaginary position similar to a position you are seeking. It would be helpful if this individual were "interviewing" you for a position that you want with a company that you like. Also, they should select the questions without your assistance. You should schedule the practice interview as you would a real interview and dress accordingly.

Anything you can do in this practice interview session to create a realistic atmosphere will be helpful. In this manner, you will continue to sharpen your interviewing skills. If possible, have a third individual observe the scenario and provide feedback upon completion of the sample interview. After listening to the critique, you will want to reflect on the process and determine what segments of the interview can be improved.

GUIDELINES TO DISCUSSING COMPENSATION

Compensation is one of the most important but most often misunderstood areas of a career campaign. It is common for an individual to be confused by terms such as salary, bonus, or compensation.

Salary is the amount you receive in your gross or total pay. This amount can be expressed as an annual sum, or in the case of an hourly employee, it is the wage paid per hour. Compensation is defined as salary plus bonus. Benefits such as insurance, stock options, car, club allowances, or other perks should not be calculated as part of salary or compensation. They are simply defined as "benefits."

HELPFUL HINT

When an employer requests your compensation, respond by stating your salary is $X and bonus (if applicable) was $Y last year.

CURRENT COMPENSATION

Always tell the search firm or your prospective employer, when asked, your exact salary. Prospective employers will usually contact your previous employer to verify your salary. However, due to the confidentiality of this information, your previous employer will not release this information, or he or she may have a policy that only allows him or her to verify information (answer "yes" or "no" questions) regarding salary and compensation. Therefore, the candidate may have to verify his/her own compensation by submitting a copy of their last W-2 and/or paycheck. Remember, always keep a copy of your last check. If you want your previous employer to release additional information about your compensation, job performance, etc., you will need to sign a release authorizing your previous employer to provide this information.

In addition, if your salary is $129,000, do not round it up to $130,000. If your previous employer's policy is just to verify a salary figure, he or she may indicate, "No, he did not earn $130,000," and you may lose a job opportunity. Also, remember that failure to provide accurate salary information when hired is grounds for dismissal.

After responding to an interviewer's question about current earnings, it is acceptable to ask, "Is there a salary range for the position we are discussing, or does it depend largely on the person you select?" If the answer is "Yes, there is a range," then you may ask, "Are you able to tell me what it is?" It costs you nothing to ask!

This exchange is merely an information-gathering procedure and is not to be construed as negotiating for an offer. Usually, this kind of conversation will **occur early** in the interview process – even before a material interest has been mutually established. A discussion of compensation is not itself an indication that the interviewer is contemplating offering you a position.

Another area where compensation can be confusing is when to list your salary in a letter. The following chart will assist you in determining the proper course of action. Also, for your review, the chart includes when a resume should be enclosed with the letter.

Marketing Letter	Include Salary	Include Resume	General Comments
Search Firm/ Employment Agency	Yes	Yes*	They must have your salary to determine if any current job openings match your background.
Networking	No	Yes	Salary information does not need to be divulged.
Cover Letter to Corporations	No	Yes	Since your marketing letter is unsolicited, it is in your best interest not to include salary information.
Direct Mail to Companies	No	No	Since your marketing letter is unsolicited, it is in your best interest not to include salary information.
Ad-Response Letter	Only if ad requests this information.	Yes	Remember, if you cannot follow directions in the ad, the company may wonder if you can follow directions on the job.

* If you are changing careers or industries and do not have a broad skill base in this new area, you may want to identify your current salary and indicate your salary requirements are open.

SALARY HISTORY

If an ad requests salary history, it is not necessary to provide a complete recap of previous salaries. It is acceptable to provide your last or current salary figure. The term "salary history" started after World War II, when the economy was in transition from "guns to butter" and the inflation rate was low and stable. After World War II, it was natural and necessary for employers to request an individual's salary history and compare his or her percent of salary increases to inflation rates. The salary increase for high-performance individuals always exceeded the inflation rate. Although the term is still used today, it is not necessary to provide a complete salary history. Your most recent salary will provide the information the employer requires. If you provided the employer with a salary history, he or she may review your percent increases and offer you less than he or she and you anticipated.

FUTURE COMPENSATION

Search firms and employers will often ask one of the following questions:

- What would you like to earn?
- What type of compensation are you looking for?

In most cases, an interviewer asks what salary you are seeking because he or she is trying to decide:

- Whether his or her position carries a salary level equal to your desires or level of expectation.
- How realistic you are in your salary desires.
- Whether you are competitively priced compared to other candidates who may be under consideration.

Your response to each of these questions should always be, "I am open." "I am open," means you are "Open to listen to a competitive offer." An offer is more than just compensation. In other words, the salary part of the offer may be less than you were previously earning, but perhaps the insurance coverage, 401(K) plan, pension, savings program, or other plans may more than make up the difference. In some cases, search firms or employment agencies may continue to ask what compensation you want. It is important to continue to respond by indicating that you are "open." Do not change your vocabulary; certainly do not use the term "negotiable." The world has very few real negotiations; after all, when was the last time you really negotiated your own salary? Also, many companies do not negotiate. Their first offer is their last and only offer.

Why not provide your future salary requirements? Let us look at the case of three individuals applying for the same position. Since the company may not share the salary level of its position, any salary figure you provide could be incorrect. In this example, let us assume the desired salary for the new position is $85,000 and your current salary is $80,000. We will also assume each individual has the same skills and background.

- Candidate A indicated his or her salary "requirement" is $80,000. The employer may make an offer to this candidate, but it will probably be at the salary figure the candidate specified ($80,000). Therefore, this candidate lost a $5,000 increase. But the company satisfied the applicant's requirements.

- Candidate B indicated his or her salary requirement is $90,000. Since this is $5,000 more than the company is willing to pay, this candidate will not receive an offer.

- Candidate C responded with "**I am open.**" This indicates they are open to listen to any offer. As we have discussed, salary is only part of an offer. If you convince the employer you can make a positive impact on their company, you stand a better chance of obtaining a higher salary.

I have seen numerous individuals totally wreck their opportunities for economic advancement by mishandling compensation issues. The simple phrase "I am open to listening to a competitive offer," will place you in the strongest position. Obviously, it indicates to a potential employer that you are indeed flexible.

Employers can come at you from a number of different directions:

"What are you looking for?"
"What's your salary requirement?"
"What's it 'gonna' take to get you?"
"If you don't have a figure in mind, can you give me a salary
 range?"

PLUS

"For an exciting opportunity, would you consider a salary cut?"

The answer to all of these questions is the same, "I am open," or "I am open to listening to a competitive offer." You are advised that if an employer presses you time and time again with the same question, the best strategy is to repeat the same answer time and time again. The employer will get the idea that you are not going to tip your hand.

In the earlier mentioned three scenarios, anytime an individual responded with a specific figure to the question of "hoped for, wished for, anticipated compensation," invariably, after that meeting, the individual would wonder if the figure quoted was too much and if he or she therefore, blew himself or herself out of the water. Or was it too low and left money on the table? To avoid either possibility, the "open" position is strongly suggested.

You may also want to communicate that you are seeking an opportunity in which you can perform and advance in both position and compensation as a result of your performance. You are not merely seeking another job. The determining factor of compensation is responsibility followed by performance. You are not looking for a job but rather a career.

Another question candidates often hear is, "I do not have anything at your current salary level right now, but I have a position that is $5,000 below your current salary; would you be interested in something at that level?" You already know the answer; "I am open." Once again, you need to understand the entire offer. Perhaps the person you would be reporting to will be retiring in six months and you will be trained for his or her job.

HELPFUL HINT

A company may press you that it absolutely must have your anticipated salary. Example: "I cannot possibly present you to my boss without providing him with this information." In response, you should repeat your most current salary and indicate:

"I am open."

Be tough, hang tight, and do not be the first one who blinks.

THE OFFER

As outlined in Chapter VIII, "Evaluating and Handling the Offer of Employment" beginning on page 347, always request the offer be put in a confirmation letter. If the company is unable or unwilling, you should send it written confirmation including the salary offer, title, benefit package, and any other pertinent information. Always express enthusiasm when thanking the company for the offer but request a reasonable amount of time to carefully review the total compensation and benefit package. Twenty-four to forty-eight hours should be sufficient time to complete your evaluation. For executive level positions, a week or longer is not unreasonable. If you are going to take longer than a week (five business days) to think about an offer, make sure you advise the potential employer you are doing so.

If you are still having difficulties with the salary offer and it is not acceptable, your options are:

1. Accept – The only remaining action is to discuss a start date.

2. Reject – No further action is required except to send a polite letter declining the offer.

3. Review offer with the employer with an objective of increasing the offer!

If you decide to review the offer, realize there is always a possibility the offer could be withdrawn. To reduce this possibility, make sure you review the offer over the telephone, not in person, and prepare a written script outlining what you want to say. For example:

> *Mr. Smith, I want to thank you for your offer to work for the ABC Company as a Quality Control Manager. I am excited about this opportunity, but I would appreciate it if you would once more review with me the scope, responsibilities, and authority of this position.*

Since the company and the people you are talking with want you to accept the position, otherwise they would not have provided you with an offer – they may try to convince you that this is a very responsible position. After they have completed their review, your response should be:

> *In light of these important and broad responsibilities, I would appreciate it if you could review the salary offer. I am really looking forward to working with the company and would like to start the position as soon as possible, but please take whatever time you need to review this matter. If we can resolve this last issue, I would like to discuss a start date.*

Do not be alarmed if they are not able to provide you with an immediate answer. The individual you are talking with may not have the authority to increase the salary offer. As an alternative, you may be able to request an employment bonus. This is a one-time payment, which could be used to defer certain employment or relocation expenses.

NEGOTIATING THE OFFER OF EMPLOYMENT

I have had the opportunity to counsel and serve as a backroom negotiator for many of my individual clients in their dealings with corporate America. There are a few sound principals I would like to pass on for the readers' review. These principles obviously have been honed as a result of over twenty-five years in assisting people negotiate their own employment offers, and having those skills further honed by serving five years earlier as a chief spokesman during more than sixty labor negotiations. The process of negotiating an employment offer has some subtle differences from labor contracts or negotiations involving outside vendors, etc. What I have found is that almost all businessmen and women don't do a good job of negotiating. It is a very subjective topic, and because it is so subjective, it distorts the individual's perception of what is really taking place. As a result of many errors or miscues, I have developed the following guidelines to assist the job hunter.

1. Accept this fact: You are not the best negotiator because you are the person who is going to potentially benefit from your success. The anticipated rewards many times are mentally reaped before they are physically achieved. Keep this distinction in mind. Next, how often have you successfully negotiated an employment offer? What makes you think you are an expert in this endeavor? Your subjective involvement is not the best asset to have as an objective negotiator.

2. Know where you are going. If the difference between what the company's offer is and where you want to be, or the objective you want to achieve is in your opinion, after some soul-searching, small, then my best advice is leave it alone and accept the offer. The negotiation process has the wonderful potential and significant opportunity to leave hurt feelings on one side or another. The objective is to try to have both sides feel that they are equally "winners" in these discussions called negotiations. Your objective is not to "win" a short-term job negotiation – but rather avoid losing a long-term career opportunity.

3. It is important to keep in mind that most individuals want to move at a speed that is faster than the corporation is capable of moving. Individuals who have received an offer and wish to negotiate the offer upward want to move quickly. That is not the style of most corporations. Companies move at glacial speed! Many times the person making the offer is not at liberty to change the offer. Additional salary might be beyond his/her level of authority, and thus this decision may have to be bumped up the chain of command. An important principle here is to go slowly. Don't seem over-anxious.

4. The place of negotiation should not be in the employer's office. Any individual who goes into a potential employer's office to negotiate an offer is in a psychologically defensive position. He or she is going into an area, possibly an office or a conference room, where he/she is not comfortable in, it's new, and the employer would have the psychological advantage. Rather,

to neutralize the company's advantage, negotiations should be done over the phone. The individual would do a much better job of negotiating in the comfort, safety, and familiarity of his or her own kitchen, living room, etc. rather than going into the lion's den.

5. Assume the company knows that it's been over a year since your last salary increase. Whose fault is that?

6. While money is the most negotiable item, it doesn't hurt to ask about other items. Certain benefits, for example, pension plans, are controlled by federal regulations to ensure they are administered equitably with all people within the same defined class of participants. Whether an item is negotiable or not will never be ascertained unless the candidate asks, "Is this item negotiable?"

7. Candidates are well advised not to view the negotiating process like a metronome or a pendulum on a grandfather's clock. Offers are not always greeted with counteroffers. Counteroffers are not always greeted with a response. The delicate part of negotiation must be honed. For most job hunters, this is a process that they will do only a few times in their business life. Most frequently when an offer is presented to an individual, the individual has one trump card to play, the counteroffer. Unfortunately, most individuals play that counteroffer not knowing whether their offer is going to leave money on the table or blow them out of the water because they have requested far too much from the employer. Further complicating the process is the fact that many employers make only one offer and do not wish to engage in the negotiation process for fear of earning a reputation of being easy to negotiate with and are willing to back off their first offer. Many times the first offer is the final offer.

8. No offer should be negotiated without seeing it in writing first. In other words, to avoid misinterpretation and faulty logic in forming a negotiating strategy, the offer should be expressed in writing and what is termed a "letter of confirmation." Only after seeing it in writing and reviewing the various options does the candidate decide how and where he/she might wish to negotiate the offer.

9. As indicated above, a safe tactic is for the individual to ask the employer to rethink his or her offer without making a counteroffer. This strategy is most effective for the uninitiated negotiator or first-time negotiator. It ensures that one is not overplaying or underplaying his position. Only when the company's final offer is on the table is the person faced with the decision to accept, reject, or attempt a counteroffer.

10. A strategy that is preferred by corporations is simply to get all items out on the table – don't try to nickel and dime a company. This leads to bad feelings and an assessment that the candidate is hard to deal with or at best is holding something back. The strategy that applicants use too frequently is to get salary issues out of the way first and then move onto other items of significant importance. This tactic leads to hard feelings. Items should be

brought out on the table for discussion and not left for any last-minute "surprises." Let everyone know what the total cost is of the entire package.

11.   Items agreed to in previous negotiations should always be confirmed in writing. The applicant is making a major mistake leaving this to the memory of both parties. All major agreements should be reduced in the final analysis to writing, to avoid misunderstanding or misinterpretation.

12.   With the exception of pension and those benefits controlled by the Internal Revenue regulations as to their administration, almost all things are free game in today's business climate. Therefore, some additional thinking and planning must go into the negotiation process. The strategy of "one more item" is not looked upon favorably. Present a list of "requests," not demands, and greet the company's representative appropriately. Look at his/her body posture, eye contact, voice inflection, degree of nervousness, hesitation, etc. All figure dominantly in the process.

The foregoing assumes that you are meeting face to face. It is still my strong recommendation to avoid face-to-face meetings so that the above-mentioned items cannot be read from your own body posture, hesitation, or nervousness.

The individual again is advised that the greater the negotiation list of priorities, the greater the chance that the employer could come back and say simply, "We are just too far apart, and therefore we are withdrawing our offer. Best wishes for continued success with your future employer." Every negotiation involves give and take. Be prepared to know what your priorities are and what items you can give or sacrifice. In all negotiations involving potential employment, the number of rounds or meetings is significantly fewer than the candidate believes.

In summary, take your time, go slowly, go very slowly; a lot is at stake.

EVEN YOUR LAST JOB TITLE IS NEGOTIABLE

One of my individual clients, as a result of her company's attempt to reorganize, lost her position as Vice-President. After applying herself diligently in her job campaign, approximately four to five months later, she secured a new position. The new position with a larger company carried an enhanced benefit plan and a nice adjustment in salary and bonus, and was apparently a good career move. My client, however, traded her VP title for a Director's title to receive those better benefits and an increased compensation plan.

The new company she joined was a manufacturer and distributor of fiber optics, which are key components of data transmission and telecom operations. Given the volatility of this particular market, there was a natural concern that her position could be eliminated in the future. She felt comfortable she could explain why the job elimination took place. The problem would not be the explanation of the potential job loss but getting in front of the decision-maker in the first place and having the platform to explain why she was on the market. Her resume would show a length of employment with her previous employer ending with the ascension to the rank of a Vice President. The next position would be Director and then, after a brief potential period of time, she could be unemployed.

Recognizing this would further diminish her marketability, the issue became how do you handle this particular situation, at least on paper?

Right or wrong, titles imply responsibility. And it is responsibility that is the best determinant of compensation. The problem of apparent career "downslide" as suggested by diminishing job titles can be overcome when an offer of employment is extended to a candidate by simply requesting that if for any reason he/she must leave, is asked to leave, or separated in an involuntary manner other than for cause, on the last day of employment, all records will be changed to indicate a previously held job title. In other words, if this person was going to leave her director position, then on the last day of employment, the records would reflect that the title was changed to Vice President. A Manager's title would change to Director, etc. This strategy is fairly easy to accomplish. Corporations realize that there is no cost involved. The agreement to change the job title on the last day of employment must be presented, discussed, and hopefully agreed upon when the individual is interviewing and is considering an offer of employment. Once the offer has been accepted, all leverage on this point is lost. The bottom line is that this particular candidate was a Vice President, although currently operating in a Director-level capacity with broader responsibilities, enhanced compensation and benefits. If she should be separated, the last position she would show is that of a Director, not a Vice President, indicating a potential reduction in responsibility. To avoid this interpretation, she successfully negotiated with her new employer a potential change in job status in the highly "unlikely event" of an involuntary separation. The issue, of course, becomes mute if she is again promoted to the Vice President level.

In summary, job titles may not always be the best indicator of worth, but they are a significant indicator of progress and career pathing.

HOW TO BE COMPENSATION SMART

To be successful in obtaining the "right" offer, you must have a compensation strategy.

- **Be confident** in your salary discussions but realistic in handling compensation issues.

- **Sell yourself** and your skills and demonstrate how you can benefit the company.

- **Be confident** in all your discussions. A positive mental attitude is the sign of a winner.

- **Be realistic** and realize that you will probably not receive an offer that is 20 percent higher than your previous salary. Most individuals receive the same salary or a small increase. Salary increases in the 20 - 25% range should be strongly pursued when you are relocating to a new area on behalf of your new employer. Why? Simply because the full costs of relocation are seldom ever covered by the company's "full" relocation program. If you disagree, check out the list on page 369 and page 370.

- **Do not be misled** by compensation surveys. Job functions, responsibilities, and titles can differ from region to region.

- If the employer uses the HAY system or other predetermined salary ranges for a position, you may still obtain the salary you require by convincing the employer you have the experience to successfully assume additional responsibilities. These new responsibilities may place you in a higher salary range.

You are well advised to keep in mind that you can always move a company further and faster on salary than on any other issue. Certainly it is obvious that not all companies negotiate salary offers. Certain companies have adopted a posture over the years that they will make a fair offer, stick to it, and will not negotiate. Therefore, again, it is helpful to stress the point that when pressed on salary issues to reply, "I am open to a competitive offer." This positions the company to make its best offer in light of what it evaluates as your skill sets, what you bring to the party, and, obviously, what your most recent or current salary-compensation package was.

There are a number of things and items that can be presented in a compensation negotiation. Salary is most negotiable of all items if the company is going to be in a position to listen to your requirements or suggestions. A one-time hiring bonus can be requested. This is an attempt to level the difference between your past or current compensation and the company's offer. Company benefit plans, or individually constructed benefit plans for retirement, etc., would not be an item for negotiation. These plans have to be qualified with the IRS for the company to receive a tax deduction. And the qualifying plans must be administered to all employees in the designated class in a non-discriminatory manner. Individuals at the executive level are well advised to investigate executive compensation programs, severance arrangements, etc. Severance arrangements can be negotiated up front during the hiring process for such items as a separation agreement and providing outplacement services in the "highly unlikely event" there is a separation. Being the first on the block to receive a car allowance, club membership, or other unique perks is usually very, very difficult to achieve. If they are established for a general level of executive, they can most times be readily obtained. Again, assuming that it is an ongoing or current practice.

The basis for any bonus arrangements should be clearly understood. When that bonus is paid, how or what indices of performance must be achieved to receive the maximum amount of compensation under the bonus plan should be clearly spelled out. It is amazing the number of people who will accept the company's word that there will be a bonus paid but have no idea of the basis or the percentage range of base salary that is applicable to the individual being hired. Many accept a bonus-eligible position without even knowing if bonuses were paid in the prior year.

Employment contracts are rare. It costs nothing to ask, but these agreements are distributed very, very rarely in publicly held companies. My best advice to you is to secure a 10K report, which indicates who has employment agreements granted by the Board of Directors and what duration these agreements are for. Keep in mind, an employment agreement does not prohibit an individual from being separated but does bind the corporation to maintain the terms and conditions of employment for the remainder of the contract. An individual would be prudent to invest in an attorney when negotiating an employment agreement. Employment contracts, generally, are covered by "local state law," which varies from state to state. So local counsel is recommended. Provisions and agreements should be made regarding the cessation or continuation of the employment agreement in light of the company being sold or merged with another employer.

In all items dealing with negotiation or review of salary offers, compensation packages, termination agreements, and employment contracts, the universal fault in this process lies with the desire of the individual applicant to conclude these negotiations too quickly. This is understood, but it also leads to many errors in the process. Corporations are like glaciers and move at glacier speed. They don't like to be turned, stopped, or accelerated. They move at one speed – dead slow! Think back; how many times were you able to speed up the corporation's decision-making, slow it down, or turn it to the right or left? The applicant is strongly advised to proceed slowly regarding this issue. It is not a matter that can be concluded quickly. It requires thought, resolve, and expert counsel. The individual you will be talking to or negotiating with may not have sufficient authority to grant the requests or acknowledge the points that you have made. He or she must forward them up the "chain of command," which, of course, will take additional time. Be willing to accept the speed of your anticipated new employer.

WHAT YOU SHOULD KNOW ABOUT STOCK OPTIONS
Which Is Not an Optional Subject

Any discussion regarding compensation would not be complete without a comment or two on the subject of stock options. The following was derived from information supplied by Mark Cooter, CPA, PFS, Elliott Davis, LLP, Greenville, South Carolina.

STOCK OPTIONS – A FUTURE RIGHT TO PURCHASE STOCK, USUALLY COMMON STOCK, IN A COMPANY

With the emergence of many of the dot.com stocks in the year 2000 came an accelerated usage of stock options. Almost abruptly with the increase of using stock options as a form of compensation came the market decline of the stock market in the year 2001, which saw many of these option programs becoming worthless. It is well to keep in mind that **STOCK OPTIONS ARE NOT A SUBSITUTE OR GUARANTEE OF CASH.** Stock options are an attempt to link someone to the future performance of the company, e.g., usually given to executives and/or sales personnel.

Incentive Stock Options

There are various kinds of stock options. Some of the more typical include an Incentive Stock Option and a non-statutory or a non-qualified stock option, which will be discussed later on in this section. Another incentive plan to consider is phantom stock, also to be discussed later.

Incentive Stock Options, (ISO), which must meet statutory requirements of the Internal Revenue code, are also called qualified stock options, and these are predominately given to middle-management individuals and below. Incentive Stock Options must be granted at the fair market value at the date of grant. Of all stock options that are granted, 90 to 95 percent are of the incentive type.

The ISO Agreement must meet the following IRS requirements per Section 422 of the Internal Revenue Code:

1. The option agreement must be in writing.
2. The option agreement must specify, at a minimum, the number of shares subject to the option, the exercise price, the restrictions on exercise, if any, and the term of the option. Additional provisions may and frequently are included in the option agreement provided such provisions are not inconsistent with the option being an ISO.
3. The option agreement must provide that the option cannot be exercised more than ten years (five years in the case of a 10 percent owner) after the date on which the option was granted.
4. The option agreement must provide that the option cannot be transferred other than by will of the laws of descent and distribution. The option agreement may give the optionee the ability to specifically designate the optionee's beneficiary. The exercise of an option by a legal representative of the optionee, such as during the disability of the optionee, or an exercise by the estate of the optionee, will not violate the probation on transfer.
5. The option agreement must not designate the option as an NSO (Non-Statutory option or non-qualified) agreement.

For the stock of a publicly traded corporation, the value is determined by the price of the common stock on the date of the grant. For non-public corporations, the value is determined by an appraisal Pre-I.P.O. (Initial Public Offering).

The value of an Incentive Stock Option is not negotiable because of statutory requirements under the Internal Revenue Code. What is negotiable is the quantity of the options being given at the time of employment. For most executives, the number of options is as negotiable as the executive's salary. For mid-management and below, the number of options becomes less negotiable as salaries become less negotiable.

By IRS code, ISOs have various caps. For example, Incentive Stock Options carry $100,000 per year limitation; to the extent that the individual is granted his stock options that exceed $100,000, such options shall be treated as non-qualified options. A company cannot discriminate against a class of employees but rather can issue stock to employees with (X) number of years of service. This would, of course, go across all lines for classification of employees.

The vesting schedule whether it is three, four or five years is set in the ISO plan and established by the Board of Directors. The schedule of vesting is not a negotiable item. Most vesting schedules are on a step basis. For example, if there were a three-year vesting schedule, the individual would be one-third vested after the first year, two-thirds vested after the second year, and wholly vested after year three. Or, the individual could have cliff vesting. For example, an individual would be 100 percent vested after five years.

If, for example, an individual has a stock option with five years of vesting with 1,000 shares, and the individual either leaves voluntarily or involuntarily, or dies during the first year, the individual is vested in 200 shares of stock. The decision to exercise an option *must* be made within ninety days of leaving the company, whether the separation is voluntary or involuntary.

A company is under no obligation to inform an individual of his or her exercisable rights after separation. Thus, it is extremely important to check the terms of your option agreement and to review the agreement before leaving the corporation. Unless specified in the Option Agreement, separation for cause is not grounds for declaring your option agreement null and void.

Upon exercise, the actual shares can be sold for cash, held for future appreciation, or a combination. If exercised and sold, the income is taxed at ordinary rates. Alternatively, although there is no immediate ordinary income tax effect on exercised and held shares, there can be dramatic Alternative Minimum Tax (AMT) ramifications. But this strategy of buy and hold can be effectively implemented to achieve lower capital gain rates when sold. Your tax advisor should be consulted for further recommendations/advice.

Non-Qualified Stock Options

The second type of stock options is the Non-qualified Stock Option or NSO. These types of stock options are traditionally given to senior executives and corporate officers and are much easier to negotiate than the Incentive Stock Options (ISO). There is no $100,000 cap with a Non-qualified Stock Option, and these types of stock options are not given to all classes of employees. NSOs are typically granted at fair market value; however, they can be issued below fair market value (rarely), can be issued in any amount, and are negotiable between the candidate and his or her immediate supervisor. There is a vesting schedule set by the Board of Directors.

Unlike ISOs, NSOs are taxable at ordinary tax rates at the time of exercise. This decreases the likelihood of utilizing a buy/hold strategy to obtain lower long-term capital gain rates.

Phantom Stock Plan

Another incentive plan is a Phantom Stock Plan. It is usually granted by smaller and privately held corporations. There is no equity in Phantom Stock. The grant of phantom stock is treated as an unfounded and unsecured promise to pay money in the future based on the value of the company.

What happens in a Phantom Stock Plan is first the company has an initial appraisal of the value of the company and the shares, determined by the Board of Directors, divided into the value the company gives the price of the share. Share price and number of shares are both negotiable because they are non-statutory. Phantom Stock, since there are no shares of common stock involved or any other type of equity arrangement, is treated similar to a cash-bonus incentive at time of redemption. Tax is due upon the redemption of the phantom stock. If an individual redeems and holds the phantom stock and the company goes down the tube, an individual could lose everything.

In summary, the Phantom Stock Plan is a form of deferred compensation.

An employee who participates in a Phantom Stock Plan is entitled to receive at some later specified date (perhaps retirement) cash equal to the value of the phantom shares. That is, the employee is entitled to cash equal to the excess of the stock value at the time of the cash payout over the value of the company's stock at grant.

Phantom Stock Plans have not gained in popularity simply because, first, there has to be an annual outside appraisal performed on the company to determine its value. Second, there are potential problems for minority versus majority stockholders to agree on the value of the corporation and, thus, price of shares.

CONFIDENTIAL

SEVERANCE PACKAGE

Never tell the potential employer the details of your severance package. The compensation level and length is privileged information and should not be disclosed to the future employer.

If an employer knows your severance package has or will be exhausted, he or she may view you as desperate and reduce the offer. Likewise, potential employers may not like to hire individuals who "double dip" and are still collecting a salary from a previous employer. When asked if you have a severance package or to explain what your severance package is, simply indicate that your previous employer has always treated you fairly and has put together a fair severance package, which he or she has asked you to keep confidential.

COMPENSATION AND HAPPINESS

Although salary is fundamental in paying bills and providing the necessities and sometimes the luxuries of life, the old adage is true – money does not buy happiness. It is more important to find a company and position that is right for you, one that will be interesting and will provide you with fulfillment and happiness. Happiness cannot be purchased.

CHAPTER VIII.

EVALUATING

AND

HANDLING THE OFFER
OF EMPLOYMENT

**Checking Your Map And Compass
One Last Time — Are You There?**

N

EVALUATING THE EMPLOYMENT OFFER

You Are Almost At Your Destination . . . .

This is it! All of your diligence has finally paid off, and you have received an offer of employment. How do you decide whether to accept?

An offer is good news. Any offer, no matter how large or small, provides positive feedback. The truly wise candidate does not have an unrealistic view regarding the amount of salary he or she is worth. Remember that the offer of employment is the only true sign that the company not only believes you are a potential good "fit" for the job but is also willing to put money on that estimate. Expectations of candidates rise unrealistically because the candidate thought the interview was outstanding, only to later be dashed when the offer is not forthcoming.

Good corporations always try to treat prospective employees with the highest degree of respect and decorum. Treatment like that may lead a candidate to think that the company has a high degree of interest in his or her background. Often the manner in which a company handles an offer of employment or negotiation may give you a barometer reading into the organization, i. e., positive or negative insight.

Now that the job offers start to present themselves, perhaps the real challenges in a job-search campaign are just beginning. To properly evaluate a job offer, you must first consider the offer against other alternatives – how the offer matched up against the job requirements you established during your campaign and how the job will serve both your short-term and long-term career objectives.

When an offer is made – before accepting – try to find out:

- When is the first salary or performance review?
- What usually happens then?
- When is the next review?
- Are raises accompanied by promotions?
- Are promotions accompanied by a raise?
- What is the top of the range for the position being offered?
- Is there room for growth, i. e., salary increase?
- If you believe the salary offered would be in a different range with higher limits and a different title, you may have a good point for negotiating.
- If there are annual increases, does the whole range move up? Or, what happens when someone hits the top of the range?

There are a host of questions one can consider in evaluating the attractiveness of an employment offer. Following are a few of those questions to which I strongly recommend due diligence be given.

- How will your performance be measured?
- What criteria of performance does the company use to determine your performance level?

- If you are rated average, above average, or excellent, how do these performance evaluations translate into salary increases?
- Have all of the company benefits programs been explained and given to you in written form?
- When do these programs commence?
- What is the employee cost, if any, of your participation in these programs?
- If the company has a pension program, when does full vesting occur?
- What are the deductibles, if any, under a current major medical program offered by the prospective employer?
- Does the company use a Management by Objectives (MBO) program?
- Are financial reviews tied to MBO programs?
- Request a copy of the pension formula if the company maintains a defined benefit-pension plan. Then use that formula to do a sample pension calculation.

If a position requires the use of special tools, equipment, clothing, protective gear, etc., whose responsibility is it to provide these items in terms of cost and subsequent ownership? The following question, given today's market, is not inappropriate: "In the highly unlikely event of involuntary separation from the company, does your corporation provide individual Outplacement services for a person at my level?"

FINALLY, LET'S TALK BENEFITS

I have held discussing this subject to almost the very end because I feel that benefits, although hugely important, should not play a critical part in the interviewing process. The only time I would discuss benefits is, of course, after the offer has been extended and before acceptance or rejection. Why? Simply because benefits are always enjoyed off the job; they are not enjoyed on the job. During the interview process the applicant is well advised to stress what he or she can contribute to the organization, not what the applicant can enjoy in his or her leisure off-work hours. Benefits, of course, are extremely costly to the employer. Some of them range in excess of 40 percent of the salary dollar. Additionally, many benefits are taxable as income. The following list of benefits includes both taxable and non-taxable, and the individual would be again advised when discussing these benefits to get a clarification as to whether these costs would in fact be reviewed by the IRS as income and therefore taxable.

Following is a list of benefits that are legitimate topics for discussion when a job offer is made:

1. **Signing bonuses.** Signing bonuses generally range in the 5 to 10 percent category and can run up to as high as 75 percent, or even 100 percent of the total amount of the salary offers. Signing bonuses in the 75 to 100 percent range are not unheard of but are extremely rare. For the recent MBA or MS graduate, signing bonuses can go up to approximately $20,000.
2. **Cafeteria-style flexible insurance plans.** Under a cafeteria-style of insurance, employees can design the plan to best suit their needs. This is highly desirable since older employees obviously have different needs than a young family or a family with young children.

3. **Medical insurance.** Not all medical insurance is the same. Typically, oral surgery is covered under a major-medical insurance program; some cover psychotherapy and eye-care plans. Many companies have gone to HMOs (health maintenance organizations) or PPOs (preferred-provider organizations). Many times medical insurance includes unmarried couples or significant others.

4. **Prepaid legal plans.** These plans are not necessarily in high usage but are very attractive to employees with the exception that they generally have a provision against initiating legal action against their current or former employer.

5. **Dental insurance.** Because of the high cost of dental bills, this type of insurance is very popular. Although some plans have lower deductibles and a higher company-paid portion.

6. **Pension or 401K retirement plans.** Vesting under these plans differs from company to company as well as the amount of contribution that a company will fund for its employees. One of the best ways to determine how lucrative a company's pension or 401K plan would be to ask Human Resources to do a sample pension calculation using some very conservative estimates of salary, career life with the company, etc.

7. **Profit sharing.**

8. **Stock options.** These are not a substitution for cash!

9. **Long-term or short-term disability insurance.** The big questions here are what is meant by disability, and what is meant by long-term or short-term.

10. **Life insurance.**

11. **Performance bonuses.**

12. **Promotions and raises.**

13. **Vacations.**

14. **Paid sick leave and personal days.**

15. **Comp (compensation) time.**

16. **Equity stake in the company.**

17. **Flexible hours.**

18. **Telecommuting.**

19. **Job-sharing.**

20. **Childcare.**

21. **Elder care.**

22. **Tax preparation assistance.**

23. **Executive physical program.**

24. **Outplacement assistance.** For a spouse or significant other in the event the employee of the company is transferred or relocated.

25. **Tuition reimbursement.**

26. **Professional association dues.**

27. **Professional seminar and conference fees.** Including travel and meals.

28. **EAP (Employee Assistance Programs).** May include items and services such as financial planning, retirement counseling, drug or alcohol abuse counseling, etc.

29. **Outplacement services.**

30. **Bonus programs.**

31. **Company car.**

32. **Car allowance**

33. **Office equipment.** Such as laptop computer, cell phone, or calculator.

34. **Administrative support or assistant.**

35. **Second cars with their insurance, gas, tires, and maintenance.**

36. **Health club.**
37. **Executive dining privileges.** There may be some tax ramifications on providing this privilege.
38. **Relocation expenses.**
39. **Sabbaticals.**

A STRATEGY TO HELP GUIDE YOUR DECISION

Always ask for time. Except under special circumstances, never accept an offer on the spot. **Express enthusiasm and thanks for the offer and, upon receiving your letter of confirmation, request a reasonable amount of time to carefully weigh the offer.** Use a phrase such as, "**I very much appreciate your offer and will give it thoughtful consideration.**" During this grace period, you must resolve other potential opportunities and come to a wise decision based on your alternatives and insights. Agree upon a follow-up date with the potential employer. Then, should you need additional time, be sure to advise your potential employer of the fact as soon as your requirement for more time becomes apparent.

– The ins and outs, pros and cons of speeding it up and slowing it down. When "it" refers to the almighty job offer. –

Obviously it is highly desirable to be able to select a job or career opportunity from more than one alternative. The advantages of having more than one job offer to consider are obvious. While money and bonuses are important, not all companies place the same emphasis on their benefit policies and programs. Vacation eligibility, relocation-allowance packages, comparative cost of living in different geographic areas, including differentials in state income tax make the task of selection one that should not be taken lightly. Nevertheless, the reality of today's market simply doesn't afford the majority of job hunters this luxury. Specifically, the job hunter of today will probably have to make a career decision based on a single job opportunity. It is rare that more than one employment opportunity presents itself to give the job hunter the luxury of comparing two or more offers.

Also rare is the situation where the candidate may be presented with a job offer and wishes to delay responding with a decision until an additional company is heard from. This process is called "slowing it down" or "buying time" to enable the job hunter to have a maximum amount of information on hand and to compare and contrast various offers. Remember that any job offer, whether it is high, low, or average, is an expression of corporate love and should be treated appropriately.

First, I will deal with "slowing it down." Basically, what can the job hunter do to buy more time so as to compare a possible second or third offer?

REMEMBER: **Corporations have a tendency to move at glacial speed. Glaciers don't like to be changed, turned, or stopped unless they want to.**

SLOWING IT DOWN

There are a number of activities that, if performed selectively and in a professional manner, will slow down the employment process, but each has its risks. The more of these activities utilized, the more the potential employer will conclude that the candidate is playing games, or worse, incapable of making a decision. (Let the hunter beware.) Each risk must be weighed carefully with the understanding that should the potential employer become dissatisfied or discouraged with the candidate's actions, an offer can be quickly withdrawn. Additionally, corporations do not like to be used as bargaining pawns. In other words, to be used as leverage against another corporation. **The reader is well advised to understand the risks of tampering with the timing of an offer once it has been communicated**. Following is a list of short delaying tactics that might be used to obtain additional time.

1. **Employment offers should always be expressed in written form**. This is called the letter of confirmation, which simply confirms all terms and conditions of employment on paper. A professionally run human-resources organization will usually have this correspondence prepared at the time that the offer is made. If it is not, request that a letter be sent to you, thereby buying additional time while it is prepared and sent.

2. **Details of an offer can always be negotiated, but if the offer is a sound one, strong prudent advice is to let it alone**. Don't attempt to negotiate an offer just to buy time. An employment offer should be negotiated if:

    - The offer is not totally acceptable, or
    - There is some confusion with the details that were previously discussed but were not reduced to written form.

    Assuming then that there is no negotiation and the candidate has requested a letter of confirmation, the next strategy would be to request, if it has not been presented, **an explanation of the full benefits program that would be enjoyed were the position to be accepted**. This explanation should include all costs as well as when eligibility would commence for various programs. Rarely is there one individual within any corporation who is totally capable of a knowledgeable discussion of all benefits. These questions should be directed to your potential supervisor – not the Human Resources department. Remember, you are trying to buy time!

3. Guaranteed to buy some time is **a request for a sample pension calculation**, given some prudent but conservative assumptions about retirement age as well as income. This is not a bad question to ask. First, it probably will take the benefits department a bit of time to get back to you with a written estimate of your pension income. Second, it communicates the fact that you are thinking about retiring from this company.

4. **When an offer has been extended, it is unreasonable to assume that a person can go five working days without some communication to his/her potential employer**. This is the time for thinking. Corporations get jittery if an offer has been extended and no communication is forthcoming, so the candidate is advised to commence some communication. Acknowledge receipt of the offer; acknowledge the excitement the

offer has brought and that the candidate wishes to give it reasonable thought and consideration. Job candidates are advised to NEVER just "disappear" in hopes that the lack of communication or the difficulty of being reached will provide ample time for receipt of an additional offer.

5. Assuming steps 1 through 4 have taken place and you know that in five days you will not be in a position to receive another offer, **it is always advisable to communicate your position early to avoid doubt or the assessment that you are indecisive**.

6. In twenty plus years of counseling executives regarding offers of employment, I have heard many different strategies for postponing the decision to accept or reject a company's offer. This includes "the dog ate" your employment offer. **Without question, the alternative that produces the least risk, least embarrassment, and the highest rate of deferment is called the "honesty approach."** It is important to keep in mind that this approach must be implemented very shortly after one has received the letter of confirmation of the employment offer. This approach is generally quite simple and goes something like the following:

Using the telephone, place a call to the party who signed the letter of offer. If you don't get through on the first try, leave a message that you tried to respond to his or her letter and would look forward to a phone call at his or her earliest convenience. It is always preferable to use a delaying tactic via telephone rather than to journey into a potential employer's place of business and meet eyeball to eyeball. This would place the job candidate in a defensive posture and is not recommended. When telephone communication is possible, a script similar to the following might be appropriate:

> Mrs. Smith, this is Bob Jones. I wanted to take the opportunity to call you today and share with you that I have received your letter confirming the offer of employment to join XYZ Corporation. I have reviewed it and compared it to my notes, and both documents are in agreement. I must share with you how excited I am about the prospect of joining your organization. However, as you know, I have been prudent in my search for the right career opportunity. I have talked to many corporations and search firms and have given my word that I will not make a career decision (*not* job decision, which implies short term) until the eighteenth of the month (assuming that date is ten business days into the future.) While your offer and the opportunities that we discussed are indeed exciting and I am very close to indicating my acceptance of your offer, I feel that I must honor my commitment and hope that you can see your way clear to the eighteenth when I will be in a position to respond. I take great pride in honoring commitments that I have made and hope that you will find this slight postponement reasonable and professional.

7. **A slightly more aggressive stance** would be, "As you have probably interviewed other candidates to insure the best possible hiring fit, I am taking a little more time because I am not interested in a job but in a strong career move, which I believe I have found."

8. **All else having failed, and if pressed by your potential boss for a decision today, then there is no other course but to provide him with that decision**. You accept or reject the offer or express regrets that you will not be in a position to give him or her a

decision until the eighteenth. A delay of two weeks is not unreasonable, but to stretch it to three weeks would certainly send the wrong signal.

Note: It is imperative to be mindful of two issues:

    A. Life is based on timing.
    B. This is a *business* decision based on *your* life.

Therefore, when accepting an offer, you have not necessarily made a lifelong commitment. If another organization you may have had substantive conversations with wants to pursue you further, be open. If a desirable offer should then come from this other organization, there is nothing wrong with negotiating and accepting the offer. You must politely tell the first company that your circumstances have changed, and you won't be starting with it as planned. You are sorry for any inconvenience this may cause.

This happens all the time. It may feel uncomfortable to you, but if handled well, all parties will end up with the appropriate fit. Especially you!

SPEEDING IT UP

Again, the reader would be well advised to review the statement "corporations move at glacial speed, and glaciers don't like to be changed, turned, or stopped unless they want to be." The same advice holds true when the job hunter is trying to accelerate the decision making process with the perspective employer. Most business people fail to reflect on how they were unable to change or accelerate the decision-making mode of their previous employer. Think about what leverage you have now as an "outsider." The best advice that can be offered is simply, **"Don't do it."** However, if you must speed things up, honesty is still the best policy. Prepare a telephone script that says to your potential employer, "I am in receipt of a job offer from another corporation and have a week or possibly ten days to consider it. I believe my career direction and long-term commitment might be better served exploring career opportunities with your organization. Will you share with me if you would be in a position to make that type of decision by the end of next week?"

Obviously, many different individuals who really didn't have an offer from another employer have used this tactic. Consider the consequences of a potential employer saying, "We're sorry, but we can't change or expedite this process. This position is too critical." Where does that leave you?

This tactic can be used after a second or third meeting. It should never be tried after a first meeting because it is too early in the interview sequence. **The only way to ensure that you know what a potential employer is thinking is to reject all other offers.** Obviously, this is an alternative that should be avoided. The old adage of "curiosity killed the cat, but satisfaction brought him back" only works with cats!

This entire process must be done **in a professional and businesslike manner**. All of the relationships you form are very important to your future. However, it is **your** search, **your** career, **your** future, and **your** life. Make sure that your actions and decisions remain focused on these principles.

1. **Request a confirmation letter** – Always review the verbal job offer, point by point, with your potential employer to ensure there is a complete, mutual understanding. Tell

your prospective boss that upon receiving the confirmation letter, you will give serious consideration to the offer and get back to him/her with your decision. Do not sever your present employment relationship or cut loose from other job opportunities until you receive the confirmation letter. This letter should include **starting date, title, reporting relationships, salary, initial salary review date, and any other negotiated items**. If your potential boss informs you that such a letter is against company policy, prepare in duplicate your own confirming letter and ask your potential boss to sign and return a copy. A reluctance to do so should be taken as a danger sign. The inability of a reputable company to reduce an offer to writing may well be grounds enough for rejecting the offer.

2. **Finalize your alternatives** – Any other potential opportunities will need to be resolved. Be tactful yet forceful. Ideally, you would like to have other good offers to compare. Be careful not to inflict mortal wounds; you never know when you might like to rekindle a potential opportunity. Remember that an offer is the highest level of interest you can achieve in a job campaign. Do not confuse possible interviews with offers. They are not on the same level.

3. **Make overall career considerations** – How will this job serve your career objectives and aspirations? What skills and experiences will you gain to enhance your career development? How will this job serve your career five or ten years from now? Is this position an entry to another position? Can you be promoted to a higher-level position? Will the position provide additional breadth and challenge? How much visibility does the position provide?

   Review the following factors when making a career decision:

Accountability	Decision-making authority	Promotion
Achievement	Flexibility	Relocation
Approval	Intellectual challenge	Reporting relationship
Autonomy	Location	Social contacts
Benefits	Management style	Span of responsibility
Bonuses	Perks	Special expenses
Company Size	Physical challenge	Stability
Compensation	Power	Status
Creativity	Professional growth	Travel Variety

4. **Evaluate** –

   A. **The company** – Do not rely on the company "spin." Do your homework. What is the history and growth record of the company? Size? Relationship to other companies within the industry? Financial posture? Product lines and diversification? Forecasts and trends? Reputation? Have you obtained the company's annual report, last three quarterly reports, 10-K Report, or a D & B credit report?

   B. **The industry** – What is the history and growth record of the industry? Problems? Government intervention? Relationship to general economic conditions? Some industries follow definite cyclical patterns. Future trends and potentials? Compensation levels?

5. **Construct a checklist to aid and clarify your decision-making process** – List all areas of concern and then rate each as a plus or minus. For example:

Area of Concern	+	-
Compensation	+	
Benefits		-
Commuting Time	+	
Working Environment	+	
Promotional Opportunities		-
TOTAL	**3 (+)**	**2 (-)**

If the compensation is less than adequate you may –

Negotiate upward – Discretion is paramount, but you may do well to negotiate the offer. However, you must realize that the first offer may be the only offer, and you could risk losing the job opportunity. If you decide to negotiate, do not do this in the employer's office. That is his or her turf – the area where he or she is secure, not you. Prepare a phone script to cover all your concerns. Great care must be exercised when negotiating for greater compensation or fringe benefits. Plan what you want to say ahead of time. You should develop a written script to make sure that you cover all of the salient parts. Then call the employer from a place where you feel secure. Have the employer redefine the scope and authority of the position. If the salary does not appear to correspond with job responsibilities, you may begin negotiating for a higher salary. You should also discuss the possibility of a one-time hiring bonus, shorter duration for initial salary review, perks, and fringe benefits. Besides the possibility of acquiring better monetary rewards, you may gain some valuable insights about your potential employer and how you can expect to be treated.

6. **Ask yourself** – "Will I be happy in this position?"

7. **Remember that there is no –**

   A. **Job security** – There is no such thing. With mergers, technological changes, and management changes, even the most secure jobs have a way of disappearing.
   B. **Employment security** – Employment security has little to do with age, gender, race, religion, or ethic origin. It is a function of continually increasing your achievements, broadening your knowledge and skills, increasing your business and professional contacts, and equipping yourself with effective job search techniques and strategies.

8. **Checklist for evaluating job offers –**

Once the job offer is received, the applicant is well advised to consider the following items. This thought-provoking list is provided as a guide in making a decision about your job offer. Consider each item and its importance in the overall picture. You are near the end of your campaign, and you don't want to overlook this last bite of very important "trail mix."

Has the job offer been reduced to a written format? Yes _____ No _____

Has the written job offer included all the salient points that were discussed verbally when the offer was first explained? Yes _____ No _____

In other words, were all details covered to your satisfaction, or were some points "inadvertently" left off the written offer? Yes _____ No _____

Have all the fringe benefits been explained to your satisfaction? Yes _____ No _____

Do you know what the cost is? Yes _____ No _____
Do you know when the benefits start? Yes _____ No _____
Do they cover dependents? Yes _____ No _____

Is there an agreed-upon start date? Yes _____ No _____

Do you know when the first date is for salary-review purposes? Yes _____ No _____

Are you clear as to what the performance indices are to measure your contributions to the organization; i.e., how will your performance be measured? Yes _____ No _____

How does the performance-measurement system translate into a salary increase? In other words, if you are rated as an "average" performer, do you know how this differentiates in percent of increase from "above-average" to "excellent" performer? Yes _____ No _____

Does the new employer provide severance and outplacement assistance in the highly unlikely event of an involuntary separation or a change in ownership? Yes _____ No _____

If you have been granted stock options, has the stock-option plan been fully explained to you? Yes _____ No _____

For example, do you know when the options are exercisable, and what the vesting procedures are? Yes _____ No _____
Is there other pertinent information as to any provisions of this stock-option plan? Yes _____ No _____

Is relocation involved? Yes _____ No _____

Has the relocation program been fully explained to you? Yes _____ No _____
Do you know what costs are reimbursable and what costs are not covered by the relocation program? Yes _____ No _____

Does the relocation package include a gross up or
reimbursement provision so as not to incur
income-tax liability?   Yes _____ No _____

If the co-captain on your marriage team is also employed outside
of the home and relocation occurs, does your new company provide
spousal outplacement assistance, i.e., assistance to find new
employment in a comparable position with an employer within
commuting distance of your new home?   Yes _____ No _____

Do you know what the next logical promotion/career path
position is from the position you are accepting?   Yes _____ No _____

Has the vacation and holiday policy been explained?   Yes _____ No _____

Have you received a copy of the pension formula if the
company maintains a defined pension plan, thereby enabling
you to use a formula to do a sample pension calculation? Yes _____ No _____

Have you done a cost-of-living comparison between your
existing home and the proposed location with your new
employer?   Yes _____ No _____

Have you done a comparison of state income-tax rates
between your current state and the state to which you will
be moving?   Yes _____ No _____

If you are relocating to a new city, does that city have a
city income tax?   Yes _____ No _____

If you are relocating, have you completed at least one, if
not more, house-hunting trips to assess not only living
conditions but also schools, areas of cultural interest,
shopping centers, etc.?   Yes _____ No _____

Is the salary you have been offered with your new employer
at the top of the pay grade, or is there room for
advancement?   Yes _____ No _____

Does this position have a written job description?   Yes _____ No _____

Have you asked yourself these questions:

   Does this position meet my needs, both present
   and future?   Yes _____ No _____
   Do I understand why I am interested in this position? Yes _____ No _____
   Does this position fit into my career path?   Yes _____ No _____
   Will I have fun in this job?   Yes _____ No _____

Ask yourself this question:

> If I leave my new employer, will my new resume be
> an enhancement over my existing resume?　　　　Yes ＿＿　No ＿＿

Will my family be happy with my job change?　　　Yes ＿＿　No ＿＿

Will my family be happy in a new location?　　　　Yes ＿＿　No ＿＿

Will my commuting time and commuting costs be
increased?　　　　　　　　　　　　　　　　　Yes ＿＿　No ＿＿

Does this position carry an expense account?　　　Yes ＿＿　No ＿＿

Does this position have an employment contract?　Yes ＿＿　No ＿＿

Does this position have a termination agreement?　Yes ＿＿　No ＿＿

Finally, what does your "gut feeling" say about this position?

Are you going with your "gut feeling"?　　　　　Yes ＿＿　No ＿＿

9. **Make your decision/implement your decision.**

10. **Thank supporting individuals** – Be **sure** to thank all those individuals you contacted in your job-search campaign for their help and let them know about your new position. I suggest that you send an "Eagle has landed" letter to all of your network contacts. (See page 379 for an example.)

11. **Continue selling yourself** – The first day of your new job should mark the beginning of your personal public-relations campaign. Sell yourself to your new company. You should start a concerted effort to make your achievements known, internally and externally. The best way to a better job is to let your achievements and capabilities speak for you. Making your achievements known is as important as the achievements themselves.

Internally, be a "doer," get involved. Send periodic memos or updates to your boss regarding your involvement and project status. Learn the success patterns of those who have risen in your company. Continually plot and refine the course needed for your advancement.

Externally, become actively involved in job-related organizations to cultivate as many contacts as possible. This can create unlimited opportunities. You must be ready to act when these opportunities arise.

Finally, all future job-search campaigns must be oriented toward matching what you most enjoy doing with where you can do it best.

TERMINATION AGREEMENT

Question: Why should we discuss divorce when we are not even married yet?
Answer: Because it is the best time to get a corporate prenuptial agreement.

A friend of mine once shared the following comment regarding his marriage: "If my courtship was rocky, why should I believe my marriage would be anything different?" Herein lies a significant kernel of truth. If the interview process leaves an individual with a few doubts and along comes an offer of employment, and if that offer of employment is the only one the individual is considering, then by default it becomes a very good offer. In this day of mergers, acquisitions, divestitures, hiring freezes, hiring frosts, rightsizing, downsizing, reengineering, cutbacks, and cost initiatives, the employment, a.k.a. courtship, may indeed be very sound. But many times the aforementioned events can turn a sound relationship into no relationship.

Therefore, I would suggest that when an individual receives a written Letter of Confirmation containing all the details surrounding the employment offer to join a corporation, serious thought should be given to submitting a Termination Agreement or clause, which can be inserted into the redraft of the Letter of Confirmation. A Termination Agreement is just that. It details from your perspective as the employee significant points, which have been agreed upon in advance that surround the termination. It *is not* an Employment Contract. This will be discussed shortly. The following is a simple, but effective example of a Termination Agreement or clause to be placed into a confirmation letter upon being hired.

Suggested Termination Agreement

In the unlikely event of an involuntary termination or change in company ownership, the Company agrees to provide up to one (1) year of full salary continuation with full benefits, or until re-employment, whichever event comes first. In addition, the Company agrees to provide full executive outplacement services through the outplacement firm of my choice. Fees associated with these services will be fully assumed by the Corporation.

This Termination Agreement will be invalid if separation occurs as a result of theft, dishonesty, substance abuse, or any other proven illegal act.

The above agreement contains several points, which are negotiable. For example, one year of full salary could be reduced to ten-months, nine-months, or six-months of salary continuation with the employee picking up the cost of insurance, etc., after six months, or the individual is provided not full executive outplacement but a level of outplacement services, which is slightly reduced, and at less cost to the employer.

It is my experience that termination agreements can be negotiated with a fairly high level of success if the employee submits his or her own agreement right after an offer has been extended. If there is another item to be negotiated, then it should be included in that list of negotiable items. It should not be hung out as one "additional" item to discuss. This nickel and dime approach, which corporations do not like, rarely is successful. A key part of securing this type of language in a Confirmation Letter is the concept first expressed in writing, then verbally discussed. From my experience, discussing first and submitting appropriate language later almost always leads to foolproof, 100 percent disaster.

For example, I had the opportunity to work with a Vice President of Research and Development, whose salary was in the low six-figures. He had just been separated, as was his entire department after a venture capital buyout. After an exhaustive search, he found an employer that he liked. He proposed after receiving his Letter of Confirmation of the Offer of Employment that a Termination Clause be inserted in the agreement. Unfortunately, this individual was sourced through an executive-retainer search firm, and our candidate chose against better advice to discuss this agreement verbally with the search consultant. The search consultant then discussed it with the HR representative, who then discussed it with the Head of Research & Development. The upshot of so many people getting involved in the discussion of this agreement was that no written document was submitted beforehand, and by the time this "agreement" was presented to the President, it was so convoluted that our candidate was made to appear that he was requesting a lifetime agreement. Again, what he should have done was to submit the verbiage in writing and discussed it later to avoid misinterpretation.

In a similar manner, I was working with a very sharp woman, who was in Human Resources, who presented this agreement only to be told by the Vice President of Human Resources that he, himself, did not possess such an agreement in his letter of offer. Our candidate, being very sharp, replied simply, "I am surprised. I thought if anyone had this agreement, it would be myself and certainly yourself." The point was well taken. The Vice President of Human Resources pushed for the inclusion of this clause in the offering letter, and it was granted. Later, the Vice President indicated to our candidate that he was most happy to see that this verbiage was included because at the next opportunity, he was going to push for similar verbiage in his own agreement since he had a subordinate that had a Termination Agreement, and he did not.

Finally, this concept, again, should be introduced prior to an individual's acceptance of an employment offer. Once the individual accepts an employment offer, all leverage is lost on this issue.

EXECUTIVE EMPLOYMENT AGREEMENT:
ISSUES FOR CONSIDERATION

The following excellent information comes from my friend Eugene Jacobs, Attorney at Law, at the Chicago law firm of Seyfarth Shaw. I thank him for permission to reproduce this information here.

I.   INTRODUCTION:

This discussion outline is primarily intended to assist an executive in focusing upon the compensation, employee benefits, and other employment related issues most relevant to him/her as the executive considers executive level employment opportunities. It is also intended to serve as a framework to facilitate the negotiation and preparation of an executive employment agreement where appropriate.

II. PRELIMINARY ISSUES:

1. What are your present career objectives?

2. What is your negotiating leverage vis-à-vis this prospective employer?

3. Have you performed appropriate due diligence regarding this employment opportunity?

4. What are industry norms regarding compensation/employee benefits pertaining to this prospective employer?

5. What are internal equity norms (how are other executives treated regarding compensation/employee benefits) at this prospective employer?

6. Who is the prospective employer's representative in your discussions/ negotiations?

7. What are your priorities vis-à-vis compensation, employee benefits, title, duties, and responsibilities of the position?

8. What are the anticipated "hurdle" issues pertaining to this employment opportunity?

9. What is the prospective employer's view regarding the utilization of an executive employment agreement?

10. What is the appropriate negotiation strategy to employ under the circumstances?

III. SPECIFIC EXECUTIVE EMPLOYMENT AGREEMENT ISSUES:

1. **Identify the parties to the Employment Agreement.**
   a. Identity of the employee.

   b. Identity of the employer.

      i. Distinguish whether employer is parent or subsidiary.

      ii. If executive is employed by subsidiary, executive may seek parent-corporation guarantee of compensation matters.

2. **Specifically engage the executive as an employee.**

   a. Agreement should specifically provide that employer employs executive and executive agrees to be employed by employer.

3. **Identify the executive's duties and responsibilities.**

   a. Identify executive's titles, if any.

      i.   If appointment to office requires Board action, make appointment subject to election by Board.

      ii. If executive is to serve on Board, determine who needs to commit to voting shares to ensure election (and make appropriate commitment in Agreement). For public company, commitment may involve commitment to vote shares or simply a commitment to recommend executive for election.

   b. Describe executive's duties and responsibilities, as feasible.

   c. Specify that executive is required to spend full business time and efforts on employer matters except vacations, sick leave, charitable and civic activities, and similar exceptions.

   d. Where appropriate, identify party or parties to whom executive reports.

      i.   Is executive responsible to the Board and/or one or more other officer(s)?

4. **Specify the term of employment.**

   a. Employment for a fixed term.

      i.   If employment is for a fixed term, consideration should be given to renewal options; specify notice requirements for exercise/non-exercise of renewal options.

   b. "Evergreen" provision in which term automatically renews.

      i.   If Agreement "evergreens" (i.e., automatically renews), determine whether renewal occurs periodically (e.g., each year of three year Agreement) or only at end of term.

5. **Compensation/Benefits Issues.**

   a. Salary.

      i.   Amount and payment timing should be specified.

      ii. Salary should be subject to withholding requirements.

      iii. Timing of salary reviews should be agreed upon or increases should be specified.

363

b. Determine type of incentive compensation.
   i. Annual and/or long-term cash-based.

   ii. Real or phantom equity arrangements.

   iii. Consider whether to specify method of calculation and timing or method of payment.

c. Standard employee benefits should be considered.

   i. Ascertain whether executive is to be included in or excluded from standard employee-benefit plans.

      (A) Pension plan(s).

      (B) Health/dental/vision benefits.

      (C) Life insurance.

      (D) Disability insurance.

      (E) Vacations.

      (F) Expense reimbursement.

d. Ascertain whether executive will receive additional/executive level benefits.

   i. First-dollar medical care/annual physical.

   ii. Additional insurance (health, life, and/or disability).

   iii. Automobile.

   iv. Clubs (dining, health, country; initiation fees and/or dues).

   v. Memberships in business organizations.

   vi. Signing bonus.

   vii. Relocation program.

   viii. Loan for new housing.

   ix. Payment of legal fees incurred regarding preparation of any disputes under the Agreement.

   x. Payment of financial/estate planning fees.

xi.   Indemnification regarding amounts paid, including legal fees, in connection with any restrictive covenant litigation initiated by former employer.

xii. Directors and officers's liability insurance coverage and/or indemnification for acts and omissions as an executive.

6. **Termination Provisions.**

a. Agreement should distinguish between "favored" termination events (that result in most generous severance, executive career-transition assistance and fewest non-competition and confidentiality restrictions) and "disfavored" termination events (that result in greatest forfeitures by executive and restrictions on activities).

b. Termination by executive without "good reason."

   i.   Such termination is generally subject to non-competition and confidentiality restrictions on executive.

   ii.   Such termination should be subject to reasonable specified notice requirement.

   iii. Such termination could cause forfeiture of all or part of deferred compensation, executive career-transition assistance, incentive compensation and/or other executive benefits; alternatively, forfeiture would only occur if specified advance notice of termination not given or if non-competition or confidentiality restrictions are violated.

c. Termination by employer "without cause."

   i.   Non-competition restriction may not apply (confidentiality restriction generally will apply).

   ii.   Identify whether payments and benefits continue and, if so, whether for the Agreement term or a shorter period of time.

   iii. Should also be subject to reasonable, specified notice requirement.

d. Termination by employer "with cause."

   i.   Non-competition and confidentiality restrictions generally will apply.

   ii.   Defining "cause" for termination is generally a difficult negotiation issue.

     (A) Who determines?

     (B) Opportunities for cure?

   iii. Definition of "cause" may include:

     (A) Commission or conviction of criminal offense (may be limited to serious crimes and/or crimes involving honesty or moral turpitude).

     (B) Bad rating or request of termination from government regulators, if applicable.

     (C) Activity viewed as detrimental by government regulators, customers, Board.

     (D) Material breach of agreement.

   iv. Such termination could cause similar forfeitures as in b. iii. above.

 e. Termination by executive for "good reason."

   i. Treatment of continued payments and benefits, and extent of restrictions on executive's activities, should be similar to termination by employer "without cause" in c. above.

   ii. Good reason typically includes either during the term of the Agreement and/or a specified period following a change of control:

     (A) Cuts in pay/benefits.

     (B) Reduction of duties/title.

     (C) Relocation without executive's consent.

 f. Termination due to death or disability of executive.
   i. Treatment as "favored" or "disfavored" event of termination varies. Generally depends on the kind of benefits otherwise payable in the event of death or disability.

7. **Severance provisions.**

 a. Circumstances under which severance pay and benefits, including executive-level career-transition assistance, will be paid or provided should be clearly identified.

   i. Termination of executive "without cause."

     ii.   Termination by executive for "good reason."

     iii.   Completion of Agreement term without renewal by employer.

     iv.   Change in control.

  b. If severance benefits are paid following a change in control, care should be taken to avoid payments being construed as "excess parachute payments" within the meaning of Section 280G of the Internal Revenue Code of 1986. Agreement may cap payments to avoid Section 280G excise tax or provide for gross up of tax amount.

8. **Restrictions upon future employment.**

  a. Executive may be prohibited from engaging in competition against the employer after termination of the executive's employment.

     i.   The enforceability of such restrictions varies dramatically from state to state.

     ii.   Generally, restrictions must contain reasonable limitations upon activity, duration, and geographic scope.

  b. The Agreement may include a basis for seeking injunctive relief.

  c. Such restriction may also include a restriction prohibiting the solicitation of employees.

9. **Restrictions upon disclosure of confidential information.**

  a. Employers generally seek to protect their confidential information by prohibiting executive from disclosing confidential information either during the term of employment or after termination.

  b. The information, which is confidential, must be identified.

     i.   Customers.

     ii.   Processes, formulas, or plans.

     iii.   Employer information regarding suppliers, costs, sales, or other financial data.

     iv.   Marketing or other strategic business plans.

  c. The Agreement may include a basis for seeking injunctive relief.

  d. Include a provision in the Agreement that employee will not use or disclose confidential information/trade secrets of former employer.

10. **When applicable, patent rights to executive's inventions are generally transferred to the employer.**

   a. The Agreement should cover both inventions that occur during working hours through the use of employer assets and those inventions that occur outside of the work environment without the use of employer assets but relate to the employer's business. Similar protection is generally extended to copyright rights.

11. **Miscellaneous matters.**

   a. Executive's employment Agreement is generally assignable by the employer in connection with transactions.

   b. Consideration may be given to dispute resolution concerning the Agreement through the arbitration process. Arbitration may be a simple, cost-effective mechanism for resolving disputes. Pros and cons of arbitration should be carefully weighed.

      i. If arbitration is selected, enforcement of the non-competition and confidentiality restrictions may be excluded from the arbitration process.

   c. Select the state law and forum, which will govern enforcement of the Agreement.

   d. Provide for severability of unenforceable provisions.

      i. If certain provisions are deemed unenforceable, the balance of the Agreement should remain in force.

   e. Provide that the written Agreement represents the entire agreement between the parties.

      i. This will help eliminate claims of oral promises.

   f. Provide extension of directors and officers's liability insurance/indemnification following termination of employment.

HIDDEN COSTS ASSOCIATED WITH RELOCATION

I suggest when evaluating an offer for employment that involves relocation that you consider the following checklist of possible hidden costs.

HOUSE-HUNTING TRIPS

- Ground transportation to/from airport
- Airline tickets
- Car rental
- Hotel accommodations
- Meals
- Laundry and cleaning
- Child-care costs
- Long-distance phone calls

PURCHASE OF NEW HOME

- Market values/purchasing power differences for different areas
- Mortgage rate differentials
- Closing costs:

  Down payment
  Application fees
  Origination fees
  PMI insurance
  Homeowners insurance service fees
  Discount points
  Mortgage insurance
  Funding fees
  Title insurance
  Recording fees
  Closing escrow fees
  Attorney's fees
  City and state taxes
  Document-preparation fees
  Interest from closing date to end of
    the month

- Survey
- Home-rating service
- Inspections (well, termite, roof, septic)
- Tax-service fees
- Carpeting allowance
- Cleaning costs (draperies, carpets, etc.)

- Draperies (if not included with house)
- Home-insurance rate differential
- Costs for extras on new construction, such as:

  Chair rail
  Paddle fan
  Crown molding
  Upgrade ceramic baths
  Upgrade carpet and pad
  Dishwasher
  Window grills
  Sod
  Garden window in kitchen

- Decorating or redecorating
- Miscellaneous hardware
- Heating/cooling cost variations
- Property tax differential
- Mid-year tax planning costs

SALE OF OLD HOME

- Realtor's fees
- City and/or state taxes
- Attorney's fees
- Survey
- Inspections (well, termite, roof, septic)
- Payment of point system
- Painting and repair work
- Management fees (if home is rented prior to sale)
- Maintenance fees
- Double mortgage payment (if home has not been sold)

RENTAL OF NEW HOME
(If none purchased initially)

- Rental fees
- Furniture rental fees
- Appliance rental fees
- Rental insurance
- Storage of excess furniture and personal items
- Damage and security deposits for rental unit

MOVING EXPENSES

- Cost per pound of goods (interstate versus intrastate)
- Limit on pounds moved and paid for by hiring company
- Packing charges
- Transportation for second car or boat
- Special item charges (e.g., antiques)
- Storage fees
- Plants
- Loss of food in freezer and refrigerator
- Rider insurance policy

EXPENSES INCURRED DURING RELOCATION

- Vehicle registration and stickers
- Driver's licenses
- Auto insurance rate differential
- State and local tax differential: income, personal property, real estate, sales
- Cost-of-living index (see Rand McNally's "Places Rated Almanac Listed by City")
- Clothing costs due to climate differences
- Religious and business-organization fees
- Conversion of automobile emission standards to meet state laws
- Modification of automobile(s) for operation in a different climate
- Cost of check printing
- Telephone and cable installation
- Deposits for utilities (electric, gas, telephone, water, etc.)

If the above information appears confusing and a little overwhelming, I would direct your attention to the Internet to consult the site http: //verticals.yahoo.com/cities. This Web site is probably the most user friendly and has the most information on costs when comparing your existing location to your proposed relocation site. This site will give you information on all the following:

Cooling index	Population
Electricity costs	Population density
Heating index	Property tax
Home-purchase costs	Property tax rate
Median family income	Local income tax
High-school-graduation rates	State income tax
Bachelor-degree rates	Sunny days per year
Job growth	Annual precipitation
Crime index	Air quality
All insurance rates	Average January low
Average commute time	Average July high
Unemployment rate	

I have used this Web, site, and it is indeed helpful. Probably the most surprising cost that people incur when they relocate is the cost of a city income tax. Some cities have an income tax. This is a relatively new phenomenon, which a lot of people are not familiar with. Basically, it works as follows: whether you live in a city that has an income tax or live out of the city, you could be taxed if your place of business is in the city that has the income tax. It's always an excellent question to request personal income-tax information based on city income tax, state income tax, and even county income tax.

There could be some pleasant surprises. For example, when relocating at the present time, there are nine states that do not have a state income tax. They are Alaska, Florida, Nevada, New Hampshire, South Dakota, Tennessee, Texas, Washington, and Wyoming. Moving from a state that has a 6 percent personal income tax to one of these states, along with a 10 percent increase, would in effect produce a 16 percent increase. Assuming, of course, there is no difference in the cost of living.

The data in the Web site is compiled by ACCRA, P. O. Box 407, Arlington, VA 22210. The company can also be reached at 703-522-4980 and will provide information for one or two sites on request. The most comprehensive information still remains on the above Web site.

Bottom line, it's simple. What you don't know and don't ask can hurt you. I have seen too many of my individual clients fail to address these taxation and cost-of-living questions to my satisfaction, and they might have made an imprudent relocation decision if I hadn't slowed them down. What happens is that individuals who are unemployed get very excited about the prospects of joining a new company and commencing a new employment relationship. The end result is that in their excitement, haste makes waste, and they fail to address all of the important issues that could make a financial difference on the economic part of the decision to relocate.

SO, YOU'VE DECIDED TO RELOCATE

You've studied the company's offer. All negotiations have been completed. The cost-of-living comparisons have been completed, and now it's time to think about buying a new home and, of course, selling your existing home or condominium. Assuming that the reader of this section of the guide is not an apartment dweller, or even if he/she is and may be considering buying a home or condominium for the first time, the following comments will be very helpful. They were collected during a series of conversations with my good friend Kathy Rogoff, who is a professional residential realtor with the firm of Coldwell Banker in Greenville, South Carolina.

The basic principle when buying a home is to get educated and to know your market. This is going to take some digging and asking the right questions of the right people. The following key points should be thoroughly digested and are worth the buyer's time and energy to get the necessary information.

☑ It seems like everybody knows a "good" realtor. Good realtors are those individuals who have established a sound realty practice and have received most, if not all, of their business by referral. Once you have identified a realtor, you want to make sure that he/she provides you with comparable data on sales of the type or size home you are looking for. Certainly it would not be unreasonable to ask for a full year's list of past sales. Included in the past sales history should be the price per square foot and the sales-to-list price percentage, which are key pieces of data.

☑ If your family has children, or you plan to start a family, educate yourself on local schools. Good realty agents should be able to give test scores, which are updated yearly, and certainly it would not be inappropriate to visit various schools where one could meet and visit with teachers and inquire about extracurricular activities that the school offers. It would indeed be unfortunate if an individual came from a soccer family and such a sport was not offered at the local neighborhood school where one contemplated sending one's children. Check on bus routes. Are children to be picked up, or do they have to be carpooled?

☑ Certainly have any contemplated house inspected by a professional, bonded home rater, or inspection service. This is money well spent and can save major expenditures in the future. Know the age of the heating, ventilation, and air conditioning systems and inquire about a home-warranty insurance policy. The premium for this policy can be paid by you, the buyer, or seller and can be made a part of the contract-negotiation process.

☑ Your lending agent should explain in great detail what the closing costs are expected to be. It is prudent to do a title search. Lenders do require a title search but do not always require surveys or CL-100s. Ask your realtor to go to the tax records and see what the seller paid for the house you are contemplating buying. Check that the taxes were paid and what the amount was and what these taxes covered.

☑ Ask for a year's utility bill, and inquire what the utilities actually include. This is particularly significant if the prospective homeowner has previously had well water and will be moving into an area where he/she is going to experience the "pleasure" of paying for city water.

☑ One of the major elements that has a direct bearing on insurance, of course, is the distance of the contemplated house from the nearest fire hydrant. Inquire about the financial stability of the city or county. If the city or county has to cut back on fire protection, security, etc., these again are going to increase the costs of insurance coverage. Inquire about whether there are any assessments in progress.

☑ When considering a particular area of the city, depending on, of course, the size of the city, your realtor should be able to provide you with the average number of days a home is on the market. Specifically, one can inquire how long the property that you are interested in has been on the market. Select a realtor who has a Web site. This can be verified by checking Realty.com.

☑ Make sure to get a **CL-100** letter from a reputable pest-control company, which will detail termite inspection and moisture content of the home in question. If there is no city water, have a well inspection and an analysis of the water for lead, uranium, etc. Radon, a hazardous gas, is prevalent in many parts of the country. Be sure to have a home inspector check on radon levels, especially in basement homes. If the property has not had a recent survey, it behooves the prospective buyer to commission a recent survey. Your potential neighbor may actually have his/her driveway on your property.

☑ If one is moving into a community or a subdivision, inquire about whether or not there is an architectural-review committee to determine if additions to your new house have to be approved, or if one is allowed to put up a fence and what type of fences are permitted, etc.

☑ Is there a homeowners' association? If so, is it mandatory that the new homeowner join the association, and, if so, what is the cost? Does the cost cover swimming pools, tennis courts, entranceway, clubhouses, etc? What are the regulations? Does the association permit boats in the driveway, etc?

SELLING YOUR HOME

Coldwell Banker has an excellent booklet called the Home Enhancement Guide, which lists a number of items that the homeowner can simply do to make his/her home more sellable and enhance the potential for a quick sale. Perhaps of significance is the fact stated early in this booklet that within fifteen seconds, a potential buyer has already developed an opinion of the property that he/she may or may not be interested in buying. Bottom line, the first impression is critical. No thought better explains this point than "Would I buy this house?" Meaning, of course, what do I have to do to get my home in shape?

Certainly, getting a minimum of two market opinions will assist you in pricing your home. Your realtor should assist you in understanding the competition. How many houses have sold, and at what prices during the last year? As in buying a home, the seller should know what is the average number of days a similar house has been on the market. Have prospective real-estate agents give you their recommendations. Know all of your closing costs and know all of your realtor's fees. Certainly use a realtor that has a Web site for greater publicity. Are there restrictions on placing "For Sale" signs in the neighborhood or on the property? Probably some of the best advice is simply to fix what's wrong. Disclose, Disclose, Disclose. Failure to disclose is a disaster waiting to happen because a home rater will undoubtedly find what is wrong with the house that the seller has failed to disclose.

Almost all real-estate agencies will provide the seller with tips and suggestions on how to increase the marketability of your home. Included in these books are not only suggestions for the interior and exterior but also the surrounding yard or grounds to enhance the sales features of your home. Suffice to say that the following is a short list of principles to increase a home's sales appeal. These points greatly simplify the voluminous checklist that most realtors offer.

- ☑ Fix it or replace it.
- ☑ Paint it or scrub it.
- ☑ If it smells bad, it is bad; throw it out.
- ☑ Organize it or sell it at a garage sale.
- ☑ Think small – detail show loving care.
- ☑ Use colors that are neutral, then add lots of light.
- ☑ The best smell is no smell.
- ☑ The kitchen launches more torpedoes than any other room in the house and can quickly sink a deal.
- ☑ Use mirrors to enhance the perception of size and elegance.
- ☑ Let the realtor earn his/her commission.

HOW TO ASSESS IF YOUR JOB IS IN JEOPARDY
Are the Red Flags Blowing in the Breeze?

The thrust of this guide is to provide job-hunting assistance to either the person who is unemployed or the person who is employed but seeking to make a job change. Many of the individuals that I have worked with in my consulting practice have been absolutely blindsided by the news that they have been eliminated, downsized, or laid off with no hope of recall. It is only appropriate that I offer some thoughts to the person who may be employed and not necessarily motivated to seek employment elsewhere but nevertheless should be keenly aware of what direction the trade winds are blowing and which red flags are fluttering.

Red flags are terms which are synonymous with potential danger signals regarding the health of any business organization. The more red flags that flutter in corporate breezes, the more signs that the corporate health of the organization could be in dire straits. I have attempted to put together a list of elements that one could look for to see how one's own particular corporation is faring.

I am amazed at the number of people who work for publicly held companies that do not take the time to read the literature on their own companies, specifically the 10K, the Annual Report, the 10Q, and quarterly earnings report. These individuals would be well advised to take a hard look at some of the other subtleties of corporate health.

These red flags include the following:

- Has overtime been slashed?

- Has the number of production or manufacturing shifts been reduced from three to two, or two to one?

- Are inventory levels increasing?

- Has there been a slowdown in inventory turns?

- Has travel cost been severely curtailed?

- Have wage and salary guidelines been tightened or reduced?

- Have budgets been cut back, particularly sales, advertising, and training?

- Has there been a series of key management separations?

- Has there been a number of what I call "take-it-for-granted" items eliminated, such as the quarterly company newspaper, Christmas party, the summer picnic?

- Have car allowances been reduced or eliminated?

- Are there hiring freezes or hiring frosts? (A hiring frost is almost as severe as a hiring freeze, but on various special occasions, unique individuals to the corporations can be hired or replaced).

- Has there been a consolidation of functions or departments?

- Has there been an increased number of functions or activities outsourced?

- Are similar companies in your industry facing significant downturns or economic reverses?

- Does the company gather a significant portion (in excess of 50 percent) of its total annual sales revenue from one or two key clients?

- How many key clients or accounts has the company lost in the last year versus how many major clients or accounts has the company won in the same period of time?

- Has the company been forced to cut the prices of its products and/or services?

- Has there been at least one downsizing in the last twelve months?

- Have plants been closed or consolidated?

- Have product lines been phased out without the introduction of new updated products?

- Have capital budgets been slashed?

- Has capital been expended for modernization in updating of plants, machinery, or equipment?

- Has the company suffered any economic reverses in the court system because of product liability, trade infringements, patent infringements, anti-trust violations, etc.?

- When employees leave the organizations, are they replaced in kind, or are those positions consolidated into other positions?

- Has secretarial/administrative support been consolidated to where people share assistants and secretaries?

- Have certain benefits been curtailed, or have the employee-participation rates or costs been increased?

- Has tuition reimbursement been curtailed?

- Are shipments or the number of trucks calling upon a company's shipping docks reduced, indicating fewer shipments of products?

- Has there been an abnormal number of "strangers" or "visitors" coming through the reception area or walking through the plant to review the plant operations?

- Have there been offers to the employees for early retirement or buyouts in efforts to reduce employee head counts?

- Has the company decided to change its method of distribution, or has it decided to increase the amount of products being manufactured by outside vendors?

- Have the company's customers or traditional targets for the sale of the company's products suffered any changes or turndowns in their market?

- Have any of the company's products been subject to recall or product-liability judgments?

- What has been the reputation of new management? For example: Al "Chain Saw" Dunlop has had the reputation, and richly earned, of a slash, cut, and burn CEO in an effort to increase profits.

- How does your salary compare with people in your department?

- How does your age compare to others in your work group or at a comparable level of employment?

- When individuals are terminated, are they receiving adequate or fair severance packages?

- Has career pathing become an increasingly vague issue? In other words, have the previous paths to increased responsibility with enhanced compensation now become doubtful avenues for progression?

- Are more critical decisions being delayed due to more "analysis"?

- Does your current job title include any of the following words:

    *Coordinator
    *Special Projects
    *Trainer
    *Specialist

In summary, the more of these red flags that flutter in your corporate breeze, the stronger I suggest that it is time to update or initiate active use of your job-campaign materials.

FOCUS TIME

Over the years, I have had the opportunity to work with many tough business executives who prided themselves on being sharp as well as tenacious negotiators. Many times when an offer was presented, these same individuals were not the most astute negotiators of their own job offer. There are basically two explanations for this. When an individual is offered the opportunity to join an organization, the employment offer becomes very subjective and emotional. It becomes *your* offer, *your* dollars, *your* career path, and very few individuals over the course of their business career really have the opportunity to strategically negotiate a business offer regarding their own salaries. The subjective involvement is too great for most individuals to remain strong, objective negotiators.

The second problem job applicants have is that they have willingness to move far too fast. They expect the potential employer to move faster than the company can, or in all likelihood is going to, move in the negotiations process. In fact, the offering party many times does not have the authority to go above the stated offer of employment. The individual in haste to conclude the negotiations commits many fouls or errors in judgment.

In summary, if the variance between the offer and what is expected is large and one is willing to risk losing the opportunity for resumed or continued employment, an attempt should be made to have the company reconsider its offer. If the variance in the offer versus the desired package is small, then offer should be left by itself and accepted.

Consider for a moment the alternative of presenting a counter salary offer with a request for a one-time early salary review based upon a six-month review or a one-time hiring bonus equal to 5 to 10 percent or higher of your starting salary. There are many avenues to take towards reaching a satisfactory compensation package. The key is to move at a pace that is not too fast and to remain focused.

THE EAGLE HAS LANDED!

FOLLOWING UP WITH
YOUR CONTACTS AFTER ACCEPTING AN OFFER

Once again, I want to stress the importance of follow-up when you accept a job offer. Be wise and courteous and inform all of your networking contacts of your success. They will be pleased to share in your success and will remember the courtesy displayed through your job campaign.

A sample announcement letter follows:

$$\boxed{\textbf{SAMPLE 55}}$$

ROBERT T. THOMAS
1424 Main Street
Anywhere, State 99999
(765) 555-1212

SAMPLE "EAGLE HAS LANDED" LETTER

Note: To be used *after accepting* an offer.

January XX, 20XX

Mr. Herbert Cooper
1221 Jane Street
Pittsburgh, PA 19199

Dear Herb:

Recently I wrote to you and asked for your thoughts and suggestions regarding my career search. I am most pleased to inform you that I will begin my new position as Director of Manufacturing at the ABC Manufacturing Company in Plantville, Indiana, early next month. Initial challenges include plant layout and conversion of the machining process to automation.

I certainly appreciate your encouragement and support over the last several months, and I hope that we will remain in contact. If I can be of assistance to you in the future, please do not hesitate to call upon me.

Sincerely,

Robert T. Thomas

In Summary, I have covered many topics through this program and the tools that you have acquired will make you successful in finding a new career opportunity. Take a moment to reflect upon the various skills that are now in your hands:

You know how to develop job opportunities via:

- ✓ the telephone
- ✓ effective marketing of yourself
- ✓ direct mail letters
- ✓ network contacts
- ✓ Internet

- ✓ search firms
- ✓ cover letters
- ✓ ad-response letter
- ✓ targeting your campaign.

You have learned how to:

- ✓ interview successfully
- ✓ ask pertinent and helpful questions during the interview
- ✓ evaluate the employment offer.

And you have learned the importance of follow-up in a successful job campaign.

The opportunities are out there. I know this, and you know this. The next move is yours, and I am confident that your diligence will pay off!

Remember that a job-search campaign takes a minimum of four to six hours per day to be successful!

Success is not a place. It's a journey!

CHAPTER IX.

JOURNEY'S
END

A FINAL COMMENT AND LASTING THOUGHT

A frequently asked question in many of today's interviews is, "What is your greatest strength?" This question essentially asks what are you bringing to the party, or how are you going to help our company?

I have been asked this same question many times by individuals seeking the "right" or "best" answer. Of course, there is no right answer but only the reply that correctly fits you and the total of your skills and lifetime of experiences.

For myself, one of my strengths is my fear of failure. I have never liked to lose. I never have and never will get used to losing. I am an awkward loser and proud of it! Show me a graceful loser, and I will show you a person who has had a lot of practice! In fact, in my own career, I have celebrated a number of victories, but I have never lost a battle, a contest, a project, or an assignment. Rather, I have experienced what I'd call "a few" delayed victories. Victories by themselves have little meaning unless they are compared to one's lifetime of experiences and losses.

Unfortunately, most people do not get every interview they want, and most interviews do not end in a job offer. Possibly these experiences are looked upon as failures or losing out to someone else. They should not be!

View the campaign process as one filled with "delayed victories," as there are no perfect jobs or job applicants. Use the campaign time to learn, as well as unlearn, to attack, and attack again, long-held beliefs and methods of doing things. Take each "delayed victory" as a learning moment to recharge your batteries and again recommit yourself to the objective at hand. Learn from your "delayed victories" rather than have them become excuses for a Victory Denied!

Lawrence A. Stuenkel

It is not whether you get knocked down that counts, it is whether you get up.

- Vince Lombardi

Index

NOTES

NOTES

NOTES

NOTES

NOTES

Enjoy your CD-ROM!

This CD is compatible with MAC, Unix or Windows Operating Systems.

From Here To There
A Self-Paced Program for Transition in Employment

Copyright 2002
Lawrence A. Stuenkel